Hillier's
Fundamentals of Motor Vehicle Technology

Book 2

Powertrain Electronics

Hillier's
Fundamentals of Motor Vehicle Technology
5th Edition

Book 2
Powertrain Electronics

V.A.W. Hillier, Peter Coombes & David Rogers

Nelson Thornes
a Wolters Kluwer business

First published in 1966 by:
Hutchinson Education
Second edition 1972
Third edition 1981 (ISBN 0 09 143161 1)
Reprinted in 1990 (ISBN 0 7487 0317 9) by Stanley Thornes (Publishers) Ltd
Fourth edition 1991

Fifth edition published in 2006 by:
Nelson Thornes Ltd
Delta Place
27 Bath Road
CHELTENHAM
GL53 7TH
United Kingdom

07 08 09 10 / 10 9 8 7 6 5 4 3 2

A catalogue record for this book is available from the British Library

ISBN 978-0-7487-8099-0

Cover photograph: Aston Martin V12 Vanquish by David Kimber/Car and Bike
Photo Library

Page make-up by GreenGate Publishing Services, Tonbridge, Kent

Printed and bound in Slovenia by Korotan – Ljubljana Ltd

CONTENTS

LIST OF ABBREVIATIONS

4WD	four-wheel drive		HCCI	homogeneous charge compression ignition
ABD	automatic brake differential		HEGO	heated exhaust gas oxygen (Ford)
ABS	anti-lock braking system		HT	high tension
AC	alternating current		IC	internal combustion
A/D	analogue to digital		ISG	integrated starter–generator
ASR	traction control		LED	light emitting diode
ATF	automatic transmission fluid		LOS	limited operating strategy
CAN	controller area network		LSD	limited slip differential
CBW	clutch-by-wire		MAP	manifold absolute pressure
CD	capacitor discharge		MIL	malfunction indicator lamp
CI	compression ignition		MTM	mechatronics transmission module
CO	carbon monoxide		N_2	nitrogen
CO_2	carbon dioxide		NO	nitric oxide
CPU	central processing unit		NO_2	nitrogen dioxide
CSC	cornering stability control		NO_x	oxides of nitrogen
CTX	constantly variable transaxle (Ford)		NTC	negative temperature coefficient
CVT	continuously variable transmission		O_2	oxygen
DC	direct current		OBD	on-board diagnostics
DDC	dynamic drift control		OHC	overhead cam
DRP	dynamisches repelprogramm – German for dynamic control program		Pb	lead
			PCU	powertrain control unit
DSG	direct-shift gearbox		ppm	parts per million
EBD	electronic brake force distribution		PTM	Porsche traction management
ECU	electronic control unit		PWM	pulse width modulated
EDC	electronic diesel control		SAE	Society of Automotive Engineers (USA)
EDL	electronic differential lock		SUV	sports utility vehicle
EEC	European Economic Community (now EU)		RPM	revolutions per minute (abbreviated to rev/min when used with a number)
EGR	exhaust gas recirculation		TCS	traction control system
EOBD	European on-board diagnostics		TCU	transmission control unit
ESP	electronic stabilisation programme		TDC	top dead centre
EU	European Union		VBA	variable bleed actuator
EUDC	European extra-urban driving cycle		VE	verteiler – German for distributor (VE is used by Bosch for a type of diesel injection pump)
EVAP	evaporative emissions			
GT	grand touring		WOT	wide open throttle
H_2O	water			
HC	hydrocarbon			

ACKNOWLEDGEMENTS

We should like to thank the following companies for permission to make use of copyright and other material:

Audi AG
BMW (UK) Ltd
Robert Bosch Ltd
Butterworth-Heinemann
Haldex Traction AB
Haynes Publishing Group
Jaguar Cars Ltd
LuK GmbH & Co
Porsche Cars (GB) Ltd
Siemens VDO Automotive
Toyota (GB) Ltd
Valeo
Volkswagen (UK) Ltd

Every effort has been made to trace the copyright holders but if any have been inadvertently overlooked the publishers will be pleased to make the necessary arrangement at the first opportunity.

Although many of the drawings are based on commercial components, they are mainly intended to illustrate principles of motor vehicle technology. For this reason, and because component design changes so rapidly, no drawing is claimed to be up to date. Students should refer to manufacturers' publications for the latest information.

Chapter 1

INTRODUCTION TO POWERTRAIN ELECTRONICS

what is covered in this chapter . . .

- Application of electronics and computers
- 'Electronic systems' or 'computer controlled systems'
- Electronic control units (ECUs)
- Sensors: a means of providing information
- Examples of different types of sensor
- Obtaining information from analogue and digital sensor signals
- Actuators: producing movement and other functions
- Examples of different types of actuators
- ECU/actuator control signals

1.1 APPLICATION OF ELECTRONICS AND COMPUTERS

1.1.1 The increased use of electronic and computer controlled systems

Modern motor vehicles are fitted with a wide range of electronic and computer controlled systems. This book details most of these systems and explains their operation, as well as giving guidance on maintenance, fault finding and diagnosis.

However, it is important to remember that electronic or computer control of a system is often simply a means of improving the operation or efficiency of an existing mechanical system. Therefore many mechanical systems are also covered, especially where their function and capability has been improved through the application of electronics and computer control. See *Hillier's Fundamentals of Motor Vehicle Technology Book 1* for explanations of the basic mechanical systems that still form a fundamental part of motor vehicle technology.

There are of course many electronic systems that do not influence or control mechanical systems; these pure electric/electronic systems are also covered.

There are many reasons for the increased use of electronic systems. Although vehicle systems differ considerably in function and capability, they rely on the same fundamental electrical and electronic principles that must be fully understood before a vehicle technician can work competently on a modern motor vehicle.

1.1.2 Why use electronics and computer control?

Most people who witnessed the cultural and technological changes that occurred during the last 30 years of the twentieth century would probably regard the electronics revolution as having had the greatest impact on their working lives, significantly affecting the rest of their lives as well. Although we are primarily concerned with the motor vehicle here, electronics have had a substantial and fundamental impact on the way we live and particularly on the way we work. Electronic systems affect almost all aspects of our lives, with the design and production of consumer products being particularly affected. Domestic goods, entertainment systems and children's toys have all changed dramatically because of electronics. While all of the above examples are obvious and important, electronics has also enabled computers to become everyday commodities for professional and personal use.

Why have electronics had such an impact on our lives and the things we buy and use? A simple answer could be that they are now much more affordable, but this alone would not be a complete answer. The application of electronics to so many products has enabled dramatic improvements in the capability and function of almost all such products. A simple example is the process of writing a letter, which progressed from being hand written to being created

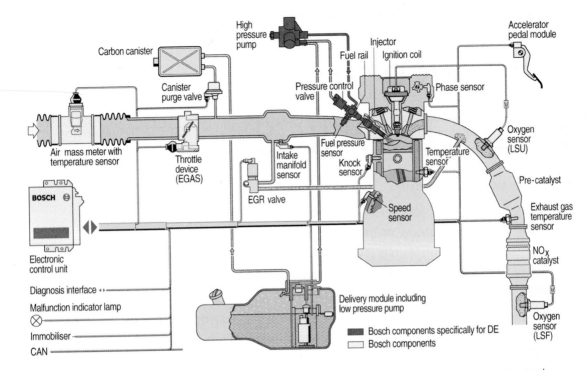

Figure 1.1 Components used in a typical modern electronic computer controlled vehicle system (engine management system)

on a mechanical typewriter. The mechanical typewriter was improved by the use of electronics, but the introduction of the computer allowed businesses and then individuals to produce letters with much greater stylistic freedom. The computer allows the user to correct errors, check spelling, change the layout and achieve a more professional letter than was ever possible with any of the previous methods. This book has been produced using computers, with the author typing the original text and producing some of the illustrations on computer. The original documents were then passed electronically (by e-mail) to the production company, which used computers to create the final style and prepare the book ready for printing (the printer also uses computers and electronics).

Apart from the quality improvements already mentioned computers have brought greatly increased speed; this book would have taken much longer to write and produce without the benefit of electronics and computers. This is true of virtually everything that makes use of electronics. Speed and efficiency are important, but improvements in almost every way can be achieved using electronics and computers.

So if we go back and again ask the question 'Why use electronic control?' we can perhaps now provide a number of answers, including improvements in speed, in capability or function and in quality. The fact that electronics are now much more affordable and electronic components considerably smaller than in the past, facilitates wide use of electronics, resulting in all of those benefits so far discussed and many more.

1.1.3 Why use electronics and computer control on the motor vehicle?

Since the late 1960s motor vehicles have been fitted with an increasing range of electronics and computer control. Cost and size reductions are obviously important because of the production volumes of vehicles, space considerations and the need to keep down the price paid by consumers (the people and companies that buy the vehicles).

Reducing emissions and improving safety
Electronics and electronic control (or computer control) have become increasingly necessary in motor vehicles. For example, without electronic control of vehicle systems (primarily the engine management and emission control systems), emissions from engines could not have been reduced by so much. Legislation has imposed tighter control on emissions; a balance has been struck between what is wanted and what can be achieved. The legislators seek continued reductions in emissions and the vehicle manufacturers have been able to achieve tremendous results, but without electronics it would not have been possible to reduce emissions to anywhere close to the current low levels.

Safety is another area where electronics have enabled improvements. The design of a motor vehicle is very dependent on computers that can analyse data and then help to incorporate improved safety into the basic vehicle structure. Safety systems such as anti-lock brakes (ABS) and airbag systems could not function anywhere like as efficiently or reliably without the use of electronics.

Consumer demand

One other important issue is consumer demand or expectation. Not very long ago, only the most expensive vehicles had electronic or computer controlled luxuries. However, it is now expected that cheaper high volume vehicles will also have electronically controlled systems, including the ABS and airbag systems. In fact ABS is now standard on vehicles sold across Europe. Further examples include: air conditioning with electronic control (climate control), electric seat adjustment (often using electronic control), sophisticated in-car entertainment systems (CD and DVD systems, etc.), as well as driver aids such as satellite navigation or dynamic vehicle control systems. In fact, consumer expectations for more and more electronically controlled vehicle systems is only matched by the desire of vehicle manufacturers to sell more and more of these systems to the consumer. When new or improved systems and features are developed, the vehicle manufacturing and sales industries are only too willing to offer them to consumers, who then develop an expectation.

Without electronics, almost all of these new safety systems, the modern emission systems and other systems would not be affordable, and would certainly not be as functional or as efficient.

> **Key Points**
>
> Electronic controls are now used for almost all vehicle systems
>
> Emissions regulations are a key factor in the increasing use of electronic and computer control

1.2 'ELECTRONIC SYSTEMS' OR 'COMPUTER CONTROLLED SYSTEMS'

1.2.1 Different levels of sophistication and functionality

Electronic enhancement or computer control

Although different people will provide different definitions of electronic systems and computer controlled systems, it is possible for the purposes of this book to clearly separate the two types of system, as follows.

Electronic systems

An electronic system uses electronics to improve the safety, size, cost or efficiency of a system, but the electronics do not necessarily control the system.

For example the evolution of motor vehicle lighting systems shows how electronics can be used on a simple system. Figure 1.2 shows a headlight circuit that is switched on by the driver when the light switch is turned to the appropriate position. When the switch is in the correct position, it allows electric current to flow from the battery directly to the light bulbs. The disadvantage of this type of circuit is that all of the current passes through the light switch and through all of the wiring; the switch and wiring must therefore be of high quality and able to carry the relatively high current (which creates heat).

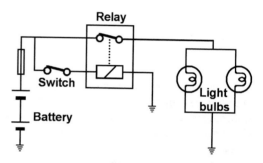

Figure 1.3 Simple headlight circuit with a relay

Figure 1.3 shows the light circuit fitted with a relay. When the driver turns the light switch to the appropriate position, it allows electric current to pass to the relay, which is then 'energised'. However, to energise the relay requires only a very low current; therefore, the switch and the wiring will be subjected to neither high current nor heat, and can be produced more cheaply. When it is energised, the relay contacts (or internal switch) are forced to close (owing to the magnetic field created by current flowing through the relay winding), which then allows a larger electric current to pass from the battery through to the light bulbs.

If the relay is located close to the light bulbs, the wire carrying the high current is relatively short, and because the longer length of wire between the switch and the relay carries only a low current, it can cost less than the wire required in Figure 1.2. As well as the reduced cost of the wiring, the reduced current and heat passing through the light switch and much of the wiring provides a safety benefit, allowing a less expensive switch to be used.

Figure 1.4 shows almost the same wiring circuit as Figure 1.3 but the relay has been replaced by an electronic module. The electronic module performs the same task as the relay but does not contain any moving

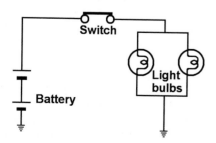

Figure 1.2 Simple headlight circuit

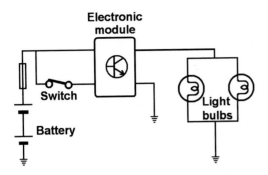

Figure 1.4 Simple headlight circuit using an electronic module

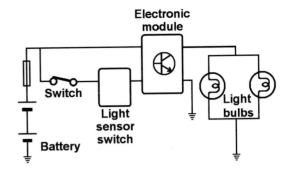

Figure 1.5 Headlight circuit with an electronic module and a light sensor switch

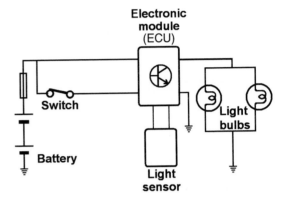

Figure 1.6 Computer controlled headlight circuit with a light sensor

parts: there are no contacts or internal switch. The module can consist of very few simple electronic components (transistors and resistors, etc.), which are inexpensive and reliable.

Note, however, that the module does not control the lighting circuit (as is also the case with the relay); it simply completes the lighting circuit in response to input from the driver (when the light switch is turned to the appropriate position).

Computer controlled systems

A computer controlled system could generally be defined as a system in which some of the actions or functions are automated, as opposed to being controlled by the driver or passenger. Using the simple example of the light circuit again, computer control could automatically switch on the lights when it became dark, such as at night or when the vehicle passes into a tunnel.

For control to be automated, the computer would need information from a sensor. A light sensor can be used to detect the amount of light and pass an electrical signal (proportional to the amount of light) to the computer. The computer would then respond to the electrical signal; i.e. if the signal had a specific value or went above or below a certain value, the computer would then switch on the lights.

It is possible that a simple version of an automated light system could use a sensor that is simply a switch, which provides either an on or off signal to the computer. When the light fades to a certain level, the switch could close, thus completing the light circuit. Figure 1.5 shows a headlight circuit where a light sensor has been included between the light switch (operated by the driver) and the electronic module. This is effectively the same circuit as shown in Figure 1.4, with the addition of a simple light sensor switch. In this example, the sensor simply forms part of the circuit between the main switch and the electronic module; therefore if the light switch is in the on position, the lights will be switched on when the natural light fades below the specified level. This type of system would **not** represent a fully computerised system.

However, Figure 1.6 shows a similar circuit where the electronic module is replaced by a more sophisticated computer module or electronic control

unit (usually referred to as an ECU). In this example, the light sensor is directly connected to the ECU and provides a signal that varies with the amount of light, i.e. the voltage generated by the sensor could increase or decrease as the light reduces. The computer would then effectively make the decision as to when the lights were switched on.

It is then in fact possible to increase the functionality of the computer by adding more sensors. For example, a rain sensor could be fitted to the vehicle to provide automatic operation of the windscreen wipers. The signal from the rain sensor could then also be passed to the light system ECU, thus allowing the ECU to switch on the lights when the rain sensor detected rain.

Although the above example is relatively simple, it shows that a modern computer controlled system uses a computer or ECU to control actions and functions, depending on the information received. Many computer controlled systems make use of a large number of sensors passing information to the ECU, which may in turn be controlling more than one action or function. The above examples of headlight circuits represent ECU controlled functions, i.e. switching on a light bulb. However, when an ECU controls an action, it usually does so by controlling what is referred to as an actuator. Electric motors and solenoids are typical actuators that can be controlled by an ECU; a number of examples will be covered and explained within this book.

An ECU controlled system

As shown above, an ECU receives information from sensors, makes calculations and decisions, and then operates an actuator (or provides signals for electronic components such as digital displays).

The essential point to remember is that an ECU cannot achieve its main objective, which is to operate an actuator or electronic component, unless the appropriate signals are received. This is true of all ECU controlled vehicle systems, and almost all other computers: some form of input signal is required before a calculation and control process can take place. Even a normal PC (personal computer) used to write a letter requires inputs from the keyboard and mouse before the words are displayed on the monitor or before the letter can be printed or e-mailed.

Figure 1.7 shows the basic principles of almost all ECU controlled systems, whereby a sensor produces some form of electrical signal, which is passed to the ECU. The ECU uses the information provided by the signal to make the appropriate calculations, and then passes an electric control signal to an actuator or digital component such as the dashboard display.

Figure 1.8 shows a more complex arrangement for an ECU controlled system. This example would be typical of an early generation fuel injection system where the ECU is controlling a number of actuators and where a number of sensors are used to provide the required information.

Actuators that could be fitted to an engine management system

- Fuel injector solenoid (for fuel quantity control).
- Idle speed stepper motor (for idle speed control).
- Exhaust gas recirculation solenoid valve (part of an emission control system).
- Turbocharger wastegate solenoid valve (controlling turbocharger boost pressure).
- Ignition coil (in this instance, the ECU is in fact controlling the ignition timing when it switches the ignition coil on/off, although strictly speaking the ignition coil is not an actuator).

Sensors that could be fitted to an engine management system

- Engine coolant temperature sensor.
- Air temperature sensor (ambient).
- Air temperature sensor (intake system).
- MAP (manifold absolute pressure) sensor (an intake manifold pressure/vacuum sensor for an indication of engine load).
- Crankshaft position sensor (identifies the crankshaft position for ignition and fuel injection timing, and also indicates engine speed).
- Camshaft position sensor (providing additional information for ignition and fuel injection timing).
- Throttle position sensor (indicates the amount of throttle opening and the rate at which the throttle is opened or closed).
- Boost pressure sensor (indicates the boost pressure in the intake manifold that has been created by the turbocharger).
- Lambda sensor 1 (indicates the oxygen content in the exhaust gas passing into the catalytic converter, which enables the ECU to correct the fuel mixture).
- Lambda sensor 2 (indicates the oxygen content in the exhaust gas leaving the catalytic converter, which helps the ECU assess if the catalytic converter is functioning efficiently).

The ECU controlled system shown in Figure 1.8 is in fact typical of a modern engine management system, although this example does not show all of the sensors and actuators that could be fitted. The example does however illustrate a number of sensors and actuators that can be controlled on a typical vehicle system that is fully computer controlled. The engine management system is a good example of the absence of driver input to the control of the system (apart from placing a foot on the throttle to select the desired speed).

Key Points

All complex systems can be considered as having inputs, control and outputs

Sensors usually provide inputs, and actuators are controlled by ECU outputs

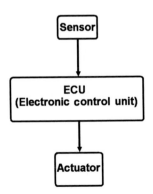

Figure 1.7 ECU controlled circuit with a single sensor and single actuator

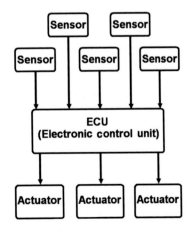

Figure 1.8 ECU controlled circuit with multiple sensors and actuators

See *Hillier's Fundamentals of Motor Vehicle Technology Book 3* for more detailed information about the electronic components used in an ECU.

1.3.1 Decision making process

The electronic control unit is often referred to by many other names, such as electronic control module, black box or simply the computer. However, the most commonly used name is the electronic control unit, which is generally abbreviated to ECU.

Although the ECU can provide a number of functions and perform a number of tasks, it is primarily the 'brain' of the system because it effectively makes decisions. In reality, however, an ECU makes decisions based on information received (from sensors) and then performs a predetermined task (which has been programmed into the ECU). Whereas a human brain is capable of 'free thinking', an ECU is very much restricted in its decision making process because it can only make decisions that it has been programmed to make.

To compare free thinking with programmed decision making, imagine a car driver approaching a set of traffic lights when the green 'go' light is replaced by the amber 'caution or slow down' light. The driver can make a decision either to slow down, or to accelerate and get across the lights before the red 'stop' light is illuminated. This decision is based on an assessment of the conditions; different drivers will make different decisions, and in fact one driver could make different decisions on different occasions even if the conditions were identical. To make a similar decision as to whether to slow down or accelerate, an ECU would also assess conditions such as vehicle speed and distance to the traffic lights, as well as road conditions (wet, icy, etc.). The ECU would then make the decision based on the programming. If the conditions (information) were the same on every occasion, the ECU would always make the same decision because the programming dictates the decision (not free thinking).

In reality, ECUs and computers in general are progressively becoming more sophisticated, and their programming is becoming increasingly complex. ECUs can adapt to changing conditions and can 'learn', which allows alternative decisions to be made if the original decision does not have the desired effect. A human can make a decision based on knowledge or information; if the first decision does not then produce the desired result, an alternative decision can be made because the human brain possesses the ability of free thinking. Modern ECUs do have a similar capability but it is a programmed one, designed by humans.

The decision making capability of an ECU is therefore dependent on the volume and accuracy of information it receives, and the level of sophistication of the programming.

1.3.2 Control

Having been designed with the capacity to make a pre-programmed decision, an ECU can then be used to control other components. A simple example is the use of an ECU to switch on an electric heater when the temperature gets cold. Information from a temperature sensor would inform the ECU that the temperature was falling; it could then switch on an electrical circuit for the heater.

With a simple version of this system, the ECU could be programmed to switch on the heater at a predetermined low temperature, and switch off the heater when the temperature has risen to a predetermined high temperature. Such a system would result in the temperature rising and falling in cycles as the heater was turned on and off. Note that the temperature sensor could be a simple switch that opened or closed at a predetermined temperature, providing an appropriate signal to the ECU.

A more sophisticated system could however be designed to maintain the temperature at a more constant level. If the ECU was designed so that it could control the electric current passing to the heater, this would enable the heater to provide low or high levels of heat. The ECU program could include the assessment of how quickly or slowly the temperature was falling or rising, so that the ECU could switch on part or full power to the heater. If the temperature was falling rapidly, the ECU could switch on full power to the heater. If the temperature was falling slowly, the ECU would need only to switch on part power to the heater. In this more sophisticated system, the temperature sensor would have to indicate the full range of temperature values to the ECU, i.e. the signal from the sensor would have to change progressively with change in temperature; the ECU could consequently assess the rate at which temperature was changing.

With the appropriate information from one or more sensors, the ECU can be programmed to provide the appropriate control over a component (such as the heater). The achievement of better or more sophisticated control of a component inevitably requires more sophisticated and complex programming of the ECU. However, to achieve the required level of sophisticated control usually requires a greater amount of more accurate information, i.e. a greater number of sensors, each of which should provide more accurate information.

For example, compare an older fuel injection system with a modern engine management system. Because of tighter emission regulations and continuous efforts to improve economy and performance, the modern engine management system ECU must carry out many more tasks with greater levels of control than older systems. Figure 1.9 identifies some of the components in an early

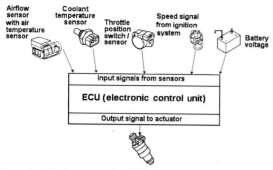

Figure 1.11 Modern ECU and components

Figure 1.9 Earlier generation ECU controlled fuel injection system

type of computer controlled fuelling system, which has relatively few sensors and relatively few actuators, so that the ECU has only a small number of tasks or control functions to perform.

Figure 1.10 lists the components from a modern engine management system where the ECU has a much larger range of tasks to perform. The number of sensors and actuators is therefore much greater than on earlier systems. On the modern system, the ECU controls a much larger number of other components, and in fact has some control over other systems such as the air conditioning system (the engine management ECU can influence the operation of the air conditioning compressor, so that the compressor, which is driven by the engine, is switched off when full engine power is required).

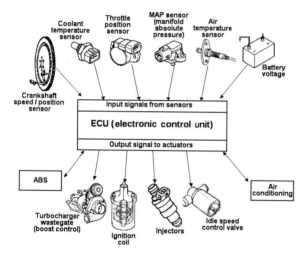

Figure 1.10 Modern engine management system. The system has a large number of sensors and actuators and the ECU therefore has a large number of tasks and control functions to perform including influence of other systems

1.3.3 ECU components and construction

Hillier's Fundamentals of Motor Vehicle Technology Book 3 provides a detailed explanation of the components and operations of ECUs, but a brief explanation is required at this stage to enable the reader to appreciate the complexity of the ECU.

Main casing

An ECU (Figure 1.11) is, amongst other things, a computer. Readers who use PCs or laptops will know that they produce a considerable amount of heat. In many cases an electric fan is used to move cooling air around the PC or laptop to remove some of the heat. The more powerful the computer, the more heat it produces. An ECU is a powerful computer, and therefore produces heat that must be removed or dissipated. Although some very early ECUs were located on the vehicle so that a cooling fan could help remove some of the heat, ideally they need to be located where they are unlikely to be exposed to moisture, as well as being isolated from vibrations and kept away from engine heat. In general, therefore, although not always, ECUs are located within the passenger compartment. The ECU main casing is usually an alloy casting which, because it can be bolted to the vehicle bodywork, should help to dissipate heat.

Microprocessor

As previously mentioned, a computer is regarded as the brain of a controlled system; the ECU contains one or more microprocessors which are the main decision making components. As with a normal PC or laptop, the microprocessor receives information to enable it to make calculations (effectively the decisions). The microprocessor then provides an appropriate output signal, which is used to control an actuator or influence another system (usually by communicating with another ECU). Figure 1.12 shows the essential functions within the ECU and the essential tasks of the microprocessor.

If we refer back to the example of the ECU controlling a heater (section 1.3.2), the decisions as to when to switch on the heater, and whether part or full power should be used for the heater, are calculated or decided by the microprocessor.

Amplifier (output or driver stage)

Microprocessors operate using very weak signals, i.e. low voltage and current, so would not be directly

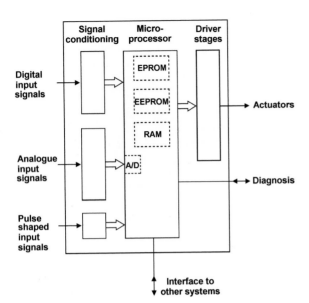

Figure 1.12 Signal processing in the ECU

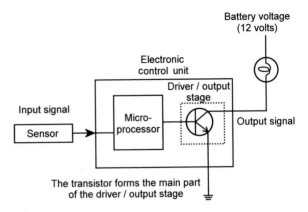

Figure 1.13 Power transistor functioning as a switch in a light circuit

connected to the heater (section 1.3.2), which uses much higher voltages and currents. The same applies to an ECU that is controlling a vehicle system; most vehicle systems operate on 12 volts with relatively high currents, which are much higher than the voltages used within microprocessors. To overcome the problem, the output or control signal from the microprocessor will usually be passed to some form of amplifier. The amplifier receives the control signal from the microprocessor and then provides an amplified or stronger signal to the actuator.

The final part of the amplifier system is often referred to as the **output**, **power** or **driver** stage. The driver stage amplifier often contains a power transistor, which may be seen mounted on the outside of the ECU casing to help with heat dissipation. A simple power transistor can be regarded as a switch that will switch a high power circuit on or off when an appropriate signal is received from a low power circuit. Therefore, if the transistor is connected into the 12 volt circuit for an actuator, or, for this example, a light bulb, it will switch the light bulb on or off when the appropriate low voltage signal is received from the microprocessor. The signal from the microprocessor could be a simple on or off signal: the power transistor would then switch the 12 volt circuit on or off.

Figure 1.13 shows a simple circuit where a light bulb is switched on or off using a power transistor. Note that the transistor is switching the earth or return part of the 12 volt circuit. The transistor receives a signal from the microprocessor and effectively emulates or copies the signal onto the 12 volt circuit.

There are a number of ways in which a power transistor can switch or affect a higher power circuit. Although a simple on or off function is commonly used, a transistor can emulate or copy a progressively

changing input signal. Therefore, if the signal passing into the transistor progressively rises and falls in strength, the transistor can progressively increase and decrease the current flow passing through the high power circuit.

High speed switching of circuits
The ECU on a modern vehicle system is often tasked with switching a circuit on and off at very high speed and frequency, such as when an ignition coil or fuel injector is switched on and off (which could occur as often as 100 times a second on an engine operating at high revolutions per minute). Therefore the decision making process in the microprocessor would produce an output signal that switches on and off at this frequency, and the power transistor would also switch on and off the 12 volt or power circuit at the same frequency.

Memory
Computers, including ECUs, have a **memory** which is stored in a memory microchip. There are different types of memory, but all of them essentially store a description of the tasks that the ECU must perform. When the microprocessor is making calculations, it will refer to the memory or 'talk' to the memory to establish what task should be performed when certain items of information are received. As an example, if we again refer to the computer controlled heater system covered in section 1.3.2, the information received by the microprocessor could indicate a low temperature; the microprocessor would then refer to the memory to find out what task to perform. The memory would indicate that the task is to switch on the heater.

The memory contains all of the necessary operating details applicable to the system being controlled by the ECU. For example, if the ECU is controlling a fuel injection system, all the information about the fuelling requirements are contained within the memory. Therefore, if the information passed to the microprocessor includes engine speed, engine temperature, throttle position, etc., the microprocessor refers to the memory to find out how long an injector should be switched on for (how long the injector should remain open so that the correct quantity of fuel can be delivered). These operating details are placed or 'programmed' into the memory either at the time of ECU manufacture or at a later time using dedicated equipment (in both cases, this is referred to as the software program). In many cases, it is possible to reprogram the memory using modified software, which can be useful if it is found that the original program has a minor fault, such as causing a hesitation when the vehicle is under acceleration.

In the memory systems discussed so far, once the memory chip has been programmed with the operating details, this program remains permanently in the memory chip. However, there are situations where the memory details change. A simple example is when a memory chip might receive information relating to the number of miles or kilometres that the vehicle has travelled; this information could be used to calculate fuel consumption. However, when the driver resets the memory, the information is then erased, i.e. it is not permanent. The memory chips that store this type of information can lose it when the power is switched off, so it is often necessary to provide a back-up power supply using a small battery (usually contained within the ECU) to prevent loss of data. Note that some ECUs have a permanent power supply from the vehicle battery (even when the ignition is switched off). In these cases, the memory will be retained as long as the vehicle battery is not disconnected.

Analogue and digital signals

An **analogue signal** can be regarded as a signal or indicator that continuously changes from one value to another. A good example is a speedometer using a needle to sweep around the gauge with changes in speed: the visual display is an analogue type display, which shows progressive change.

A signal that relies on a change in voltage can also be analogue. An example is the change in voltage that occurs when a simple lighting dimmer control is altered from the 'dark' to the 'bright' position. If a voltmeter were connected to the output terminal of the dimmer control (which is usually a variable resistor), the voltage would be seen to progressively increase and decrease when the control was altered.

A voltage signal produced by many sensors can be an analogue signal. An example is a throttle position sensor, which uses a variable resistor in much the same way as the light dimmer switch: when the throttle is opened or closed, the voltage progressively increases or decreases (Figure 1.14).

Although earlier electronic systems relied on analogue signals and in fact the electronics were analogue based, modern computers and electronic systems are generally digital systems.

A **digital signal** provides a stepped or pulsed signal. A digital display can be used on a speedometer to

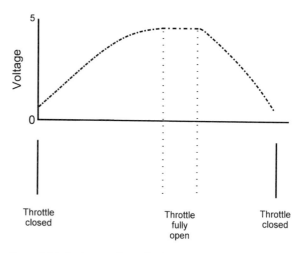

Figure 1.14 Analogue voltage signal produced by a throttle position sensor

display speed in steps. These steps could be in increments of 5 km/h or 5 mile/h. In such a case the driver would only see the display change when the speed increased by 5 km/h or 5 mile/h. Digital electronic signals are also structured in steps, which generally consist of electrical pulses.

ECUs on modern vehicles operate using digital electronics. However, in basic terms, the digital process consists of on and off pulses. In effect there are only two main conditions that the ECU works with: the on and off parts of the digital signal.

Signals that are either passing into, passing out of or passing within an ECU should ideally also be digital signals. These on and off pulses can then be counted by the ECU (counting either the on parts or the off parts of the signal). Alternatively the on and off pulses can be used as a reference by the ECU, which could result in the ECU performing a predefined task. The ECU does in fact examine the digital signal in a number of ways, which allows the ECU to extract different information from the signal such as speed or frequency (Figure 1.15a).

In reality, when a digital signal is being used as an information signal passing into the ECU, it does not necessarily have to be exactly on or off. An example could be a light switch in a 12 volt circuit, which would produce an on signal of 12 volts and an off signal of zero volts. However, the ECU could be programmed to accept any voltage above 9 volts as being on, and any voltage below 3 volts as being off. Therefore, if the signal voltage from a sensor progressively changes between zero volts and 12 volts (an analogue signal), the ECU could still respond to the same programmed voltage thresholds of 9 volts as an upper limit and 3 volts as a lower limit (Figure 1.15b). We should not therefore always refer to a digital signal as being fully on or off, but regard it as having upper or lower thresholds, which can be monitored by the ECU as reference points.

Figure 1.15 Analogue and digital signals
a Digital signal, where the pulses could be used to provide speed or frequency information
b Analogue signal where the ECU locks on to the 3 volt and 9 volt thresholds reference points
c Principle of analogue to digital converters

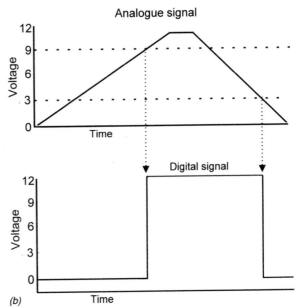

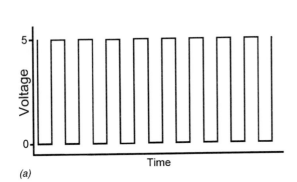

(a)

(b)

The 9 volt threshold is identified when the voltage is rising
The 3 volt threshold is identified when the voltage is falling

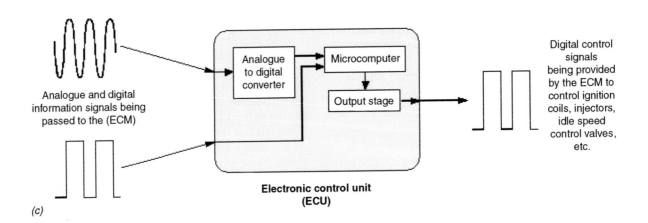

(c)

Analogue to digital converters

Because ECUs ideally require a digital signal, some form of conversion is necessary to change the analogue signal from a sensor into a digital signal.

An example could be a temperature sensor, which is used as a means to switch on a cooling fan. The ECU could switch on the cooling fan when the sensor signal voltage reaches the 9 volt threshold, but the ECU would not switch off the fan until the sensor voltage fell to the 3 volt threshold (Figure 1.15b). The ECU would therefore ideally require a modified signal that only identified or 'locked on' to the 9 volt and the 3 volt thresholds. In effect, this modification process takes place within the ECU: an analogue signal is passed to the ECU, which contains a converter that converts the analogue signal into a digital signal. Because many sensors produce analogue signals that need to be converted to digital signals to enable the microprocessor to function, a device known as an analogue to digital converter (A/D converter) is used.

Figure 1.15c shows the principle of an A/D converter and an indication of a typical analogue signal and a digital signal. Refer to *Hillier's Fundamentals of Motor Vehicle Technology Book 3* for more information on analogue and digital signals as well as on A/D converters.

Note that an ECU can also contain converters that change digital signals into analogue signals. This might be necessary if the actuator operates using an analogue signal. A simple example is a fuel gauge, which may require an analogue signal to enable the gauge needle to indicate the fuel level. Although the microprocessor is accurately creating the applicable digital signal, it would need to be converted to some form of analogue signal to operate the gauge. In reality, more and more actuators are using digital signals.

The complete ECU

A fully operational modern ECU will contain those components detailed above. Although many other electronic components are required to make an ECU operate, those discussed so far are the main functional components.

In conclusion therefore, the ECU receives information from sensors (the information might be either digital or analogue). The digital information passes directly to the microprocessor, but the analogue information must be converted to a digital signal before being passed to the microprocessor. The microprocessor then assesses the information, refers to the programmed memory to find out what tasks to perform, makes the appropriate calculations and passes an appropriate control signal to the relevant actuator (or provides signals for an electronic component such as a digital display). Where the actuator is operated using higher voltages and currents (such as a fuel injector), the weak digital signal from the microprocessor will need to be amplified using a power transistor or final stage.

The essential point to remember is that an ECU cannot achieve its main objective, which is to operate an actuator or electronic component, unless the appropriate signals are received. This is true of all ECU controlled vehicle systems and almost all other computers: some form of input signal is required before a calculation and control process can take place.

Note: Understanding of the ECU and an ECU controlled system enables a technician to perform diagnostic processes much more easily. If the function of each sensor and each actuator is understood, a relatively quick diagnosis can be carried out. Although specialised test equipment can be used, knowledge of the system operation greatly improves the ability to perform quick and accurate diagnosis.

Hillier's Fundamentals of Motor Vehicle Technology Book 3 provides an in-depth examination of the operation and construction of some sensors and actuators. In other chapters details of specific sensors and actuators are dealt with in relation to specific systems. However, the following two sections provide a general understanding of sensors and actuators commonly used on vehicle systems.

> **Key Points**
>
> ECUs contain one or more microprocessors that carry out calculations and follow lists of instructions
>
> ECUs contain A/D converters that act on sensor inputs, and D/A converters, as well as driver circuits to control outputs

1.4   SENSORS: A MEANS OF PROVIDING INFORMATION

1.4.1 Sensor applications

It has previously been explained that an ECU controlled system requires information to enable the ECU to make the appropriate calculations and decisions, which then in turn enables it to control actuators or electronic devices. The greater the amount of information that can be supplied to the ECU, the greater the control capability and number of different control functions.

An ECU controlling an earlier generation of electronic fuel injection system may have required only four or five sensors to provide the required information to it. This is because the ECU would only have been required to control the fuel injectors and therefore only limited amounts of information were necessary. However, later systems that also included control of the ignition system, idle speed and emissions devices (thus forming an engine management system) would have as many as 20 sensors, or more in some cases. As well as controlling more systems, modern ECUs require more accurate information from the sensors in order to meet stricter emissions legislation. Sensors have therefore become more sophisticated as well as increasing in number.

Whatever a sensor might be required to measure, e.g. temperature or movement, it must be able to provide a signal to the ECU that can be interpreted by the ECU.

Although the different types of electrical signal are covered later in this section, an example of change in the electrical signal would occur when temperature changes which, for most temperature sensors, results in an increase or decrease in the signal voltage passed from the sensor to the ECU.

Figure 1.16 indicates the more common examples of parameters that sensors must detect or measure on modern vehicle systems. Many other sensor applications are not included in the chart, but it does provide a good indication of the types of information and the types of applications for many sensors.

From Figure 1.16, it is possible to appreciate that sensors perform a wide variety of measurement tasks. The parameters most commonly measured are:

- **temperature** (of fluids or exhaust gas)
- **movement** (angular and linear), including rotational sensing such as crankshaft speed
- **position** (angular and linear), primarily for partial rotation of components or partial linear movement but also including exact angular position of rotational sensors, e.g. the angle of rotation of a crankshaft at a given time
- **pressure/vacuum**
- **oxygen**, using a specific type of sensor used to measure the oxygen content in the exhaust gas.

Figure 1.16 Sensors and sensor applications

Measurement task	Common applications	Additional applications
Engine coolant temperature	Fuel/ignition/engine management/emission control	Cooling fan, driver information display
Air flow (engine load sensing)	Fuel/ignition/engine management/emission control	
Air mass (engine load sensing)	Fuel/ignition/engine management/emission control	
Ambient air temperature	Fuel/ignition/engine management/emission control	Driver information display/air conditioning
Intake air temperature	Fuel/ignition/engine management/emission control	
Engine oil temperature	Fuel/ignition/engine management/emission control	
Throttle position	Fuel/ignition/engine management/emission control	Automatic transmission/anti-wheel spin/other vehicle stability control/air conditioning
Engine speed	Fuel/ignition/engine management/emission control	Automatic transmission/anti-wheel spin/other vehicle stability control
Engine intake vacuum/pressure (engine load sensing)	Fuel/ignition/engine management/emission control	Automatic transmission
Crankshaft angle position sensor	Fuel/ignition/engine management/emission control	
Camshaft angle position sensor	Fuel/ignition/engine management/emission control	
Fuel pressure	Fuel/ignition/engine management/emission control	
Fuel tank pressure	Fuel/ignition/engine management/emission control	
Boost pressure	Turbocharger/supercharger	**Note:** Information from other engine management sensors will also be used for controlling turbo or superchargers
Oxygen (oxygen content of exhaust gas)	Fuel/ignition/engine management/emission control	
Exhaust gas temperature	Fuel/ignition/engine management/emission control	
Position sensor for exhaust gas recirculation valve	Fuel/ignition/engine management/emission control	
Wheel speed (vehicle speed)	Anti-lock brakes/vehicle stability control	Driver information (vehicle speed)/ automatic transmission/airbag
Brake pedal position (on or off)	Anti-lock brakes/vehicle stability control	
Acceleration/deceleration sensing (sideways movement as well as forward and backward movement)	Anti-lock brakes/vehicle stability control	Airbag/other safety systems
Steering angle	Vehicle stability control	Power steering

Mechanical and electronic sensing devices

Although some sensors use a combination of mechanical and electrical components, which respond together to movement, position or pressure (and occasionally temperature), wherever possible most modern sensors only use electronic/electrical components. A typical example is a pressure sensor, which in the past used an aneroid capsule that deformed when the pressure changed (Figure 1.17). The deformation of the capsule caused a rod to move; the rod could be connected to a variable resistor which altered the voltage in the sensor's electrical circuit. Later types of pressure/vacuum sensor use an electronic component with no moving parts. Exposure to pressure or vacuum causes the resistance of the component to change; this change in resistance then alters the voltage in the signal circuit (see Figure 1.17).

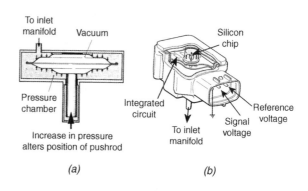

Figure 1.17 Two types of pressure sensor
a Capsule type pressure sensor using mechanical components
b Electronic type pressure sensor

1.5   EXAMPLES OF DIFFERENT TYPES OF SENSOR

Note: The explanations contained within this section cover a number of commonly used sensors with examples of the types of signal they produce. Although other types of sensor are used in automotive applications, they will generally be adaptations of those covered below. However, other sensors are covered in applicable sections within this book. For those readers wishing to have more detailed explanations of the electrical and electronic background to these sensors, see *Hillier's Fundamentals of Motor Vehicle Technology Book 3*, which provides advanced studies on electrical and electronic theory.

1.5.1 Temperature sensors

Temperature sensors (Figure 1.18a) are used in a wide variety of applications, especially in engine control systems, i.e. ignition, fuel and engine management. Additional applications include air conditioning systems, automatic transmissions and any system where temperature control or temperature measurement is critical to the system operation.

Temperature sensors are manufactured using a resistance as the main component. The value of this resistance changes with temperature. This type of resistor is called a **thermistor:** the term is an amalgamation of therm (as in thermometer) and resistor. Because the sensor resistance forms part of an electrical 'series resistance' circuit (other resistances are contained within the ECU), when the temperature and therefore the resistance changes, the voltage and current in the circuit also change. The ECU, which of course forms part of the circuit (Figure 1.18b) and supplies the reference voltage, will now have a signal voltage that changes with temperature.

As with almost all modern ECU controlled systems, a reference or starting voltage is applied to the sensor circuit. This reference voltage originates at the ECU, which reduces the traditional 12 volt vehicle supply to a stabilised or regulated voltage, typically around 5 volts. Note however that, because this circuit is used only to provide a low power signal (and not to operate an actuator such as an electric motor), current flow in the circuit is very low. The current flow passes from the ECU, through the temperature sensor resistance and then returns to the ECU. Because the circuit is a series resistance circuit, when the sensor resistance changes the current in the circuit also changes, thus providing the required temperature related signal.

There are generally two main types of resistance based temperature sensors:

- With the first type, the resistance within the sensor decreases when the temperature increases. This type is referred to as having a 'negative temperature coefficient' (NTC).
- With the second type, the resistance increases when the temperature increases. This type is referred to as having a positive temperature coefficient (PTC).

Temperature sensor analogue signal
With very few exceptions, temperature sensors produce an analogue signal. The exceptions are sensors using a switch, or contacts which close or open at specified temperatures. In these cases the signal will be either on or off.

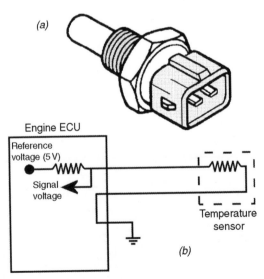

Figure 1.18 Temperature sensor
a *Typical appearance. The example shown is a coolant temperature sensor from an engine management system*
b *Wiring for a temperature sensor*

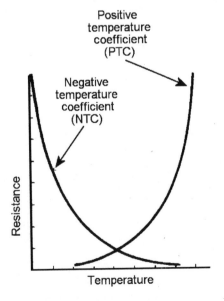

Figure 1.19 *Analogue signal voltage for a typical temperature sensor circuit. Note the progressive change in voltage as the temperature rises and falls*

The analogue signal voltage produced by sensors with a thermistor progressively increases or decreases with changes in temperature. Because it is common practice to use NTC sensors, where the resistance reduces as the temperature increases, the signal voltage will generally also reduce as the temperature increases. The typical signal voltage from a temperature sensor circuit ranges from approximately 4.5 volts when the temperature is low, down to approximately 0.5 volts when the temperature is high. More specific values are quoted in Chapter 3, which describes how these sensors are used in a fuel injection system.

Figure 1.19 shows the typical analogue output signal voltage from a temperature sensor circuit when temperature changes occur. Note that because the signal is analogue, the change in voltage is progressive.

1.5.2 Rotational speed sensors

Variable reluctance type

Rotational speed sensors are used to detect speed or revolutions per minute (rev/min) of a component; two common examples are an engine crankshaft and a road wheel. In both cases, the rotational speed information is required to enable the ECU to perform its calculations. For an engine system, the crankshaft speed information is used for the calculation of fuel and ignition requirements, as well as for emission control. The wheel speed information is used to enable calculations for anti-lock braking, wheel spin control and other vehicle stability systems. The wheel speed information can of course also be used to calculate road speed or distance travelled; this information is then displayed to the driver or can be used to calculate fuel consumption and other information.

In most cases, rotational speed sensors work on a simple principle, similar to that of an electrical generator: when a magnetic field is moved through a coil of wire it generates an electric current. The rotational speed sensor uses an adaptation of this principle, which relies on altering the strength of the magnetic field (or magnetic flux). This is achieved by passing a ferrous metal object (iron or steel) close to or through the magnetic field. The strength of the magnetic field or flux increases or decreases when the metal object is moved close to or away from the magnetic field; this change in magnetic flux causes a small current to be generated or induced within the coil of wire. These sensors are often referred to as **inductive** or **magnetic variable reluctance** sensors.

Rotational speed sensors are often constructed with a permanent magnet located inside or adjacent to a coil of wire. When a metal component (reluctor) passes close to the sensor, the magnetic field or flux is altered. However, the reluctor often takes the form of a disc, which has one or more 'teeth', each of which acts as a reluctor. Therefore, as each tooth passes the sensor, it causes an electric current to be produced within the coil of wire.

As shown in Figure 1.20a, a crankshaft speed sensor can be located adjacent to the front or back of the crankshaft, and a disc with one or more teeth, mounted on the crankshaft, can be used as the reluctor disc. For wheel speed sensors, a similar arrangement is used, but the reluctor disc is located on the rotating portion of the wheel hub, and the sensor is mounted so that it is close to the reluctor disc. Figure 1.20b shows a similar sensor used to measure wheel speed rotation (ABS wheel speed sensor); note that the reluctor has a large number of reference points.

Rotational speed sensor analogue signal

When each reluctor tooth passes the sensor, the change in the magnetic field or flux produces a small low voltage electric current. As each tooth passes the sensor,

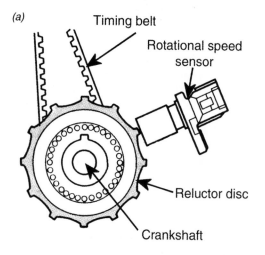

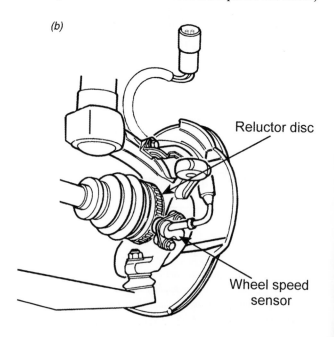

Figure 1.20 Typical arrangement for simple rotational speed sensor.
a Crankshaft speed sensor with a number of reluctor teeth (reference points)
b Wheel speed sensor

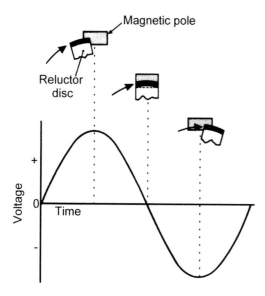

Figure 1.21 *Analogue signal produced by a rotational speed sensor. Note that the voltage progressively increases and decreases as the reluctor tooth approaches and leaves the pole of the sensor magnet*

the voltage increases and decreases, resulting in a continuously changing voltage as the crankshaft or wheel rotates. In fact, the current flow oscillates one way and then the other within the circuit, and the voltage oscillates from positive to negative. The voltage increase and decrease is shown in Figure 1.21; note that the highest voltage is produced when the reluctor tooth is approaching the pole of the sensor magnet, and the lowest voltage is produced when the reluctor tooth is leaving the magnet pole. If there is no movement of the reluctor tooth, there will be no current or voltage produced, irrespective of the position of the reluctor tooth. The signal voltage progressively increases and decreases with the rotation, so the signal is in analogue form. The ECU, which has an inbuilt timer or clock, is therefore able to count the number of pulses over a given time, and thus calculate the speed of rotation.

It should be noted that there are variations in the way in which some rotational position sensors operate. Some sensors use an 'exciter coil' which has a small voltage applied to it, allowing a stronger signal to be produced. Other types use a **Hall effect** system to produce a signal. Both of these types of sensor are discussed in *Hillier's Fundamentals of Motor Vehicle Technology Book 3*.

Rotational angular position sensor

In some cases, it is beneficial to be able to calculate or assess the position of a rotating component such as a crankshaft. If there is a means by which the ECU can determine the position of the crankshaft during its rotation, it is possible to control accurately the timing of ignition and fuelling. By adapting the previously described rotational speed sensor system, it is in fact relatively easy to provide an angular position reference.

If, for example, the crankshaft reluctor disc has only one reluctor tooth, this tooth could be the reference to crankshaft angle and could therefore indicate top dead centre (TDC) for piston number 1. In fact, this single tooth could also provide the speed reference as well, although the signal will only be produced once for every crankshaft rotation. It is, however, common practice to provide a number of teeth around the reluctor disc (60 teeth is not uncommon), and for each tooth to represent a particular angle of crankshaft rotation. If there were 60 reluctor teeth, each tooth would represent 6° of crankshaft angle rotation. However, to establish a master reference or master position point, it is normal practice either to miss out one tooth or make one tooth a substantially different shape from the other teeth (Figure 1.22). Whichever method was used, the signal from the sensor would contain one voltage change that was different from the rest of the signal, and therefore provide a master reference point such as TDC for number 1 piston.

With a possible 60 reference points (or more in some cases), the ECU is now able to calculate crankshaft speed and the rotational position of the crankshaft very accurately. In fact, the ECU can assess any increase or decrease in crankshaft speed as each tooth passes the sensor. Assuming there were 60 teeth or reference points on the crankshaft reluctor disc, this would enable the ECU to assess the change in crankshaft speed at every 6° of crankshaft rotation. Control of ignition timing, fuelling and emissions would therefore be far more accurate than if only one reluctor reference tooth were used.

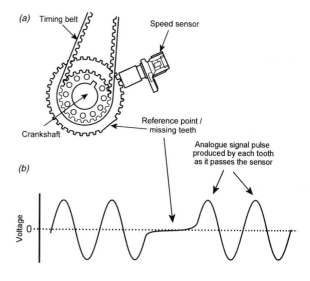

Figure 1.22 *Variable reluctance crankshaft position/speed sensor with master reference point*
a Crankshaft reluctor disc with a master position reference point (missing tooth)
b Note the different shape of the signal created by the missing tooth

(a)

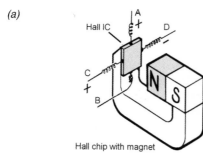

Hall IC

Hall chip with magnet

vane to deflect
flux away from Hall I C

Hall I C

Hall chip assembly with vane
deflecting magnetic flux

(b)

Voltage

(c)

HT rotor arm

Magnet

Vanes on rotor disc

Hall IC / chip

Figure 1.23 Hall effect pulse generator
a Hall effect pulse generator
b Digital signal produced by a Hall effect pulse generator
c Hall effect system located in an ignition distributor

Many engine management systems have a position sensor, which indicates the rotational position of the camshaft, in addition to a crankshaft speed/position sensor. The camshaft sensor is included because a crankshaft TDC position reference usually relates to more than one cylinder, e.g. cylinders 1 and 4, or cylinders 1 and 6, so the ECU is not able to calculate which cylinder is on the compression stroke and which cylinder is on the exhaust stroke, whereas a camshaft only rotates once for every engine operating cycle, i.e. a master reference for any of the cylinders will pass the sensor only once for every engine cycle. Therefore a camshaft position sensor can indicate to the ECU the position of cylinder 1 only (or any other cylinder chosen to be the master reference cylinder), so it is possible for the ECU to control injectors individually, timing them accurately to each cylinder. It is also necessary to have a cylinder reference signal for the modern generation of ignition systems that use individual ignition coils for each cylinder (there is no distributor rotor arm to distribute the high tension (HT) to each spark plug).

Rotational speed/angular position sensor (Hall effect)
Although performing a similar task to the variable reluctance type sensors described above, the Hall effect sensor provides a digital signal as opposed to an analogue signal.

Hall effect principle
Figure 1.23a shows a Hall integrated circuit (IC) or Hall chip. When a small input electrical current is passed across chip terminals A to B (input current), and the chip is exposed to a magnetic field (magnetic flux), a small current is then available across C to D (output current). A permanent magnet is located close to the Hall chip, but the magnetic flux can be prevented from reaching the Hall chip if a metal object is placed between the magnet and the chip. On the example shown in Figure 1.23a, the metal object that is used to block the magnetic flux is in fact a rotor or trigger disc, which is mounted on a rotating shaft. The rotor disc has a number of vanes and cut outs which, when the rotor is turning, alternately block and allow the magnetic flux to reach the Hall chip. The result is that the flow of current across the chip terminals C to D will be switched on and off in pulses. This pulsed signal can provide a speed reference signal to an ECU. Figure 1.23b shows a typical digital signal produced by a Hall effect pulse generator.

Hall effect ignition trigger
On some earlier generations of electronic ignition systems, but also on some engine management systems, a Hall effect pulse generator was located in the ignition distributor body (Figure 1.23c). The rotor disc had the same number of cut outs and vanes as cylinders. The rotor disc was mounted on the distributor shaft and

rotated at half engine speed, i.e. one complete rotation of the rotor for every engine cycle, which is two crankshaft rotations. If the rotor had four vanes and cut outs (for a four-cylinder engine), it would provide four pulses for every engine cycle. The pulsed digital signal would be passed to an ignition amplifier or to an ECU, which would then switch on and off the ignition coil circuit, thus producing the high voltage for the spark plugs (see Chapter 2).

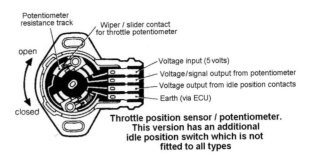

Throttle position sensor / potentiometer. This version has an additional idle position switch which is not fitted to all types

1.5.3 Position sensors for detecting small angles of movement

The rotational position sensors described above are designed for use on fast rotating components such as crankshafts. However, there are a number of components that may only partially rotate, and not in fact do so continuously. A very common example is a throttle butterfly or throttle plate. The throttle butterfly is located on a spindle and may rotate through less than 90 degrees, from idle through to the fully open position. On engine management systems and on older fuel and ignition systems, the ECU requires information relating to the throttle position to make accurate calculations for fuelling and ignition timing, as well as for some other control functions.

Almost all modern throttle position sensors (see Figure 1.24) use a potentiometer (variable resistance), which is usually connected to the throttle butterfly spindle, although some types are connected to the throttle pedal or throttle linkage. The potentiometer provides a signal voltage that increases and decreases when the throttle is opened and closed, equipping the ECU with information about the angular position of the throttle butterfly. Additionally, the ECU can detect the rate at which the voltage increases or decreases, enabling the ECU to calculate how quickly the driver is intending to accelerate or decelerate. Information about rate of change of throttle position enables the ECU to provide more accurate fuel and ignition timing control.

Throttle position sensor analogue signal
The throttle position sensor provides a progressively increasing and decreasing voltage when the throttle is opened and closed. As with many other sensors, the throttle position sensor requires a reference voltage, typically around 5 volts. The voltage is applied to the potentiometer resistance track, and a wiper or moving contact moves across the track when the throttle is opened or closed. Because the resistance along the track increases from a low value (possibly as low as zero ohms) to a high value, the voltage at one end of the track could be 5 volts whilst at the other end it could be as low as zero volts. As the wiper moves along the track, the voltage at the contact point (wiper onto the track) will change as the wiper moves. The wiper moves with the movement of the throttle; therefore different throttle positions will result in different voltages at the

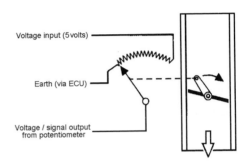

Figure 1.24 Throttle position sensor and potentiometer schematic layout

wiper contact point (see Figure 1.25). The wiper is then connected back to the ECU, which uses the voltage value as an indication of throttle position.

Although there are variations in the construction of throttle position sensors and the signal voltages, it is quite common to have a low voltage of around 0.5 volts to indicate the throttle closed position and a higher voltage around 4.5 volts to indicate that the throttle is fully open.

Note that some throttle position sensors, especially older designs, have contacts that open and close when the throttle is opened and closed. In these sensors one

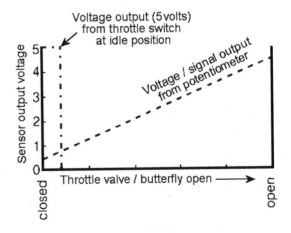

Throttle position sensor output / signal voltage

Figure 1.25 Analogue signal produced by a throttle position sensor compared with angle of throttle opening

set of contacts is arranged so that they close when the throttle is fully closed. A second set is also used to indicate when the throttle reaches a certain opening point, e.g. 60% open, an indication that the driver is accelerating or requires more power. Some throttle sensors have a combination of contacts and a potentiometer, although this type is now becoming less common.

There are other components fitted to ECU controlled vehicle systems that also use position sensors similar to the throttle position sensor, and these are dealt with in the relevant chapters.

1.5.4 Pressure sensors

There are generally two main types of pressure sensor: a mechanical type and an electronic type.

Mechanical type

One simple mechanical type makes use of either a diaphragm or capsule, which is exposed to the pressure, or depression (Figures 1.26a and 1.26b).

For example, a pressure sensor can be used to sense engine intake depression (often referred to as engine vacuum). Because engine intake depression varies with engine load and throttle position (and other factors), the sensor can pass a signal to the ECU that indicates the engine load. As a result, the ECU can control fuel quantity and ignition timing, although in fact information is required from other sensors (including engine speed and throttle position) to enable the ECU to calculate the true engine load accurately.

If the diaphragm type sensor (Figure 1.26a) was used to sense engine intake depression, the lower chamber would be exposed to atmospheric pressure and the upper chamber would be exposed to engine depression (a lower pressure unless the engine has a turbo or supercharger). When the upper chamber pressure alters (with engine operating conditions) it will cause the diaphragm to deflect or move within the casing. The diaphragm can be connected to a lever, which acts on a potentiometer, causing a voltage change in the potentiometer circuit (using the same principle as the throttle position sensor potentiometer described in the previous section). The signal voltage from the potentiometer is passed to the ECU, which is then able to control functions such as fuelling or ignition timing in response to the pressure changes. Note that on the diaphragm type sensor with a potentiometer, the signal is analogue and would progressively change in the same manner as a throttle position sensor, but in this case the changes occur with changes in engine intake pressure.

The diaphragm type sensor is in most cases too simple and inaccurate to be used for modern vehicle systems such as an engine management system; however, the principle of operation is used for some applications. A more widely used type in the past was the capsule type, whereby a capsule is sealed and

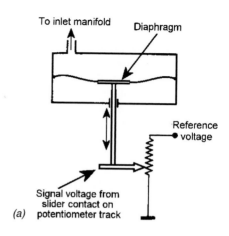

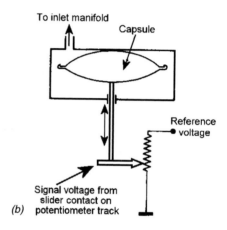

Figure 1.26 Pressure sensors and potentiometer circuits
a Diaphragm type
b Capsule type

therefore kept at a fixed pressure, and is subsequently exposed to the vacuum or depression; when the pressure outside the capsule is lower, the capsule contracts, moving the rod and potentiometer slider. There are other mechanical methods for converting pressure change into an electrical signal, although mechanical pressure sensors are rarely used on modern vehicles.

Electronic type

Electronic pressure sensors are much more reliable and accurate than mechanical sensors and have no moving parts (Figure 1.27). A solid state component or silicon chip is exposed to the pressure or depression, which puts the chip under a strain; the strain alters with pressure change. The change in strain causes a minor change in length or shape of the crystal. The change in shape or length alters the resistance of the chip; therefore, if the chip forms part of an electrical circuit, the result will be a change of voltage in that circuit. Note that, on some electronic types, the component under strain is effectively a thin diaphragm made of silicon.

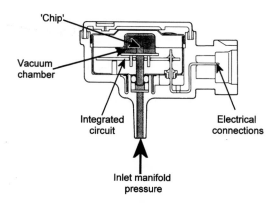

Figure 1.27 Electronic type MAP sensor

Pressure sensors can be used to measure the atmospheric pressure, fuel line and fuel tank pressure.

Pressure sensor analogue or digital signal

Electronic type sensors can produce an analogue or a digital signal, depending on their design. The analogue signals are generally simple voltage changes that increase and decrease according to changes in pressure. Typically, a voltage of around 0.5 volts would indicate a strong engine intake depression (low pressure) such as would occur at idle speed or low load conditions (throttle closed or almost closed). When the throttle is initially opened this allows the intake pressure to rise (almost no depression), which results in an increase in voltage to approximately 4.5 volts.

Note that not all analogue pressure sensors operate in the same way; therefore voltage values may differ. Some sensors may provide a high voltage when the depression is strong, and a low voltage when there is almost no depression.

Digital pressure sensors generally provide a digital pulse, which has a frequency that changes with the change in pressure. In effect, the signal provided to the ECU is a simple one consisting of many on/off pulses. The ECU effectively counts the pulses and compares them against the in-built clock or timer within the ECU. When the pressure changes, the frequency of pulses provides the ECU with a reference to the pressure.

Refer to section 1.6 for examples of analogue and digital signals.

MAP sensors

It is general practice to refer to the atmospheric pressure as being zero; this is often the value shown when a pressure gauge is not connected to a pressure source, i.e. the pressure gauge is not being used. We therefore refer to this as **gauge pressure**. However, the atmospheric pressure is of course not zero, but is in fact approximately 1 bar (approximately 14.5 lb/in^2 or 101 kilopascals), even though a gauge may indicate this as being zero. Therefore a gauge pressure of zero indicates a pressure of around 1 bar. Note, however, that some gauges are calibrated so that they indicate the actual or 'absolute' pressure.

Absolute pressure is therefore the true pressure value as opposed to the traditional gauge pressure. If a gauge reading indicates 2 bar, this would in fact be 2 bar *above* atmospheric pressure (which is already at 1 bar); the absolute pressure is therefore 3 bar.

The same applies to a pressure that is lower than atmospheric pressure. If the gauge pressure reading were lower than zero, e.g. a negative value such as 'minus 0.25 bar', this would be equivalent to an absolute pressure of 0.75 bar (1 bar minus 0.25 bar).

When a complete vacuum is formed (i.e. there is no pressure at all) the absolute pressure is zero. For this reason we should not refer to engine intake depression as being a vacuum. Intake manifold depression is a low pressure but it is not a true vacuum.

Sensing manifold absolute pressure

Pressure sensors that are used to sense engine intake depression generally now measure absolute intake pressure. These sensors are therefore referred to as manifold absolute pressure sensors (MAP sensors). The intake pressure is dependent on a number of factors including: throttle opening angle, engine load, air temperature and density, engine speed, etc. Engine condition affects the intake pressure; therefore this factor also affects the sensed pressure value. Therefore the absolute pressure value provides a more accurate indication of engine operating conditions.

MAP sensors are generally of the electronic type and may still provide either an analogue or digital signal.

1.5.5 Airflow sensing

As an alternative to the MAP or pressure sensor method of assessing engine load, many engine management systems and older fuel and ignition systems used airflow sensors. There are two types of commonly used airflow sensors: mechanical or electrical/electronic.

Mechanical

Mechanical airflow sensors are usually referred to as **flap** or **vane** type airflow meters. A hinged flap is exposed to the airflow; because the flap is spring loaded to the 'closed' or stationary position, increasing the airflow will cause the flap to open to a greater angle (Figure 1.28). The flap is connected to a sophisticated potentiometer; as with a throttle position sensor potentiometer, when the flap moves it results in a change in voltage at the potentiometer wiper contact. A more detailed explanation is provided in Chapter 2.

When an engine draws in increasing volumes of air on the induction strokes, this causes an increase in the air volume passing through the intake trunking, which is where the airflow meter is located. Therefore changes in throttle position and engine speed or load will affect the airflow, thus enabling the airflow sensor to provide a relevant voltage signal to the ECU. The ECU is then able to calculate the engine load and provide the required amount of fuel.

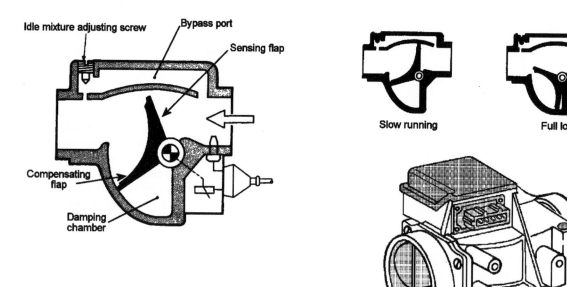

Figure 1.28 *Flap or vane type airflow sensor: cutaway view and picture/drawing*

Vane type airflow sensor analogue signal

As described above, the airflow sensor contains a potentiometer, which provides a signal voltage that progressively rises and falls as the vane or flap is moved by the increasing or decreasing airflow. The signal is therefore an analogue signal and is similar in appearance to the signal produced by a throttle position sensor (Figure 1.25).

Measuring air volume not air mass

It is important to note that the flap type airflow sensor measures air volume but not air mass. For a given volume of air, the mass can increase or decrease along with temperature and pressure changes. The greater the mass of air, the greater the amount of fuel required to maintain the correct air:fuel ratio. Through measuring only the volume, the flap type sensor is slightly limited in its capacity to provide totally accurate information to the ECU. As an example, if for a given volume of measured air the density were to reduce, this change would not be registered by a flap type sensor and would not therefore result in a reduction in fuel delivered to the cylinders; in effect the mixture would be too rich. The inaccuracies are quite small, but because emission regulations demanded tighter controls, the flap type sensor became less popular and was largely replaced by the electrical/electronic types of airflow sensors described below.

Electrical/electronic

Electrical/electronic airflow sensors generally operate on what is referred to as the **hot wire** principle. Hot wire sensors are affected by air density and can therefore provide an indication of airflow, which accounts for the mass of air rather than just the volume. These airflow sensors are often called mass airflow sensors; an example is shown in Figure 1.29.

The principle of operation relies on the fact that, when air passes across a pre-heated wire it will have a cooling effect. As the temperature of the wire changes, so does its resistance. On mass airflow sensors, the sensing wire

1 Hybrid circuit, 2 Cover, 3 Metal insert,
4 Venturi with hot wire, 5 Housing, 6 Screen,
7 Retaining ring.

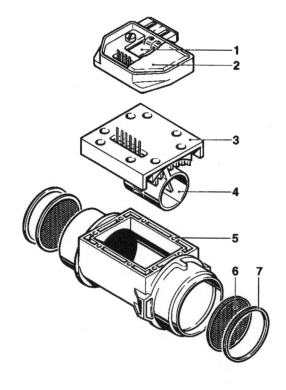

Figure 1.29 *Hot wire airflow sensor*

is heated by passing a current through the wire. When changes in airflow cause a change in the temperature and therefore changes in the resistance of the wire, the voltage then changes in the electronic circuitry contained within the sensor assembly. This circuitry (explained in Chapter 3) compensates for the change in sensing wire resistance and applies increased or decreased current to the wire to maintain the desired temperature. The change in required current flow is converted to a voltage signal that can be monitored by the ECU, i.e. the airflow mass or a change in the airflow mass results in an appropriate voltage signal passing from the sensor to the ECU.

On some types of hot wire system, the wire is occasionally heated when the engine is switched off to a much higher than normal temperature, which burns off any contamination or deposits on the wire that could otherwise affect measurement accuracy. A variation on the hot wire system is a **hot film** sensor. The operation is much the same as for the hot wire sensor but an integrated film type heated sensing element is used instead of the heated wire.

1.5.6 Oxygen (lambda) sensors

Reducing pollutants in the exhaust gas

Oxygen sensors (Figure 1.30) are used on modern motor vehicles for a very specific task: measuring the oxygen content of the exhaust gas. Whilst the oxygen sensor is not critical to the direct efficiency of the engine, it is critical to the efficiency of the exhaust emissions control system (the control of which is generally integrated into the engine management system). The catalytic converter plays the major part in reducing the pollutants contained within the exhaust emissions; the converter, in simple terms, creates a combustion process. For a catalytic converter to work efficiently, it must be fed with exhaust gases that contain the required amount of oxygen. The oxygen sensor is used to measure the oxygen content and provide a signal to the ECU which will in turn control fuelling to ensure that the exhaust gas has the correct oxygen level.

Correct air/fuel mixture

As detailed in *Hillier's Fundamentals of Motor Vehicle Technology Book 1*, efficient combustion in an engine relies on the air and petrol mixture (air:fuel ratio) being correct. The theoretically correct mixture is approximately 14.7 parts of air to 1 part of petrol (by weight); this was generally referred to as the **stoichiometric** air:fuel ratio, but is now referred to as lambda 1.

Although the air:fuel ratio varies under different operating conditions, e.g. cold running, light cruise or load conditions, modern engines do operate close to the ideal air:fuel ratio for much of the time. On a modern engine, the engine management system uses the information from various sensors to enable the ECU to calculate the required amount of fuel, thus keeping the air:fuel ratio as close as possible to the desired value.

The catalytic converter provides a further combustion process (for those exhaust gases that have not been completely burned within the engine's combustion process), this additional combustion process also requires a correct air:fuel ratio. The unburned or partially burned gases within the exhaust contain unburned or partially burned petrol; therefore if an amount of oxygen is added and the temperature within the converter is high enough, those unburned and partially burned gases will combine and ignite, hopefully creating a complete combustion of those gases (thus reducing the pollutants).

Monitoring the oxygen in the exhaust gas

In reality, the exhaust gas can contain enough oxygen to enable the unburned and partially burned fuel to ignite. However, to ensure that the correct amount of oxygen is present in the exhaust gas, the air:fuel ratio supplied to the engine must be precisely controlled, e.g. an excess of petrol (rich mixture) would lead to reduced amounts of oxygen being passed to the exhaust gas. The oxygen sensor therefore senses the oxygen content of the exhaust gas and passes a signal back to the ECU, which if necessary can alter the fuelling to correct the air:fuel ratio, thus resulting in the exhaust gas having the correct oxygen content.

Although the previous explanation provides a brief understanding of the purpose of the oxygen sensor, the operation of the catalytic converter and the oxygen sensor are in fact much more complex. These topics are therefore explained in greater detail in Chapter 2, dealing with petrol engine emissions control systems.

Oxygen measurement

(Refer to Chapter 3 for additional information.)

A typical oxygen sensor is illustrated in Figure 1.30. The sensor uses a natural process that, when specific quantities of oxygen are passed through a certain material, a small voltage is produced. Zirconium oxide is one commonly used material for an oxygen sensor element.

When the sensor is located in the exhaust pipe, one side of the sensing element is exposed to the exhaust gas whilst the other side is exposed to the atmosphere. Around 20.8% of the atmosphere consists of oxygen, whilst the exhaust gas typically has around 0.1% to 0.8% oxygen; therefore there is a substantial difference in the oxygen levels on the two sides of the sensing element, causing a small voltage to be produced. The

Figure 1.30 Typical appearance of an oxygen sensor

exact voltage will depend on the amount of oxygen in the exhaust gas. The voltage produced by the sensor is then passed to the ECU, which can alter the fuelling as necessary to ensure that the oxygen content is correct. The process is almost continuous: the sensor monitors the oxygen level and passes a signal to the ECU, which corrects the fuelling; this fuel correction then changes the oxygen level which is again monitored by the oxygen sensor, and so the process continues in a loop. This kind of process is often referred to as a **closed loop** operation.

Note that for the sensors to operate efficiently, they must be at a high temperature (typically above 350°C). The exhaust gas will provide heat but some sensors have electrical heating elements built in to the sensor body to speed up and stabilise the heating process.

Because the oxygen sensor is effectively monitoring what is now referred to as the lambda value, the oxygen sensors are commonly referred to as **lambda** sensors. However, different manufacturers (of vehicles and sensors) do use different terminology. One example is the widely used Ford term 'heated exhaust gas oxygen' (HEGO) sensor.

Pre-cat control

As detailed above, the combination of the lambda sensor and the ECU effectively controls the fine tuning of the air:fuel ratio to enable the catalytic converter to operate efficiently. The lambda sensor is located upstream (in front of) the catalytic converter and is therefore able to measure the oxygen level in the exhaust gas passing into the converter. The position of the lambda sensor in front of the catalytic converter is referred to as pre-cat control because the combinaton of lambda sensor and ECU controls the oxygen content before it reaches the catalytic converter. This arrangement is shown in Figure 1.31.

Post-cat monitoring

European legislation (and legislation in other continents) demands that an additional function is now incorporated into emission control systems. This function is part of a broad range of **on-board diagnostic** (OBD) functions. One aspect of OBD is that some form of monitoring should take place to ensure that the catalytic converter is performing efficiently.

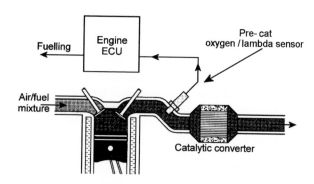

Figure 1.31 Arrangement of catalytic converter and oxygen sensor with pre-cat exhaust gas monitoring

This can be achieved by placing a second oxygen sensor after or downstream of the catalytic converter (post-cat). This arrangement is shown in Figure 1.32.

If the catalytic converter is not working, the same level of oxygen will exit the converter as entered it. The second lambda sensor signal (post-cat) will therefore be identical to the pre-cat lambda sensor signal. In such cases the ECU will establish that the catalytic converter is not working and will illuminate the dashboard warning light. A fault related code or message would also be accessible from the ECU using appropriate diagnostic equipment.

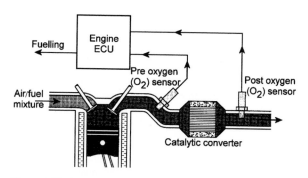

Figure 1.32 Arrangement of catalytic converter with two lambda sensors for pre-cat measurement and post-cat monitoring and oxygen sensor

1.6 OBTAINING INFORMATION FROM ANALOGUE AND DIGITAL SENSOR SIGNALS

As discussed in section 1.3.3, a modern ECU uses digital electronic processes. However, many sensors might provide only an analogue signal, which must be converted by the analogue to digital converter that is contained within the ECU. Analogue signals produced by sensors vary quite considerably, although essentially

they all provide a progressive change in voltage and can therefore be treated in a similar way by the analogue to digital converter (A/D converter).

Some examples of typical analogue signals produced by some sensors are shown and discussed in this section.

1.6.1 Temperature sensor signals (analogue)

Temperature sensors generally provide a signal voltage that changes progressively with the change in temperature (section 1.5.1). Therefore, when the temperature increases, the voltage will either decrease or increase (depending on whether the sensor is an NTC or PTC type). The voltage levels on a temperature sensor circuit generally range from a maximum of approximately 5 volts to a minimum of zero volts (although for normal operation a typical range is approximately 4.5 to 0.5 volts).

In converting the analogue signal into a digital signal, the ECU can use a number of voltage threshold points as reference points, which in effect divide the operating voltage range into steps (Figure 1.33). When the temperature changes and the voltage consequently decreases or increases, each step up or down could be counted to give the ECU an indication of temperature. If each step of 0.5 volts represented a 10° rise in temperature, the ECU would be able to count the number of steps up or down and relate this to a temperature value, thus enabling changes in fuelling and ignition timing, etc. In reality, if a greater number of reference points or steps can be created between the maximum and minimum voltages, the ECU is able to assess smaller changes in temperature, thus providing improved accuracy.

It is also of interest to note that if the typical sensor signal voltage is between 0.5 volts and 4.5 volts (when the engine and sensor are operating correctly), then any voltage above or below those values could be regarded as incorrect. An incorrect voltage is most likely to occur as a result of a faulty component (sensor) or wiring fault. The ECU could therefore be programmed to illuminate a fault light on the dashboard and furthermore to provide some form of coded message, which could be read or interpreted by diagnostic equipment.

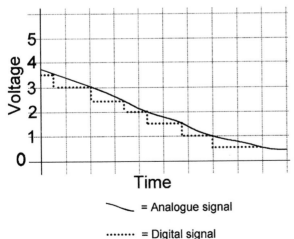

— = Analogue signal

········ = Digital signal

Figure 1.33 Analogue temperature sensor signal with conversion to a digital signal

1.6.2 Throttle position sensor signals (analogue)

As highlighted earlier (section 1.5.3), a throttle position sensor is used to indicate the angle of opening of the throttle butterfly. Although some earlier throttle position sensors relied on switches and contacts, almost all modern types use a potentiometer (variable resistor). The form of the output signal from a potentiometer is very similar to that from a temperature sensor, i.e. it progressively increases and decreases. Therefore when the throttle is opened and closed, the voltage increases and decreases.

Assuming that the progressive or analogue increase and decrease in voltage is converted to a digital or stepped signal (in the same way as a temperature sensor analogue signal is converted into voltage steps), the ECU can establish the angle of opening of the throttle and the rate at which the throttle is opened and closed (Figure 1.34). The ECU can count the up or down steps in voltage to calculate the angle of opening, but can also calculate the speed at which the steps occur, thus providing an indication of how quickly the throttle position is changing. The ECU can then provide the appropriate adjustments to fuelling, ignition timing, etc.

1.6.3 Airflow sensors and MAP sensors (analogue)

Airflow sensors and MAP sensors can provide analogue or digital signals depending on their design. The analogue types produce a voltage that increases and decreases when the airflow volume or mass changes (airflow sensors) or when the manifold intake vacuum/pressure changes (MAP sensors). As with temperature and throttle position sensors, progressive increases and decreases in voltage are converted into a digital or stepped signal so that the ECU can monitor the changes. The ECU can therefore adjust the fuelling, ignition timing and other functions as necessary, when airflow, air mass or intake manifold pressures change.

The analogue signals and the subsequent converted digital signals are therefore similar to those created by the throttle position sensor (Figure 1.34), although, for the airflow sensor, it is the change in the airflow that causes a change in the voltage.

1.6.4 Crankshaft/camshaft speed and position sensors (analogue)

As described in section 1.5.2, this type of sensor generally uses the principle whereby moving or altering a magnetic field or magnetic flux generates a small voltage. Reluctor teeth are located on a rotating component such as a crankshaft or camshaft, so when

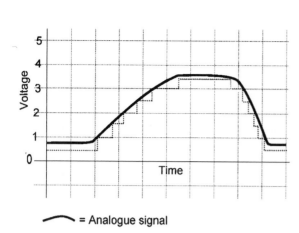

= Analogue signal

········· = Digital signal

Figure 1.34 Analogue throttle position sensor signal with conversion to a digital signal

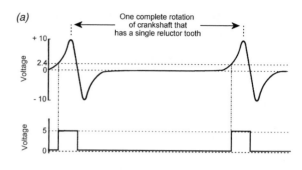

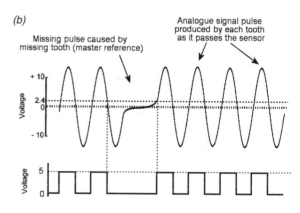

Figure 1.35 Crankshaft speed/position sensor signal with conversion to a digital signal
a Signal produced by a crankshaft speed sensor with a single reluctor tooth
b Signal produced by a crankshaft speed sensor with many reluctor teeth and one missing master reference tooth

the teeth approach or leave the magnetic field (created by the magnet within the sensor), positive or negative voltages are generated. The voltage changes form the analogue signal that is then passed to the ECU. As with other analogue signals, the A/D converter changes the signal into a digital format that can then be used by the ECU (Figure 1.35).

The ECU is able to count the number of pulses, and, because it has a clock or timing device, is then able to calculate the speed of rotation of the crankshaft or whatever rotating component is used to generate the signal. To achieve this speed calculation, there needs only to be one tooth on the reluctor disc. However, if a number of teeth are located around the reluctor disc, including a master tooth (a missing or differently shaped tooth), the ECU is then able to monitor each of the individual pulses generated by each of the teeth. The ECU is able to calculate how many degrees the crankshaft has rotated from the master position. If, for example, the master position is TDC for cylinders one and four, the ECU can assess how many degrees of rotation the shaft has rotated from TDC. This could enable the ECU to implement other control functions that are crankshaft position dependent, such as opening a fuel injector.

It is also possible for the ECU to assess the speed of the crankshaft as each tooth passes the sensor. When a cylinder is on the power stroke, the crankshaft speed will increase, but when the cylinder is on the compression stroke, the speed will decrease. Additionally, if a particular cylinder has a fault which reduces its combustion efficiency, then the acceleration of the crankshaft during the power stroke will be less than for a good cylinder, leading the ECU to assume that a fault exists which could prevent petrol from burning (causing high emissions). The ECU can therefore switch off the fuel injector for that cylinder.

Note that the ECU will also have information from the oxygen sensor, which might indicate that the oxygen content is too low, i.e. there is excessive unburnt fuel. The ECU can use this information, along with the crankshaft acceleration/deceleration information, to decide whether the fuel injector for the defective cylinder should be switched off.

1.6.5 Wheel speed sensors (analogue)

Most wheel speed sensors are identical in operation to the crankshaft speed/position sensors. The main difference is that, although the rotating disc or reluctor disc contains a number of reluctor teeth, there is no master reference tooth. The ECU counts the pulses generated by the teeth; by combining this information with the in-built clock information, the speed and acceleration or deceleration of the wheel can be calculated. An ECU on an ABS system is therefore able to establish whether a wheel is accelerating or decelerating at a different rate from the other wheels, which would indicate that a brake was locking one wheel. Many other vehicle systems use the information from the wheel speed sensors: these are discussed in the relevant sections of the book.

Note that the analogue and converted digital signals produced by a wheel speed sensor are virtually identical to the crankshaft speed/position sensor (Figure 1.35b). However, there is no master reference tooth; therefore the signal from the wheel speed sensor is a continuous series of pulses.

1.6.6 Engine knock pressure sensors (analogue)

Although not previously covered in this chapter, the engine knock sensors are electronic structure borne vibration sensors. A solid state component or silicon chip (usually referred to as a **piezo** chip or crystal) can be used to sense pressure changes (section 1.5.4). If this type of chip is built into a sensor that is attached to the engine (cylinder head or cylinder block), it can be used to detect high frequency vibrations in the engine casings when ignition knock occurs (Figure 1.36).

Ignition knock is caused when isolated pockets of spontaneous combustion occur within the combustion chamber, as opposed to the progressive and controlled combustion process that should occur. Because modern engines operate very close to the limits at which combustion knock can occur, any small variations in fuel quality or hot spots within the combustion chamber can very quickly cause knock to occur: in effect, the ignition timing may be slightly advanced for the conditions at that time. The knock sensor detects the knock and passes a signal to the ECU, which in turn slightly retards the ignition timing until the knock disappears.

Knock sensors are discussed in detail in Chapter 2, but in simple terms, the sensor produces a small electrical signal, which is dependent on the frequency of the vibrations; this signal is then used by the ECU to control the ignition timing. The signal provided by the knock sensor is analogue but it is very irregular because there is not a consistent rotation or movement of a component to create the signal. Although the engine does produce regular vibrations, the combustion process also causes irregular vibrations to occur. The sensor signal therefore contains voltage spikes caused by all vibrations, which are filtered by the ECU so that it is able to analyse correctly combustion knock should it occur.

Note that some knock sensors must be tightened to the correct torque setting when fitted to the engine; over- or under-tightening can affect the capacity of the sensor to detect the appropriate vibration frequencies.

1.6.7 Oxygen (lambda) sensor signal (analogue)

Owing to the complex nature of the oxygen (lambda) sensor signal and the interpretation of the signal by the ECU, a full explanation of the signal and how the ECU responds to the signal is provided in Chapter 3 on petrol engine emissions control systems.

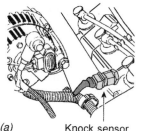

Typical appearance of a knock sensor

(a)   Knock sensor located on a cylinder head

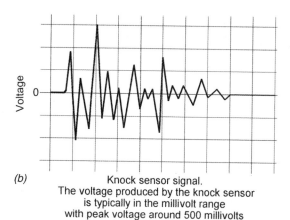

(b)   Knock sensor signal.
The voltage produced by the knock sensor is typically in the millivolt range with peak voltage around 500 millivolts

Figure 1.36 Knock sensor
a Knock sensor located in the engine block
b Signal produced by knock sensor

Key Points

Sensors convert physical quantities into signals

Position sensing is often achieved using a simple potentiometer

A knock sensor is an accelerometer

1.6.8 Hall effect pulse generator (digital)

As briefly described in section 1.5.2, Hall effect sensors produce a digital signal that consists of on/off pulses. Hall effect sensors can therefore be used to provide speed or position related information to the ECU. Such sensors are used on some ignition systems, where the sensor is located in the distributor body, the sensor having one cut out and plate for each cylinder reference. Hall effect sensors are also used as camshaft position sensors; in such cases, the rotor might contain only one cut out or plate, which would result in one master reference signal being passed to the ECU. Because the sensor is mounted on the camshaft, the ECU can determine the position (e.g. TDC) of one of the cylinders on a multi-cylinder engine. This is not possible with a crankshaft sensor, because a master TDC reference on a crankshaft will usually represent TDC on two cylinders, e.g. cylinders one and four or one and six.

The signal produced by a Hall effect ignition trigger on older systems needs only to provide a trigger signal for spark timing. Therefore one pulse of the signal corresponds to the ignition timing point for each cylinder; there is no requirement for a master reference (Figure 1.37a). On a four-cylinder engine, the ignition coil would produce four high voltage outputs (to create a spark at a spark plug), but the distributor rotor arm would direct the spark to the appropriate cylinder.

On later ignition systems (usually integrated into an engine management system), the distributor is no longer used; there is often one individual coil for each cylinder. The ECU therefore needs to be given information regarding the position of one of the cylinders, for example, which cylinder is on the compression stroke. Once the ECU has established a reference to one of the cylinders, it can provide the ignition coil control for that cylinder; then the ECU can control the rest of the coils in turn at the appropriate intervals of crankshaft rotation. Remember that the ECU will be receiving speed and angular position information from a crankshaft sensor. However, to provide the master reference for one of the cylinders, a Hall effect pulse generator, attached to the camshaft, is often used. The camshaft rotates once for every engine cycle, so the sensor needs only to provide a single pulse (Figure 1.37b), which indicates that the chosen cylinder is on the compression stroke (or any other stroke or position, so long as the ECU is programmed with this information).

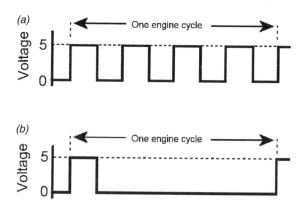

Figure 1.37 *Digital signals produced by a Hall effect pulse generator*
a Signal produced by a Hall effect pulse generator with four pulses per engine cycle (four-cylinder engine) which is used on a simple ignition system as a trigger reference signal for the four ignition sparks
b Signal produced by a Hall effect pulse generator with one pulse per engine cycle. The signal is used as a master reference for ignition or sequential injection timing

Note that injection system control can also rely on a camshaft located Hall effect trigger. If the injectors are operated in sequence, i.e. in the same sequence as the cylinder firing order, the ECU will also require a master reference signal.

ACTUATORS: PRODUCING MOVEMENT AND OTHER FUNCTIONS

1.7.1 Completing the computer controlled task

If we re-examine the purpose of ECU controlled systems, the objective is to control a function or task using the speed and accuracy that a computer or ECU provides. Therefore, when the ECU has received the required information and made the appropriate calculations, the ECU will provide a control signal to a component, which will then perform a task. In general, those components that receive a control signal and then perform a function or task are referred to as **actuators**.

Mechanical and non-mechanical actuators
The term **actuation** is generally assumed to mean that something is moved or actuated, and, in a high percentage of cases with ECU controlled systems, this is true. The ECU control signal that is passed to the actuator causes some form of movement of a component, such as opening an air valve or moving a lever (Figure 1.38a). However, there are some cases where mechanical movement does not occur, such as

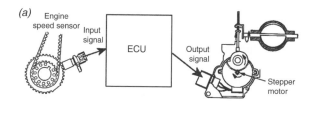
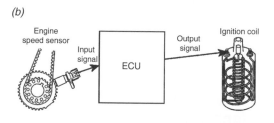

Figure 1.38 *ECUs and actuators*
a ECU controlled circuit with a single sensor and single actuator which performs a mechanical task
b ECU controlled circuit with a single sensor and single actuator which performs an electrical task

when a light bulb is switched on or off, or when an ignition coil is switched on or off (Figure 1.38b). Another example of non-mechanical actuation is where the ECU provides a signal to a digital dashboard display to enable the driver to view engine and vehicle speed as well as other information. However, even when no mechanical movement takes place, when an ECU provides a control signal to a component, that component will usually be referred to as the **actuator**.

Communication signals between different ECUs

Another example where an ECU provides a control signal that does not result in mechanical movement is the communication of one ECU with another, or with another electronic device.

An example of ECUs communicating is when the engine management system ECU provides output signals to an automatic gearbox ECU (Figure 1.39); the engine management ECU might provide a digital information signal to the gearbox ECU that indicates engine load information. The engine management ECU is able to calculate engine load conditions because it receives information from sensors such as the airflow sensor, the throttle position sensor and temperature sensor. Therefore the engine management ECU can provide a single 'engine load' signal to the gearbox ECU that provides sufficient information for the gearbox ECU to make its own calculations (also using information from other sensors on the gearbox system). In this example, the engine management ECU is not directly providing an actuator signal but it is providing a signal which assists the gearbox ECU to make its own calculations, so that it can provide a control signal to a gearbox actuator. In reality, the engine management ECU is still providing control signals to the engine management system actuators, but the information signal that is being passed to the gearbox ECU is an additional function that reduces the need for the gearbox system to duplicate the sensors used in the engine management system.

On many vehicles where the engine management ECU passes information to the gearbox ECU, the reverse also applies: the gearbox ECU passes information back to the engine management ECU. For instance the gearbox ECU might inform the engine management ECU that a gear change is taking place, e.g. third to fourth gear. The engine management ECU can then momentarily reduce the engine power, which makes the gear change smoother. The engine management ECU can achieve this by slightly retarding the ignition timing or slightly reducing the amount of fuel injected, and in some cases (if the ECU also controls the throttle opening electronically) by slightly closing the throttle. Each of these actions would result in a momentary reduction in engine power.

1.7.2 Actuators and magnetism

There are essentially two types of mechanical movement actuators: one type is the solenoid and the second is the electric motor. There are a number of variations in solenoids and electric motors, but, in general, solenoids are used to achieve linear movement and motors are used for rotary movement (although it is possible for motors to be used to create linear movement, via a mechanical mechanism, or it is possible for solenoids to create rotary movement, via a linkage).

The operation of mechanical actuators (solenoid and electric motor types) relies on magnetism. *Hillier's Fundamentals of Motor Vehicle Technology Book 3* explains in detail the way in which magnetic fields are created and used for electric motors, solenoids and generators, etc. However, the essential fact is that, when a current is passed through a coil of wire, a magnetic field is created around that coil of wire. The magnetic field can then be used to create movement.

Solenoid type actuators

In a simple solenoid (Figure 1.40a), a soft iron plunger is located within the coil, but the plunger is free to move with a linear motion. When an electric current is passed through the coil of wire and the magnetic field is created, this will cause the plunger to be attracted towards or through the coil. When the current is switched off, the spring will return the plunger back to the start or rest position. Different designs and

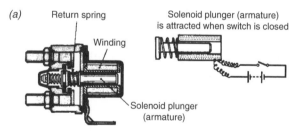

(a)

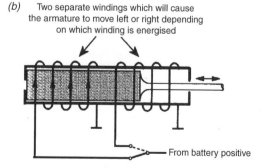

(b) Two separate windings which will cause the armature to move left or right depending on which winding is energised

Figure 1.40 Simple solenoids
a Simple solenoid
b Double acting solenoid

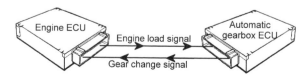

Figure 1.39 Communication between engine management and automatic gearbox ECUs

constructions of solenoids allow many different tasks to be performed. For example, the double acting solenoid (Figure 1.40b) uses two coils of wire. One coil creates a magnetic field, which moves the plunger in one direction, and the other coil creates a magnetic field, which moves the plunger in the opposite direction.

It is also possible for the ECU to regulate or control the average current flow and voltage passing through the coil of wire by altering the duty cycle and frequency of the control signal pulses (see section 1.8). With this control process, it is possible to control or regulate the strength of the magnetic field. If the plunger is moving against a physical resistance such as a spring, it can be moved further by increasing the strength of the magnetic field. Reducing the magnetic field will result in the plunger moving back slightly. Additionally, when a double acting solenoid is used, the plunger movement can be controlled in both directions; in fact one magnetic field can be used to oppose the other. This allows an ECU to move and position the plunger with reasonable accuracy.

Solenoid plungers can be connected to a number of different types of mechanisms or devices that will perform different tasks or functions; various solenoid actuators are covered in the relevant chapters within this book.

Electric motor type actuators

A simple electric motor operates on similar principles to the solenoid, but instead of the magnetic field causing a plunger to move with a linear motion, the magnetic field forces a shaft to rotate. Figure 1.41 shows a simple electric motor, which in this example has a permanent horseshoe shaped magnet with a north and south pole. A single loop of wire, which would normally be attached to a rotor shaft, is fed with an electric current, thus creating an electromagnetic field around the loop

of wire. When the electromagnetic field is created, north and south poles will exist around the loop of wire. These north and south poles will either be attracted to or repelled from the north and south poles of the permanent magnet. Remember that like poles repel each other and unlike poles attract each other.

When the current is initially passed through the wire loop, e.g. from connection A to connection B on the wire loop, if the electromagnet north pole is adjacent to the permanent magnet north pole (and the two south poles will also be adjacent to each other), this will force the shaft to rotate (Figure 1.41a). When the shaft then rotates through 180°, the north poles will be adjacent to the south poles, and because unlike poles attract each other, the motor will not rotate any further.

However, in the diagram it can be seen that the pair of semi-circular segments (or commutator) is attached to the ends of the wire loop and therefore rotates with the loop. The electric current passes from the power supply to **contact brushes** which rub against the segments as the shaft rotates. Therefore, when the shaft and the segments have rotated through 180°, the two segments are now *not* in contact with the original brushes, but they are in contact with the opposing brushes. This means that the electric current will be flowing from connection B to connection A (Figure 1.41b), which is in the opposite direction around the wire loop. The result is that the north pole of the electromagnet is now a south pole, and the south pole is now a north pole, which will cause the shaft and wire loop to rotate another 180°; the process is then repeated.

The simple electric motor in Figure 1.41 shows how magnetism can provide continuous rotary movement; the resulting rotary motion can operate various devices. Simple examples include fuel or air pumps, and wiper motors operate on the same principles.

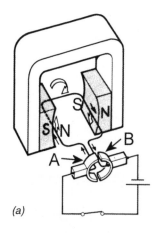

(a)

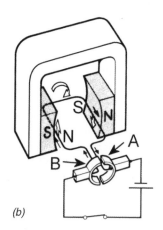

(b)

Figure 1.41 Simple electric motor. Note that the primary and secondary windings are wound around a soft iron core to concentrate and intensify the magnetic field
a Current passes from A to B creating north and south poles on the electromagnet. The like poles will cause the shaft and wire loop to rotate

b When the rotor has turned through 180°, the commutator arrangement causes the current to flow in the reverse direction around the wire loop (from B to A), therefore changing the north pole to a south pole and the south pole to a north pole. The like poles will again repel and cause the shaft to rotate through another 180°

However, many of the electric motors used on ECU controlled vehicle systems are often more complex and sophisticated in the tasks they have to perform, and in their design and construction. Many of the motors do not in fact perform a complete rotation, or they may be controlled so that they rotate in small angular steps. These types of motors are controlled by using different types of wire loops (usually coils of wire) and using different designs of commutator. In addition, by applying control signals from the ECU that have changing duty cycles, pulse widths and frequencies, it is possible to rotate motors partially so that they start and stop in any desired position. The partial rotation can be progressive from one position to another, or it can be achieved in a series of steps.

The capacity to control the rotation of motors accurately allows them to be used for a variety of tasks such as opening and closing air valves in small increments (used for idle speed control). Other examples of ECU controlled motors are dealt with individually in the following sections and in other chapters of this book.

Magnetism and non-mechanical actuators

There is one main actuator used on motor vehicles that uses the effects of a magnetic field but does not produce mechanical movement – this is the ignition coil.

An explanation of how an ignition coil works is provided in Chapter 2 of *Hillier's Fundamentals of Motor Vehicle Technology Book 1*. It is sufficient here to highlight the basic principles of ignition coil operation, which rely on the movement of a magnetic field or magnetic flux to induce an electric current into a coil of wire.

When a current is passed thorough a coil of wire, it creates a magnetic field; this is the same principle as used in electric motors. Additionally, as is the case with an electrical generator, when a magnetic field moves through a coil of wire (or the coil is passed through a magnetic field) it causes an electric current/voltage to be generated within the coil of wire. The faster the magnetic field moves relative to the wire, the greater the voltage produced. An ignition coil relies on both processes.

On most vehicles, the voltage in the vehicle electrical system is only around 12 volts, which is not sufficient to create a spark or electric arc at the spark plug gap. The ignition coil must provide a way to increase the voltage from 12 volts to many thousands of volts. A principle that is used in electrical transformers is also used for ignition coils: there are two coils of wire, one of which has many more windings than the other. In an ignition coil a secondary coil can typically have 100 times more windings than the primary coil (see Figure 1.42).

The process

The process relies on current (using the vehicle's 12 volt supply) passing through the smaller coil or primary winding to create a magnetic field. The build up of the magnetic field is relatively slow, but once the magnetic field has been established at full strength, it can be maintained for a very brief period so long as the current continues to flow. However, when the current is switched off, the magnetic field collapses extremely rapidly, in fact very much more quickly than the speed at which it was created.

Whilst the magnetic field is collapsing, the lines of magnetic force are collapsing across the same coil of wire that created it (primary winding); this causes a current/voltage to be produced within the primary winding. Because the speed of collapse of the magnetic field is very rapid, it causes a much higher voltage to be produced within this coil of wire, sometimes as high as 200–300 volts. Therefore, the speed of collapse is used to step up the voltage from 12 to typically 200 volts. However, 200 volts are still not sufficient to provide the spark at the spark plug under the conditions that exist in the combustion chamber (high pressure and other factors make it difficult for an arc to be created at the plug gap).

To achieve the desired voltage necessary to create the spark, a secondary winding is used, as mentioned above. The secondary winding can be adjacent to the primary winding, although one winding is often wrapped around the other. When the magnetic field is created, the secondary winding is also exposed to the magnetic field. Therefore, when the magnetic field collapses, as well as creating a voltage in the primary winding, it also creates a voltage in the secondary winding. Because the secondary winding may have 100 times the number of turns or windings, 100 times the voltage can in theory be produced. If 200 volts could be produced in the primary winding (owing to the rapid speed of collapse of the magnetic field), then in the secondary winding it should theoretically be possible to produce 20 000 volts (100 times greater).

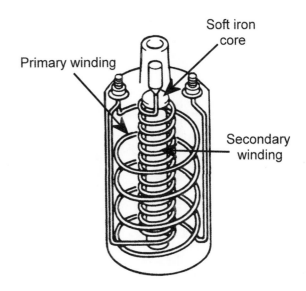

Figure 1.42 Simple construction of an ignition coil

For most petrol engines, the required voltage to produce a spark at the spark plug (under operating conditions) is around 7 000 to 10 000 volts; therefore a coil that is able to produce 20 000 volts is more than capable of producing a spark. There is therefore sufficient additional voltage available to overcome many minor faults such as a plug gap that is too large or contaminated.

Key Points

Actuators convert electrical signals into actions

Common actuators, such as fuel injectors, are solenoid operated

1.8   EXAMPLES OF DIFFERENT TYPES OF ACTUATORS

1.8.1 Solenoid type actuators

There are many different types of solenoid type actuators used on motor vehicle systems, a number of which are covered within this book. The following examples deal with two types that are used for totally different tasks.

The first example is a fuel injector, which provides very rapid opening and closing of a small valve with the result that fuel flow into the engine (into the intake manifold or combustion chamber) can be accurately controlled; the amount of movement required to open and close the injector is very small.

The second example is the use of a solenoid as an air valve. In this example, the valve forms part of a pressure/vacuum circuit which is used to control a turbocharger wastegate. The valve does not have to operate at the same speed as the injector, but it will require greater movement.

Fuel injector

Fuel injectors are high precision components used to control the flow of fuel into the engine. The injectors are usually located in the intake manifold and therefore inject fuel in the region of the intake valves. On some modern petrol engines, the injectors are located so that

fuel is injected directly into the cylinder. Modern diesel engines that now use electronic control for the fuel system also use electronically controlled solenoid injectors that inject fuel directly into the combustion chamber.

Figure 1.43 shows a typical construction for a solenoid type petrol injector. The injector has a 12 volt supply from the vehicle's electrical system, which is usually a permanent supply (via a relay) whilst the ignition is switched on (engine running). The earth circuit for the injector passes through the ECU, which acts as the control switch.

The injector must open and close very rapidly and at high frequency. The opening and closing time can often occur in around three thousandths of a second (3 milliseconds or 3 ms), and injectors might open and close more than 7 000 times a minute.

Solenoid air valve

The example shown in Figure 1.44 is a relatively simple solenoid that is used to control the pressure acting on a diaphragm. The pressure is produced by a turbocharger, which causes the intake manifold to be subjected to pressure (when the turbocharger is operating) as well as the normal vacuum levels for low load engine conditions (when the turbocharger is not operating).

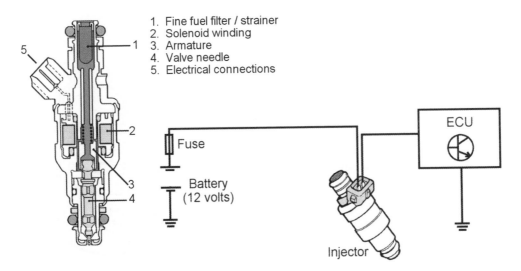

1. Fine fuel filter / strainer
2. Solenoid winding
3. Armature
4. Valve needle
5. Electrical connections

Figure 1.43 Solenoid type petrol injector and basic wiring

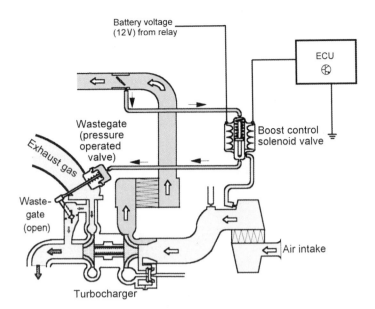

Figure 1.44 Solenoid operated air valve

When the pressure produced by the turbocharger becomes too high for engine safety, the ECU will cause the solenoid to operate and thus open the valve. This will allow pressure from the intake manifold to act on the diaphragm in the wastegate, which in turn will open and allow pressure from the turbocharger to escape (often into the exhaust system or other separate pipes that lead to the atmosphere).

To switch the air valve, the solenoid receives a permanent power supply whilst the engine is running, and the ECU controls the earth circuit. The solenoid air valve does not have to operate at the same speed and frequency as the fuel injector, but the movement of the valve is usually much greater.

1.8.2 Examples of electric motor type actuators

Electric motors used on modern vehicles systems can be categorised into three main types: full and continuous rotation; full rotation with controlled positioning; and partial rotation with controlled positioning.

- Continuous rotation motors are effectively conventional electric motors; the example used in this section is a motor that is used to drive a fuel pump.
- Full rotation motors with controlled positioning are used to position a mechanism or device such as an air valve or a throttle butterfly. In most cases, the motor may rotate through more than one complete turn, but it can be stopped at a desired position. Some stepper motors used for idle speed control operate on this principle.
- Partial rotation motors use the same principles of operation as a normal motor but the angle of rotation is limited. The example used in this section is a motor that is used to control an air valve, which

in turn controls the volume of air passing into the engine at idle speeds.

Continuous rotation fuel pump motor

The example shown in Figure 1.45 is a conventional type electric motor, which is used to drive a fuel pump. In this example, the motor and pump assembly are mounted outside the fuel tank, although for many applications, an adaptation of this type of pump is located inside the fuel tank.

The pump will receive a power supply, which is usually fed via a fuel pump relay (often forming part of an engine management system relay). The pump will usually have a permanent earth connection.

Electric fuel pump

1 Suction side, **2** Pressure limiter, **3** Roller cell pump, **4** Motor armature, **5** Check valve, **6** Pressure side.

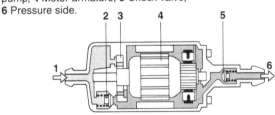

Operation of roller-cell pump

1 Suction side, **2** Rotor plate, **3** Roller, **4** Roller race plate, **5** Pressure side.

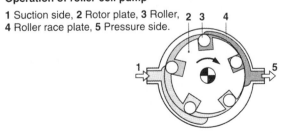

Figure 1.45 Electric motor driven fuel pump

Idle speed stepper motor with full rotation and controlled positioning

In the example shown in Figure 1.46, the motor is able to rotate fully (possibly for more than one complete rotation) but it can be positioned electrically by switching on and off the current passing into the motor. The motor contains more than one set of magnets and electromagnets. This construction enables the ECU to switch on and off each electromagnet, which enables the motor to rotate in small steps in either direction. The different control signals to the stepper motor will therefore have a series of on/off pulses which can be positive or negative to achieve clockwise or anti-clockwise rotation of the motor.

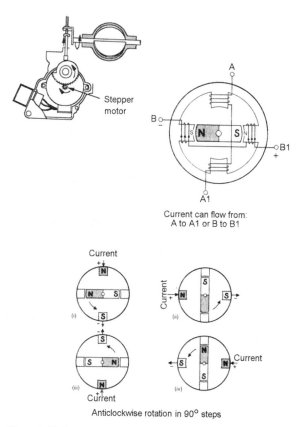

Current can flow from:
A to A1 or B to B1

Anticlockwise rotation in 90° steps

Figure 1.46 Stepper motor

Idle speed partial rotation motor (rotary idle valve)

In this design (Figure 1.47), the motor armature is restricted by mechanical stops from rotating through more than approximately 60°. Connected to the end of the armature is an air flap or air valve assembly which, when opened and closed, will regulate the air passing into the engine, thus enabling idle speed to be controlled.

In the simplest type, a spring keeps the motor armature rotated against one of the mechanical stops. However, when an electric current is applied to the motor (creating electromagnets), this will cause the armature to rotate against the spring. The ECU controls the average current flowing in the circuit by altering the duty cycle of the control signal. The greater the average current, the more the armature will rotate against the spring force. By continuously altering the duty cycle it is then possible to alter the angular position of the armature.

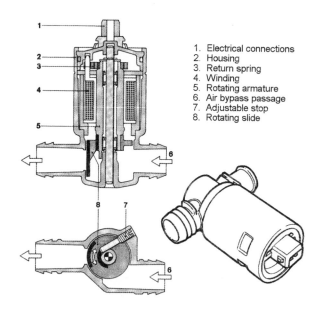

1. Electrical connections
2. Housing
3. Return spring
4. Winding
5. Rotating armature
6. Air bypass passage
7. Adjustable stop
8. Rotating slide

Figure 1.47 Rotary idle valve using partial rotation motor

1.9   ECU/ACTUATOR CONTROL SIGNALS

1.9.1 ECU functioning as a switch in a circuit

The control signal provided by the ECU to an actuator is most commonly a digital signal, which effectively switches the actuator on or off; this is achieved in most cases by making the ECU a part of the actuator electrical circuit. The ECU is therefore acting as a sophisticated switch that makes or breaks (switches on or off) the actuator circuit (Figures 1.48a and 1.48b).

As previously described (see the text about amplifiers in section 1.3.3), the ECU usually contains a final stage power transistor, which is effectively the actuator circuit switch. The low voltage signal from the ECU's microprocessor simply controls the power transistor, which then replicates or copies the control signal. But because the power transistor is the switch within the actuator circuit, when the microprocessor control signal is on or off, it causes the power transistor to switch on or off, thus making or breaking the actuator circuit.

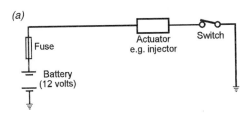

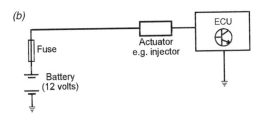

Figure 1.48 Switching an actuator circuit
a Normal switch controlling an actuator circuit
b ECU acting as the switch and controlling the actuator circuit.
Note that the power transistor in the ECU directly switches the
circuit in response to the signal from the ECU microprocessor

Note that for most ECU controlled actuator circuits, the ECU (power transistor) forms part of the earth or return circuit (negative path). The positive path from the power supply (the battery) can be directly connected to the actuator or it may contain a switch such as an ignition switch. Fuses and relays are also generally connected into the positive side of the circuit. The ECU, which provides the controlling function, is therefore making and breaking (switching on and off) the earth or negative side of the circuit.

Most control signals provided by the ECU are therefore simple on/off pulses that cause the power

transistor to switch on and off the actuator circuit. However, it is not just simple on or off control that is provided by the ECU: most control signals will cause the actuator to switch on or off for different lengths of time and at different speeds or frequencies (measured in hertz (Hz)).

When examining the control signal, the duration of the on or off period can be referred to as **pulse width**. It is however general practice that the pulse width refers to the on time only.

Figure 1.49a shows an on/off control signal where the on time or pulse width is ½ second, and the off time is also ½ second. In this case the frequency is 1 hertz, which means that the actuator is switched on and off once every second.

Figure 1.49b shows a similar signal, but the on time is ¼ second, with the off time being ¾ second. The frequency is therefore still 1 hertz but the on and off times are different.

Figure 1.49c shows a control signal with equal on and off times but the frequency is 10 hertz.

The completion of the on and off process is one complete cycle of operation or 1 cycle. Therefore, when the signal completes one on and one off pulse, this is also referred to as 1 cycle. If there are 10 cycles within one second, this is a frequency of 10 cycles per second, which is referred to as 10 hertz (10 Hz).

If the durations of the on and off times are the same, this is referred to as a duty cycle of 50%, i.e. the on time is 50% of one cycle. If however the on time is ¼ of the total cycle time then this is referred to as a duty cycle of 25%.

Figure 1.50a shows two control signals, each with a 50% duty cycle. Although the durations and frequencies of the two signals are different, the duty cycles are 50% in both cases. Figure 1.50b shows two control signals,

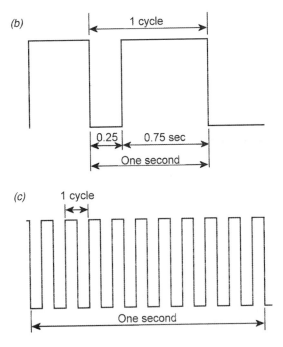

Figure 1.49 ECU control signal duration and frequency
a ECU control signal with equal on and off duration of ½ second
and a frequency of 1 hertz
b ECU control signal with on duration of ¼ second and off
duration of ¾ second but with a frequency that is still 1 hertz
c ECU control signal with equal on and off duration, but with a
frequency of 10 hertz

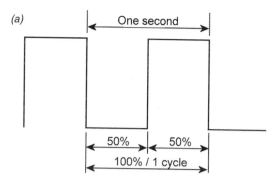

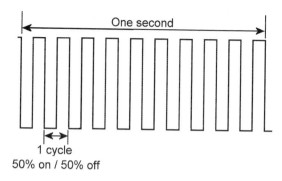

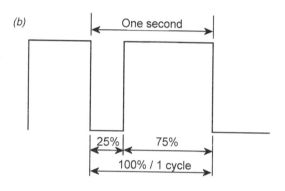

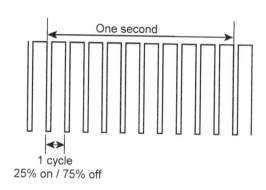

Figure 1.50 Duty cycles
a Control signals with 50% duty cycle
b Control signals with 25% duty cycle

each with a 25% duty cycle, and again, although the durations and frequencies are different, the duty cycles are the same.

Important note: In the control signal examples illustrated, the off time is shown as the higher portion of the pulse, i.e. as a voltage level. The on time is therefore shown as zero volts. When a switch (in this case the ECU) is connected into the earth or negative path of an actuator circuit, the earth circuit will in fact be at zero volts when the circuit is switched on and at battery level voltage when the circuit is switched off. It is important to note when using test equipment, such as multimeters or oscilloscopes, that the measurements displayed may be the reverse of the expected readings, e.g. the duty cycle could be shown as 25% instead of 75%.

1.9.2 Using the signal to control the actuator

By understanding that the duration (pulse width), duty cycle and frequency of the control signal can be altered, it is possible to understand how an actuator can be controlled so that the task it performs can be varied. An example is a fuel injector, which can be provided with a control signal where the duty cycle or pulse width varies. This means that the injector can be opened for longer or shorter time periods, thus allowing different quantities of fuel to be delivered to the engine.

The control signals affect how the actuator operates in different ways because the actuator is altering the current flow in the circuit. It was explained previously that the ECU is effectively an on/off switch, but this is only part of the whole story.

Altering the control signal duty cycle

Altering the duty cycle or pulse width has the effect of altering the average current flow and applied voltage in a circuit.

As an example, a simple 12 volt light circuit is switched on and off by a simple switch (Figure 1.51a). When the circuit is switched on, the voltage on the power supply to the bulb will be 12 volts. Because the light bulb has a 2 ohm resistance, the current will therefore be 6 amps and the bulb will produce its maximum light output. However, when the switch is off, the voltage and current will both be zero and the bulb will produce no light.

If the light switch could be switched on and off very rapidly, for example at 100 times a second

(Figure 1.51b), and the duty cycle was 50%, i.e. the on and off pulses were both 50% of 1 cycle (of equal duration), the result would be that the light would be on for only half of the time. This means that the average voltage, the average current and the average amount of light produced by the bulb would also be 50% of the maximum value had the bulb been switched on all the time.

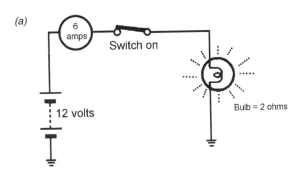

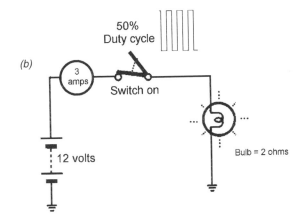

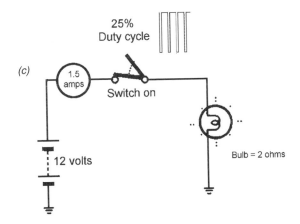

Figure 1.51 Altering the duty cycles to affect the average voltage and current
a Simple 12 volt light circuit and switch
b Average voltage and current in a light circuit with a 50% duty cycle
c Average voltage and current in a light circuit with a 25% duty cycle

In this example where the bulb is rapidly switched on and off, the average voltage on the power supply circuit is 6 volts because this is 50% of the maximum supply voltage (50% of 12 volts). The average current is therefore 3 amps (50% of 6 amps). The total amount of light produced by the light bulb should in theory be 50% of the light that would have been produced if the bulb had been illuminated for all of the time.

If the duty cycle was changed so that the on time was only 25% of the total cycle (Figure 1.51c), then 12 volts would be available to power the bulb for only 25% of the time, but zero volts would be supplied for 75% of the time. The average voltage would therefore be 25% of 12 volts, i.e. 3 volts. The average current would therefore also be 25% of the maximum 6 amps, i.e. 1.5 amps. The average amount of light produced would therefore in theory also be 25% of the maximum.

If this same process of altering the duty cycle is applied to a control signal that is being used on an actuator such as an electric motor, it is then possible to alter the power produced by the motor. The same applies to any actuator control signal, where altering the duty cycle will influence the way in which the actuator functions.

Altering the control signal timing and frequency

If the control signal consists of simple on and off pulses, an actuator will also be switched on and off. It is therefore possible to provide the on and off pulses at a specified time. A common example is when a fuel injector used on a modern fuel injection/engine management system is required to open at a certain time in the engine operating cycle. The injectors on some modern systems will open just before, or at the start of, the intake stroke (possibly just before or just as the intake valve opens). A sensor (usually the camshaft position sensor) is used by the ECU as a timing reference to calculate when the intake stroke is about to start, allowing it to provide the on pulse in the control signal at the right time.

The frequency of the control signal also affects how an actuator behaves. For instance, a simple solenoid could be used to open and close a small valve (which could be allowing fuel to pass through a pipe). If the control signal had a 50% duty cycle, and provided on and off pulses that occurred very slowly, e.g. every 10 seconds, the solenoid would open the valve for 10 seconds and close the valve for 10 seconds. Although this would regulate the flow of fuel in the pipe, it is not a very effective means of control. If, however, the control signal pulses occurred 100 times every second (100 hertz), this would mean that the solenoid would be trying to open and close 100 times a second. The solenoid would in fact adopt a half open position i.e. it would never reach the fully open or fully closed positions. Therefore, altering the duty cycle will affect the average opening time of a solenoid controlled valve, but it is more effective if the frequency is high (such as 100 hertz) than it is if the frequency is low.

Web links

Engine systems information
www.bosch.com
www.sae.org
www.imeche.org.uk
www.picotech.com
www.autotap.com
www.visteon.com
www.infineon.com
www.kvaser.com (follow CAN Education links)

Teaching/learning resources

Online learning material relating to powertrain systems:

www.auto-training.co.uk

Chapter 2

ENGINE MANAGEMENT – SPARK IGNITION

what is covered in this chapter . . .

- Emissions, reliability and durability
- Electronic ignition systems (early generations)
- Computer controlled ignition systems
- Distributorless and direct ignition systems
- Spark plugs

2.1 EMISSIONS, RELIABILITY AND DURABILITY

This section relates to systems covered in chapters 3, 4 and 5.

2.1.1 Emissions legislation

The introduction of electronic engine control systems was a result of a number of factors, most of which still apply. As noted in Chapter 1, affordable electonics enabled vehicle manufacturers to make increasing use of electronic components and electronically controlled systems. However, in the 1960s through to the early 1990s, it was in many cases still less expensive to fit more traditional fuel and ignition systems, such as carburettors and contact breaker ignition. At some stage therefore, vehicle manufacturers needed some motivation to fit electronic systems that in the early stages were still more expensive to produce and to develop than the existing components at that time.

Probably the single biggest factor in the increasing use of electronic systems was the introduction of emissions legislation. It is generally accepted that the USA was the leading country in introducing legislation that forced a reduction in emissions levels produced by engines and vehicles in general. Legislation forced vehicle manufacturers to develop and fit electronic systems to engines. This process really started towards the end of the 1960s, when electronics had just reached a level of capability and cost that enabled manufacturers to start to build systems that used electronic components.

What did make things slightly difficult was that different states in the USA had different problems; therefore they had different requirements and different legislation. **Smog** is one particular problem (Figure 2.1) that captured everyone's attention. Smog is a term that became commonly used with reference to fog that was *not* naturally formed in the atmosphere: it was created from smoke that had been produced by factories, houses and of course cars. Burning fossil based fuels such as coal, petrol, diesel and even wood produces smoke, and many towns and cities around the world suffered with smog. One of the most famous is London, which had for many years had a serious smog problem. In fact, ever since entertainment films have been made, it has been common to depict London (even in the 1800s) as having a serious smog or fog problem.

The smog in London had been present for too many years for it to be blamed entirely on motor vehicles, but when certain weather conditions existed (which could have produced normal fog), smoke produced by coal or wood fires in houses and smoke from the factory chimneys added to the problem. Although motor vehicles must have started to contribute to the problem, the relatively low number of vehicles in use up until the 1960s was not sufficient to be the major cause.

Figure 2.1 Smog in a city

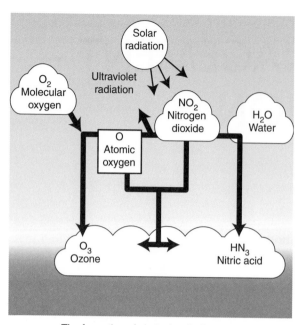

The formation of photochemical smog

Figure 2.2 Heat and exhaust gases can cause smog and other pollution, especially in certain types of geographical location

The smog problem that occurred in Los Angeles, California, which became very serious in the 1950s and 1960s, occurred because Los Angeles lies in a valley where there is often little or no wind and a lot of heat. In isolation, this could be regarded as a natural problem, but in reality smog developed because of emissions from the burning of fossil fuels. Los Angeles had a high concentration of motor vehicles that, even in the 1960s, spent a lot of time in traffic jams in what was a confined area. Therefore a combination of location, weather conditions and burning fossil fuels caused extremely serious problems.

Whilst smog can be quite thick and therefore makes driving hazardous, the real problem is a health issue. Serious illness, such as respiratory problems, can be caused by smog and many deaths have also been attributed to smog. The acids contained within vehicle related smog cause damage to buildings as well as people. Athens in Greece is a particular case where acids are destroying many of the ancient buildings.

Motor vehicles were a contributing factor to smog problems so they became a focus of attention for legislators. Legislation dealing with factories and fires in houses has also been brought in. In the UK, the Clean Air Act restricted the use of many types of fossil fuels in both homes and factories, and London is now significantly free of serious smog.

Vehicle emissions are a broad subject and smog is only one of a number of problems influenced or created by such emissions. Therefore, within this chapter, emission problems are referred to and explained where applicable, but particular reference should be made to the emissions section.

If we appreciate that vehicle emissions can cause or contribute to serious health and environment problems, then we must accept that any effort to reduce the problem is justifiable, even at a cost. The Los Angeles problem, amongst others, was without doubt a major talking point that captured the attention of the public: the consumers that buy motor vehicles. Therefore any reasonable added cost for the vehicle became relatively acceptable. The vehicle manufacturers were therefore tasked by legislators to reduce the level of vehicle emissions. It is perhaps coincidental or fortunate that at a time when emissions problems were a major focus of attention for legislators, electronics were becoming very much more capable and affordable.

Note: In the USA, diesel engines are very rarely fitted to passenger vehicles. The cost of petrol was and remains low compared to most countries and the petrol engine was more acceptable as a means of powering large American cars. Emissions legislation and technical developments in the USA were therefore focused on the petrol engine rather than the diesel engine. Europe and other regions were therefore able to take advantage of legislation and technical changes made in the USA, and it was not until more recent times in Europe that diesel engines have become a target for substantial emissions reduction (and therefore technical change).

Engine maintenance

Engine design in the 1960s had not really changed too much for many years. Although improvements had been made, such as overhead valves instead of side valves, the main objective was to improve engine performance, which at that time primarily meant more power. In the USA, in particular, vehicles were generally much larger than in the rest of the world, and because petrol was very inexpensive in the USA, large fuel thirsty engines fitted in large heavy vehicles were accepted as normal.

Engines in the USA at that time were usually of V8 configuration with typical capacities of 4 litres to 7 litres. Emissions levels from these large engines were very high, especially when the engine was at idle speed (when measured as a percentage of the total exhaust gas, some pollutants were at their highest levels at idle speed). It was therefore obviously going to be very difficult to change vehicle and engine design suddenly, so the changes were generally planned over a relatively long period of time.

However it was recognised that one major factor that could help to reduce emissions was to ensure that regular maintenance was performed correctly, but ideally, the need for regular maintenance on the fuel and ignition systems should be reduced or even eliminated. For those readers who have never worked on older vehicles with carburettors and contact breaker (points) ignition systems, it may be difficult to appreciate that it was necessary to clean and adjust the carburettor regularly and to adjust or replace the contact breaker in ignition systems. Ignition or fuel systems would not suddenly become inefficient at a particular interval, such as 16 000 km or 10 000 miles: the reality was that ignition and fuel systems progressively deteriorated. Therefore, immediately after 'perfect' maintenance had been carried out, systems would progressively become less and less efficient, until a time was reached when the inefficiency was unacceptable. Hopefully, regular maintenance was performed before systems became too unacceptable.

See *Hillier's Fundamentals of Motor Vehicle Technology Book 1* for an explanation of carburettors and contact breaker ignition systems.

Loss of efficiency of fuel and ignition systems

Carburettors would progressively accumulate a build up of deposits in the airways and petrol jets (small holes through which fuel passed). This build up of deposits would then alter the air/fuel mixture, which could result in reduced combustion efficiency and high emissions. It was also common for the carburettor to require slight adjustment of the idle mixture setting, to further compensate for build up of deposits, and even a change in the weather. Another major factor that made it necessary to adjust the idle mixture setting was the deterioration in the way the engine was performing, which was caused by wear of the contact breakers in the ignition system.

Progressive wear on the contact breakers was an acceptable part of the design, and it was possible to adjust them to compensate for wear until such time as the wear was too excessive. Contact breakers on very old vehicles may have required replacement after as little as 5 000 miles (8 000 km) but even the improved versions still required regular adjustment and were traditionally replaced at main service intervals, which could be between 5 000 and 10 000 miles (8 000 and 16 000 km).

One particular problem related to wear on the contact breakers is that it can reduce the quality or strength of the spark, because a worn set of contact breakers (or an adjustment that is out of specification) will not allow sufficient time for the ignition coil to build up a strong magnetic field. This results in weak electrical output from the ignition coil and therefore a weak spark. The result is that the combustion of the air–fuel mixture will not be efficient; this results in high emissions of pollutants.

A second problem with worn contact breakers is that, as the contact breakers wear, the ignition timing changes. See *Hillier's Fundamentals of Motor Vehicle Technology Book 1* for a full explanation of this. However, in simple terms, wear in the contact breaker mechanism causes the contact breakers to open earlier or later. The opening time of the contact breakers causes the ignition coil to provide the electrical energy that in turn causes a spark at the plug, so wear in the contact breakers affects spark timing.

Incorrect ignition spark timing will reduce combustion efficiency, with the result that emissions of pollutants increases, power is reduced and more fuel is wasted. When ignition timing is incorrect (usually retarded or later than specified), the engine will not idle smoothly. However, it is possible on older vehicles to adjust the air/fuel mixture at idle speed, which helps to smooth out the way the engine is operating. This is generally achieved by making the mixture richer than normal, i.e. an excess of fuel. This in turn can also create higher emissions.

A third problem with contact breakers is that, each time the contacts open, a small arc can occur across the contacts. Although this problem was very much reduced by the introduction of a condenser or capacitor in the contact breaker circuit, arcing progressively damaged the two contact points on the contact breakers.

Other systems requiring maintenance

It was more than just simple carburettor and contact breaker maintenance that resulted in increasing emissions. Older engine designs included many components and systems that required regular maintenance, which involved cleaning, adjustment or replacement. Those areas requiring regular maintenance included:

- valve operating clearances
- spark plugs, which required regular changing or resetting of the plug gap
- engine oil, which required regular changing
- engine breather systems
- contact breakers and ignition timing
- fuel systems (carburettors).

Each of the above listed items would progressively wear, or their operating performance would progressively deteriorate. In turn, this would either affect combustion efficiency (which would increase exhaust emissions), or would result in excessive engine oil fumes and emissions. Without regular and correct maintenance, many of those items listed above would end up operating 'out of specification', which means they would be operating outside their intended design limits. The net result was that the engine would be operating very inefficiently and excessive emissions would be produced.

2.1.2 Reliability and durability

Even if an engine was maintained at the recommended regular intervals, wear and progressive deterioration in operating performance still occurred between the maintenance intervals, thus causing an increase in emissions. Ideally therefore, those adjustable items, or items that wear and deteriorate between maintenance intervals should be redesigned to avoid any reduction in operating performance between maintenance intervals (or for longer if possible). In effect, designers were trying to create much improved reliability and durability of engine components and systems so that emissions did not increase significantly between maintenance intervals. In fact, one piece of legislation called for ignition systems to be able to operate without maintenance for 50 000 miles (80 000 km).

Ignition system developments

A number of design changes were made over a period of time to various engine components and systems. However, one particular engine system benefited from the use of electronics: the ignition system.

Early designs of electronic ignition (fitted as original equipment) were designed to eliminate the contact breakers (see section 2.2). An electronic module functioned as the on/off switch for the ignition coil circuit, so the current passing through the coil circuit was no longer being controlled by a mechanical switch; arcing at the contacts was therefore eliminated. Additionally, higher currents could be passed through the electronic module, which enabled more magnetic and electrical energy to be created within the ignition coil.

With the contact breakers eliminated as a means of switching the ignition coil circuit, the spark still had to be provided at the correct time. The electronic module therefore needed a reference or trigger signal so it would be able to switch off the ignition coil circuit at the appropriate time, thus creating the spark at the spark plug. Most earlier ignition systems used an 'inductive' or magnetic sensor, which was located within the distributor body (effectively in the same place as the previously used contact breakers).

The inductive or magnetic sensor (often referred to as a pulse generator) operated in the same way as modern speed/position sensors or rotational speed sensors (see section 1.5.2), but usually used one reluctor tooth for each cylinder. When each reluctor tooth passed the sensor magnet, it caused a small electrical pulse to be induced into the coil of wire (adjacent to or wound around the magnet). The electrical pulses were used by the electronic module as a reference point for each cylinder, thus allowing the electronic module to switch the ignition coil circuit at the appropriate time. The ignition system delivered the high voltage to a rotor arm (as was the case with contact breaker systems), and the rotor arm directed the voltage to the appropriate spark plug.

Figure 2.3 shows a comparison between a typical contact breaker ignition system and an early generation electronic ignition system, whilst Figure 2.4 shows a typical inductive ignition timing sensor and an early type ignition module.

On the early generations of electronic ignition, the automatic timing advance and retard mechanisms were identical to those used on contact breaker systems. The centrifugal 'bob weight' system was used to advance the timing with increase in engine speed and the vacuum operated system was used to retard or 'back off' the

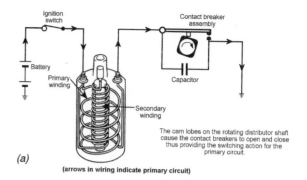

(a)

(arrows in wiring indicate primary circuit)

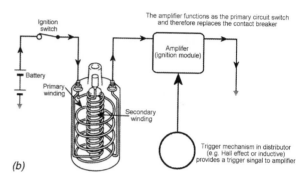

(b)

Figure 2.3 *Schematic layout of ignition systems*
a A contact breaker ignition system
b An early generation electronic ignition system

timing when a high load was applied to the engine. The advance and retard mechanisms were linked to the inductive sensor base plate and to the rotor shaft (as on contact breaker systems) enabling relative angular movement between the inductive sensor magnet and the reluctor teeth, which affects the triggering timing (and therefore the ignition timing).

2.1.3 Progress in electronic system capability

Electronic ignition systems were certainly much more reliable and efficient than contact breaker systems. What we would now regard as simple electronics allowed considerable improvements to be made in the ignition system (as described above) but mechanical devices were still relied on to alter the ignition timing when engine speed and load changed. Fuel systems, however, even into the 1980s (certainly in Europe) continued to rely on the carburettor as the means by which fuel and air were mixed in the correct proportions. Designers had made dramatic improvements to the capability and accuracy of carburettors, by adding various mechanical devices and some electronic control functions onto the basic carburettor. The carburettor actually developed into a complex and often unreliable device. There was therefore a growing demand to find an alternative method of delivering fuel to the engine.

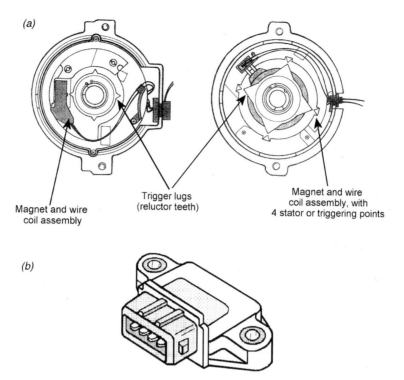

(a)

Magnet and wire
coil assembly

Trigger lugs
(reluctor teeth)

Magnet and wire
coil assembly, with
4 stator or triggering points

(b)

Figure 2.4 Inductive pulse generator and ignition module
a Two types of inductive pulse generator that were located in the distributor body
b Typical appearance of ignition amplifier/module

Emissions legislation in the USA, Europe and many other countries was becoming increasingly tough for vehicle manufacturers to comply with, but electronics were developing at a very rapid pace, which enabled many design changes to be made to ignition and fuel systems. While the early use of electronics improved reliability and durability, electronics latterly developed to the level of being able to control the engine systems; this was a fundamental turning point in vehicle technology.

The remaining sections within this chapter detail more modern ignition and petrol systems, which are generally now integrated as part of an engine management system. Ignition timing is now controlled electronically instead of mechanically, and fuel systems are also electronically controlled (via electronic fuel injection). Although some fuel injection systems used in the late 1970s (through to the early 1990s) were mechanically based, even these systems were improved by the use of electronic control. In the end, however, mechanically based ignition or fuel systems were effectively no longer able to provide the accuracy and control (at a cost effective price) that are now necessary to maintain the low emissions levels demanded by legislation.

Other benefits

Although emissions reductions are often regarded as the only motivation for using electronics on engine systems, the truth is that there are many other benefits. In

general, when engine efficiency is improved, this usually results in better fuel economy and higher engine power, as well as improved engine smoothness and reliability. Using electronically controlled systems allows engine designers to change certain design features so that there are fewer compromises.

For example, when ignition timing is electronically controlled, compression ratios can be increased to a point where they are almost at their extreme limits (which improves combustion efficiency). High compression can result in combustion knock or pre-ignition in the engine (especially if the fuel quality is poor); this problem can be accelerated if the ignition timing is only very slightly incorrect. Because the old mechanical timing controls were relatively inaccurate, it was not possible to risk damage that could be caused by high compression. Therefore ignition timing throughout the speed and load ranges of an engine were generally set on the 'safe side', slightly retarded from the ideal value.

However, with electronic control and monitoring, the ignition timing can be more accurate, which reduces the risk of detonation and knocking, and, if knock sensors detect any combustion knock, then the timing can be retarded slightly to reduce the problem.

The above is just one instance where engine design can be improved through the application of electronics. The net result is that engine efficiencies are improved so that power and economy as well as emissions are all substantially better than was the case with older non-electronic systems. Although we do tend to focus on ignition and petrol injection, other engine systems have also been improved through electronic control; examples include variable valve timing and even engine cooling systems.

Whilst it is often the case that existing mechanical systems are improved through electronic control, sometimes totally new systems are introduced which may not have been possible with mechanical control. A good example is electronic diesel injection which is not an evolution of mechanical diesel injection, but a new way of delivering diesel fuel to the engine with accuracies and control that were not previously achievable.

Growing similarities between diesel and petrol systems

Perhaps it is ironic to note that the modern electronic 'common rail' type diesel injection systems bear a close relationship to petrol injection systems, with the use of electronic injectors and many sensors that are almost identical to those of a petrol system. Conversely, some modern petrol engines make use of direct petrol injection, whereby the injectors are positioned in the cylinder rather than in the traditional location of the intake ports. Diesel engines have of course traditionally always had direct injection into the cylinder (or more accurately: into the combustion chamber).

Whilst the fundamental difference between petrol and diesel engines remains the way in which ignition occurs (spark for petrol and heat generated from high compressions for diesel), the systems used for fuel delivery are now very similar.

The continuous pace of development

Many electronically controlled engine systems are covered within the rest of this chapter, but such is the pace of development that innovations are introduced on a regular basis. However, if the reader has an understanding of the fundamental aspects of engine operation along with an understanding of electronic control, it is relatively easy to embrace any new developments.

> **Key Points**
>
> A key driver for emissions has been changes in regulations
>
> Regular maintenance and accurate settings of ignition and fuel systems reduces emissions and improves fuel consumption

2.2   ELECTRONIC IGNITION SYSTEMS (EARLY GENERATIONS)

This section deals initially with those ignition systems that were not necessarily integrated into engine management systems. However, the design of these separate ignition systems incorporates many features and components that were then used for ignition control on engine management systems. By studying many of these components and design features independently, it becomes easier to understand the complete operation of petrol engine management systems, which are covered in section 3.2.

2.2.1 Disadvantages and limitations of mechanical ignition systems

Those readers who are not totally familiar with mechanically based ignition systems (contact breaker systems with mechanical advance and retard mechanisms) should refer to *Hillier's Fundamentals of Motor Vehicle Technology Book 1*.

There are many disadvantages associated with mechanical ignition systems; the main disadvantages are:

- the contact breaker mechanism wears (causing incorrect ignition timing and low ignition coil output)
- at higher engine speeds, there is insufficient time (ignition dwell time) for the ignition coil to build up

a strong magnetic field thus reducing ignition coil output; this is made worse by higher engine operating speeds
- there is arcing at the contact breaker contact faces (causing reduced ignition coil output)
- maximum current flow passing across the contact breakers is limited because excessive current will promote arcing and cause the contact breaker faces to burn away
- ignition timing control is inaccurate, which restricts the potential for engines to operate close to their limits of efficiency
- at high engine speeds, contact breakers are not able to open and close quickly and accurately: there is a tendency for contact breaker bounce (points bounce) to occur (this causes the contact breakers to bounce open before they should do, thus causing incorrect spark timing and reduced coil output). Contact breaker systems are therefore not suited to the high engine speeds that are now typical for the modern engine
- weaker fuel mixtures can be more easily ignited with larger spark plug gaps but this requires more energy to be produced by the ignition coil, and such levels of energy are not available from contact breaker systems under all operating conditions; the following sections explain how greater energy levels are produced.

All of the above limitations and problems reduce engine efficiency, leading to high emissions, reduced engine power and higher fuel consumption. It was necessary therefore to replace the mechanical contact breaker with an electronic switch for the ignition coil primary circuit.

Figure 2.5 is a schematic diagram of a contact breaker ignition system. Note that, as with almost every design of coil ignition system, the primary circuit for the ignition coil is switched on the earth circuit, in this example by the contact breakers.

2.2.2 Main requirements of electronic ignition systems

The fundamental requirements of an ignition system have not changed much since the day that ignition systems were first used on a petrol engine. The primary requirements are to provide a spark or arc at a spark plug that is strong enough to ignite the air–fuel mixture; this spark must occur at the correct time in the operating cycle. There have been other requirements introduced over the years such as suitable interference suppression, higher engine speed operation, etc., but the basic requirements are much as they always were.

What has changed however is the quality of spark and the standards of performance (reliability and timing accuracy). These changes continue through to today's ignition systems where they form part of an engine management system. We can therefore look at the overall requirements of an ignition system at this stage, and as the reader progresses through this ignition section (and the engine management section), it is then possible to see how the later generations of ignition system are able to provide improved quality and standards of performance.

High voltage

A fundamental requirement of the ignition system is that it should produce a sufficiently high voltage from the ignition coil at all speeds to enable the air–fuel mixture to be initially ignited under cylinder pressure (compression pressure). The spark or arc produced at the spark plug must produce sufficient heat to cause ignition of the mixture. Many thousands of volts (kilovolts, or kV) are used to create or initiate the spark.

Voltage requirement (firing voltage)

A typical voltage requirement for a modern engine is in the region of 7 kV to 12 kV or slightly higher (assuming all components are good), while on an older engine, the requirements were slightly lower at around 6 kV to 10 kV. Note however that, irrespective of how much voltage the coil can produce, the voltage delivered by the coil is dependent on the conditions that exist in the high voltage ignition circuit and in the combustion chamber. Remember that electricity will take the easiest path to earth, so if the circuit from the coil passed directly to earth (in effect a short circuit), the energy or voltage requirement would essentially be zero, because this is the easiest route without resistance or barriers to electrical current flow. If, however, gaps and resistances exist in the circuit, a higher voltage will be required for the flow of electricity to reach earth. The major factors affecting ignition systems are listed below.

- **Plug gap** – with a gap in the electrical HT circuit (high tension or high voltage circuit), the energy required for the electrical flow to jump the gap and reach earth will be large. The larger the gap, the higher the voltage requirement; plug gaps are generally larger than in the past to assist in igniting weaker fuel mixtures. It is also true that the plug gap can become fouled or contaminated, which in

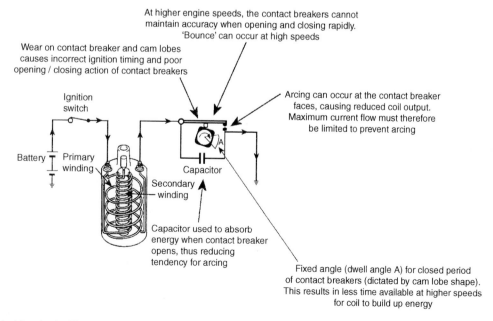

Figure 2.5 Contact breaker ignition

some cases will make it more difficult to create a spark, this also increases the voltage requirement.

- **Resistance** – if we add resistance to the plug leads and possibly also to the spark plug (to provide suppression), again this will mean that a higher voltage is required. Additionally, as plug leads and other HT components deteriorate, the resistance generally increases, which increases the voltage requirement.

- **Cylinder pressures** – with modern high compression engines the high pressure at the plug gap makes it more difficult for electricity to reach earth and a higher voltage is again required. It is also interesting to note that if the ignition timing (spark timing) is slightly retarded so that the spark occurs at TDC instead of slightly before, the cylinder pressures at this time will be higher; this will also create a higher voltage requirement. A worn engine that has a low cylinder pressure will therefore require a lower voltage.

- **Air:fuel ratio** – although a minor factor, it is also interesting to note that it is more difficult for a spark to be generated across air than it is across vaporised petrol. When a spark is created, it ionises the mixture. Vaporised petrol ionises much more readily than air, so it is more difficult to create a spark in a weak mixture; again, a higher voltage is required.

The important thing to remember is that electricity is effectively 'lazy', but it will always try to reach earth, i.e. complete the circuit. If the voltage requirement is low, then the voltage delivered by the ignition coil will be low. If however, there are resistances and gaps, etc. in the circuit, these will result in a higher voltage being delivered by the coil. Because electricity will always attempt to reach earth, even if there are restrictions or resistances, the voltage delivered by the coil will increase in line with the requirements, until such time as there is insufficient energy in the coil.

Figure 2.6 shows the output voltage produced by an ignition coil during one ignition cycle for one cylinder. Note that 'firing voltage' is at a high voltage value, which is necessary to initiate the spark at the spark plug gap (under operating conditions). The rest of the voltage levels are detailed in the following paragraphs.

Maintaining the spark (spark duration)

Since the introduction of emissions regulations, because engines generally operate on weaker or leaner mixtures (a greater proportion of air), it is more difficult initially to ignite the air/fuel mixture. Additionally, when a weaker mixture is used, flame spread throughout the mixture can be less effective at igniting *all* of the mixture. To help overcome these problems, a slightly higher initial spark voltage is required, but a spark of

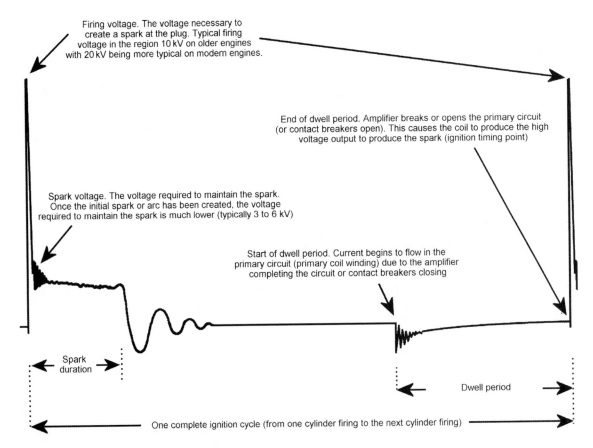

Figure 2.6 Output voltage from an ignition coil through one ignition cycle

longer duration is also required to maintain the temperature at the spark plug, thus helping to ignite or maintain the combustion of all of the mixture.

Modern ignition systems produce a spark that can last typically around 2 ms (2 milliseconds or 2 thousandths of a second) or more, whilst older engines (with relatively rich mixtures) had spark durations of around 0.5 ms. The coil needs to produce sufficient energy or voltage to create the spark initially, but there must also be sufficient energy available from the coil to maintain the spark for longer periods than was the case with older systems that ignited richer mixtures.

The spark voltage and spark duration periods shown in Figure 2.6 illustrate that once the spark has been initiated, a much lower voltage is then required to maintain the spark: once the ionisation process has been started, maintaining that process does not require such a high voltage.

When almost all of the coil energy has been used to initiate and maintain the spark, the energy remaining in the coil will be insufficient to keep the spark going; therefore the spark will extinguish. The small amount of remaining energy then tends to oscillate backwards and forwards within the system until there is no usable energy remaining.

Coil charge time (dwell period)

If the coil is visualised as a container that stores electrical energy, it is clear that a fully charged coil will be able to maintain a spark for longer than a partially charged coil. Because the coil energy is now used to initiate and then maintain the spark for longer periods, modern ignition coils must be able to build up energy (charge up) much faster than those on older systems. Current flows through the coil primary winding are increased by reducing the resistance of the coil primary winding, which enables faster charging of the coil. Additionally, the charge up period (previously referred to as the ignition dwell period) is controlled on electronic systems such that there is a longer time available to build up the coil energy.

As well as ensuring the coil provides enough energy to initiate and maintain the spark for longer, higher engine speeds add another demand because they mean less time for the coil to build up energy, so ignition systems must be able to charge the coil (build up the coil energy) in even less time.

In Figure 2.6, the indicated dwell period is the period when current flows through the primary winding, allowing energy to be built up within the coil. A switch located in the primary circuit is used to switch on and off the flow of current. On old systems this switch was the contact breaker, and when the contact breakers closed, this would complete the circuit and allow current to flow. On modern systems, the contact breakers are replaced by an electronic switch, which is usually part of an amplifier or module (or in many cases it is incorporated into the engine management ECU).

On older type contact breaker ignition systems it would take as long as 10 ms for the current to reach its maximum flow rate (typically 4 A maximum). As an example, on an old type four-cylinder engine operating at 6000 rev/min (Figure 2.7), the whole ignition cycle for a cylinder (the time between the spark on one cylinder to the spark on the next cylinder) would take only 5 ms (5 thousandths of a second). However, it is not possible to allocate the whole of the ignition cycle to building up coil energy because some of that time must be available for the coil to deliver the energy to produce the spark. Typically, around half of the total ignition cycle was used for building up coil energy; in our example, this would mean 2.5 ms (2.5 thousandths of a second). If it takes 10 ms to reach maximum current flow in the coil primary circuit, then at high engine speeds there would only be around one-quarter of that time available, which would restrict coil energy.

On an engine operating on relatively rich mixtures, the low coil energy was not so much of a problem but on modern high speed engines with weaker mixtures, the coil energy must be higher than on older ignition systems. Modern coils operating with modern electronically controlled ignition systems can build up sufficient energy in around 3 or 4 ms or less. Although the coils may not be fully charged at high engine speeds, the charge level is sufficient. However, many modern engines now use one coil for each cylinder, which on a four-cylinder engine means that a coil has four times as long to build up the energy as engines using a single coil for all cylinders. This is especially important on an engine with six, eight, ten or 12 cylinders, because the more cylinders there are, the less time is available between ignition cycles. Remember, on a four-cylinder engine, there are two sparks for every crankshaft revolution. On a 12-cylinder engine there are six sparks for every crankshaft revolution, which means there is only one third of the time available compared to a four-cylinder engine.

Dwell angles and dwell percentage

On old ignition systems that used contact breakers to switch on and off the primary current the contact breakers were set so that they were closed for typically around 50% to 60% of the ignition cycle, i.e. the dwell period. On an old type four-cylinder engine with contact breakers and a distributor, the distributor shaft would rotate through 90° for each ignition cycle (for one cylinder). A dwell period of 50% would equate to 45° of distributor rotation. It was therefore common in the past to quote the charge-up time as being the 'dwell angle'.

When contact breakers were fitted and adjusted, the objective was to achieve the specified dwell angle; by adjusting the position of the contact breaker within the distributor, the correct dwell angle could be obtained. Because the mechanical setting and operation of the contact breakers dictated this percentage, it would not change throughout the speed range of the engine. If the percentage were any larger, at slow engine speeds, the

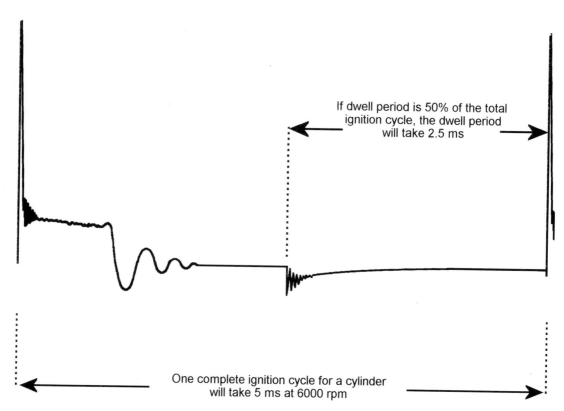

If dwell period is 50% of the total
ignition cycle, the dwell period
will take 2.5 ms

One complete ignition cycle for a cylinder
will take 5 ms at 6000 rpm

Figure 2.7 The charge up time (dwell period) on a four-cylinder engine

current flow in the primary circuit would be too long and the circuit and coil would overheat. If the percentage were any smaller, at high engine speeds there would not be enough time to charge up the ignition coil. The percentage used was therefore a compromise.

However, once the correct dwell angle was set, it would not change with engine speed, so when the engine speed increased, the whole ignition cycle had to take place within less time. Therefore there was less time to charge up the coil.

Modern electronically based ignition systems are able to control the dwell period. In effect, the dwell time is controlled so that it is ideally the same duration at all engine speeds. Therefore, if the ignition coil takes only 2 ms to build up the required energy, then the dwell time would be 2 ms at all engine speeds. There are situations where at high engine speeds there may not be quite enough time available but a number of other design changes have overcome this problem (as discussed in the following sections).

Spark timing

The spark must occur at the correct time, at all engine speeds and loads. When the mixture is initially ignited, it must have sufficient time to combust and for the gases to begin to expand before the piston has moved too far down the cylinder on the power stroke. Ideally, the mixture should initially be ignited just before the piston reaches TDC on the compression stroke; this should allow for the mixture to begin to combust and then for

the heat to cause the gases to start to expand just as the piston reaches TDC. The subsequent expansion of the gases then forces the piston back down the cylinder.

If the spark occurs too soon (with over-advanced timing), the gases will start to expand before the piston reaches TDC and the expansion will try to force the piston down the cylinder before it has reached TDC, which means that some of the energy created by the gas expansion will be pushing against the rising piston; this can result in combustion knock occurring because of the premature ignition timing.

If the spark occurs too late (with over-retarded timing), the expansion of gases will be late and the piston may be already on its way down the cylinder (on the power stroke). The effect of the gas expansion will therefore be wasted.

Speed related timing advance

If we accept that it takes a certain period of time for the fuel to ignite and then combust or burn sufficiently to create the heat and expansion of the gases, then in general this time period will theoretically not change significantly when the engine speed changes (assuming all other conditions remain the same). The burn time does in fact change with engine speed, but for the following example, it is assumed that the time remains constant.

If we assume that the time allowed for the burning process to take place and create the maximum pressure in the cylinder is around 4 ms (4 thousandths of a

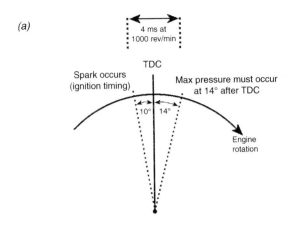

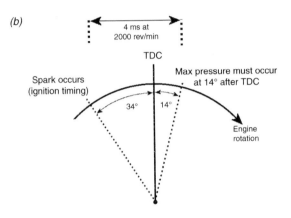

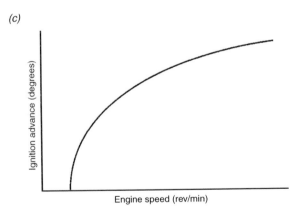

Figure 2.8 Ignition timing advance related to engine speed
a Burn time takes 4 ms. At 1000 rev/min, 4 ms gives 24° of crankshaft rotation. If the maximum pressure must occur 14° after TDC, then the spark must occur 10° before TDC.
b Burn time takes 4 ms. At 2000 rev/min, 4 ms gives 48° of crankshaft rotation. If the maximum pressure must occur 14° after TDC, then the spark must occur 34° before TDC.
c Typical ignition advance requirements

second), then the spark must occur 4 ms before the maximum pressure is required. In reality, the *maximum pressure* created by the gas expansion is usually required just after the piston has passed TDC, i.e. it is just beginning the downward stroke.

If in the following example (see Figure 2.8a) we assume a burn time of 4 ms, then at 1000 rev/min the crankshaft would rotate through 24° during the 4 ms burn time. If we also then assume that maximum gas pressure should occur at 14° of crankshaft rotation after TDC, then the spark should occur at 10° before TDC.

If the engine speed is increased to 2000 rev/min, i.e. doubled, 4 ms will still be needed for the burn time (Figure 2.8b). Because the crankshaft is now rotating at twice the previous speed, it will rotate through 48° during the 4 ms burn time. Therefore, the spark must occur 48° before the maximum pressure is required (which remains at 14° after TDC). The spark must therefore occur at 34° before TDC.

Further increases in speed would therefore also require additional advances in the ignition timing, but because the burn time does in fact not remain constant (conditions within the cylinder change with speed), the amount of additional advance required for increases in engine speed gradually reduces. Figure 2.8c shows an approximate advance curve related to engine speed. Note that different engine designs and combustion chamber designs will have different advance characteristics, so the advance curve illustrated shows a trend, rather than indicating exact values of spark timing advance.

As previously mentioned, older type mechanical advance mechanisms are not accurate enough to provide the exact advance curve needed for modern engines. Therefore electronic systems now control the timing advance process as described later in section 2.3.

Load related timing advance/retard
When an engine is operated at light load, it is possible to operate on weaker mixtures than when the engine is operated under high load conditions. On modern engines, the mixture is controlled by the engine management system using the oxygen sensor monitoring process (as discussed in sections 1.5.6 and 3.2), and there is not so much change between the mixture settings for light and heavy load conditions (compared with older engines). However, when weaker mixtures are used for light load conditions this causes a requirement for a different ignition or spark timing.

A weaker mixture takes longer to burn, so the spark timing will require additional advance. Additionally, under light load conditions, the throttle valve (butterfly) is only partially open, thus restricting the flow of intake air; this means that a lower volume of air is drawn into the cylinder, and during the compression stroke, the cylinder pressures and temperatures are lower, which also has an effect on the burning process. Under these conditions, it is therefore necessary to advance the timing slightly to account for the slower burn time.

When the engine is again placed under load and the mixture is no longer weak (cylinder pressures will also be higher), the amount of timing advance can be reduced back to the load setting.

On older ignition systems with mechanical advance mechanisms, the speed related timing advance provided the main advance setting and when the engine was under higher loads, a vacuum operated system would retard the timing; this type of load dependent system was referred to as a **timing retard system**. In effect there was a speed related advance system and a load related retard system.

Incorrect timing

If the ignition timing is incorrect, as previously mentioned, it can cause two problems: first, over-advanced timing can cause combustion knock: the premature expansion of the gases will be wasted because the piston is still rising on the compression stroke when the gases are expanding; second, over-retarded timing will result in the maximum pressure occurring when the piston has already travelled too far down the cylinder: therefore the expansion of the gas will again be wasted. In effect, both over-advanced and over-retarded timing will cause a reduction in power.

The ignition timing can also affect the emissions; over-advanced timing can cause incomplete combustion of the mixture which will result in high levels of unburned or partially burned fuel entering the exhaust gas. In addition, higher temperatures will be created in the cylinder (the pressure rise will be higher), which can result in increases of oxides of nitrogen (see section 3.5). However, over-retarded timing can in some cases help to reduce emissions, although this might also cause poor combustion: some older emission control systems used retarded timing under certain operating conditions to ensure that combustion continued later in the engine cycle, helping to burn some of the partially burned exhaust gases.

Interference suppression

Ignition systems create considerable **electrical noise**; this is the effect of providing a high voltage to a spark plug, which causes radio frequency energy around the wires carrying the high voltage. Suppression is achieved by using resistances built into the high tension (HT) cable and/or the spark plugs and rotor arm (where fitted on older systems). Apart from the fact that the interference causes electrical noise (crackles, etc.) on the vehicle radio, television and other audiovisual equipment can be affected (even if it is some considerable distance from the vehicle). Legislation limits the levels of interference.

2.2.3 Electronic switching of the coil primary circuit

The coil primary circuit carries a relatively high current for an extremely short period of time. On a contact breaker system, the resistance of the coil primary winding was typically around 3 ohms, which would mean the current flow in the 12 volt primary circuit would reach a maximum of 4 A (which was the

maximum that could be used on a contact breaker system without causing excessive arcing and damage). On older slow running engines, this current level was sufficient to enable the coil to build up a reasonably strong magnetic field and therefore produce an acceptable output voltage. Note, however, that fuel mixtures were relatively rich (containing an excess of petrol) which enabled the mixture to be ignited with a relatively weak spark. However, if a stronger spark is required, this can be generated by either increasing the current flow in the ignition coil primary circuit (lowering the resistance of the coil primary winding) or maintaining the current flow in the primary circuit for longer periods (a longer dwell time). Both options would result in accelerated damage to the contact breakers. In addition, higher engine speeds and multi-cylinder engines reduce the available time for increasing the dwell period (the coil charge time).

Using an electronic switch instead of a mechanical switch provides a number of benefits. One is improved reliability because there are no moving parts and no arcing at the contacts, but an electronic switch also enables higher current flows to exist for longer periods. The simple type electronic switch, which is a power transistor, simply switches on and off the coil primary circuit at the appropriate time, but note that the transistor will perform the switching task only when an appropriate electrical trigger signal is provided.

Figure 2.9 shows a simplified example of how a transistor functions as a switch by comparing a transistor to a water valve. Note that the main water flow from the collection point C cannot flow through the valve and be emitted at E when the valve is closed. However, if a small flow of water is allowed to pass into the base of the valve B this will cause the valve to open and allow the main water flow to pass from C to E.

For the transistor, the principle is much the same. The main electrical circuit cannot flow through the transistor from the collector to the emitter (C to E) until a small voltage or current is applied at the base B. It is therefore possible to provide a small electrical signal at B (a low current or voltage) to control a much higher current and voltage, which are passing through the transistor from C to E.

See *Hillier's Fundamentals of Motor Vehicle Technology Book 3* for a more detailed explanation of how transistors operate.

2.2.4 Electronically assisted ignition

Some early generations of electronic ignition system used a contact breaker to provide the small electric signal to the transistor. Figure 2.10 shows a simplified circuit where the transistor is the switch for the ignition coil primary circuit. In this example, however, the contact breaker is used only as a means of switching on and off a low current signal to the transistor. Therefore

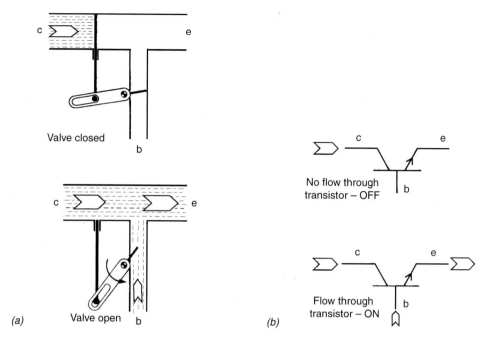

Figure 2.9 Principle of a transistor using a water valve as a comparison
a A water valve closed and open
b A transistor switching on and off

the contact breaker can be operated in exactly the same way as on a traditional contact breaker ignition system, but the contact breakers do not carry the high current. A resistor is used in this example in the contact breaker circuit to reduce the current flow passing to the B or base terminal of the transistor.

Where a simple transistor is used to switch the coil primary circuit, it is often referred to as the 'ignition module' or 'ignition amplifier', although in truth the transistor is not strictly speaking amplifying the trigger signal but merely switching the coil primary circuit in response to a trigger signal.

The contact breaker triggered system shown in Figure 2.10 would eliminate the high currents passing through the contact breaker, and higher currents could then be allowed to flow in the ignition coil primary circuit. However, the accuracy of the ignition timing is still dependent on the contact breaker, which would still suffer from mechanical wear. A non-mechanical trigger mechanism is therefore required.

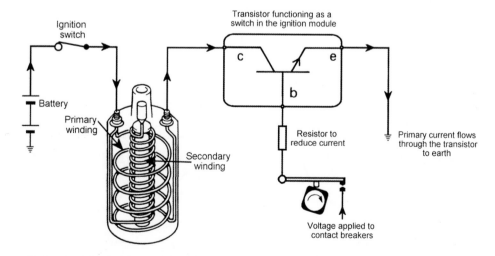

The transistor is functioning as a switch. When the contact breakers are closed, current flows through the transistor base (b) and causes the primary circuit current to flow from the collector (c) to the emitter (e).
The circuit iillustrated provides an indication of how this type of system operated, however additional components would be required in the ignition module to enable correct operation.

Figure 2.10 Using a contact breaker to control the switching of a transistor in an ignition circuit

There are a number of ways that an electrical signal can be created that will act as a means of triggering the power transistor in an ignition coil primary circuit. As explained above, a contact breaker can be used to switch on and off a trigger circuit, but more accurate and reliable methods are generally non-mechanical. The following section covers the most common types of non-mechanical trigger mechanism that were used for electronic ignition systems.

The vast majority of early generation electronic ignition systems used either an inductive or Hall effect trigger system, although a few systems did use an optical trigger. Although we can refer to these systems as being non-mechanical, mechanical components are used, but the important fact is that the trigger signal passed to the ignition module is created by a non-mechanical process, i.e. there is no mechanical switch.

A number of constructional and design variations existed for all three trigger systems, but for each of the examples mentioned in the following section, the general operating processes form the basis for other variants of each type.

2.2.5 Inductive ignition trigger

Inductive pulse generator

Figures 2.11 and 2.12 show two different types of inductive trigger or pulse generator. Both types were located in the ignition distributor body and as such physically replaced those components originally used for contact breakers. On earlier generations of electronic ignition, both types were also connected to the mechanical/vacuum advance mechanisms (inherited from the contact breaker systems).

Both examples operate on the same principle of using a reluctor with the same number of reluctor teeth (or triggering lugs) as the number of cylinders, i.e. four reluctor teeth for four cylinders. A permanent magnet and inductive coil (coil of wire) are located adjacent to the reluctor. When the reluctor is rotating, each of the reluctor teeth passes the magnet and inductive coil assembly, which will produce a small electrical pulsed signal. This electrical signal is an analogue signal. The pulsed signal is then passed to the ignition module (power or switching transistor), which uses the pulses as a trigger or reference point to switch the ignition coil primary circuit.

The example in Figure 2.11 shows a magnet and inductive coil assembly located to one side of the reluctor. The iron reluctor is mounted on the distributor shaft and therefore rotates with the shaft. The example shown in Figure 2.12 operates in much the same way as the example in Figure 2.11, but the construction is slightly different. The magnet is a circular disc which is located concentrically with the distributor shaft; the inductive coil is also concentric with the magnet. The **stator**, or pole for the magnet, consists of fingers (one for each cylinder) which protrude upwards. A rotor or reluctor, which also has one reluctor tooth for each cylinder, is located on the distributor shaft; the reluctor teeth are formed as fingers that protrude downwards and pass adjacent to the stator fingers.

In both examples, when the reluctor teeth or fingers pass the stator or stator fingers, this causes an electrical signal to be produced as explained below.

Generating the pulse

When a reluctor tooth is aligned with the permanent magnet or stator (as shown in Figure 2.11), it allows the magnetic flux to flow from the stator, across the reluctor and back again. When the distributor shaft is rotating, the reluctor teeth will inevitably move away from the stator, providing a gap between the reluctor teeth and the stator. This gap results in a greater **reluctance** of the magnetic field or magnetic flux, i.e. the flow will be less.

In effect, when the reluctor teeth approach the stator, the flow of magnetic flux will increase. The flow of magnetic flux will be at its maximum when the teeth and stator are in alignment, and it will reduce when the reluctor teeth move away from the stator. When the flow of magnetic flux changes, i.e. increases or

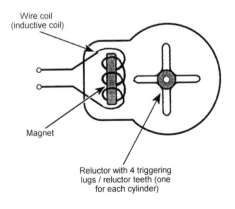

Schematic layout of inductive pulse generator

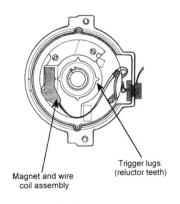

Inductive pulse generator located
in distributor body

Figure 2.11 Inductive pulse generator with the magnet and inductive coil located at the side of the reluctor

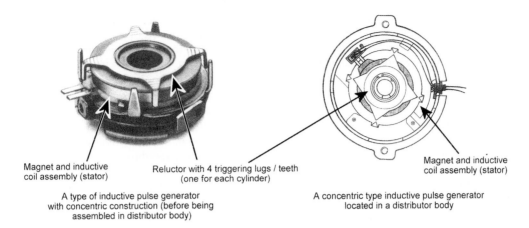

Magnet and inductive
coil assembly (stator)

Reluctor with 4 triggering lugs / teeth
(one for each cylinder)

Magnet and inductive
coil assembly (stator)

A type of inductive pulse generator
with concentric construction (before being
assembled in distributor body)

A concentric type inductive pulse generator
located in a distributor body

Figure 2.12 Inductive pulse generator with the magnet and inductive coil located concentrically around the reluctor

decreases (owing to rotation of the reluctor), this causes a small electrical current to be produced in the inductive coil. The voltage generated is at its greatest when the change in flux flow is at its greatest; this occurs just as the reluctor teeth are approaching or leaving alignment with the stator.

Figure 2.13a shows the voltage output from the inductive sensor, or **variable reluctance** sensor as it is sometimes called. There are four electrical pulses (for a four-cylinder engine) produced during one complete rotation of the reluctor. A positive voltage is produced as the reluctor teeth approach alignment with the stator (magnet); as the reluctor teeth leave alignment with the stator, a negative voltage is produced. The output signal is therefore an analogue **alternating current** (AC).

As described above, when the reluctor teeth approach or leave the stator (Figure 2.13b) this causes a large change in magnetic flux, which therefore produces higher voltage (positive or negative). However, when the reluctor teeth are close to alignment and in alignment with the stator, the result is very little or no change in the flux, which means that less voltage is produced. When the reluctor is directly in alignment with the stator, there is no change in magnetic flux: therefore the voltage produced is zero.

Note: The gap between the reluctor teeth and the stator is effectively set during manufacture. However, on some types of construction it is possible to alter the gap. If the gap is not correct, this will affect the magnetic flux and the strength of the signal produced. Reference should always be made to manufacturer's specifications.

Reference point for ignition timing

It is normal practice to use the change or 'switch over' from positive to negative voltage, i.e. the zero voltage point, as the reference point for ignition timing. The ignition module will therefore use this 'zero volt' point of the electrical signal as the reference to switch off the ignition coil primary circuit, thus creating the high voltage and a spark at the plug.

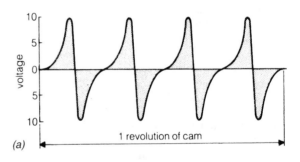
(a)

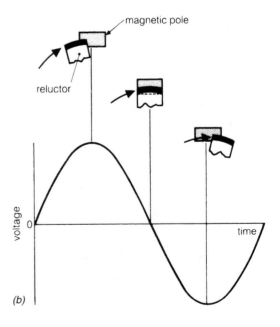
(b)

Figure 2.13 Rotation of the reluctor
a One rotation of the reluctor produces four pulses as an analogue signal
b Voltage levels produced when the reluctor teeth are in different positions relative to the magnet (stator)

The ignition coil will produce its high voltage output when each reluctor tooth is aligned with the stator: on a four-cylinder engine there will be four high voltage outputs from the coil for every rotation of the distributor shaft. The output from the coil must therefore be distributed to the appropriate spark plugs at the correct time (when each of the cylinders is close to TDC on the compression stroke); this is achieved by passing the high voltage from the ignition coil to the centre of a rotor arm located within the distributor. When the distributor shaft and rotor arm are rotating, the rotor arm will direct the high voltage to the contact segments in the distributor cap, which allows the voltage to pass to each of the spark plug leads and spark plugs in turn (Figure 2.14). It is therefore important to note the exact location of each spark plug lead on the distributor cap to ensure that the voltage is directed to the correct spark plug at the correct time.

Wiring circuit for an inductive pulse generator

Inductive pulse generators generally have two wiring connections to the ignition module. Effectively, these two wires provide a positive and a negative path for the electric current. However, remember that the current is an alternating current which means that the flow alternates within the wiring; each wire therefore alternately carries positive and negative flows. Figure 2.15 shows the wiring for a typical inductive sensor and ignition module.

The wiring diagram (Figure 2.15) shows two wires carrying the pulsed signal from the inductive pulse generator to the ignition module. Because the module forms part of the earth circuit for the ignition coil primary circuit, the power supply from the ignition switch passes to the coil positive terminal (usually marked terminal 15) and then through the coil primary winding to the ignition module. The module functions as the switch for the primary circuit; therefore the circuit must pass through the power or switching transistor in the module before it is connected to earth. If the ignition module contained only simple passive electronics, no power supply would be required for the module, but it contains active electronic components that require an additional power supply and earth connections.

On some applications, a third wire has been used which is wrapped around the two signal wires. The third wire is connected to earth or ground, acting as a screen or shield against interference from other electrical systems. Also note that when only two wires are used, one of the wires may be wrapped around the other, which provides a form of screening.

The inductive sensors can usually be classified as **self-generating**, which means that no additional power

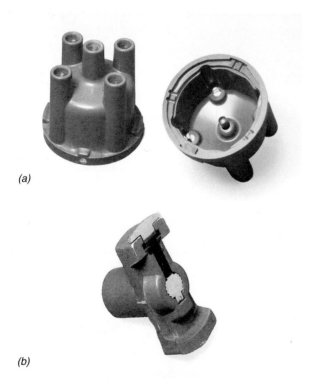

(a)

(b)

Figure 2.14 Rotor arm and distributor cap (allowing a high voltage to be directed to the correct spark plug)
a Distributor cap
b Rotor

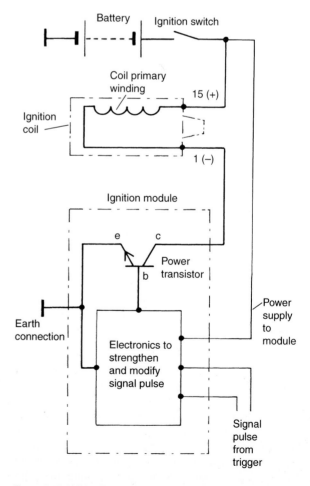

Figure 2.15 Wiring for a simple inductive trigger ignition system

supply is required to enable the pulsed signal to be produced. Therefore the two wiring connections simply provide a complete circuit for the inductive coil. There are however some examples where an electric current is used to enhance or create the magnetic field; in such cases the same wiring that provides the current to the sensor also carries the pulsed signal.

Advantages and disadvantages of inductive pulse generators

Inductive pulse generators are relatively inexpensive to produce and generally reliable and accurate, even when working in the harsh environment of a vehicle's engine. Inductive pulse generators produce an analogue signal, which, when passed to an ECU that is operating with digital electronics, will require an analogue to digital converter (A/D converter). When the analogue signal is supplied to the early types of ignition modules (a simple power transistor switch), some simple circuitry within the ignition module is used to reshape the pulse so that the applicable reference points are recognised, i.e. the zero volt timing reference point.

The inductive pulse sensor operates using the same principles as a conventional electrical generator and, as is the case with a conventional generator, the voltage produced increases with the increase in rotational speed of the rotor (or reluctor). Therefore, when the engine speed increases, the voltage produced by the inductive pulse generator also increases, ranging from around 0.5 volts at slow speeds to a possible 100 volts at high speeds. If, therefore, there is any deterioration in the strength of the magnetic flux, and the engine is turning over very slowly during starting, it is possible that no signal will be produced.

Also of note is that, on the example shown in Figure 2.11, where the magnet and inductive coil assembly are located to one side, it is possible for an erratic or unusable signal to be produced if wear exists in the distributor shaft bearings. If a distributor shaft bearing is worn, the shaft can wobble during rotation; this in turn can result in the air gap between the reluctor teeth and the stator changing. The usual problem encountered is that the air gap for one reluctor tooth is too small whilst the gap for the opposite tooth is too large. It is not uncommon in these cases for the pulse signal to be missing a trigger pulse for one and sometimes two cylinders. This will mean that one or two cylinders may not receive a spark at the spark plug.

2.2.6 Hall effect ignition trigger

As mentioned previously, when a sensor produces an analogue signal (such as the inductive ignition trigger), if the signal is then passed to an ECU that operates with digital electronics, an analogue to digital converter is required to enable the ECU to interpret the signal. It is therefore an advantage if the sensor is able to provide a digital signal.

A digital signal also has other advantages relating to the very defined reference points that can be provided. In the previous section (2.2.5) it was stated that the analogue signal produced by the inductive sensor would change with engine speed: the voltage produced by the sensor increases with increases in engine speed. In fact, the whole 'shape' of the signal changes. However, with a digital signal such as the signal produced by a Hall effect sensor, the reference points are consistent, irrespective of engine speed.

Hall type systems are often referred to as **Hall effect switches** or **Hall effect** pulse generators. Figure 2.16a shows a typical construction of a Hall effect ignition trigger located in an ignition distributor; Figure 2.16b shows a separate view of the Hall trigger assembly.

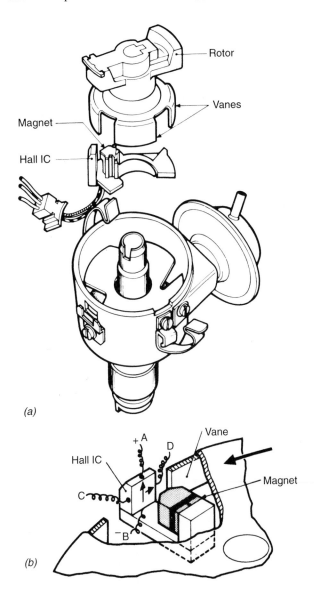

(a)

(b)

Figure 2.16 Hall effect pulse generator
The rotor has four vanes which causes four pulses to be produced (a digital signal) during one rotation of the rotor
a A Hall effect ignition trigger in an ignition distributor assembly
b A Hall effect pulse generator

Hall effect digital pulse

The construction and operation of the Hall effect sensor is described in Chapter 1. The signal produced is a square wave: Figure 2.17 shows a typical digital signal produced by a Hall effect ignition trigger. Here, there are four pulses produced during one rotation of the rotor, which would indicate that the rotor has four vanes and would be used on a four-cylinder engine.

With a digital signal, it is possible to make use of at least two definitive reference points on the signal. One reference point is when the voltage increases from zero to 5 volts (or whatever voltage is used on the sensor). The second option is when the voltage drops from 5 volts down to zero. Therefore, either the rise or the fall in voltage can be used as the reference point for the ignition module to switch off the ignition coil primary circuit. When working on Hall effect systems, it is therefore necessary to refer to the manufacturer's instructions to find out whether the ignition timing point occurs when a vane is just leaving the air gap (between the magnet and the Hall chip), or when the vane is just entering the air gap, because this will dictate whether the voltage is rising or falling.

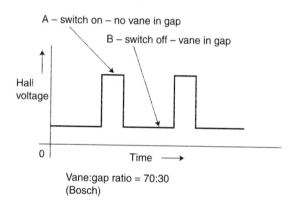

A – switch on – no vane in gap

B – switch off – vane in gap

Hall voltage

Time

Vane:gap ratio = 70:30
(Bosch)

Figure 2.17 Digital signal produced by a Hall effect pulse generator

For most Hall effect systems, there will be the same number of vanes as there are engine cylinders. This means that on a four-cylinder engine with a single ignition coil, there will be four vanes, and the ignition coil will therefore produce four high voltage outputs for every rotation of the Hall effect rotor/trigger disc. As with the inductive ignition trigger system, it is therefore necessary to pass the high voltage coil output to a rotor arm in the distributor cap, which will then direct the voltage to the four spark plugs in turn.

Wiring for Hall effect pulse generator

Figure 2.18 shows the wiring for a simple Hall effect triggered ignition system. The Hall effect pulse generator initially requires two wiring connections for the input (a power supply and earth connection) to enable it to function; Figure 2.16b shows the circuit passing across the Hall chip terminals A and B. However, the signal produced at the Hall chip should also have two connections (positive and negative paths), but the negative or earth path is shared with the earth path of the input, which means that there is a total of three connections between the Hall effect sensor assembly and the ignition module.

Note that it is common practice to mark the terminals on the Hall sensor connector plug with three symbols: +, –, and **0**. The + terminal is the power supply (often stabilised at 5 or 8 volts), the – terminal is the earth terminal and the **0** terminal is the output terminal for the digital signal.

The ignition module will require a power supply and earth connection, and the module again forms part of the earth circuit for the ignition coil primary circuit.

2.2.7 Optical ignition trigger

Optical ignition triggers have been used on a number of ignition systems and also for some other applications where a digital signal is preferred to an analogue signal;

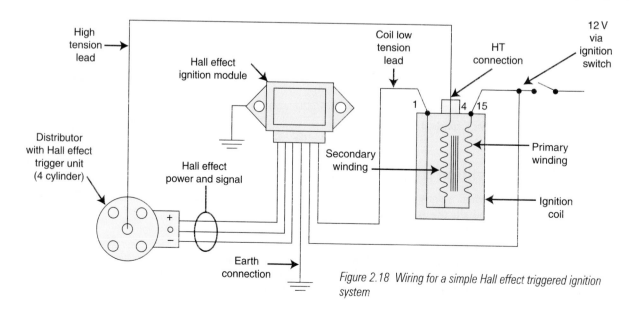

Figure 2.18 Wiring for a simple Hall effect triggered ignition system

the optical system provides an alternative to the Hall effect system.

Producing the optical trigger digital pulse

A light emitting diode (LED) produces a small light when an electric current is passed through it; conversely a phototransistor produces a small electric current when it is exposed to light. Therefore, if an LED is used to project light onto a phototransistor, the phototransistor will produce an electric current.

As illustrated in Figure 2.19, an LED and phototransistor can be located, as an assembly, inside the distributor body. If a 'chopper disc' is located on the distributor shaft so that the vanes or shutters of the chopper disc pass between the LED and phototransistor, the shutters will prevent the light from the LED from reaching the phototransistor. If the chopper disc has four shutters (as shown in the illustration), then when the disc rotates (with the distributor shaft), each time a shutter blocks the light from the LED then the phototransistor will not produce an electric current. However, when the gaps between the shutters are in line with the LED and phototransistor, the light will reach the phototransistor thus producing the electric current. The four shutters and gaps would result in four on/off pulses of current being produced by the phototransistor in one rotation of the distributor shaft and shutter disc; this version would therefore be used on a four-cylinder engine.

The optical system produces a digital pulse (Figure 2.20), which can be at a lower voltage than that provided by the Hall system (sometimes as low as 2.4 volts). However, the signal from the optical system is sufficient for the ignition module to identify the rise in voltage or the fall in voltage as the signal alternates from on to off.

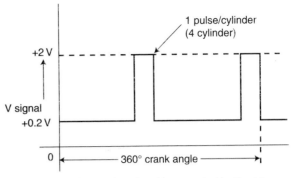

Figure 2.20 Digital signal produced by an optical ignition trigger

Wiring for optical ignition trigger

The LED requires a power supply and earth connections (Figure 2.21). The power supply will usually be passed from the ignition module to the LED. Note that the voltage will be stabilised by components within the module. The phototransistor will also require two connections to the module (positive and negative paths) to carry the signal produced by the phototransistor. There will therefore be four connections between the optical sensor and the ignition module. The module will also require its own power supply and earth connections, and, as with inductive or Hall systems, the module will form part of the earth circuit for the ignition coil.

Advantages and disadvantages of an optical system

The optical ignition trigger system provides a true digital signal, which is especially useful when the signal is passed to an ECU that operates with digital electronics. Optical systems are also generally reliable and relatively inexpensive.

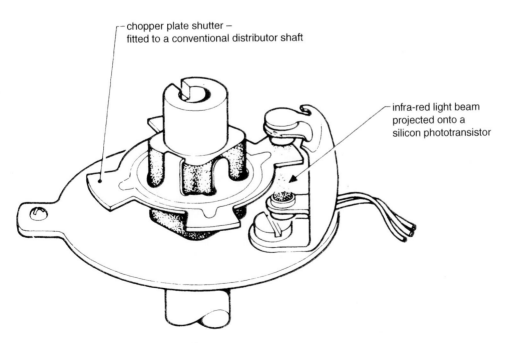

Figure 2.19 Optical ignition trigger assembly

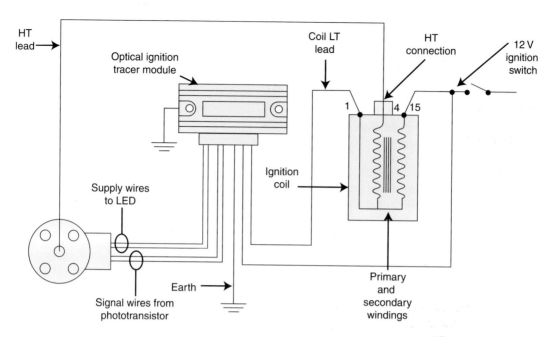

Figure 2.21 Wiring for an optical ignition trigger

The main disadvantage with an optical system is the importance of keeping the LED and phototransistor clean. A build up of dirt or oil on the components would reduce the efficiency or prevent the system from functioning.

2.2.8 Ignition modules/amplifiers: early types

With earlier types of electronic ignition, the ignition module simply functioned as the electronic switch for the ignition coil primary circuit. Assuming that a trigger mechanism such as an inductive trigger (as described in section 2.2.5) was used as a means of providing the timing reference signal, the module simply switched the primary circuit on and off thus forming a non-mechanical circuit switch. There were several variations of early systems but the basic objective was to eliminate any mechanical switching, and this was achieved with an inductive trigger (or Hall effect type) and a transistor that acted as the primary circuit switch.

Ballast resistor and dwell period
Early generations of electronic ignition systems, often had a ballast resistor in the primary circuit (as did many contact breaker systems). The resistance of the ballast resistor altered with temperature, and the temperature change was dictated by the length of time that current flowed in the primary circuit. As with a contact breaker system, the dwell period was a fixed percentage of the ignition cycle, e.g. 60%. Therefore, at slow engine speeds when an ignition cycle took a relatively long time, the current flowed through the primary circuit for 60% of this period, causing the resistor temperature and its resistance to increase, thus reducing the current

flow. However, when the engine speed increased, the time available for the current flow reduced thus reducing the temperature of the resistor; the resistance of the ballast resistor therefore also reduced thus increasing the current flow in the primary circuit.

The action of the ballast resistor therefore allowed a high current to flow in the primary circuit when there was reduced time available at high engine speeds but, when the engine speed was low, the current flow was reduced to prevent overheating of the coil and wiring (i.e. it is an output control ballast). The result was that the ignition coil could build up to an acceptable energy level at high as well as low speeds.

The ignition coils would have a primary winding resistance of typically 1.5 ohms (or slightly less), which would allow for a rapid build up of current flow. The ballast resistor would also have a resistance of approximately 1.5 ohms, so the total resistance in the circuit was approximately 3 ohms, which, with the 12 volt supply, would result in a current of 4 A. When the resistance of the ballast resistor increased at low engine speeds, this would then reduce the current flow. For many systems, the dwell percentage was often more than 60%, which meant that there was a longer period for charging the coil. So long as the ballast resistor functioned correctly, then the system would not overheat at low speeds.

Dwell periods on the early systems were generally a fixed percentage (fixed dwell angle). In the same way that a reference point on the trigger signal was used as a reference to the timing point, it was also possible to use another reference point on the signal as a reference to starting the dwell period. Some systems might have used an electronic device within the ignition module to control the dwell period.

Ignition timing advance and retard

With early generations of electronic ignition, the ignition timing advance and retard mechanisms remained much the same as for a contact breaker system: mechanical advance mechanism to alter the timing with engine speed and a vacuum operated retard system to alter the timing with changes in engine load. See section 2.2 in this book and section 2.28.8 in *Hillier's Fundamentals of Motor Vehicle Technology Book 1.*

2.2.9 Ignition modules: later types with dwell control and constant energy function

Improving the coil output at all engine speeds

One of the main problems with early electronic modules was that the dwell period was a compromise (as was the case with contact breaker systems); this meant that the dwell period was too long at slow engine speeds and too short at high engine speeds (hence the use of a ballast resistor as described in the previous section).

The next generation of ignition modules therefore provided a facility to alter the percentage of dwell depending on the engine speed. In effect, when the engine was at low speeds and an ignition cycle lasted a relatively long time, the dwell percentage was a small percentage of the long ignition cycle time. When the engine was at high speeds and the cycle time was much shorter, the dwell percentage was increased.

Example of dwell control

As an example, to achieve a good quality spark, if we assume that a current that flows for 2.5 ms is needed to allow the coil to build up the required amount of energy (magnetic field strength), then this in theory would be the same irrespective of engine speed. At 1000 rev/min on a four-cylinder engine, the ignition cycle for one cylinder would last for 30 ms, so the required 2.5 ms would represent one-twelfth of this period i.e. 8.33%.

If the engine speed is then increased to 2000 rev/min (twice the speed), then one ignition cycle will now last for only 15 ms (half the time). However, the coil would still require 2.5 ms of charge up time, which represent one sixth of the total 30 ms i.e. 16.66%. In effect, the charge up time remains the same but the percentage of the whole cycle changes in proportion with the change in engine speed.

As a last part of the example, if the engine speed is now increased to 6000 rev/min, the ignition cycle for one cylinder will last for only 5 ms. The coil charge up time will remain at 2.5 ms, which now represents 50% of the ignition cycle.

It is therefore possible with this type of dwell time control to operate an engine at high engine speeds and still provide a long enough dwell period for the coil to build up strong energy levels.

The actual control of the dwell period is not necessarily as precise as in the explanation above, and there are several variations in the exact dwell time provided depending on the ignition system module design. However, the objective is to ensure that the dwell time is sufficient for all engine speeds, thus allowing the ignition coil to provide a reasonably consistent output at all speeds.

For engines with more than four cylinders, the dwell time will have to be slightly less because of the shorter time available for one ignition cycle for each cylinder. However, on more modern ignition systems, developments have included one coil to provide a spark for two cylinders and more recently, systems now provide one coil for each cylinder. In both cases, the time available for each coil to charge up is considerably increased. These systems are explained in greater detail later in this section.

Controlling dwell for specific conditions

Although the system can control the dwell to suit engine speed, there are some operating conditions where it is an advantage to enable the coil to provide greater energy levels than normal. The usual examples are to provide a slight increase in dwell time at starting and at low engine speeds. Starting inevitably requires a strong spark, and at idle speed where emissions are critical, a better quality spark helps to ensure improved combustion. This is especially true with engines operating on relatively weak mixtures, which then benefit from long spark durations.

Constant energy control and high energy coils

It is obviously an advantage to use an ignition coil that has a rapid build or charge up time, and this can be achieved by using a coil with a low primary winding resistance (low inductance). Many modern ignition coils have a primary winding resistance that is as low as 0.5 ohms, which is one-sixth of the resistance of older contact breaker system coils. Therefore, the potential current flow through the primary winding on a modern coil could be as high as 24 A (12 volts through a resistance of 0.5 ohms). In fact, such potentially high current levels would be too high and could damage the wiring and the coil winding. However, another major benefit of the low resistance primary winding is that the build up of current flow is much quicker than with primary windings of higher resistance. With this fact in mind, it is then possible to allow an initial rapid build up of current flow but to then limit the current so that it does not reach levels that are too high; the coil will be able to produce high energy levels due to the rapid build up time but without the problem of high currents damaging the system components.

Later generations of electronic ignition modules and modern ignition systems use a method of current control or 'current limiting' in conjunction with low resistance ignition coils. The process of current control is generally carried out in one of two ways, both methods relying on a 'feedback' or 'closed loop' system. In effect, the system monitors the current flow in the primary circuit and when it rises to a predetermined level, the current in the primary circuit is then either restricted or the dwell time is reduced; both methods will prevent overheating that would otherwise be caused by an excessive current level that lasts for long periods.

Feedback system

The feedback systems are relatively simple in operation and rely on a resistor that forms part of the primary circuit, i.e. it is in series with the primary winding of the ignition coil. The resistor (referred to as a sensing resistor) is located within the ignition module, which is of course functioning as a switch on the earth path for the primary circuit. The voltage drop across the resistor will change with changes in current flow and, by passing the voltage signal from the resistor to other circuitry in the module, it is then possible to either control the current or control the dwell time accordingly.

With the current limiting systems, the 'Darlington pair' within the module is used to switch the primary current through to earth (Figure 2.22). When the voltage signal from the resistor indicates that the current has reached the predetermined level, the input voltage to the Darlington pair is reduced, which in turn reduces the primary circuit current flowing from C to E (collector to emitter). When the current is reduced, the voltage at the sensing resistor is also reduced and this voltage is then again used as the reference to control the input voltage to the Darlington pair. In effect, the process is a continuous action of monitoring and adjustment of voltages and current flow (i.e. it is a closed loop).

With dwell control systems, the same principle is used as for current limiting systems but the voltage from the sensing resistor is passed to the dwell control circuitry within the module. Dwell control therefore depends on the voltage at the sensing resistor.

A complete constant energy system

Figure 2.23 shows a simplified layout of a constant energy ignition system. The process is as follows.

- A trigger signal is passed from an inductive or Hall effect trigger to the ignition module.
- The signal will be processed by the pulse shaping device; if the trigger signal is provided by an inductive trigger, it will also be converted from analogue to digital.
- The processed signal is then passed through the dwell control device and peak coil current cut off device.
- The signal is then passed to the 'driver' which is effectively a low current/voltage switching transistor that is directly responding to the processed trigger signal. The driver responds to the trigger signal and in turn switches on and off the Darlington pair, which contains the main power transistor.
- The Darlington pair forms the final switching element of the ignition module. The primary current passes through the Darlington pair, so when the Darlington pair switches on the primary circuit, current will flow through the primary circuit thus enabling the ignition coil to build up a magnetic field. When the Darlington pair switches off the primary current, the magnetic field in the coil will collapse, thus providing a high voltage to the spark plug.
- Note that the voltage either side of the current sensing resistor is passed to a comparator, which then passes an appropriate signal either to the driver (which controls the Darlington pair), or the signal is passed to the dwell control device.

Different locations for ignition modules

There are several variations in the design of the electronic ignition systems so far discussed. Whilst in principle the systems will generally all function in the same way, the different versions produced for different vehicles have constructional variations that are either design preferences or are dictated by installation requirements.

In general, there are three basic physical layouts:

- remote module – the ignition module is remotely located away from the trigger mechanism
- integrated with the distributor body – the module is either located inside the distributor or mounted on the outside of the distributor body
- located on the ignition coil – the module is mounted on the ignition coil casing.

Figure 2.24 shows some examples of different module locations.

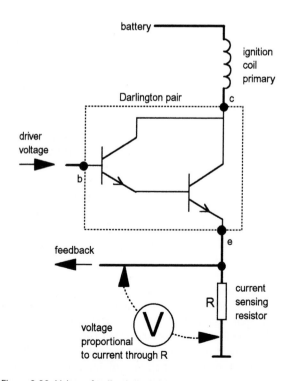

Figure 2.22 Voltage feedback control

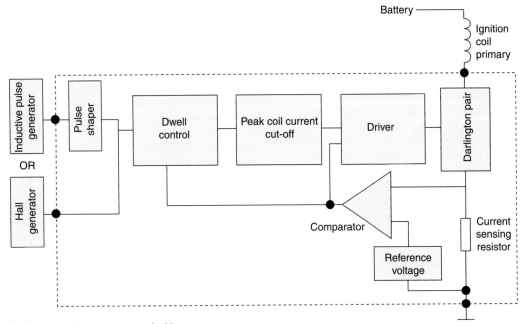

Figure 2.23 Layout of constant energy ignition system

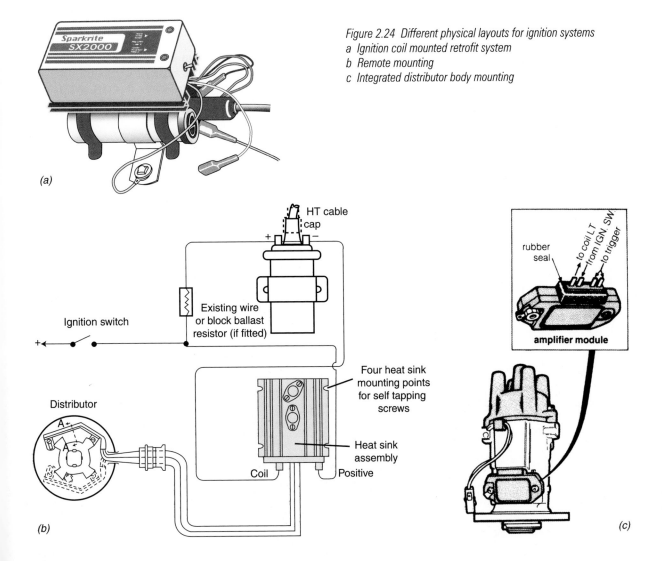

Figure 2.24 Different physical layouts for ignition systems
a Ignition coil mounted retrofit system
b Remote mounting
c Integrated distributor body mounting

2.2.10 Capacitor discharge ignition

Capacitor discharge ignition systems have been used in the past on some vehicles and were not uncommon on high performance engines. The capacitor discharge system is however not ideally suited to modern engines and is therefore seldom used on today's vehicles.

Capacitor discharge (CD) systems operate in a slightly different way to more traditional types of ignition. Although an ignition coil is still used, the coil does not store energy as is the case with most systems: the ignition coil on a CD system functions as a 'pulse transformer'. In effect, a short and relatively high voltage pulse (typically of 400 volts) is passed through the primary winding of the coil; this causes a very rapid build up of a magnetic flux (magnetic field) in the primary winding. Because the secondary winding is exposed to the rapidly created magnetic field, a very high voltage (typically around 40 kV) is then induced into the secondary winding.

To create the short 400 volt pulse, a capacitor in the module is charged (effectively during a dwell period). However, when a trigger signal is provided, the capacitor discharges its stored energy through the primary winding.

A simple capacitor discharge circuit is shown in Figure 2.25. Note that a pulse generator is still used and the trigger signal from the pulse generator is passed to a pulse shaper. The processed signal from the pulse shaper is passed to the trigger stage, and the signal from the trigger stage will cause the capacitor to discharge.

CD systems provide a short but very high voltage coil output, which is typically only around 0.1 ms in duration. This short duration spark is not effective in maintaining the combustion process with weaker air/fuel mixtures. However, the high intensity 40 kV coil output is consistent across most engine speeds and it is very effective at igniting relatively rich mixtures. One advantage of a CD system with older high performance and racing engines was that the high voltage at the spark plug could burn off any contaminants. On older racing engines, it was common on cold engines for the mechanical clearances to be large until the engine reached operating temperatures; this allowed oil to pass the piston rings and valve guides and therefore enter the combustion chambers. Oil would therefore contaminate the spark plugs and cause ignition and combustion problems. Additionally, because racing engines operated with relatively rich mixtures, carbon fouling of the spark plugs was a common problem. The high voltage at the spark plug produced by CD systems was very effective at keeping the plugs free of contaminants.

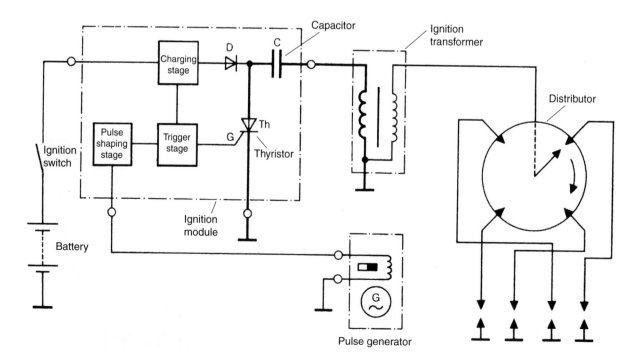

Figure 2.25 Capacitor discharge system

2.3 COMPUTER CONTROLLED IGNITION SYSTEMS

2.3.1 A further improvement in timing accuracy

Eliminating the problems of mechanical timing systems

Although earlier generations of electronic ignition systems had improved reliability and spark quality, the accuracy of ignition timing advance and retard mechanisms was still dependent on mechanical and vacuum operated systems that had not changed for many years: the timing advance and retard mechanisms were no different to those of contact breaker systems. The problem again was tighter emissions regulations, a requirement for improved fuel consumption and continued demand for improved engine power.

As is often the case with emission requirements, there are conflicts between achieving the desired emissions and also achieving economy and power. However, if the ignition timing can be more accurately controlled and if the changes in timing (advance and retard with speed and load) can be more rapidly implemented, then combustion efficiency can be improved under almost all conditions.

As mentioned in section 2.2.2, if the correct ignition (spark) timing can be provided at exactly the right time,

the gases will expand at exactly the right time and this will allow maximum possible power to be achieved (assuming all other conditions are good). However, because of minor variations in fuel quality and in other engine operating conditions, it was general practice to set the timing slightly retarded so that combustion knock and other overheating problems did not occur.

Importantly, the relative inaccuracy of mechanical and mechanical/vacuum based timing mechanisms prevented the timing being correct for all operating conditions. Even when the components were new, mechanical advance mechanisms and mechanical/vacuum operated retard mechanisms could not provide correct timing in all operating conditions.

Mechanical 'engine speed' related advance

Figure 2.26a shows two advance lines for engine speed/timing advance; the curved line shows the requirements for an engine, whilst the straight line shows what was available from a mechanical advance mechanism (bob weight and spring system). Note that the kinks or angle changes in the straight line are caused by using unequal strength springs on the bob weight system (Figure 2.26b): the weaker spring acts against the bob weights for the lower engine speeds and

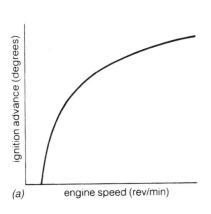

(a) engine speed (rev/min)

ignition advance requirement

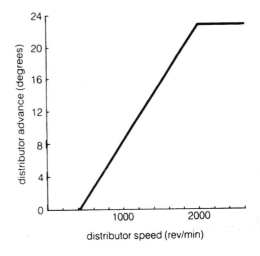

(b)

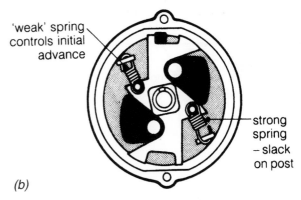

Figure 2.26 Engine speed related timing advance curve and mechanical advance mechanism
a Ignition advance curves
b Mechanical advance mechanism using unequal length springs

then, as the bob weights are flung out under centrifugal force, the stronger spring then also acts against the bob weights.

The difference between the two advance lines shown in Figure 2.26a illustrates the inability of a mechanical advance system to provide the correct timing at all engine speeds. It was therefore necessary to try to achieve the best compromise for timing advance, which meant that the timing was not correct for much of the engine speed range.

As well as not being able to provide the correct timing at all times when the system was new, when the timing mechanisms began to wear matters became worse and timing was often much too far away from the desired value to enable the engine to operate efficiently. Mechanical and mechanical/vacuum systems could not respond quickly enough to the required changes in timing and the accuracy deteriorated over time due to wear. It was therefore necessary to eliminate mechanical systems and to use electronic or computer control for the ignition timing functions.

Load related vacuum retard

Figure 2.27 shows a simple vacuum operated timing retard system. The illustration shows the mechanism acting on a base plate onto which the contact breaker assembly were mounted.

When the throttle was closed at idle speed or during deceleration (upper left diagram), the vacuum was blocked from reaching the diaphragm and therefore any timing changes were dependent purely on the mechanical bob weight system (engine speed related).

When the throttle was then partially opened (light load conditions), high manifold depression acts on the diaphragm, which in turn pulls the diaphragm

against the spring. The movement of the diaphragm pulls the linkage, which rotates the base plate in an anticlockwise direction, against the direction of rotation of the distributor shaft. This would have the effect of advancing the trigger signal and timing.

When however the throttle was then opened further (high load conditions), the intake depression would initially reduce (higher pressure), the spring would then force back the diaphragm and in turn, this would allow the base plate to move back in a clockwise direction (the same direction as the distributor shaft rotation). The opening of the contact breaker and timing would therefore retard.

Whilst the vacuum advance/retard system was reasonably effective, it could not accurately control timing for all the variations of load that occur and again a compromise was inevitable. Adding the compromise of a vacuum system to the compromise of a mechanical advance system, resulted in an inaccurate timing control system.

For electronic systems, near the trigger mechanism located in the distributor (e.g. inductive, Hall effect or optical). Refer to Figures 2.11, 2.12 and 2.19. The movement of the base plate and distributor shaft altered the timing in the same way.

Changing operating conditions

Apart from the lack of accuracy of mechanical and vacuum based timing systems, there are other reasons why greater flexibility of timing control is needed. Air/fuel mixtures need to be altered more rapidly, so the ignition timing must be altered accordingly; in addition, ignition timing requirements differ with temperature. In effect, anything that affects the speed of combustion, i.e. the flame speed through the combustion chamber

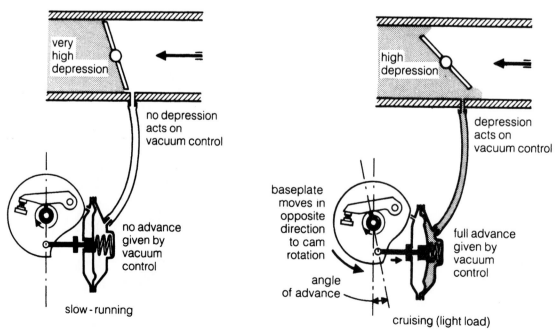

Figure 2.27 Vacuum advance/retard mechanism

and the burn time, will require a different timing advance value.

Although many adaptations to basic mechanical and vacuum systems were introduced, the accuracy and speed of change of timing remained less than satisfactory for modern requirements.

With computer control, and the use of a number of sensors, it became possible to obtain much more accurate control of ignition timing. Rapidly changing operating conditions could therefore be sensed (including rapid changes in engine speed), and the computer or ECU could then alter the timing as necessary. Systems were therefore introduced where the switching action of the ignition module was controlled by the ECU. A trigger signal is still produced by an inductive or Hall effect trigger (or other type of pulse generator), but the signal is passed to the ECU, which modifies or 'phases' the signal to achieve timing control. Figure 2.28 shows the basic layout of such a system. Note that the ignition module can be separate from the ECU or, in many cases, the module is integrated within the ECU.

The simple example in Figure 2.28 shows an ECU receiving a trigger signal provided by an inductive sensor. A vacuum pipe connects the intake manifold vacuum (depression) to a pressure sensitive component in the ECU thus providing the ECU with engine speed and load information. See section 1.5.4 for information on electronic type pressure sensors.

2.3.2 Digital timing control

If we assume that an ECU receives a trigger signal from some form of engine speed sensor, and load information via the vacuum sensor, the ECU can then calculate the required ignition timing. Within the ECU is a 'look up table' or memory, which contains all the relevant timing data applicable to the different load conditions; by comparing the conditions with the data in the look up table, the ECU can determine the timing advance required.

The look up table effectively contains a three-dimensional map of the timing requirements, a simple example of which is shown in Figure 2.29. The spark timing map provides the timing angle (crankshaft angle) related to engine speed (revolutions/second) and engine load (on a scale of 0 to 1). The example in Figure 2.29 shows a relatively small number of speed, load and timing reference points, but many more reference points can be included on a spark map.

Figure 2.30 shows the same spark timing map with the engine speed at 32 rev/s (1920 rev/min) and the engine load at 0.5 (half load). The 32 point mark on the map is therefore followed across until it intersects with the 0.5 load line; the intersect point identifies the required spark advance, which in this case is 52°.

The timing advance characteristics are established during many tests on development engines (before they go into production). Once the timing

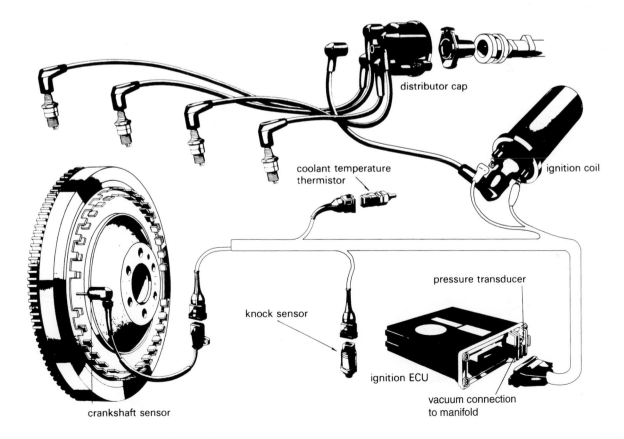

Figure 2.28 Layout of a computer (ECU) controlled ignition system

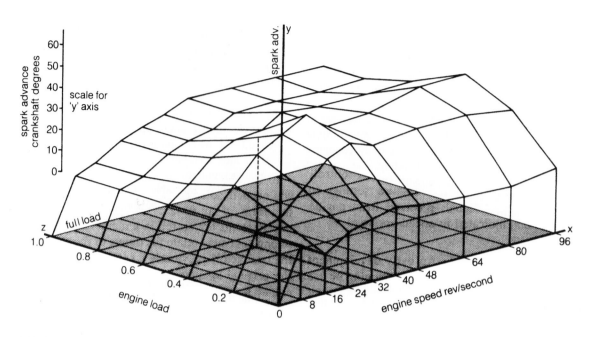

Figure 2.29 Simplified three-dimensional spark advance map

characteristics have been established, production ECUs will then have a memory and look up tables containing the applicable data.

Because accurate timing is so important to engine efficiency, performance, emissions and economy, improvements in all of these factors are achieved with a greater number of timing reference points. Figure 2.31 shows a more modern and complex spark advance map (compared with the example in Figure 2.29).

It can now be appreciated that considerable accuracy of spark timing can be achieved with the complex spark timing map. However, because the trigger signal from the inductive or Hall effect triggers (and other pulse generators) discussed so far provides only one reference point per cylinder, this is a limiting

factor in the accuracy of ignition/spark timing. Additionally, the trigger mechanisms so far discussed are usually located within the distributor body, so the rotation of the trigger mechanisms is driven by the distributor shaft which in turn is driven by a timing belt or chain. Any wear or maladjustment of the belt or chain will cause inaccuracies in the timing reference.

A more reliable and accurate means of providing a trigger/reference signal would enable the spark timing also to be more accurate. The following section (2.3.3) covers some examples of more accurate timing trigger/reference signal systems which usually have a sensor and reluctor or trigger disc located on the crankshaft.

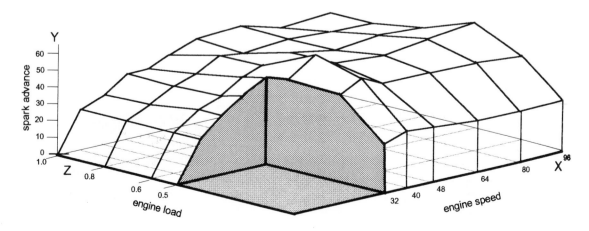

Figure 2.30 Simplified three-dimensional spark advance map showing the spark timing at 32 rev/s and half engine load

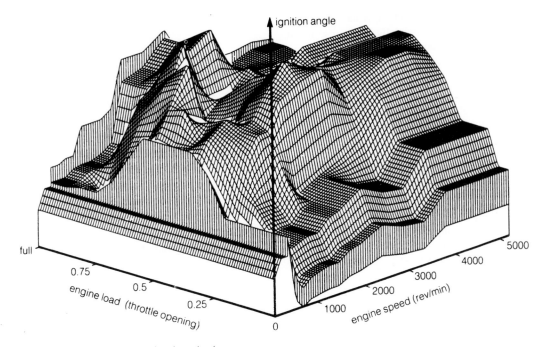

Figure 2.31 Typical modern three-dimensional spark advance map

2.3.3 Crankshaft speed/position sensors

Direct triggering reference from the crankshaft

Most crankshaft speed/position sensors are located adjacent to the crankshaft and are usually inductive sensors (Figures 2.32 and 2.33). In some cases Hall effect sensors have been used. Locating a sensor adjacent to a crankshaft allows a reluctor disc (trigger disc with the reference points) to be mounted directly on the crankshaft, with most versions being mounted either at the front pulley or at the rear of the crankshaft adjacent to the flywheel. Sometimes a reluctor disc is mounted at a convenient point on the crankshaft between the crankshaft webs, i.e. the disc is located in the crankcase.

The obvious advantage of locating the reluctor/trigger disc on the crankshaft is that there is no drive linkage (belt, chain or other mechanism); this means that the trigger or reference signal will be accurately identifying the crankshaft speed or angular position without any losses of accuracy that could be caused by drive mechanisms.

Increased number of reference points

With a crankshaft mounted reluctor or trigger disc, it is possible to use a larger diameter disc, which can more easily contain a larger number of reference points (reluctor teeth). Due to the fact that most of the crankshaft speed position sensors are of the inductive type, the reference points usually take the form of teeth located around the disc.

In most cases the trigger disc is located directly at the front or the rear of the crankshaft and can form part

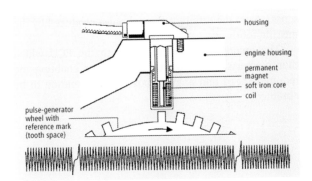

Figure 2.32 Crankshaft speed/position sensor

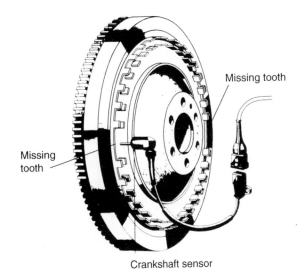

Figure 2.33 Crankshaft speed/position sensor located adjacent to flywheel

of the front pulley or part of the flywheel assembly. Because of these locations, especially if the disc has a similar diameter to the flywheel, it is relatively easy to locate a number of reference points around the disc. Some earlier examples had only a small number of reference points, e.g. two or four, but most modern systems have as many as 60 reference points. One of the reference points or teeth is usually either missing or is a different shape to the rest of the teeth; this enables a master reference signal to be produced.

Figure 2.33 shows a flywheel located inductive crankshaft speed/position sensor. Note the missing tooth, which is adjacent to the sensor in the illustration. In fact, the example shown in Figure 2.33 has two missing teeth; one missing tooth is a master reference for cylinders 1 and 4, while the other missing tooth is a master reference for cylinders 2 and 3. On this particular system, with a single ignition coil, the high voltage output from the coil is directed via a rotor arm located at the end of the camshaft (OHC type). Therefore the ECU does not need to receive a signal relating to each cylinder, but it does receive signals relating to the TDC position of each pair of cylinders (or other predefined angular position of the crankshaft).

On this system therefore, the sensor would provide the speed signal and the angular position of the crankshaft as each tooth passes the sensor; the ECU can count the number of signals as each tooth passes the sensor thus enabling the ECU to identify the angle of rotation from TDC (or from the master reference position). It is also possible on this type of system for the ECU to assess any changes in crankshaft speed as each tooth passes the sensor.

Using Figure 2.28 as an example, the ECU receives a load signal from the pressure sensor (pressure transducer), which is connected by a vacuum pipe to

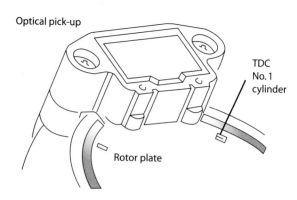

Figure 2.34 Optical speed/position sensor located in distributor body

the intake manifold. This system also uses information from a knock sensor (discussed in section 2.3.4). Also note that a coolant temperature sensor provides information to the ECU to enable changes in timing to occur with changes in temperature (temperature sensors are covered in section 1.5.1).

Note: Some speed/position sensor systems located within a distributor also have many reference points, one type being an optical system with 360 slots located around a disc (Figure 2.34). However, locating a large number of reference points around a relatively small disc requires good manufacturing accuracy and the problem still remains that any wear or maladjustment of the drive linkage to the distributor will result in incorrect timing references.

Crankshaft speed/position sensor: operation and signals

Section 2.2.5 provides an explanation of an inductive pulse generator, and the inductive crankshaft speed/position sensor operates in exactly the same way. The crankshaft sensors, however, are usually constructed so that the winding or coil is formed around the magnet and this assembly is located in the sensor body, which is then bolted or secured in some way to the engine block or flywheel housing. The sensor is located so that it will be affected by the movement of the reluctor teeth (reference points) whilst the crankshaft is rotating.

Figure 2.35 shows a typical analogue signal produced by an inductive crankshaft speed/position sensor. Note the different shaped pulse produced by the missing tooth.

The analogue signal is passed to the ECU which then converts it to a digital signal, thus enabling the required speed and angular position information to be obtained.

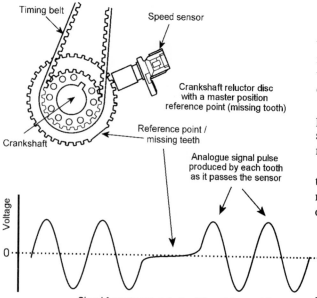

Signal from sensor, note the different shape of the signal created by the missing tooth

Figure 2.35 Analogue signal produced by an inductive crankshaft speed/position sensor

Other types of sensor signal

Almost all crankshaft speed/position sensors are of the inductive type, but where a Hall effect or optical system is used, these types will provide a digital signal in the same way as the older ignition trigger systems discussed previously in sections 2.2.6 and 2.2.7. The only differences compared with the older ignition trigger systems will be the number of signal pulses produced which will depend on the number of reference points.

2.3.4 Knock sensors

A knock sensor (Figure 2.36) is effectively a vibration sensor that responds to those vibrations in the engine that cause pressure waves to occur in the cylinder block or cylinder head. By detecting the vibrations or pressure waves, a knock sensor can detect the vibrations caused by combustion knock.

The knock sensor is an electronic pressure sensor, which with a pressure sensitive crystal that produces a small electrical pulse when it is exposed to pressure waves (such as the engine vibrations). Vibrations caused by combustion knock will result in a slightly different signal (frequency and voltage) being produced by the sensor. When the ECU receives the signal from the sensor, it is able to filter out the normal vibrations and respond to the particular part of the signal that is caused by combustion knock.

Although ECU controlled ignition timing should provide ideal timing for all operating conditions, it is possible that fuel quality could be poor (momentarily or continuously). Other factors such as the temperature in the combustion chamber can also cause short term combustion knock. In most cases, slightly retarding the ignition timing/spark advance will reduce and eliminate combustion knock.

Therefore, when the ECU detects a combustion knock signal, it will respond by retarding the spark timing a predetermined number of degrees. If the combustion knock is no longer detected, the ECU will progressively advance the timing to its correct value (so long as combustion knock does not reoccur).

An ECU can alter the timing for just the affected cylinder. When the knock occurs (when combustion occurs in the affected cylinder), the ECU will then provide the correct timing for the remaining cylinders (for example, the remaining three cylinders on a four-cylinder engine). When the affected cylinder is then due to receive its next spark, the ECU can retard the timing for just the affected cylinder.

Key Points

The main advantage of computer controlled ignition is accurate timing – that stays accurate over the life of the engine

The ideal timing setting is held in the ECU memory in the form of a look up table

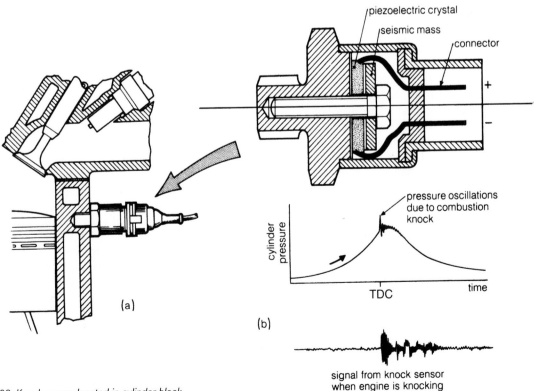

Figure 2.36 Knock sensor located in cylinder block

2.4   DISTRIBUTORLESS AND DIRECT IGNITION SYSTEMS

2.4.1 Limitations of distributor based systems

Restricted dwell time and wasted energy
All of the ignition systems covered so far have two major disadvantages when it comes to providing high energy from the ignition coil to the spark plugs; both disadvantages arise because the ignition systems use a single coil to provide a spark for all of the cylinders.

Time to build up coil energy
The first disadvantage when using a single coil for all cylinders is that it limits the time available to build up coil energy between each of the individual ignition cycles: there is very little 'dwell' time available for the current to flow through the primary winding of the coil and build up a strong magnetic field (magnetic flux).

As previously explained, on a multi-cylinder engine there is very little time between one cylinder firing and the next; the faster the engine speed and the greater the number of cylinders, the less time there is available for the ignition coil to build up sufficient energy for the next ignition cycle. On modern high speed engines which operate with relatively weak mixtures, it is essential that the energy available from the coil is sufficient to produce a powerful and long duration spark otherwise emissions and general performance will not be acceptable.

Distributor and rotor arm wasting energy
When a single coil is used to produce a spark for a number of cylinders, the energy from the coil (high voltage) is passed via a high tension cable (HT lead) to the distributor cap and rotor arm assembly (see section 2.28 in *Hillier's Fundamentals of Motor Vehicle Technology Book 1*). Note that the lead passing the energy from the coil to the distributor cap is often referred to as the 'king lead'. The distributor cap contains a number of contact points (referred to as electrodes), which in turn are connected to each of the spark plugs via additional HT leads. When the high voltage from the coil passes along the king lead to the centre electrode in the distributor cap, it is then passed to the centre of the rotor arm; because the rotor arm rotates with the distributor shaft, it is then able to pass the energy to the individual HT leads and spark plugs.

Figure 2.37a shows a basic layout of an ignition system with a single coil and Figure 2.37b shows a plan view of the rotor arm and distributor cap.

One problem with the rotor arm system is that voltage is lost or wasted when the current flow flows through all of the HT leads, and especially when the current flows across the rotor arm tip to each of the electrodes. There is a necessary gap between the rotor arm tip and the electrode, and this absorbs or uses some of the energy produced by the coil.

However, although Figure 2.37b shows the rotor arm in alignment with the electrode, in reality, the rotor arm passes through quite a large angle during the period of time that the spark exists (remember that the spark may last 2 ms or more). When an engine is operating at 6000 rev/min, the rotor arm (which rotates at half engine speed) will rotate 50 times in one second or one rotation in 0.02 s (2 hundredths of a second). During the spark duration of 2 ms (2 thousandths of a second), the rotor arm will rotate through one-tenth of a complete rotation i.e. 36° of rotation. There is therefore quite a substantial gap between the rotor arm tip and the electrodes when the energy from the coil is passing to the spark plug. This gap inevitably uses considerable amounts of valuable energy, which reduces the energy available to maintain the spark. Additionally, the rotor arm tip and electrodes will progressively deteriorate due to the arcing that occurs as the voltage or energy flows across the gaps.

It is also important to note that, when electricity has to jump the gap at the rotor arm tip, this creates electrical interference, which must be suppressed to prevent interference with other electrical and electronic devices.

Using multiple ignition coils (eliminating the rotor arm)
The next progression in ignition system design was therefore based on a desire to eliminate the distributor cap and rotor arm assembly and use more than one ignition coil. Note that there were some engines produced (typically V8 and V12 engines) that did use two coils, each of which provided sparks for half of the cylinders. However, these systems still used one rotor arm for each coil and group of cylinders: in effect there were two ignition systems.

The ultimate ignition system would have one coil for each cylinder, and this is the general rule for modern engines, where an individual ignition coil is either directly connected to the top of the spark plug or there is an HT lead from each coil to the spark plug.

There is however another solution, which is still used on some systems, and this design uses a single coil to provide a spark at two spark plugs. Although these systems are often referred to as 'distributorless' ignition systems, the same terminology can be applied to systems that use one coil for each cylinder. For the purposes of differentiation, coils that provide sparks to two cylinders at the same time are referred to within this book as 'wasted spark' systems, the reason for which will be made clear in section 2.4.2. Section 2.4.3 covers systems that use a 'single coil per cylinder'.

For both the wasted spark and the single coil per cylinder systems, the ignition systems do not require a distributor and rotor arm assembly to distribute the spark to the different cylinders: they are both therefore

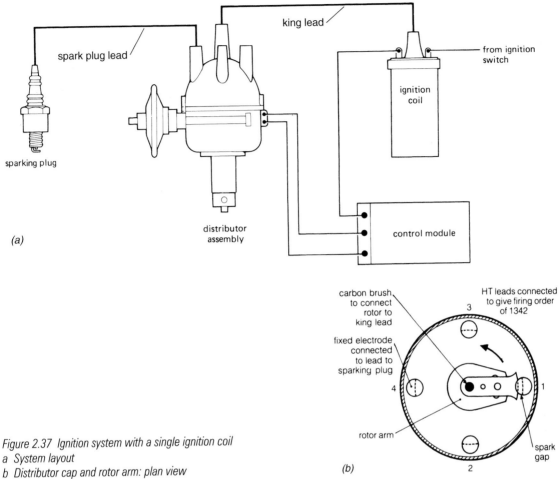

Figure 2.37 Ignition system with a single ignition coil
a System layout
b Distributor cap and rotor arm: plan view

'distributorless' ignition systems. The term 'direct ignition' is also used but this would generally refer to systems where the ignition coil is directly located onto the spark plug, i.e. there is no HT lead between the coil and spark plug.

2.4.2 Wasted spark ignition systems

Principle of operation of a wasted spark system
Providing a spark at two cylinders
For the majority of engines layouts where an even number of cylinders is used, two of the pistons will rise and fall within the cylinders at the same time. Using an in line four-cylinder engine as an example: pistons 1 and 4 rise and fall together, but when cylinder 1 approaches TDC on the compression stroke and is provided with the spark, piston number 4 is approaching TDC on the exhaust stroke. However, at the next full rotation of the crankshaft, the situation is reversed. The same process is true for pistons 2 and 3.

Therefore, with an ignition coil that can provide a spark at the spark plugs for cylinders 1 and 4 at the same time, if cylinder 1 receives a spark at the correct time (i.e. at the top of its compression stroke) cylinder 4 will receive the spark when it is on the exhaust stroke and therefore the spark to cylinder 4 is wasted. On the

next revolution of the crankshaft, the wasted spark will be at cylinder 1 and cylinder 4 will receive the spark at the correct time (i.e. at the top of its compression stroke). Figure 2.38 shows the basic principle: a pair of cylinders that rise and fall together (but on different strokes) receive a spark at the same time.

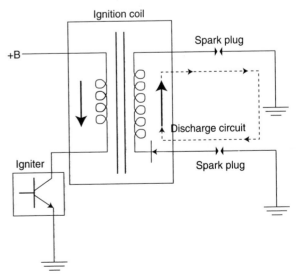

Figure 2.38 Single ignition coil providing a spark to two cylinders at the same time

Positive and negative sparks

The ignition coil on a wasted spark system operates in the same way as the conventional coils so far discussed. However, both ends of the secondary winding in the coil are connected to an HT lead and a spark plug (Figure 2.39), whereas on a conventional coil only one end of the secondary is connected to an HT lead and spark plug (the other end is connected internally within the coil to the end of the primary winding, which completes the earth path for the secondary winding).

On the wasted spark ignition coil, when the magnetic field collapses around the secondary winding, one end of the winding will be positive whilst the other end will be negative. The flow of current at the positive end of the winding will pass from the coil winding down to the spark plug and then across the plug gap to earth (the engine acts as the earth point for the spark plugs). Note that current flow is generally regarded as passing from the higher voltage to the lower voltage, and, if we assume that the output voltage from the coil in this example is 10 000 volts, current will flow from the 10 000 volts at the coil to the zero volts at earth.

The flow of current at the negative end of the winding will however be from earth (the earth electrode at the spark plug) across the plug gap and then through the HT lead to the coil. This direction of flow is caused by the fact that the voltage at the negative end of the coil winding is a minus value, e.g. –10 000 volts, which is 10 000 volts lower than the voltage at earth (which is zero volts); current is again assumed to flow from the higher to the lower voltage.

Note: Electron flow is actually opposite to the generally accepted convention: electrons flow from the lower to the higher voltage rather than from the assumed higher to the lower voltage. However, as with most explanations, it is assumed that conventional flow is from the higher voltage to the lower voltage.

Irrespective of which way the current is flowing across the spark plug gap, a spark will be provided that is sufficient to cause combustion in the combustion chamber. However, because electrons flow naturally from a hot surface, and the centre electrode is the hotter of the two electrodes, it is easier to produce the spark or arc if the current flows in a direction that matches this natural electron flow (because the voltage required is lower). Conventional coils are wired in such a way that there is a 'negative spark' at the plug gap. However, with the wasted spark coils, one spark will be a negative spark and the other will be a positive spark.

The positive spark is still effective at creating combustion but there is a tendency (because of incorrect electron flow) for the electrodes to operate at slightly lower temperatures, which can result in fouling of the plug electrodes. It is therefore necessary either to use different grades of spark plug for the positive and negative sparked plugs (which is not desirable) or to use a spark plug that is effective irrespective of the polarity of the spark.

Increased dwell time

Although the term 'dwell' is perhaps not really applicable to modern electronic ignition systems, it still used to refer to the period of time available for building up coil energy, i.e. the time for current to flow through the primary winding. We can therefore examine the 'dwell time' available for a single coil system and for a wasted spark system for a four-cylinder engine to assess the increased amount of dwell time available.

1 When a single coil is used to serve all four cylinders, the coil is required to provide a spark when each of the cylinders approach TDC. This means that in two revolutions of the crankshaft, the coil will be required to provide four sparks, which is two sparks per revolution of the crankshaft. This equates to one spark or one complete cycle of operation for the coil for every half rotation of the crankshaft.

2 When a wasted spark system is used on a four-cylinder engine, there would be two wasted spark coils: one coil for cylinders 1 and 4, and one coil for cylinders 2 and 3. If we examine the operation of the coil that serves cylinders 1 and 4, it will be required to provide a spark each time that the two pistons approach TDC, which equates to one complete cycle of operation for each revolution of the crankshaft.

With a wasted spark system on a four-cylinder engine, the ignition coils now have twice as much time available for the cycle of operation (between one spark and the next), which means that it would be possible to

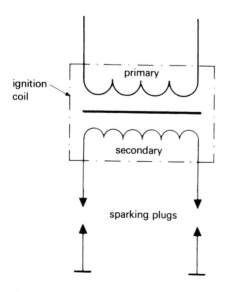

Figure 2.39 Schematic view of a wasted spark ignition coil

provide twice as much dwell time (if necessary) in order to build up the energy in the coil. Note that, whenever a wasted spark system is used, there will be twice as much time available compared with the same engine using a single coil with the same number of cylinders.

Typical operation and layout of a wasted spark system

On a wasted spark system, the coils are switched in exactly the same way as on a single coil system: the ECU calculates the ignition timing in the same way and the ECU will cause the ignition module to switch each of the wasted spark coils at the appropriate time. Because there are effectively two coils on a four-cylinder engine, there would need to be two switching modules, i.e. the ECU will be controlling two modules, each of which will switch the primary circuit for one of the coils. In reality, the modules are usually integrated into the ECU and in fact the ECU will contain two power stages (one for each coil), with all other functions such as current and dwell control being managed by the ECU.

The ECU will require information (from a crankshaft speed/position sensor) to indicate when one pair of cylinders is approaching TDC; in effect a master reference. Once this master reference has been established, the ECU can make one of the coils provide the sparks to one pair of cylinders. If the crankshaft sensor is providing many reference points in addition to the master reference (because there is a large number of teeth on the reluctor disc), the ECU can then calculate the angle of rotation of the crankshaft and make the other coil or coils provide sparks to the other pair of cylinders. As with other ECU controlled systems, a load sensor and possibly other sensors, e.g. temperature sensors, can provide information to enable the ECU to more accurately calculate the correct ignition advance angle (spark timing).

Figure 2.40a shows a basic layout of a wasted spark system, with an example of a typical wasted spark coil shown in Figure 2.40b (note that there would be one of these coils for each pair of cylinders).

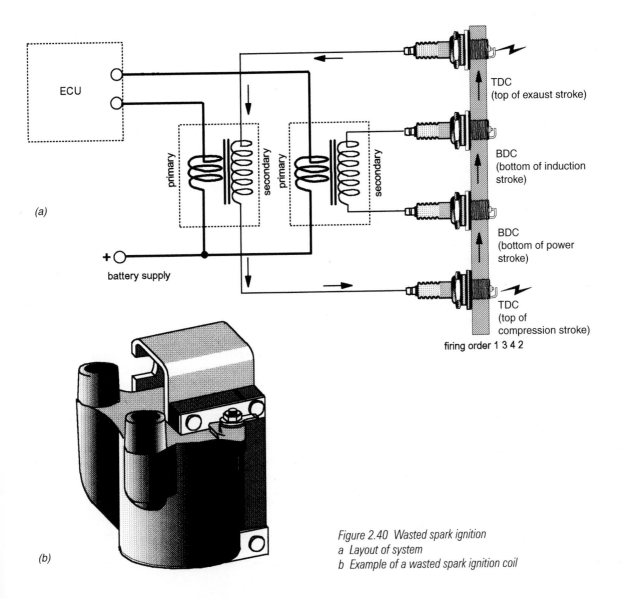

(a)

(b)

Figure 2.40 Wasted spark ignition
a Layout of system
b Example of a wasted spark ignition coil

Alternative construction and operation of wasted spark system with diode control

A development of the wasted spark system used a 'coil pack' with two primary windings but only one secondary winding (Figure 2.41).

The ECU functioned as on the previous system by switching the two primary windings alternately. The polarity applied to the two primary windings is different; therefore this will cause the magnetic field created in the primary and secondary windings to alternately reverse polarity. In turn this will cause the output current from the secondary winding to also alternately reverse polarity.

In effect, the HT voltage at point A on the secondary winding (Figure 2.41) will alternately be positive then negative, depending on which of the primary windings is active on each of the ignition cycles; the same situation will therefore occur at point B, so that when the HT coil output at A is positive, it will be negative at point B. This situation will reverse when the other primary winding is active on the next cycle.

If we assume that, on one of the cycles the current is flowing through the secondary winding from A to B (from earth through A to B and then back to earth again), then the diode at spark plugs 1 and 4 will prevent current flow. However, the diodes at spark plugs 2 and 3 will allow current to flow, thus allowing a spark to occur at spark plugs 2 and 3.

On the next cycle, the other primary winding will be active and this will cause the polarity at A to be negative and B to be positive. Therefore the diodes on spark plugs 1 and 4 will allow current to flow and sparks to occur at those plugs. However the diodes on spark plugs 2 and 3 will prevent current flow and therefore there will be no spark at plugs 2 and 3.

This design of system allows for a more compact coil assembly that will contain the two primary windings and a single secondary winding, as well as the diodes. The ECU still performs the same task as for the previously described wasted spark system, in that it controls the switching of the primary circuits at the appropriate time (spark timing). The ECU also still relies on the crankshaft speed/position sensor and a load sensor (usually a vacuum sensor) for the required information.

2.4.3 Single coil per cylinder and coil on plug ignition systems

The logical development

A high percentage of modern petrol engines are fitted with ignition systems that use one coil for each individual cylinder. The basic principle of operation for each coil remains the same as for previously described coils. However, unlike wasted spark systems, each coil can provide a negative spark.

One logical reason for using a single coil for each cylinder is the fact that in recent years there have been several engine designs with odd numbers of cylinders (five cylinders and three cylinders). A wasted spark system cannot effectively be used on engines with odd numbers of cylinders, since such a system is suited to engines where two pistons rise and fall at the same time. Older distributor cap and rotor arm systems are inefficient, so, on engines with odd numbers of cylinders, it is necessary to use one coil for each cylinder.

Another advantage of single coil per cylinder systems is that the ignition coil can be mounted directly onto the spark plug. This direct connection eliminates the need for an HT lead and therefore reduces the potential for lead and connection failure. Electrical interference is also greatly reduced. However, some single coil per cylinder systems do locate the coils remotely from the spark plugs and therefore need an HT lead. A basic layout for a single coil per cylinder system is shown in Figure 2.42.

With single coil per cylinder systems, it is perhaps obvious that the time available to build up coil energy is greater than when a single coil is used to provide a spark to all cylinders. As an example, on an eight-cylinder engine with eight ignition coils, each coil will have eight times longer to complete one ignition cycle compared with the same engine using a single coil for all cylinders. The available 'dwell' time is therefore also up to eight times longer.

The operation of the system is much as for wasted spark systems except that the ECU will now have one power stage to switch each of the ignition coils. The ECU will receive information from a crankshaft speed/position sensor and other information from load sensors, etc. In most cases, single coil per cylinder systems form part of an engine management system and the ECU is usually the same ECU that controls fuelling and other functions.

Cylinder recognition

Single coil per cylinder systems require one additional item of information from sensors compared with other ignition systems and this is referred to as 'cylinder recognition'.

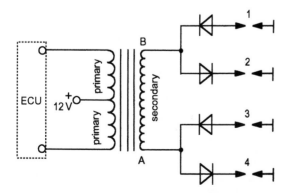

Figure 2.41 Wasted spark ignition system with diode control

Although the ECU can receive a master reference signal from the crankshaft speed/position sensor, the master reference cannot identify an individual cylinder; on a four-cylinder engine, a TDC reference for number 1 cylinder will also indicate TDC for number 4 cylinder. Therefore a separate sensor is required to identify when one particular cylinder is on a particular part of the engine operating cycle, e.g. TDC on the compression stroke for number 1 cylinder.

Because the camshaft rotates once for every complete engine cycle and the crankshaft rotates twice, the camshaft is the best place to locate a cylinder identification sensor. The sensors are generally either inductive or Hall effect and operate in exactly the same way as previously described inductive and Hall type pulse generators. However, whichever type of sensor is used, it requires only one reference point to provide the required information to the ECU.

It is quite common for a trigger lug to be located on the camshaft; this lug can look very similar to a cam lobe but it functions as the reluctor tooth for the inductive sensor; the sensor is therefore located on the camshaft cover or housing in line with the trigger lug. Each time that the trigger lug passes the sensor, a single electrical pulse will be passed to the ECU, which can then assess which cylinder is on which part of the cycle. It does not matter which cylinder or which stroke of a cylinder's cycle the signal identifies, so long as the necessary information is programmed into the ECU.

The ECU uses the cylinder identification signal to establish when a particular cylinder is on the compression stroke, and the spark will then be provided to that cylinder at the appropriate time. The ECU then uses the information from the reference points on the crankshaft speed/position sensor to calculate when the sparks should be provided to the remaining cylinders.

Cylinder recognition sensors are used for most modern petrol injection systems so, as is the case with most sensors, the information is provided to the ECU which is then able to control ignition and fuel systems.

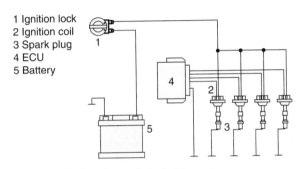

1 Ignition lock
2 Ignition coil
3 Spark plug
4 ECU
5 Battery

Figure 2.42 Single coil per cylinder ignition system
Note that the module can be located within the ECU or separate from the ECU. In some cases the module is located with the ignition coil.

Key Points

- Distributorless ignition uses the 'lost or wasted spark' principle
- Direct ignition systems use one coil for each cylinder

2.5 SPARK PLUGS

2.5.1 Function

The sparking plug provides the gap across which the high tension current (coil energy) jumps, thus creating an arc or spark that will then ignite the petrol–air mixture. Since the Frenchman Etienne Lenoir invented the anti-flashover ribbed insulator sparking plug in 1860, many detailed changes have been made, but the basic construction has remained the same: a highly insulated electrode is connected to the HT cable, and an earth electrode joined to the plug body.

2.5.2 Spark plug requirements

The basic requirement is that a spark of sufficient energy should be produced across the electrodes at all times, irrespective of the pressure and temperature of the gases in the combustion chamber. These two factors of temperature and pressure create a very hostile operating environment, as highlighted in the following paragraphs, but in addition to these basic requirements, the plug must be: resistant to corrosion, durable, gas tight and inexpensive to produce.

Pressure
Besides withstanding an operating pressure of about 70 bar during combustion, the plug must be also able to produce the high energy spark when the gas pressure within the cylinder is about 10 bar or more (at the top of the compression stroke). The voltage required to do this may be as high as 30 kV, so adequate insulation is required to prevent leakage of electrical energy to earth.

Temperature
The plug must be capable of withstanding temperatures of between 350°C and 900°C for long periods of time. The spark plug construction should ensure that electrode temperature remains between these limits, because if these limits are exceeded the plug will fail.

Above 900°C the high temperature of the electrodes causes pre-ignition, whereas below 350°C carbon will form on the insulator; this can cause fouling which allows the electrical energy to find an easier route to earth via the carbon rather than jumping the plug gap.

2.5.3 Construction

Figure 2.43 shows the construction of a typical spark plug. The example shown consists of an alloy/steel centre electrode and an aluminium oxide ceramic insulator, which is supported in a steel shell. Gas leakage past the insulator is prevented by 'sillment compressed powder seals' and leakage between the cylinder head and the plug shell is prevented either by a gasket (often a copper or alloy gasket) or by using a tapered seating (where the shell contacts the cylinder head).

An earth electrode (usually of rectangular cross section) is welded to the shell. Whilst most plugs have traditionally used a single earth electrode, there are many designs where more than one earth electrode is used. There is normally a hexagon formed on the shell to enable a socket to be used for installing and removing (tightening and loosening) the spark plug.

Ribs are formed on the outside of the insulator, which increase the length of the flashover path, and also improve the grip of the HT lead end covers (or coil end covers) that are used to prevent moisture or dirt gathering around the insulator.

Plug terms and identification

The length of the thread that screws into the cylinder head is called the 'reach' and the diameter of the threaded part indicates the 'plug size'; common sizes used are 10, 12, 14 and 18 mm.

Spark plug manufacturers use their own codes to identify their products and the variations; the letters and numbers stamped on the insulator give the following information:

- diameter and reach
- seat sealing and radio interference features
- centre electrode features, such as the incorporation of a resistor or an auxiliary gap heat range
- configuration of the firing end of the plug.

Figure 2.44 shows the position of the plug when it is screwed into the cylinder head. The gasket (where used) creates a difference between the seating height A and the plug reach.

Heat range

Heat range indicates the temperature range in which a plug operates without causing pre-ignition and without causing plug fouling due to carbon or oil deposits on the insulator.

Figure 2.45 shows the heat limits and the effect of road speed on the temperature of a typical plug. In addition to pre-ignition and carbon fouling, the graph shows that an operating temperature in excess of about

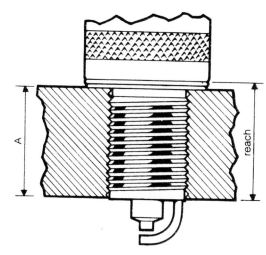

Figure 2.44 Spark plug screwed into cylinder head

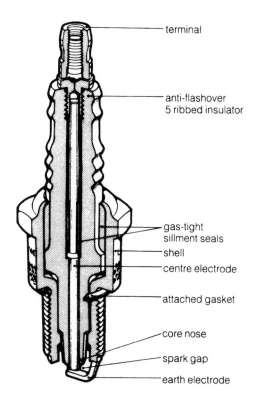

terminal

anti-flashover
5 ribbed insulator

gas-tight
sillment seals

shell

centre electrode

attached gasket

core nose

spark gap

earth electrode

Figure 2.43 Spark plug construction

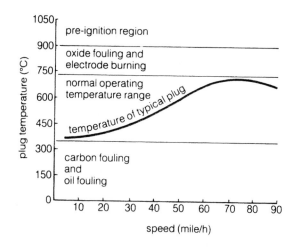

Figure 2.45 Spark plug operating temperature

750°C causes oxide fouling of the insulator and excessive burning of the electrodes.

The operating temperature of a plug depends on the four features shown in Figure 2.46, these are:

1 **Insulator nose length.** This is the distance from the top of the electrode to the body. The length of this heat flow path governs the temperature of the insulator nose; therefore if the path is made short, the plug will run relatively cool.
2 **Projection of insulator.** The amount that the insulator protrudes into the combustion chamber governs the amount of cooling obtained from the incoming air/fuel charge.
3 **Bore clearance.** The clearance between the insulator and the shell governs the amount of deposit that can be accepted before the plug electrodes are shorted out (the spark finds a shorter route to earth).
4 **Material.** Rate of heat transfer depends on the thermal conductivity of the materials used, especially the material used for the insulator.

Figure 2.47 shows two plugs with different heat ranges. The hot (or soft) plug has a long heat transfer path and is recommended for cool running, low compression engines, and other engines that are used continually at low speed for short journeys. Unless this type of plug is used on these engines, carbon will build up on the insulator, thus causing misfiring to occur after a short period of time.

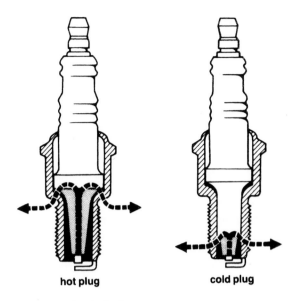

hot plug   cold plug

Figure 2.47 Spark plug heat range

At the other end of the heat range is the cold (or hard) plug. The cold plug has good thermal conductivity, and is therefore used on engines where high compressions and high combustion temperatures would cause excessive temperatures at the spark plug. This type of plug is therefore frequently used in high performance engines or engines with high power outputs for their size.

Spark plug manufacturers offer a wide range of plugs, thus enabling engines to be fitted with an appropriate type of plug to suit the operating temperatures, etc.

2.5.4 Electrode features

Materials

Spark plugs have traditionally used nickel alloy for the electrodes, which give good resistance to corrosive attack by combustion products, and also good resistance to the erosion that is caused by the high voltage arc. Both electrodes must be robust to withstand vibration from combustion effects and they must also be correctly shaped to allow a spark to be produced with minimum voltage (Figure 2.48a). Under normal conditions, erosion eats away the electrodes, so after a period of time the earth electrode becomes pointed in shape (Figure 2.48b); in this state it requires a higher voltage to produce a spark.

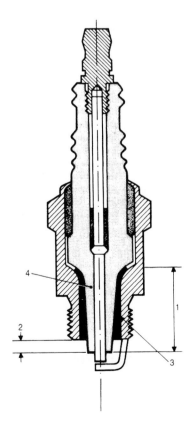

Figure 2.46 Spark plug features that affect temperature

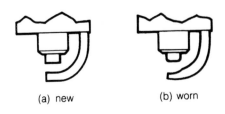

(a) new   (b) worn

Figure 2.48 Electrode wear

As previously stated, nickel alloy has traditionally been used for the electrodes. Although increasing the insulator nose length reduces the risk of carbon fouling when the vehicle is operated on short journeys, the plug can then overheat when high vehicle speeds are maintained for long periods. This temperature problem can be overcome by using more expensive materials and alloys for part of the construction of the electrodes, which can include materials such as platinum, iridium, silver or gold–palladium alloy. However, a less expensive material is copper, which can be used for the core of the central electrode and which provides good thermal conductivity (Figure 2.49).

Platinum and other materials can be used for the electrodes to overcome the problems of erosion caused by high voltage arcing. These expensive materials might be used only as a coating over the base material, so care should be taken not to scratch the coating.

Plug gaps

Spark plug gaps used to require regular adjustment, and the electrodes would require regular cleaning and even filing to ensure that their tips were the correct shape (an incorrect shape would be caused by erosion). This was very important on vehicles with older ignition systems because the eroded electrode tips would often result in larger gaps that required additional voltage for an arc to form. However, older ignition systems (primarily contact breaker systems) would produce lower voltages due to wear and maladjustment of the contact breakers. It was therefore common for poor starting and misfires to occur if spark plug maintenance and ignition system maintenance were not carried out.

On older engines, plug gaps were typically around 0.6 mm (0.24 in) but gaps on modern engines and spark plugs are more likely to be 0.8 mm and larger. These larger gaps are more suitable for engines operating on mixtures that are weaker than in the past. Of note is the fact that the larger gaps will inevitably require greater voltages to initiate the arc (spark) and to maintain the arc. It was therefore essential that the modern generation of ignition systems was developed to create and sustain the arc at the spark plug.

Electrode polarity

A lower voltage is needed to produce a spark at the plug electrodes when the centre electrode is negative in relation to the HT circuit polarity. A hot surface emits electrons and, because the centre electrode is the hotter of the two electrodes, there is a natural flow of electrons from the centre electrode to the earth electrode. Therefore, if the circuit is connected to give the same direction of electron flow as the natural flow of electrons, this will assist in producing a spark for a lower voltage.

Because the direction of electron flow in the secondary winding depends on the polarity of the primary winding, it is important that the primary winding is connected correctly. Most coils will have markings to identify the positive and negative terminals and these are usually marked as '15' or '+ve', and '1' or '–ve'. A correctly connected primary winding will therefore provide a 'negative' spark.

Key Points

Combustion takes place at different temperatures in different engines. Spark plugs are designed to operate at set temperatures so the correct heat range plug must be used

Spark plug centre electrodes use materials such as copper or even silver to aid temperature conduction

Web links

Engine systems information
www.bosch.com
www.sae.org
www.imeche.org.uk
www.picotech.com
www.autotap.com
www.visteon.com
www.infineon.com
www.kvaser.com (follow CAN Education links)

Teaching/learning resources

Online learning material relating to powertrain systems:

www.auto-training.co.uk

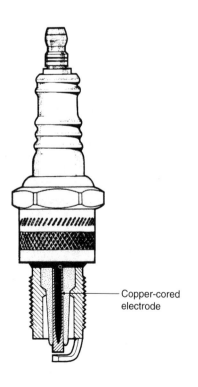

Copper-cored electrode

Figure 2.49 Copper core central electrode

ENGINE MANAGEMENT – PETROL

what is covered in this chapter . . .

- ■ Introduction to electronic petrol injection systems
- ■ Petrol injection system examples (multi-point injection)
- ■ Single-point (throttle body) petrol injection
- ■ Direct petrol injection
- ■ Emissions and emission control (petrol engines)
- ■ Engine management (the conclusion)
- ■ Engine system self-diagnosis (on-board diagnostics) and EOBD

3.1 INTRODUCTION TO ELECTRONIC PETROL INJECTION SYSTEMS

The following sections deal with sensors, ECUs and actuators that are covered in detail in other sections; see the relevant sections in Chapters 1 and 2, as well as other sections within Chapter 3.

Electronic injection systems have progressed through many developments and variations, so it would not be possible to cover all of these within this book. However, section 3.1 provides a general understanding of the systems and their components, and sections 3.2–3.4 give examples of specific injection systems along with the latest developments. Note that later injection systems form part of engine management systems, which are covered separately in section 3.6.

3.1.1 Fuel system developments

From the carburettor to electronic injection

As with ignition systems (see sections 2.2–2.4), fuel systems have evolved progressively since the motor vehicle first appeared, but, with the introduction of electronic control, fuel injection has become the dominant method of fuel delivery for the petrol engine.

The carburettor (covered in *Hillier's Fundamentals of Motor Vehicle Technology Book 1*) was almost universally used on petrol engines through until the late 1970s, when fuel injection systems began to appear on mass produced vehicles. Electronic injection was, however, used in the late 1960s to overcome

emission control problems with some vehicles intended for the American market. In the 1970s a Bosch mechanical/hydraulic system (Bosch K-Jetronic) gained favour with many European manufacturers: this system tended to lead the way until the early 1980s, when a new generation of electronic injection systems progressively became more common. The Bosch K-Jetronic and its ECU controlled variant the KE-Jetronic system are dealt with in *Hillier's Fundamentals of Motor Vehicle Technology Book 1*.

It is suggested that the first application of fuel injection was on the engine that was used by the Wright Brothers for the first manned flight of an aeroplane. However, simple carburettors were very much the only petrol delivery systems used on mass production vehicle engines for many years. Although diesel engines used a mechanical injection system until fairly recently, petrol engines relied on carburettor systems because of cost, simplicity and the fact that there was no need for high pressure delivery of petrol.

A number of cars did use petrol injection, but these were generally racing cars and not production vehicles. One notable exception, however, was in the mid-1950s, when Mercedes-Benz used an adaptation of a mechanical diesel pump on its racing engines and also on a limited production sports car (Mercedes 300SL); it is interesting to note that these systems were adaptations of diesel mechanical pump systems, which injected fuel directly into the cylinder and not into the intake system, which has been the general principle for most electronic injection systems until recently. Mercedes continued to develop its use of fuel injection with petrol engines and, in the early 1960s, several of the company's production vehicles were available with petrol injection.

So, although fuel injection was not widely used, Mercedes and a number of vehicle and racing engine manufacturers continued to develop the use of fuel injection for petrol engines. Various mechanical and electronic systems used from the early 1960s through to the 1980s were developed to improve emissions for vehicles sold in the United States, although there was an increase in the use of injection systems for the European market for higher performance vehicles and for more expensive vehicles.

It was, however, the introduction of European emissions regulations that effectively forced the use of fuel injection systems on almost all petrol engines by the early 1990s. By this time, electronic control was becoming less expensive and it was therefore inevitable that any mechanical systems would be replaced by electronic injection systems.

Fuel injection and engine management

Almost all modern petrol engines for light cars are equipped with engine management systems, which control the fuel injection, the ignition and many other functions. The engine management system is therefore effectively a number of different systems controlled by a single ECU (in most cases). The main systems (ignition and fuelling) are covered separately within this book; the integration of these systems is dealt with in the engine management section (section 3.6).

3.1.2 Advantages of electronic petrol injection

Improved efficiency and control

Compared with the carburettor, there are numerous benefits provided by a fuel injection system; most of these will become obvious in the following sections. However, almost by way of a conclusion, it is certain that an electronic fuel injection system provides an overall efficiency of fuel delivery and control of fuel quantity that could not be achieved with a carburettor; the result is improved combustion efficiency, improved engine performance (power), improved economy and reduced emissions.

Even when compared with later types of mechanical injection systems, electronic control provides a superior capacity to control fuel quantity and to embrace any changes in fuelling needed to suit changing conditions.

However, a fully electronic fuel injection system also provides the facility for integration and communication with other vehicle systems, such as the ignition and emission control systems.

Some specific advantages of electronic fuel injection are covered in the following sub-sections.

Controlled pressure difference

A carburettor operates by using 'pressure difference'. In basic terms, fuel in the carburettor float chamber (the fuel reservoir) is exposed to atmospheric pressure. Then, when air flows through the carburettor body, this creates a low pressure area around the venturi (located in the carburettor body). Therefore, the fuel in the chamber, which is at a higher pressure, flows to the lower pressure area. The airflow through to the engine then carries the fuel with it thus resulting in a mixing of air and fuel in the combustion chambers. In effect, a pressure difference is created by the air flow, so varying quantities of petrol can be drawn into the engine, depending on

- the speed of airflow
- the size of the holes or jets through which the petrol flows
- the throttle opening (the angle of opening of the throttle butterfly).

A fuel injector works on a similar principle of pressure difference, but the fuel at the injector is at a higher pressure than that of the atmosphere and therefore much higher than in the intake manifold or in the cylinder on the induction stroke. The fuel pressure is created using a pump controlled by some form of regulator, so it is always at a controlled pressure. There is, therefore, no need to create a low pressure by using a venturi, because the fuel pressure is always higher than that of the intake system or cylinder at the time when the fuel is delivered. Even on a turbocharged or supercharged engine, where the intake system pressure can be higher than atmospheric pressure, the fuel pressure will always be higher by a 'controlled' pressure difference. Fuel therefore flows into the intake system or into the cylinder in a controlled way due to this pressure difference.

Electronic petrol injection system pressures vary, but typically they are in the region of 2.5 to 3 bar. This pressure, forcing the petrol through the injector nozzle, then assists in creating good atomisation of the petrol: mixing of air and petrol is therefore much more effective.

Figure 3.1 shows a simple carburettor and a fuel injector, both of which rely on pressure difference as a means of delivering fuel.

Intermittent injection to individual cylinders

With a carburettor, the flow of air creates the low pressure that causes the petrol to flow from the carburettor to the intake system. In theory, the petrol mixes with the air: therefore, as the air enters the cylinder, the petrol also enters the cylinder. However, there is an inevitable delay from the time that the inlet valve opens (the start of airflow of that cylinder) to the time when the increasing airflow draws petrol from the carburettor; for this and other reasons, it is necessary to operate with an excess of petrol in the mixture.

Figure 3.1 Pressure difference causing a flow of fuel
a in a carburettor
b in a fuel injection system

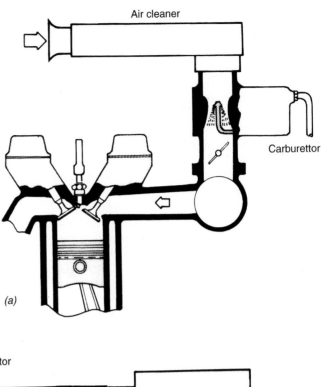

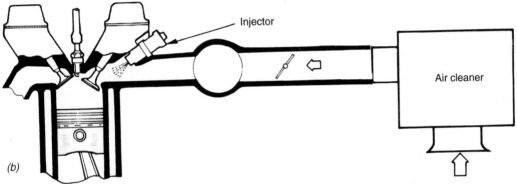

With the more commonly used mechanical injection systems (Bosch K and KE-Jetronic) the injector is in the intake port just ahead of the intake valve (Figure 3.2), so petrol is delivered directly to each individual intake port. However, the flow of petrol from the injectors on the K and KE systems is continuous all the time that the engine is running, so most of the petrol is being injected whilst the inlet valve is closed. The petrol is therefore 'waiting' in the intake port until the inlet valve opens and the air starts to flow into the cylinder. In reality, the petrol flowing from the injector is atomised sufficiently for it to mix with the air in the port, so this is a considerable improvement over the carburettor.

One big advantage of electronic injection is that the petrol injectors (located in the same place as in mechanical injection systems) are opened and closed at specific times, which in theory reduces the waiting time before the petrol is drawn into the cylinder. Although on earlier generations of electronic injection, there was some 'waiting' time, most modern systems inject at precisely the correct time so that petrol typically leaves the injectors just before the intake valve opens. Note that some modern systems inject petrol direct into the cylinder during the intake stroke.

The injection on fully electronic systems is not continuous, since the injectors open and close intermittently at predetermined times, so it is sometimes referred to as 'intermittent injection'.

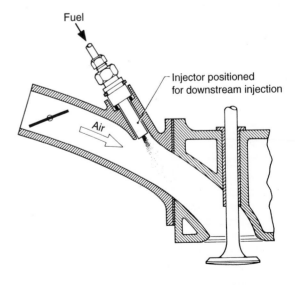

Figure 3.2 Injector located just ahead of the inlet valve

Precise fuel control

Electronic injection systems are controlled by a computer (ECU), which not only switches the injectors on and off at the appropriate time, but is also supplied with a wide range of information (by various sensors) that enable it to calculate the required fuel quantity for all operating conditions. The ECU is therefore able to deliver the correct fuel quantity at the correct time, and change that quantity as the operating conditions change. A schematic layout of a simple injection system is shown in Figure 3.3.

The injection system ECU can also communicate with other electronic systems, such as the ignition and emissions systems. In fact, there is considerable communication between the engine systems and chassis systems such as ABS and transmission, as well as with systems such as the air conditioning. This level of communication enables the fuel injection ECU to assess many aspects of a vehicle's operation, thus helping to improve the accuracy and efficiency of the engine. In turn, the fuel injection ECU can pass information to other vehicle systems, thus improving the efficiency of those other systems.

Management of these systems can be integrated so that they are all controlled by a single ECU: this process is now almost universal for engines, where an engine management system ECU controls virtually all engine functions. A similar philosophy is used for chassis systems, where the braking, and vehicle stability systems are controlled by a single ECU. Since this ECU communicates with the engine management ECU, the next step is to use a single ECU for all vehicle functions.

3.1.3   Main components and layout of a multi-point, port type electronic system

Note: This section deals with the main components required for a simple multi-point injection system. Additional components used for emission control and

for other functions are covered in subsequent sections in this chapter. Single-point injection systems (often referred to as 'throttle body' injection), where a single injector is used to deliver fuel to all of the cylinders, are covered in section 3.3. Direct injection, where the injectors deliver fuel directly to the cylinders, is covered in section 3.4.

Two sub-systems

An electronic petrol injection system effectively consists of two sub-systems: an electrical/electronic system and a fuel delivery system. This section deals with the sub-systems for multi-point injection systems, where an individual injector is used to deliver fuel to each cylinder.

The main components of both sub-systems are listed below and are also illustrated in Figure 3.4.

Electrical/electronic system (see section 3.1.4)

- *Injectors* – electrically operated fuel valves that, when open, allow petrol to flow into the engine.
- *ECU* – the computer that calculates the required amount of petrol and then opens the injectors for the appropriate amount of time.
- *Sensors* – provide the necessary information to the ECU to enable it to calculate the fuel required for different operating conditions.

Fuel system (see section 3.1.5)

- *Fuel pump* – moves the fuel from the fuel tank to the injectors; the pump provides an excess of fuel, which results in pressure being developed in the fuel system.
- *Fuel filter* – filters the fuel to remove dirt particles that could damage the system components or block the injectors.
- *Fuel pressure regulator and fuel rail* – the regulator controls the pressure of the fuel; the fuel rail acts as the distribution pipe to pass fuel to the injectors.

Note that, in addition to the main sub-systems, an idle speed control system forms part of many injection systems. These systems are covered separately in section 3.1.6.

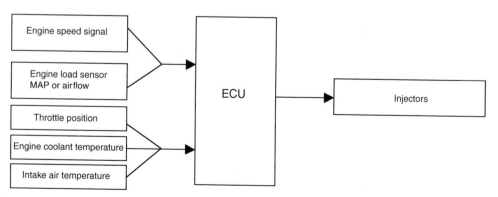

Figure 3.3 Layout of a simple electronic fuel injection system
The schematic layout shows the ECU receiving information from sensors and then controlling the fuel injectors.

L-Jetronic system overview.
1 Fuel tank, 2 Electric fuel pump, 3 Fuel filter, 4 Control unit, 5 Lambda sensor, 6 Injection valve, 7 Intake manifold,
8 Fuel pressure regulator, 9 Throttle valve switch, 10 Airflow sensor, 11 Engine temperature sensor,
12 Auxiliary air device, 13 Battery, 14 Ignition and starting switch, 15 Relay.

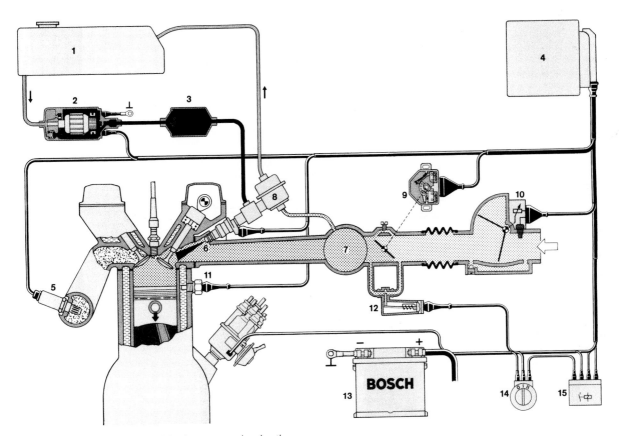

Figure 3.4 Simple electronic fuel injection system, showing the fuel and electrical/electronic sub-systems

3.1.4 Electrical/electronic system

Injector solenoid valves

Petrol injectors used on electronic injection systems are fuel valves that open and close to control fuel delivery. The injectors are solenoids with a needle valve attached to the solenoid armature, so that, when current flows in the solenoid winding, the magnetic field moves the armature, which in turn moves the needle valve off its seating and allows the fuel to flow through the nozzle. An example of an injector with a needle valve is shown in Figure 3.5a, and a different type of injector, with a disc rather than a needle is shown in Figure 3.5b. Note that a fine mesh filter is used to filter out the very small particles that can damage the injector nozzle seating.

The injector solenoid valve is connected to a fuel supply rail (Figure 3.6), or in some cases is located within the fuel rail. The fuel within the rail is regulated at a predetermined pressure, which is altered to suit operating conditions. However, the quantity of fuel delivered is largely controlled by opening the injectors for differing lengths of time.

Creating an atomised fuel spray

Fuel is fed to the injector under pressure (typically around 3 bar); because the fuel is under pressure, when it flows out through the injector nozzle a spray of finely atomised fuel is formed that is able to mix easily with the air. To further assist with creating a spray of atomised fuel, the injector needle and needle seating are designed so that the fuel is forced to exit the injector in a particular spray pattern.

In general, the fuel exiting the injector nozzle is directed so that it sprays against the back of the inlet valve. There are now many different designs of nozzle used to create a spray pattern for the fuel as it flows through and exits the nozzle. Depending on the location of the injector in the inlet port, spray pattern requirements will differ: wide and narrow angle spray patterns are used to suit the different engine applications. Some injectors provide a dual spray pattern, designed to suit engines with two inlet valves per cylinder; each of the fuel sprays is directed to the back of each of the inlet valves.

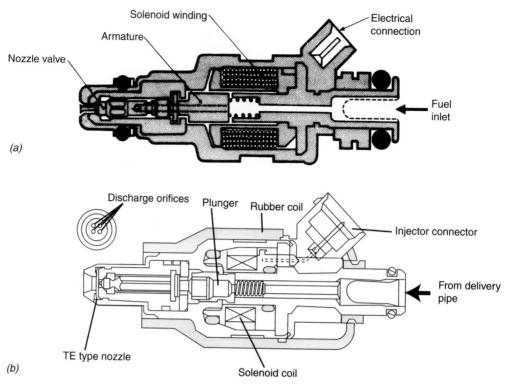

(a)

(b)

Figure 3.5 Fuel injectors
a with a needle valve
b with a disc valve

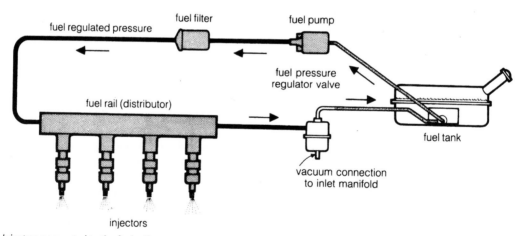

Figure 3.6 Injectors connected to the fuel rail

Many petrol injection systems now inject petrol directly into the cylinder rather than into the intake port. These systems are covered in section 3.4.

Speed of operation and opening time

With most systems, the injectors will open either once or twice for each operating cycle of a cylinder (see injector timing in the following paragraphs). Therefore, if an engine is operating at 6000 rev/min, each cylinder will complete 3000 cycles in one minute or 50 cycles in one second. An injector might therefore open and close as many as 50 times a second (once a cycle) or 100 times a second (twice a cycle).

An injector needs to open for sufficient time to allow the required amount of fuel to enter the intake port (or enter the cylinder with some types). Depending on the amount of fuel required (for example, low load and engine speed or high load), the injectors will typically be open for durations of 1.5 ms to as much as 15 ms.

Electronic control unit (ECU)

As with an ECU controlled ignition system, the fuel injection electronic control unit is the 'brain' of the system (Figure 3.7). The ECU controls the fuel injectors in response to the information received from the sensors.

Figure 3.7 Typical appearance of a fuel injection ECU

An ECU contains a programmed memory, which, in an injection ECU, contains data on how much fuel should be injected under different operating conditions. When information is received from the sensors, the ECU refers to the programmed data and switches on the fuel injectors so that they deliver the required amount of petrol (Figure 3.8). See sections 1.2 and 1.3 for an explanation of ECU operation and construction.

Fuel map and basic fuel program

Section 2.3.2 describes how a 'map' is used to provide ignition timing values on modern ignition systems. The same process is used for ECU controlled fuel injection systems: a three-dimensional map provides the ECU with the necessary references for the required quantity of fuel.

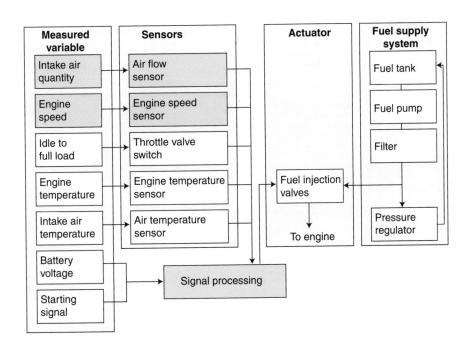

Figure 3.8 ECU processes in an injection system
Intake air quantity per unit of time and engine speed are the basic measured variables to which corrections are applied.

The map shown in Figure 3.9 gives references for fuelling based on engine load and engine speed; the fuelling references (vertical scale) are air:fuel ratios, which are expressed as lambda (λ) values. Lambda values are explained in section 3.5.1.

As noted above, the fuel map provides the ECU with references for fuel quantities for different operating conditions. However, there are some basic or fundamental trends that dictate the overall mapping or program strategy.

In theory, the amount of fuel injected is matched to the mass of air injected so that the stoichiometric air:fuel ratio is provided (the stoichiometric ratio is the ideal ratio of air and fuel to provide complete combustion). However, minor variations in air:fuel ratio are necessary for different operating conditions, so the ECU controls the injector opening time to suit the various conditions as listed below.

- **Light load conditions** – The injection duration is long enough to provide the quantity of fuel needed to give the theoretical stoichiometric ratio. Minor increases or decreases in air mass (air drawn into the engine) will result in minor changes in injection duration.
- **Acceleration and high load** – The ECU will increase the injection duration so that the fuel quantity increases to match the increase in air mass. However, under heavy load and acceleration, a slight excess of petrol is usually required (a rich mixture), so the injection duration increases to slightly more than would be required to achieve the ideal stoichiometric ratio.
- **Cold running** – When the engine is cold, the cold surfaces of the intake port and combustion chamber can cause slight condensation of the fuel and prevent complete mixing of the fuel vapour and air.

The injection duration is therefore increased slightly to provide a rich mixture, thus ensuring that sufficient fuel is available to mix with the air.
- **Idle** – When the engine is idling, the air:fuel ratio on modern engines is controlled at around stoichiometric or lambda 1. It was, however, normal on older engines for a slightly rich mixture to be provided, which helped the engine to develop sufficient power and to run smoothly.
- **Deceleration** – During deceleration, no power is required from the engine so fuel injection can be completely cut off. Depending on engine speed and whether the throttle is partially or completely closed (indicated by the throttle position sensor), the fuel injectors can be completely switched off, or the injection duration reduced, so that very little fuel is injected. Careful programming of the ECU map is necessary because, when the throttle is reopened, there can be a tendency for the engine to hesitate. A progressive cut-off and reapplication of fuel injection are necessary to ensure a smooth transition from deceleration to acceleration.

ECU switching the injectors

The ECU contains the 'power stages' or power transistors that are used to switch the injector electrical circuits on and off. As with most computer controlled systems, the ECU forms part of the earth circuit for the injectors, so the ECU is switching on and off the earth path. The injectors receive a battery voltage supply from the battery via a relay.

Having made the necessary calculations, the low current (and low voltage) microchips within the ECU will provide an appropriate signal to the power stage, which will cause the power stage to complete the earth circuit to the injectors, thus switching them on and allowing fuel to be delivered.

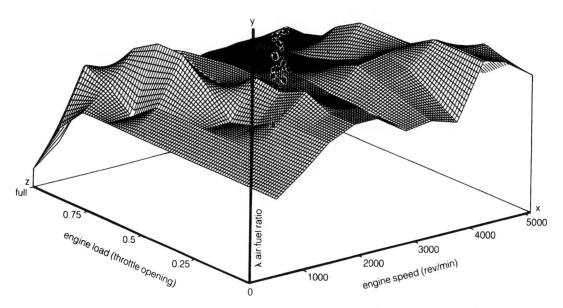

Figure 3.9 Fuel mixture map

Injector timing on earlier systems (simultaneous injection)

The ECU will switch on the injectors (by completing the earth circuit) at a predefined time in the engine operating cycle. On many earlier electronic injection systems (typically through until the early 1990s), the injectors were all opened at the same time (on four-cylinder engines), which is referred to as 'simultaneous injection'. With six-cylinder engines the injectors were generally operated in two groups of three injectors; with eight-cylinder engines the injectors were operated in two groups of four; and with 12-cylinder engines there were four groups of three injectors. All of the injectors in a group would open and close at the same time.

It was also usual for all of the injectors to be opened twice for every engine cycle, so half of the required quantity of fuel was delivered each time the injectors opened. On these older systems, the injector timing was therefore not perfect because, while one cylinder might have its injector opening when the inlet valve was open, on the rest of the cylinders, the inlet valves would be closed. As previously noted, the injected petrol would therefore be 'waiting' for a short period before it was drawn into the cylinder. Figure 3.10 shows a four-cylinder engine where the injectors are opened simultaneously twice for every engine cycle.

On earlier systems, the injector opening would be triggered by the ignition system, but the injection ECU would switch on the injectors on alternate ignition pulses: i.e., if the firing order was 1,3,4,2, then the injectors would open when the ignition system was firing numbers 1 and 4 cylinders or numbers 3 and 2 cylinders. Therefore, in a complete engine cycle (two crankshaft revolutions), in which all cylinders would have fired once, the injectors would have opened twice.

Injector timing on later systems (sequential injection)

With modern systems the injectors are usually opened individually in sequence (to match the engine firing order); this is known as sequential injection. The injectors are typically opened just prior to the inlet valve opening. All the required fuel is therefore delivered in one 'opening' of the injector (Figure 3.11). However, there are occasions where a very large quantity of fuel is required, for example during full load acceleration, where the injectors can be opened twice for every operating cycle (half the fuel quantity is delivered at each opening).

Although it is possible to use a signal from the ignition system to trigger sequential injection, many systems use separate sensors to identify one of the cylinders, for example cylinder number 1; the ECU then uses this signal as a master reference and operates the injectors in sequence at the appropriate times. The sensor is referred to as a 'cylinder identification sensor' or 'phase sensor': these are usually either inductive or Hall effect sensors.

The camshaft rotates once for every engine cycle (while the crankshaft rotates twice), so the cylinder identification sensor is usually located adjacent to the camshaft. Therefore, a single reluctor tooth or trigger lug attached to the camshaft could then cause an inductive sensor to provide a single reference signal (see section 2.2.5). Alternatively a Hall effect rotor (see section 2.2.6) attached to the camshaft could have a single 'cut out', thus producing a single reference pulse. A crankshaft speed/position sensor provides the necessary crankshaft angle and speed information.

Figure 3.10 Injector timing for simultaneous injection on a four-cylinder engine

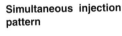
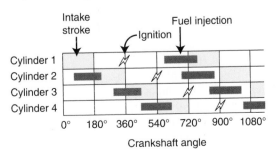
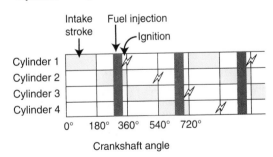

Figure 3.11 Injector timing for sequential injection on a four-cylinder engine

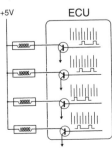
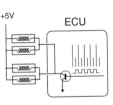

Some systems used a trigger signal provided by a sensor attached to a spark plug lead. The sensor generated a small electrical pulse that was used by the ECU as the master reference signal.

Injection duration

The ECU uses the information from the sensors to calculate the operating conditions for the engine and thus enable the correct volume of fuel to be injected. In theory, the mass of air entering the engine is the main item of information required by the ECU to enable the correct quantity of fuel to be calculated. The air mass can be measured with an air mass sensor but further information is used to assist the ECU in the calculation process. This additional information, supplied by other sensors, is covered in the following sections.

When the ECU has calculated the quantity of fuel to be delivered (effectively by noting the information from the sensors and then referring to the programmed fuel map within the memory), it will then switch on the injectors for an appropriate length of time (the injection duration). The duration will vary with the system's design and operating conditions, such as engine load, engine speed, temperature, etc., but typical values are between 1.5 ms and 15 ms.

Injectors are produced with differing nozzle sizes, so different injectors will allow different quantities of fuel to flow through the nozzle for a given opening duration. The different nozzle sizes are produced to suit larger and smaller engine cylinders, which will require correspondingly larger or smaller quantities of fuel to be delivered. A large nozzle injector used in a large cylinder will have a similar opening duration to a small nozzle injector used in a small cylinder.

Control signal

The ECU functions as the switch in the injector earth circuit. The power stage within the ECU is the switching component, and when the ECU calculates that the injector should be switched on for a specific length of time, the power stage will complete the injector earth circuit for the appropriate time period.

As with any switch that is located in the earth circuit, when the switch is 'closed' there is a complete circuit, which means that the earth circuit voltage should be 0 volts. When the switch on the earth circuit is open, current does not pass to earth and there is an 'open circuit voltage' available at the negative terminal of the injector and at the input terminal of the earth circuit switch.

On an injector circuit, therefore, assuming that a 12 volt power supply is connected to the injector, the input voltage to the injector positive terminal will be 12 volts. When the earth switch is closed (completing the circuit through to earth), then the voltage at the negative terminal of the injector and at the input terminal of the power stage or switch will be 0 volts. The switching action of the power stage therefore results in the voltage on the earth path (negative terminal of the solenoid) switching between 0 and

12 volts. In effect, this on/off switching action is the control signal produced by the ECU: this control signal is a simple on/off digital signal. The length of the on pulse of the control signal will dictate the duration of the opening of the injector.

Two examples of control signals are shown in Figure 3.12. These signals are typical of control signals when observed with an oscilloscope.

The example in Figure 3.12a shows a signal produced when the power stage switches on and off the earth circuit. The spike at point C on the signal is produced when the circuit is switched off, which causes a 'back EMF' to be produced in the solenoid winding, i.e. the rapidly collapsing magnetic field causes a voltage to be induced in the winding. The duration of injection is dictated by the pulse width B. Therefore points A, B and C on the pulse can be described as follows:

A = injector earth circuit switched off. The open circuit voltage can be measured at the injector negative terminal.

B = injector earth circuit switched on. The ECU completes the earth circuit so the voltage in this circuit is 0 volts. The width of this section of the signal (pulse width) dictates the opening time or duration of opening of the injector.

C = injector earth circuit switched off. At the end of duration B, the ECU switches off the earth circuit and back EMF is induced within the solenoid. The EMF can reach figures in the region of 40 to 60 volts on some systems, as indicated at point C.

The example in Figure 3.12b is typical of systems where current control is used by the ECU in a two-stage control process. Stage 1 is where full current is allowed to flow through the injector earth circuit (B2), which allows rapid opening of the injector; the duration of this full current period can be very short, e.g. 0.5 ms. Stage 2 is where current limiting is implemented by the ECU so that the current flow through the earth circuit is limited (B3); however, sufficient current will still flow to keep the injector open for the required period. The injector duration is varied by altering the width of the injector control signal pulse in stage 2 (B3).

A = Injector earth circuit switched off. The open circuit voltage can be measured at the injector negative terminal.

B1 = Total duration of control signal (made up of B2 + B3).

B2 = Injector circuit is switched on. At this point, the ECU allows full current to flow through the earth circuit, thus rapidly opening the injector. At the end of period B2, the current is limited by the ECU, which would in theory cause the injector to close.

B3 = When the current has been limited at the end of B2, the ECU allows a reduced current to flow which is sufficient to keep the injector open. The width of the pulse at B3 alters, which controls the duration of opening for the injector.

C = Injector earth circuit switched off. At the end of duration B, the ECU switches off the earth circuit and back EMF is produced within the solenoid. The EMF can reach 40 to 60 volts on some systems, as indicated at point C.

Sensors

The main objective of any petrol delivery system is to provide the correct mixture of air and petrol so that the combustion process is efficient and produces maximum power from the mixture. To achieve this, the fuel injection system must provide the correct quantity of petrol to suit the mass of air being drawn in by the engine, i.e. the ratio of petrol to air must be correct.

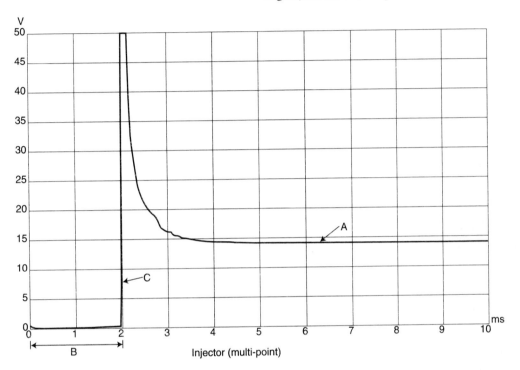

(a) Injector (multi-point)

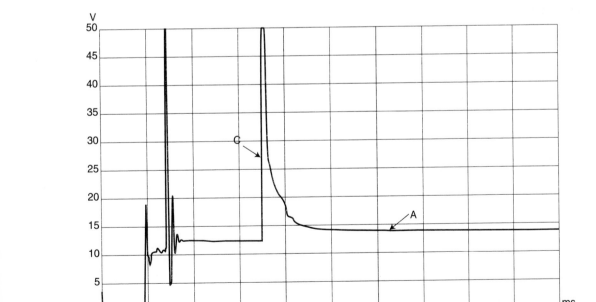

(b) Injector (single-point)

Figure 3.12 Injector control signals
a A signal produced when the power stage switches on and off the earth circuit
b A signal typical of systems where current control is used by the ECU in a two-stage control process

If we therefore assume that, at all times, the air:fuel ratio is stoichiometric (as discussed in Book 1), then the mixture delivered should be in the ratio of approximately 14.7 parts of air to 1 part of petrol by weight. This is the ratio that, in theory, will provide complete combustion of the mixture.

However, there are numerous situations that influence the air:fuel ratio: this means that the mixture can vary above or below the stoichiometric value, i.e. the mixture can have a slight excess of fuel or an excess of air (rich or weak) to suit the conditions and requirements. A simple example is with cold starting and running, where a slightly rich mixture is required. In other situations, a slightly weak mixture might be provided for better fuel economy.

In reality, with modern engines, emissions regulations force the use of a stoichiometric air:fuel ratio for a high percentage of engine operating conditions. However, the same rule applies with modern and older engines: the injection system ECU must initially calculate the fuel requirement based on the mass of air flowing into the engine.

The main information required by the ECU is therefore a measurement of the mass of air. Other sensors are, however, required to enable the ECU to 'fine tune' the air:fuel mixture. As noted previously, there are a number of factors that affect the air:fuel ratio, such as:

- temperature
- emissions control
- engine load
- driver intentions
- engine design

and other factors also slightly influence the mixture finally delivered to the engine. Therefore many additional sensors are used to give the ECU sufficient information to enable it to finely adjust the fuel quantity delivered by the injectors. The following list highlights only those sensors that might be used on a basic electronic injection system.

Note: Additional sensors are covered in the examples of injections systems in section 3.2, whilst other sensors used on modern systems are dealt with in section 3.5 (emission control); also refer to Chapter 1.

Airflow and mass airflow measurement

Airflow sensors (discussed later in this chapter) can be used to measure and transmit a signal to the ECU relating to either the volume or the mass of air that is flowing through the intake system at a given time. However, the ECU must calculate what mass of air is flowing to each cylinder at any given time, so it also requires engine speed information. Some examples of airflow and mass airflow sensors are shown in Figure 3.13.

Air mass and engine speed are the fundamental items of information required by the ECU. Although some systems use an air 'mass' sensor, others use different sensors such as manifold absolute pressure sensors (MAP sensors), which measure the manifold depression; in this case, the ECU uses the MAP sensor information along with engine speed, air temperature and other information to establish the basic fuel requirements.

Coolant temperature (Figure 3.14a)

The engine coolant temperature information enables the ECU to alter the fuel quantity (thus altering the air:fuel ratio) so that, when the engine is cold, an excess of fuel (a rich mixture) can be provided. The ECU can slightly alter the fuel quantity and mixture over the whole range of operating temperatures, thus allowing 'fine tuning' of the mixture.

Air temperature (Figure 3.14b)

The air temperature sensor information helps in calculating the air mass, because air density changes with temperature. Many air temperature sensors are incorporated within the airflow sensors. Since a high air temperature can cause 'pinking' or pre-ignition, the ignition timing might be altered by the ignition ECU to correct this, but it is also possible that the injection ECU might slightly alter the fuel quantity if necessary.

Throttle position

On early basic electronic injection systems, a simple 'throttle switch' was used to indicate when the throttle was in the closed position (idle). The switch also indicated when the throttle was around 60% open, which was a sign that the engine was under load. The most widely used type of throttle switch on earlier systems contained two sets of contacts, which closed and opened at the relevant time as the throttle was opened and closed. For both idle and load positions, the ECU provided a slight enrichment of the mixture, which helped stabilise the engine at idle and allowed additional power to be developed under load. Note that later engines, with improved emission control, operate with weaker mixtures at idle and under load conditions; the programming of the ECU and the information required are altered to suit these requirements.

Later throttle position sensors use a potentiometer or variable resistor instead of switches. With a potentiometer based sensor, it is possible to send a varying voltage analogue signal to the ECU; the signal indicates all throttle opening angles and the ECU can also calculate the rate at which the throttle is being opened and closed. The ECU is therefore able to alter the fuelling to suit the minor and major changes in throttle position (load changes). The ECU can also assess the driver's intentions, such as the intention to rapidly accelerate, by detecting the speed or rate at which the throttle is being opened.

Figure 3.15 shows an example of a throttle switch and a throttle position potentiometer.

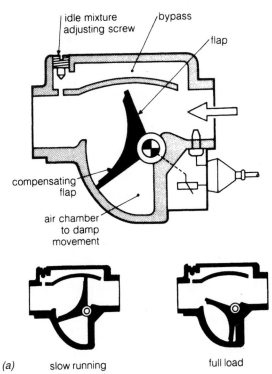

idle mixture adjusting screw

bypass

flap

compensating flap

air chamber to damp movement

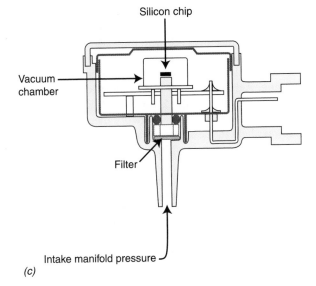

(a) slow running full load

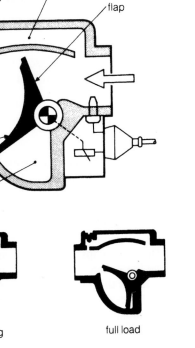

Silicon chip

Vacuum chamber

Filter

Intake manifold pressure

(c)

Figure 3.13 Examples of airflow and mass airflow sensors
a Flap type airflow meter
b Hot wire air mass meter
c MAP sensor

(b)

1

2

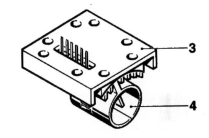

3

4

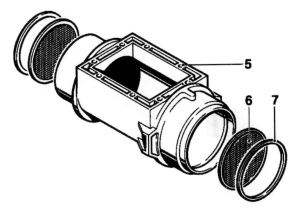

5

6 7

**1 Hybrid circuit, 2 Cover, 3 Metal insert,
4 Venturi with hot wire, 5 Housing, 6 Screen,
7 Retaining ring.**

Ignition trigger or crankshaft position trigger

As noted previously, early injection systems used ignition pulses as a means of triggering the injectors. These earlier injection systems were usually fitted to engines that also had earlier designs of electronic ignition with inductive or Hall effect triggers located in a distributor, so it was common practice to provide a signal from the ignition system to the injection ECU. This signal was often taken directly from the coil negative terminal, which would be the same terminal used to provide a signal to a rev. counter. On some ignition systems, the signal might have been a digital signal provided by the ignition module.

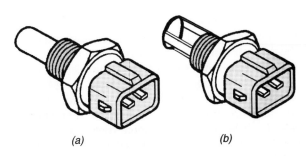

(a) *(b)*

Figure 3.14 Examples of temperature sensors
a Coolant temperature sensor
b Air temperature sensor

1 Full load contact, 2 Contoured switching
plate, 3 Throttle valve shaft, 4 Idle contact,
5 Electrical connection.

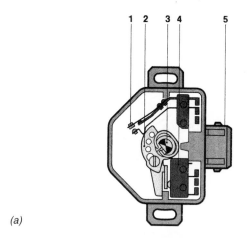

(a)

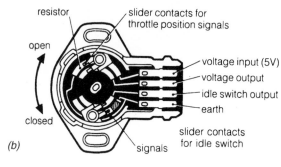

(b)

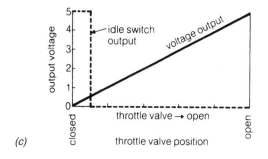

(c)

Figure 3.15 Measurement of throttle position
a Throttle valve switch
b Throttle position potentiometer
c Output from potentiometer as throttle valve opens

With those later ignition and injection systems, a crankshaft position sensor was often used. The sensor transmitted the crankshaft speed and position data to the ignition system ECU, and the ignition ECU then transmitted a digital speed signal to the injection ECU.

Whichever triggering system is fitted, the ECU can use the information as a triggering signal for opening the injectors (the injector timing on simultaneous injection systems). The ignition trigger signal also provides the ECU with engine speed information, which can be used to help calculate fuel requirements.

Figure 3.16 shows the process of an injection system that is being triggered by an early ignition system.

Other sensors

The sensors described so far provide the essential information to enable a simple injection system to operate. In fact, many early systems used only these sensors.

The need for improved emission control and efficiency led to other sensors being added, which are covered in the following sections of this chapter.

3.1.5 Fuel system

Fuel pump
Providing sufficient fuel flow

The fuel pump moves the fuel from the fuel tank through to the injectors. The pump must provide sufficient fuel for the engine to operate at full load: it delivers typically between 1 and 2 litres of fuel each minute (depending on engine size).

The fuel pumps on most systems operate at full rate all the time: there is no variation in the amount of fuel delivered by the pump, irrespective of engine speed and load. However, at low engine speeds and loads only a small amount of fuel is used, so the excess fuel flows back to the fuel tank.

Pressurising the system

Liquids cannot be compressed, but they can exist in an enclosed system under pressure. With petrol injection systems, a high volume of fuel delivered by the pump flows to the injectors and, with only a small amount of fuel able to escape through the injectors, this continuous flow of fuel causes the system to build up pressure. Although excess fuel is allowed to return to the tank, a regulator valve is used (see below) to control the pressure in the system. In theory therefore, the fuel is always held in the system at a constant pressure (see the following paragraphs dealing with pressure regulators). This combination of a high volume of fuel delivered by the pump and the pressure regulator ensures that the fuel flowing through the injectors is at a pressure that causes atomisation of the fuel when it exits the injectors.

Construction and location

With most modern systems the fuel pump is located in the fuel tank, although on many earlier systems the pump was mounted externally (Figure 3.17). In some cases, two pumps are used: one which initially moves the fuel from the tank to the main pump (which might be located too high in the vehicle for the fuel to flow into it), the main pump then moves the fuel through the fuel injection system.

The main pump is driven by an electric motor, which turns a pumping element. A number of different types of pumping element have been used: the examples shown in Figure 3.18 cover both positive displacement (a) and flow type pumping elements (b).

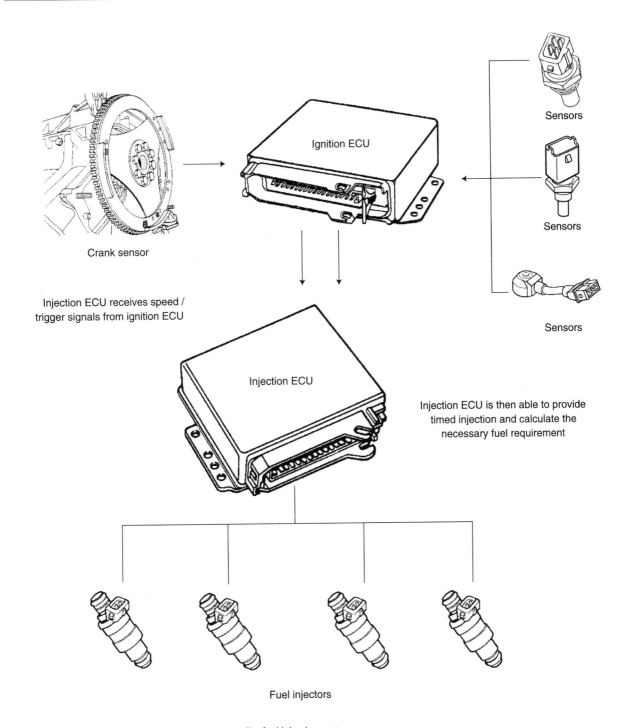

Crank sensor

Injection ECU receives speed / trigger signals from ignition ECU

Ignition ECU

Sensors

Sensors

Sensors

Injection ECU

Injection ECU is then able to provide timed injection and calculate the necessary fuel requirement

Fuel injectors

Figure 3.16 Ignition system used for triggering an earlier fuel injection system

One disadvantage of positive displacement types is that pulses are produced by the pumping action, which can cause noise and vibration in the fuel system. Flow type pumps provide much quieter operation and are therefore more widely used. However, with the latest generation of direct injection systems, positive displacement pumps are again becoming more widely used.

Fuel filter

The fuel filter is located in the fuel circuit after the fuel pump. Although different manufacturers use slightly different construction, the example shown in Figure 3.19 is typical of most filters.

The filter usually consists of a fine paper element and a strainer, which can retain any larger particles. Filters are often constructed in such a way that fuel

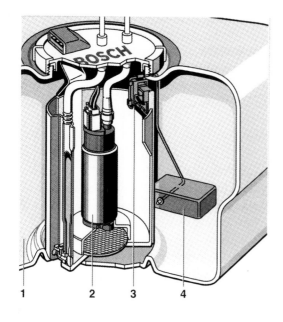

1. Fuel tank
2. Electronic fuel pump
3. Fuel level sensor
4. Float

(a)

should flow in one direction only; markings are usually provided to indicate the fuel flow. Incorrect fitment can result in collapse of the paper element.

Although fuel filters are designed to prevent any impurities and dirt from reaching the injectors, additional fine mesh filters are often also fitted in the injector inlets.

A Suction opening
B Outlet
1 Slotted washer (eccentric) 2 Roller
3 Inner driving wheel 4 Rotor (eccentric)
5 Impeller ring, 6 Impeller blades
7 Passage (peripheral)

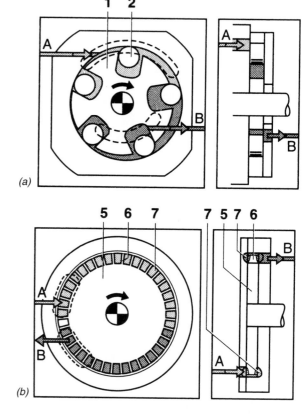

Figure 3.18 Fuel pump with positive displacement and flow type pumping elements
a Roller cell pump
b Flow type pump

Filter intake
Rotor
Relief valve
Pump spacer
Armature
Magnet
Discharge
Brush
Check valve
Diaphragm chamber
Silencer

(b)

Figure 3.17 Examples of fuel pumps
a Pump located in the fuel tank
b An external pump

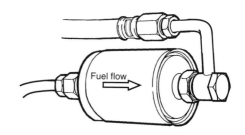

Fuel flow

Figure 3.19 Fuel filter

Fuel pressure regulator and fuel rail

The fuel rail is simply a distribution pipe that allows fuel to flow to all of the injectors. Fuel flows from the tank through the pump and filter to the fuel rail, where the injectors receive their supply of fuel. Until relatively recently, on most systems the fuel rail had an excess fuel pipe connection, which allowed unused or excess fuel to flow back to the fuel tank. A pressure regulator in the fuel rail maintains the pressure in the fuel rail at the required value: excess fuel flows from the regulator back to the fuel tank. An example of a fuel system with an excess fuel return is shown in Figure 3.20a.

Relocation of the excess fuel return pipe

A disadvantage of returning excess fuel from the fuel rail to the fuel tank is that the fuel carries heat from the engine bay back to the fuel in the tank. The temperature of the fuel in the tank therefore rises, which causes evaporation, resulting in fumes that can escape to the atmosphere. Emissions regulations require emissions from the fuel tank to be controlled. A recent change in fuel system design helps to reduce evaporative tank emissions by eliminating the return pipe from the fuel rail. The return pipe is relocated so that it collects the excess fuel from a position much closer to the fuel tank: it is connected just after the fuel filter. These systems are often referred to as 'returnless systems', although in reality a return pipe is still used. An example of a returnless system is shown in Figure 3.20b.

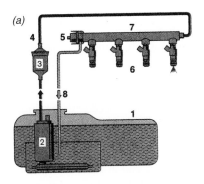

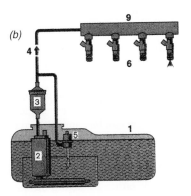

1	Fuel tank
2	Electric fuel pump
3	Fuel filter
4	Fuel injection tubing
5	Pressure regulator
6	Fuel injectors
7	Fuel rail (continuous flow)
8	Return line
9	Fuel rail (no return flow)

Figure 3.20 Fuel delivery systems
a Fuel system with excess fuel return from fuel rail
b Returnless fuel system

Pressure regulator

One principle of operation of electronic injection systems is that if the fuel pressure remains constant, i.e. the fuel exiting from the injector is always at the same pressure, then any variation in fuel quantity delivered to the cylinders can be controlled by altering the duration of the open time of the injectors. In effect, the injection 'on time' or injection duration is the only method through which the fuel quantity is regulated, and the duration is controlled by the ECU in response to information from the sensors.

A fuel pressure regulator is therefore fitted to the fuel delivery system to ensure that the fuel pressure remains constant.

Fuel pressure and engine intake pressure

One factor that must be considered in maintaining a constant fuel pressure is the change that occurs in the engine intake system pressure.

While an engine is operating, the pressure in the intake system (manifold and ports) varies with changes in engine load, engine speed and throttle opening angle. At one extreme, when the throttle is initially opened, the intake pressure is almost the same as atmospheric pressure (approximately 1 bar). At the other extreme, for example when the engine is at high speed and the throttle is suddenly closed, the intake pressure will fall (often referred to as the intake vacuum) due to the restriction of the closed throttle and the strong suction created by the cylinders. The intake pressure can reduce to a typical value of 0.5 bar, so the pressure will have fallen by 0.5 bar.

If the fuel injection pressure remained constant at a typical value of 3 bar, then the difference between the injection pressure and the intake system pressure would vary as the intake system pressure varied. The extremes of effective or true injection pressure would therefore be as follows:

1 intake system pressure = 1 bar
   injection pressure   = 3 bar
   pressure difference   = 2 bar.
   The injection pressure will therefore be 2 bar.

2 intake system pressure = 0.5 bar
   injection pressure   = 3 bar
   pressure difference   = 2.5 bar.
   The true pressure of injection will therefore be 2.5 bar.

Therefore, if the true injection pressure were allowed to vary with the intake system pressure, the quantity of fuel delivered would also vary: for the same duration of injector opening time, if the true injection pressure increased, the amount of fuel flowing through the injector would also increase.

To overcome this problem, most pressure regulators are fitted with a pressure/vacuum pipe connection to the intake system. When the intake pressure reduces, this lower pressure acts on the pressure regulator, which in turn reduces the pressure in the fuel system. In effect, as the pressure in the intake system rises and falls, the pressure in the fuel system also rises and falls by the same amount.

The relationship between intake system and fuel system pressure will therefore be as follows:

1   intake system pressure = 1 bar
     injection pressure   = 3 bar
     pressure difference   = 2 bar.
     The true pressure of injection will therefore be 2 bar.

2   intake system pressure = 0.5 bar
     injection pressure   = 2.5 bar
     pressure difference   = 2 bar.
     The true pressure of injection will therefore be 2 bar.

The following statement can therefore be made:

'Fuel system pressure is maintained by the pressure regulator at a constant pressure relative to intake system pressure.'

Figure 3.21 shows a typical pressure regulator, where intake system pressure (manifold pressure) is connected to the regulator. The operation is as follows.

- When fuel is delivered to the fuel rail and regulator, it will flow to the underside of the regulator diaphragm. A spring acts on the diaphragm and valve assembly, which holds the valve closed. However, the fuel entering the system will build up pressure to a level where it will cause the diaphragm to lift against the spring, and therefore the valve will open.

- As soon as the valve opens, the excess fuel will escape through the return port, which will cause the pressure to reduce; the valve will therefore close. In reality, the valve is constantly oscillating between the open and closed positions, with the result that

1 Intake manifold connection **2** Spring
3 Valve holder **4** Diaphragm **5** Valve
6 Fuel inlet **7** Fuel return

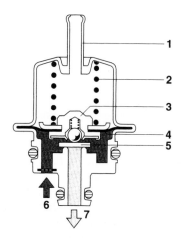

Figure 3.21 Fuel pressure regulator

the pressure is maintained at a value that is dependent on the strength of the spring.
- When the manifold pressure reduces, this lower pressure acts on top of the diaphragm and helps to lift the diaphragm against the spring. Therefore the fuel pressure will not need to be so high before it lifts the diaphragm and opens the valve.

Therefore, when there is a low pressure in the intake manifold, the fuel pressure beneath the diaphragm will be lower when the valve opens. When the intake manifold pressure is higher, then the fuel pressure beneath the diaphragm will need to be higher to open the valve.

3.1.6 Idle speed control

Stalling at idle speed
When an engine is operating at idle speed, many of the engine's processes are relatively inefficient. For example, the air flows through the intake system at a low speed, which does not help the air and fuel to mix. For many engines therefore, especially older designs, emission levels at idle speed were relatively high (as a percentage of the total exhaust gas) and the power developed by the engine was very low.

The regulations are very much focused on idle speed emissions, so for many years it has been necessary to operate engines on a weak mixture or at stoichiometric air:fuel ratios. However, these air:fuel ratios at idle speed do not enable the engine to produce good power outputs leading to a tendency for the engine to stall when any load is applied.

To overcome this problem, a means of controlling the idle speed is used which relies on regulating the airflow into the engine to ensure that the engine does not stall or run too slowly at idle. One option is to rely on the driver to control the idle speed with the throttle; this is, of course a very imprecise and impractical method. Therefore automated systems are used to regulate the airflow. In effect these systems are automatic throttle controls, and in some cases, they do physically control the throttle butterfly. However, many systems regulate the air flowing through a bypass port by using an ECU controlled air valve.

Stepper motor idle valves
See section 1.8.2 for additional information on stepper motors.

A stepper motor is effectively an electric motor that can be stopped or positioned at selected angles of rotation. Some stepper motors can be controlled so that the motor or armature will rotate and stop in increments of less than 1 degree of rotation.

Stepper motors are generally used in one of two ways to control idle speed: either by acting on an air bypass port or by acting on a linkage that connects to the throttle butterfly (throttle valve or plate). Figure 3.22a shows a stepper motor used to regulate the air through an air bypass port and Figure 3.22b shows a stepper motor acting on a throttle butterfly linkage.

The control signals for stepper motors are generally conventional digital control signals: they are on/off pulses. A stepper motor has a number of windings, each of which can be provided with an on/off control signal from the ECU, which enables the armature to be positioned accurately.

Rotary idle valve using partial rotation motors

Although this type of valve also uses a type of electric motor, the rotation of the armature is restricted by mechanical stops or limiters, so that it can only partially rotate. Bosch produces the most widely used type of rotary idle valve: see Figure 3.22c. The armature is connected to a valve that controls the air flowing through a bypass port (Figure 3.22c); the assembly is

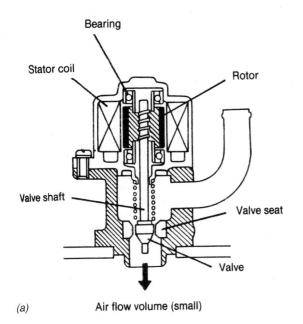

(a)   Air flow volume (small)

Air flow volume (large)

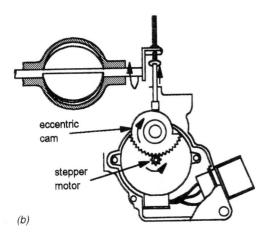

(b)

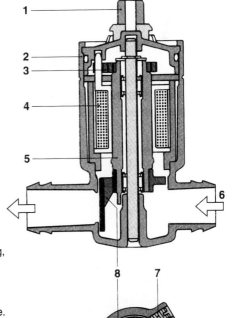

1 Electrical connection, **2** Housing,
3 Return spring, **4** Winding,
5 Rotating armature,
6 Air passage as bypass around the throttle plate,
7 Adjustable stop, **8** Rotating slide.

(c)

Figure 3.22 *Electric motors used to control idle speed*
a *Construction of stepper motor idle control valve*
b *Stepper motor acting on throttle linkage*
c *Rotary idle valve*

usually remotely located, so air pipes connect the valve assembly to the intake system throttle body.

When the throttle is in the idle or closed position, air is able to bypass the throttle butterfly by flowing through the air pipes and the rotary idle valve; the idle speed is therefore dictated by the valve position.

Earlier versions had two windings in the motor. By transmitting a control signal through each winding, it was possible to rotate the armature clockwise or anti-clockwise, depending on which control signal provided the higher current flow through the winding. Later types use a spring to rotate the armature in one direction, with a control signal flowing to a winding that will then rotate the armature against the spring; this type is shown in Figure 3.22c.

The ECU alters the duty cycle of the digital control signal (see section 1.9), which alters the average current in the circuit and the winding. This then causes a stronger or weaker magnetic field to be produced, which results in a stronger or weaker force to oppose the armature spring.

Solenoid idle valves

Several system manufacturers have used solenoid operated valves to regulate the air flowing through an air bypass port. The principle of regulating air in a port is the same as for stepper motor systems (see above), but a linear solenoid is used to control the valve instead of a rotary motor (Figure 3.23).

Although there are various designs of solenoid systems, the basic principle relies on a solenoid armature being connected to an air valve. When the solenoid armature moves, it increases or decreases the aperture in the air bypass port.

The solenoid is usually spring loaded in one direction; current flowing through the winding causes the armature to move against the spring. By increasing or decreasing the current in the circuit and winding, it is then possible to create a greater or weaker magnetic field, which creates a stronger or weaker force on the armature. Altering the current in the circuit therefore moves the armature (against the force of the spring) giving the required valve position to regulate the airflow in the bypass port and the idle speed.

Although there are variations in the control signals used for solenoid valves, a digital signal can be used where the duty cycle is altered, which in turn alters the average current flow (see section 1.9 for additional information on control signals and solenoids).

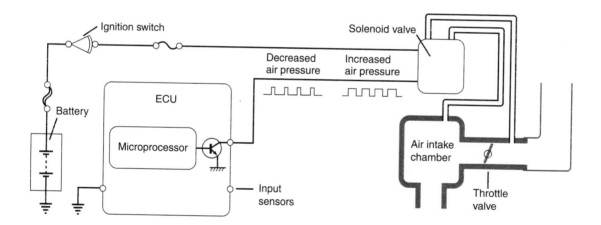

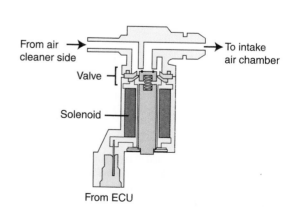

Figure 3.23 Solenoid type idle speed control valves

3.2   PETROL INJECTION SYSTEM EXAMPLES (MULTI-POINT INJECTION)

This section explains the operation of different types of electronic fuel injection systems. The examples are all multi-point port injection systems: i.e. they have individual injectors for each cylinder, with the injectors located in the intake ports. Section 3.3 covers single-point systems.

3.2.1   Example 1: Simple multi-point injection with airflow sensor

System components and layout

Figure 3.24 shows the main components used in the Bosch LE system, which was widely used by many vehicle manufacturers and was a system from which many others evolved. In addition to the main injection system components, an auxiliary air valve is used to provide a fast idle speed when the engine is cold. The air valve is not controlled by the ECU and its operation is explained later in this section. The LE2 system therefore has several sensors but only one set of actuators: the injectors. The fuel delivery system on the Bosch LE is identical to the example illustrated in Figure 3.20, so it is not described again in this section.

Airflow sensor with combined air temperature sensor

The airflow sensor provides the ECU with an analogue signal that indicates the volume of air being drawn into the engine. Air density changes with temperature, so an air temperature sensor is built into the airflow sensor assembly. The ECU therefore receives airflow and air temperature information.

Airflow sensor operation

The airflow sensor has a flap or vane that is forced to move when the air flows through the sensor body (Figure 3.25). The flap is connected to a hinge or shaft, so the angle of the flap increases as the airflow increases.

A potentiometer (variable resistor) is fitted to the sensor assembly, and the potentiometer 'wiper' or 'slider' is connected to the shaft. Therefore, when the flap moves, the potentiometer wiper moves around the resistance track of the potentiometer. This changes the voltage at the wiper, with the magnitude of this change depending on the flap position. The voltage reading at the wiper is sent to the ECU, which provides the ECU with an indication of airflow.

Potentiometer

One of the disadvantages of the flap system is the change in angular movement that occurs with increased airflow. When the airflow is low, the flap is almost at right angles to the airflow and therefore the force acting on the flap is relatively high; any small change in airflow will cause a relatively large change in the flap angle. However, when the airflow is already high, the higher forces acting on the flap will have pushed it to a position where it is almost in line with the airflow (almost lying flat in the sensor body), so any further small increases in airflow will not greatly affect the angle of the flap: it will move only a little further.

When the flap is almost at right angles to the airflow, the voltage change at the potentiometer will be quite large for a small change in the airflow. When the flap is almost in line with the airflow, however, small changes in airflow will result only in very small changes

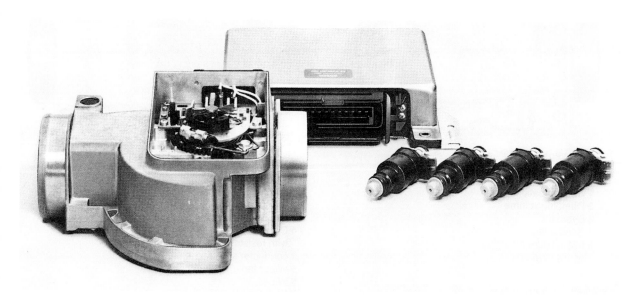

Figure 3.24 Bosch LE injection system

in voltage, which does not provide sufficient information to the ECU. The ECU ideally requires large changes in voltage to assess the airflow accurately.

The potentiometer used on the airflow meter is therefore more complex than conventional potentiometers. A thick film resistance track is used, made of several segments, each with a different resistance. The resistance of the segments is designed to compensate for the reducing angular movement of the flap as the airflow increases: as the wiper moves across the track, the output voltage is progressive and linear.

On this type of airflow sensor, 12 volts is applied to the potentiometer, and, as the wiper moves across the resistance track, the voltage at the wiper changes from typically around 5 volts at low air volumes to around 9 volts at high air volumes.

Damping chamber

A second flap (attached to the first flap) is positioned in a small chamber (referred to as a damping chamber). Air is drawn or induced into the engine in pulses or waves (each cylinder creates a single strong pulse giving as many pulses in one engine cycle as there are cylinders), so the first flap will also tend to pulsate when the airflow passes through the sensor. The second flap is also exposed to the pulsing action of the airflow, but the airflow is directed against the second flap in such a way that the pulsing on the second flap cancels the pulsing of the first flap.

If the compensating flap and damping chamber were not used, the pulsations caused by the airflow would also cause the signal from the sensor to pulsate.

Air temperature (see section 1.5.1)

An air temperature sensor is incorporated within the airflow sensor. The temperature sensor is a thermistor, which is a resistor that changes in resistance with changes in temperature. Because the sensor forms part of a series resistance circuit that has a reference voltage applied to it, when the temperature changes, the resistance and voltage in the circuit also change. The change in voltage is used as a signal to the ECU.

The ECU uses the signal for the change in air temperature in conjunction with the airflow signal (because air mass for a given airflow changes with temperature).

Mixture adjustment

A bypass port is provided on older airflow sensors so that mixture adjustments can be carried out at idle speed. This facility is no longer required with modern engine management systems, but on older engines it was needed to ensure that the idle emissions were within specified limits and to enable the engine to idle smoothly.

Figure 3.25 shows the bypass port, which has an adjusting screw at one end. If the adjusting screw is screwed fully into the port it will block the bypass port, which will force all of the air being drawn into the

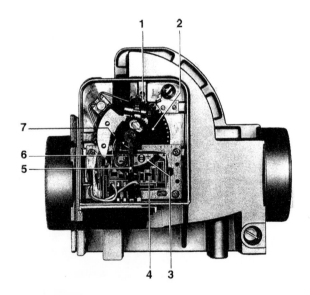

1 Compensation flap
2 Damping volume
3 Bypass
4 Sensor flap
5 Idle mixture adjusting
   screw (bypass)

1 Ring gear for spring preloading
2 Return spring
3 Wiper track
4 Ceramic substrate
   with resistors and
   conductor straps
5 Wiper tap
6 Wiper
7 Pump contact

Figure 3.25 Cutaway views of vane type airflow sensor
a Air side
b Electrical connection side

engine to flow through the main intake port and therefore move the sensing flap. When the adjusting screw is unscrewed, a small amount of air is able to flow through the bypass port, so the flap will not be affected by all of the airflow: the sensing flap will move back slightly, which will reduce the signal voltage transmitted to the ECU. Altering the adjusting screw will therefore affect the amount of air flowing through the bypass port and thus the amount of air affecting the sensing flap. The signal voltage will alter, which causes the ECU to adjust the quantity of fuel being injected. Adjusting the bypass port screw will therefore affect the fuel quantity and the mixture at idle speed.

Coolant temperature sensor
(See section 1.5.1.) The coolant temperature sensor is positioned (usually in the cylinder head) so that it can measure the temperature of the engine coolant. A signal from the sensor is transmitted to the ECU so that the fuel quantity can be altered for cold running (by enriching the mixture) as well as for other minor variations in fuelling that are required at different coolant temperatures (to provide fine tuning of the mixture). Figure 3.26 shows a typical coolant temperature sensor.

The coolant temperature sensor operates in exactly the same way as the air temperature sensor described above. The sensor resistance changes with coolant temperature, resulting in a voltage change in the circuit, which the ECU can then use as an indication of coolant temperature.

The sensor has a negative temperature coefficient (NTC), so its resistance reduces as the temperature

increases. A typical resistance for the sensor is around 7000 ohms (7 kΩ) at 0°C, falling to around 250 ohms at 100°C.

The voltage in the sensor circuit also reduces as the temperature increases. A reference voltage is applied to the sensor circuit, which on the Bosch LE2 system is around 12 volts. However, when the sensor is connected to the circuit, the resistances in the circuit reduce the voltage to a value that depends on the resistance of the sensor, which changes with temperature. For normal operation, the voltage in the circuit is around 9 volts for a very cold engine and around 5 volts for a hot engine.

Throttle position switch
As previously described, the throttle switch consists of two sets of contacts. One set closes when the throttle is closed (the idle position). The second set of contacts closes when the throttle is approximately 60% open (this value will depend on the application).

With the Bosch LE2 system, 12 volts is applied to the centre terminal of the switch. When a set of contacts closes, the 12 volt signal is transmitted back to the ECU. The ECU uses this signal as an indication of idle position or load position. The air:fuel ratio is usually enriched slightly to stabilise the idle speed and to enable the engine to produce full power. Figure 3.27 shows a throttle switch and its construction.

Timing/trigger reference
The Bosch LE2 system relies on a signal from the ignition system for information on engine speed (to assist in fuelling calculations) and as a reference for triggering the injectors. A signal is taken from the ignition coil or direct from the ignition module. In effect, every time the ignition module switches off the ignition coil (spark timing) a signal is transmitted to the LE2 ECU.

1 Electrical connection, 2 Housing, 3 NTC resistor.

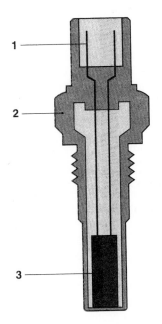

Figure 3.26 Coolant temperature sensor

1 Full load contact 2 Contoured switching guide 3 Throttle valve shaft 4 Idle contact 5 Electrical connection

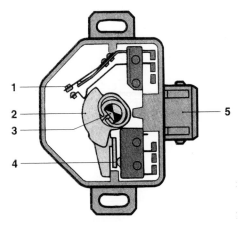

Figure 3.27 Throttle position switch

The injectors on an LE2 system operate simultaneously: they all open and close together on a four-cylinder engine. The ECU uses every alternate ignition pulse (on a four-cylinder engine) as a reference to open the injectors, so the injectors open twice for every engine cycle.

Injectors (actuator)
Simultaneous injection
The only true actuators on an LE2 system are the injectors, which are exactly as described in section 3.1.4. On a four-cylinder engine, all four injectors are opened and closed at the same time (simultaneous injection). In fact, all four injectors are connected back to the ECU at one terminal, so the power stage within the ECU switches all four injectors together (more than one power transistor might however be used). With engines of more than four cylinders, the injectors might be triggered and connected in groups of three or four.

LE2 injectors operate with a fuel pressure of around 2.5 bar above the intake manifold pressure (see section 3.1.5).

Figure 3.28 shows the control signal provided by the ECU. Note that the EMF created when the injectors are switched off causes a voltage spike at around 60 volts.

Idle speed control/adjustment
The standard LE2 system did not provide an automated idle speed control system. The idle speed was adjusted manually using a bypass port adjuster on the throttle body (Figure 3.29).

Manual idle speed adjustment
A bypass port was usually formed as part of the throttle body (Figure 3.29). The bypass port allows intake airflow to bypass the closed throttle butterfly (throttle valve). The bypass port has an adjusting screw that can be altered to allow more or less air to bypass the throttle butterfly.

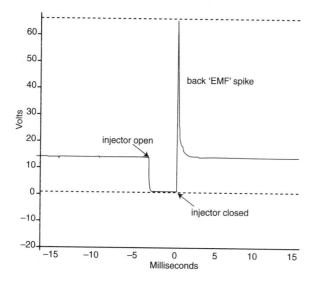

Figure 3.28 Injector control signal

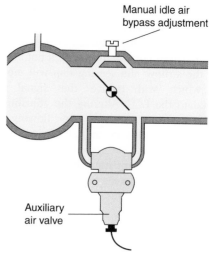

Figure 3.29 Manual and auxiliary air valve bypass ports to control idle speed

Therefore, if the adjusting screw is unscrewed, more air is allowed to enter the engine, which will increase the idle speed. Screwing in the adjuster will restrict the air, thus reducing the idle speed. This enables the idle speed to be set to the manufacturer's specifications.

On the LE2 system, when either more or less air is allowed to flow into the engine through the bypass port, the air will still have to flow through the airflow sensor. An increase in airflow will therefore cause the airflow sensing flap to move, altering the sensor signal to the ECU; the ECU will therefore increase the fuel quantity to correspond with the increase in airflow, thus maintaining the air:fuel ratio.

Auxiliary air valve (cold running)
When an engine is cold, all moving components have higher levels of friction, and the cold oil can also cause additional drag or resistance in the engine. To prevent this additional friction and resistance from stalling the engine when it is cold, the LE system provides additional air to the engine, which results in a slight increase in engine speed at idle (with the throttle closed).

An additional or auxiliary air valve is used which is connected by air pipes to the throttle body. As with the manual idle speed adjuster, the air valve is effectively a bypass port, as shown in Figure 3.29. However, instead of a manual adjusting screw, the auxiliary air valve has a temperature sensitive plate valve which is open when cold and closes when hot (Figure 3.30).

The valve assembly is exposed to two heat sources. The first heat source is an electrical heating element integrated into the air valve body. When the engine is cold the valve plate is in the open position, so when the engine is started, additional air flows through to the engine, thus providing a fast idle speed. However, when the engine is running, the full battery voltage is applied to the heating element, which heats up a bimetallic strip attached to the valve plate. As the bimetallic strip heats up, it bends, which causes the valve plate to progressively close the air bypass port.

Electrically heated auxiliary air device

1 Electrical connection
2 Electrical heating
3 Bimetal strip
4 Perforated plate

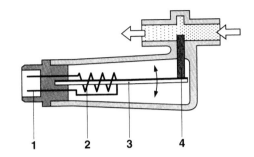

Figure 3.30 Auxiliary air valve located in the intake system

When the engine is switched off, in theory, the bimetallic strip will cool down, allowing the valve plate to reopen the port. However, the air valve is positioned so that it is exposed to engine heat, so the valve body stays hot until the engine cools down. So the port will not open again until the engine is quite cool.

It takes typically around 3 minutes (depending on the vehicle application) for the auxiliary air valve to move from the fully open to the fully closed position. In this time, the engine should have reached an operating temperature that allows it to idle at normal speed.

Electrical systems and wiring (LE2)

Although the Bosch LE system is now an old one, its basic elements are still relevant to today's injection systems. Therefore, in addition to the wiring circuit shown in this section (Figure 3.31), the operation of the circuit and some of the functions are also explained.

Power supply

Early electronic injection systems generally used battery voltage for all aspects of system operation. On the Bosch LE system, the injectors used the 12 volt supply and the sensors were also provided with a 12 volt reference voltage. Although all systems largely still use the full battery voltage for actuators such as the injectors, it is now normal practice to use a 5 volt reference voltage for sensors.

A system relay provides the system components with the 12 volt supply. The relay acts as a safety device and will switch off the power supplied to the components unless certain signals are received from the engine, etc.

The relay consists of contacts which, when closed, connect the battery voltage direct to the system components. Energising windings within the relay will cause the contacts to close when a voltage is applied to the windings.

Relay operation

The relay receives the full battery voltage supply direct from the battery (possibly fused on some applications) to terminal 30.

- When the ignition is initially switched on, the battery voltage will be applied to terminal 15 of the relay (the voltage will be applied to the energising winding). A timer circuit within the relay will cause the relay to apply the battery voltage from relay terminal 87b to the fuel pump for a few seconds (allowing the pump to operate, thus ensuring that the fuel system is under pressure). If the engine is not cranked or started, the relay will switch off the supply to the pump.
- When the ignition switch is then placed in the cranking position, the voltage will be applied from the starter circuit to terminal 50 of the relay; this will again cause the energising winding to close the contacts and the battery voltage will now be applied to all of the system components (the fuel pump, injectors and sensors). The engine should now start.
- When the engine starts, an ignition speed signal (from the ignition coil or module) is transmitted to the relay at terminal 1, which indicates that the engine is running. Because the start signal from the starter circuit will now switch off (the engine is no longer cranking), the speed signal acts as a replacement so that the relay will continue to provide battery voltage to the injection system.
- If for any reason the engine were to stop, the ignition signal would disappear and the relay would switch off the power supply to the injection system.

Injectors

All injectors will receive battery voltage from relay terminal 87 during starting and engine running. The second terminal at each injector is then connected to ECU terminal 12, which is the earth path for the injectors. The circuit passes from terminal 12 through the power stage of the ECU to earth. Therefore, when the ECU switches on the injectors, the power stage will complete the earth circuit for the injectors.

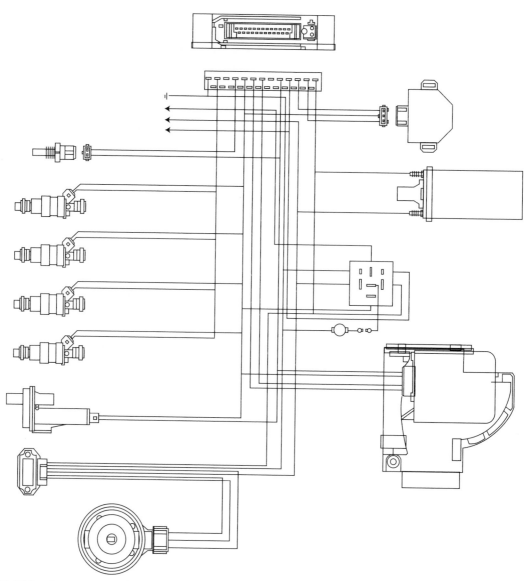

Figure 3.31 Wiring diagram for Bosch LE2 injection system

Fuel pump

The fuel pump receives a power supply from relay terminal 87b while the engine is starting and running.

Throttle switch

The throttle switch receives battery voltage at terminal 18 from relay terminal 87. When the idle contacts or the load contacts in the switch are closed, the battery voltage will then be applied from the switch terminals 2 or 3 to the ECU at terminals 2 or 3. The ECU will then have an indication of idle or engine load.

Coolant temperature sensor

The coolant temperature sensor also has a battery voltage supply from relay terminal 87. As previously noted, the sensor is part of a series resistance circuit, so, as the resistance of the sensor varies with temperature, the signal from the sensor to ECU terminal 10 will change, indicating the temperature to the ECU.

Airflow sensor

The airflow sensor is supplied with the battery voltage at terminal 9 through relay terminal 87. This voltage is applied across the air temperature sensor, which operates in the same way as the coolant sensor described above. The signal from the air temperature sensor passes from terminal 8 to the ECU terminal. The supply voltage is also applied across the potentiometer within the airflow sensor; when the wiper on the potentiometer moves (due to the airflow sensing flap moving), the voltage on the wiper contact will change, and this changing signal is transmitted from terminal 7 of the airflow sensor to terminal 7 of the ECU. Airflow sensor terminal 5 is the earth connection for the potentiometer.

Auxiliary air valve

The valve is supplied with the battery voltage from relay terminal 87 while the engine is starting and running; this will cause the heating element in the valve assembly to become hot and remain hot while the engine is running, which causes the air valve to close (so there is no fast idle).

ECU

The ECU is also supplied with the battery voltage from relay terminal 87. A speed signal is provided at terminal 1 (to enable the ECU to calculate the fuelling requirements). The cranking or start signal is supplied to terminal 4; the ECU can then provide additional injection pulses or lengthen the duration of the injection control signal (both of these will allow additional fuel to be injected for starting).

Signals from the temperature and airflow sensors are transmitted to terminals 7, 8 and 10, with the throttle switch signals passing to terminals 2 and 3. The injector control signal is provided at terminal 12, with terminals 5 and 13 being earth connections for the ECU.

3.2.2 Example 2: Multi-point system with added functionality

Note: This section should be studied in conjunction with section 3.2.1. Note also that the fuel delivery system on the Bosch M1.5 is identical to the example covered in section 3.1.5 and illustrated in Figure 3.20. It is therefore not described again in this section.

System components and layout

The system featured in this second example is again made by Bosch, but is a later system than the previously covered LE2 system. The system is referred to as M1.5 (Figure 3.32), and features a number of improvements and changes, as well as added functionality and capability. In Bosch terminology, the 'M' tends to refer to 'Motronic', the Bosch term that is generally applied to an engine management system. The M1.5 system combines the ignition and fuel injection functions as well as some other functions, which include control of the idle speed via an ECU controlled air valve.

Although this section does not deal specifically with engine management, the M1.5 system provides an insight into later fuel system developments as well as into early engine management systems. Not all of the functions and components of the M1.5 system are dealt with in this section: some are covered in greater detail in the emissions section and in the engine management section.

Sensors and sensor reference voltage

Many of the sensors used on the M1.5 system are developments of, or the same as, those used on the LE2 system (section 3.2.1). There are however some additional sensors.

One major change to the system is that the reference voltages used for the sensors are generally stabilised at 5 volts (as opposed to battery voltage). This is because

1 Fuel tank, 2 Electric fuel pump, 3 Fuel filter, 4 Pressure regulator, 5 Control unit, 6 Ignition coil, 7 High-tension distributor, 8 Spark plug, 9 Fuel injection valves, 10 Throttle valve, 11 Throttle valve switch, 12 Airflow sensor, 13 Potentiometer and air temperature sensor, 14 Lambda sensor, 15 Engine temperature sensor, 16 Rotary idle actuator, 17 Engine speed and reference mark sensor, 18 Battery, 19 Ignition and starting switch, 20 Air conditioning switch.

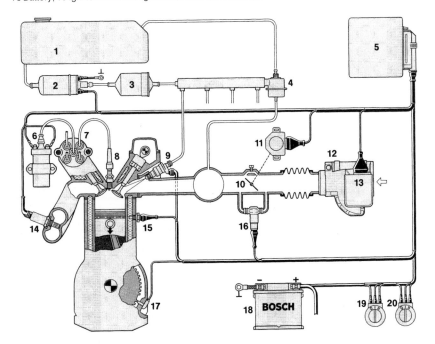

Figure 3.32 Bosch Motronic M1.5 system

the M1.5 system uses digital electronics to a much greater extent than previous systems and a 5 volt circuit is more suitable for use with electronic components.

Key Points

Standard multipoint gasoline injection systems use solenoid type injectors mounted in the inlet port spraying directly at the back of the inlet valve

The quantity of fuel delivered is a function of injector opening duration as the pressure differential across the injector is kept constant. This is achieved via the fuel pressure regulator which takes into account manifold pressure

Airflow sensor with combined air temperature sensor

The airflow sensor and the air temperature sensor operate in much the same way as the sensor on the LE2 system (section 3.2.1). However, one major change is in the idle mixture adjustment or CO (carbon monoxide) adjustment. Although the task remains the same, the adjuster on the M1.5 airflow sensor is a potentiometer instead of an air bypass adjuster. Since the reference voltage to the sensor is 5 volts, the output signal voltages during normal operation will typically be between 0.25 and 4.75 volts.

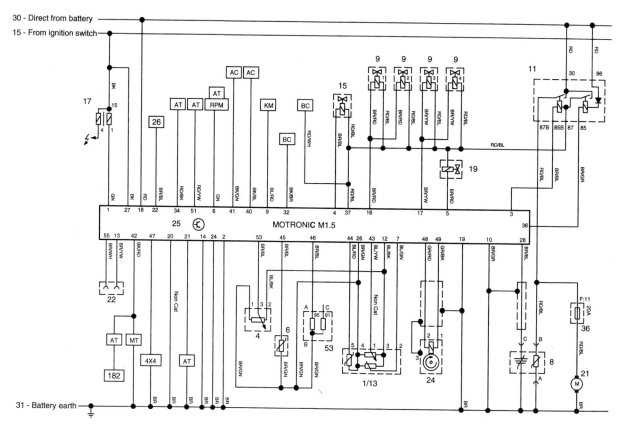

Wire colour codes : BG = Beige; BK = Black; BL = Blue; BR = Brown; GN = Green; D = Dark; GR = Grey; IV = Ivory; L = Light, OR = Orange; PK = Pink; PU = Purple; RD = Red; WH = White; YW = Yellow; TT = Transparent.

Note. *Wire colours are subject to change according to vehicle year.*

1. Airflow Sensor
4. Throttle Position Sensor
6. Engine Coolant Temperature Sensor
8. Lambda (oxygen) Sensor
9. Injector(s)
11. System Relay
13. Intake Air Temperature Sensor
15. Idle Speed Control Valve
17. Ignition Coil
19. EVAP Canister Solenoid
21. Fuel Pump
22. Self Diagnostic Plug
24. Engine Speed Sensor
25. ECM

26. Instrument Cluster Warning Lamp
36. Fuse
53. Fuel Octane Encoding Plug
182. Neutral / Park Position Switch
MT. Manual Transmission
AC. Air Conditioning
AT. Automatic Transmission
KM. Vehicle Speed Signal
RPM. Engine Speed Signal
BC. Trip Computer

Key to wiring symbols

Wiring connection   No wiring connection   Wiring screen connection

Figure 3.33 Wiring diagram for Bosch M1.5 injection system

The CO adjusting screw is connected to a small potentiometer, so when the screw is adjusted it alters the voltage at the potentiometer wipe connection. The voltage across the potentiometer is applied to the ECU. When the adjustment is made, the voltage changes and the ECU alters the injected fuel quantity, which in turn alters the mixture/CO setting.

In some vehicle applications, the system uses an oxygen sensor (lambda sensor) to control the mixture, so the CO adjuster is not used. Oxygen/lambda sensors are covered in the section 3.5.

Coolant temperature sensor

The coolant temperature sensor is a negative temperature coefficient (NTC) sensor, which operates in exactly the same way as the version used on the LE2 system. Note that the reference voltage to the sensor is 5 volts.

Figure 3.34 shows the typical resistance values for the sensor and typical voltages in the sensor circuit at different coolant temperatures. Although the values quoted are typical for many systems, some systems may have sensor resistances and voltages that differ; always refer to the appropriate specifications when testing.

Figure 3.34 Temperature against resistance and voltage for a coolant temperature sensor

Temperature, °C	Resistance (ohms)	Signal voltage
0	6,000–8,000	3.7–4.0
20	2,000–3,500	3.0–3.2
40	1,000–1,500	2.0–2.2
60	500–700	1.2–1.5
80	275–350	0.6–0.9
100	150–250	0.4–0.5

Throttle position sensor

On the M1.5 system, the throttle position sensor (Figure 3.35) is a potentiometer instead of a switch. A 5 volt reference is applied to the potentiometer. When the throttle is opened and closed, the potentiometer wiper (which is connected to the throttle butterfly shaft), moves across the resistance track, thus providing a change in voltage corresponding to the position of the throttle. The output signal is transmitted to the ECU to enable it to assess the angle of throttle opening.

When the throttle is closed (at idle) the voltage from the sensor potentiometer should be at the specified value, which is typically between 0.3 and 0.9 volts. When the throttle is opened, the voltage rises and, at full throttle, the voltage will be in the region of 4 to 4.5 volts.

Trigger/timing reference (engine speed sensor)

The M1.5 system is a combined injection and ignition system, and a single sensor is used to provide the ECU with crankshaft speed and angular position information. The crankshaft speed/position sensor is an inductive or variable reluctance sensor.

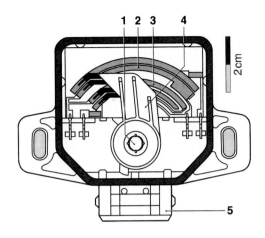

1 Throttle valve shaft	4 Wiper arm with wipers
2 Resistance track 1	5 Electric connection (4-pole)
3 Resistance track 2	

Figure 3.35 Throttle position potentiometer: Bosch Motronic M1.5 system

See sections 1.5.2 and 2.2.3 for additional information on variable reluctance sensors used to indicate crankshaft speed and position.

On the M1.5 system there is a trigger or reluctor disc on the crankshaft (different positions on the crankshaft are used for different engine applications). The disc has 60 reference points or trigger teeth, although one tooth is missing, which functions as the master reference. Figure 3.36 shows the sensor and reluctor disc.

The sensor is constructed with a permanent magnet and a winding. It is located next to the reluctor disc and as each tooth passes the sensor, it induces a small current into the winding. So, when the crankshaft is rotating, the sensor will produce an electrical pulse or signal as each tooth passes the sensor. The missing tooth will create a slightly

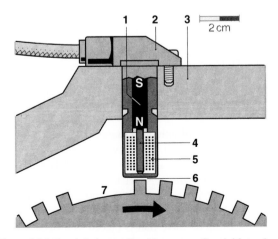

Figure 3.36 Crankshaft speed/position sensor: Bosch Motronic M1.5 system

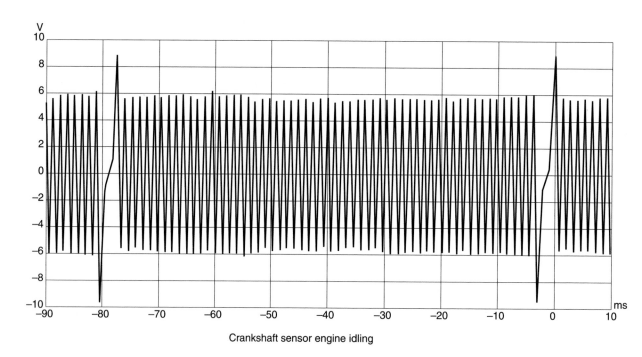

Crankshaft sensor engine idling

different pulse shape, which the ECU will use as the master reference. Figure 3.37 shows part of the AC analogue signal that would be seen when the sensor is connected to an oscilloscope.

The ECU uses the master reference signal to establish a master position for the crankshaft, e.g. TDC for cylinders 1 and 4. This can be used as a trigger reference for operating the injectors and as a master reference for the ignition timing. The M1.5 system is a simultaneous injection system, i.e. all injectors open and close together. Also note that the ignition system has a single coil for all cylinders and a rotor arm/distributor cap (connected to the end of the camshaft) to distribute the HT voltage to the appropriate spark plugs.

The additional reference points on the reluctor disc provide the ECU with angular rotation information for the crankshaft: the ECU can determine crankshaft speed as each tooth passes the sensor (each reference tooth represents six degrees of crankshaft rotation).

Injectors (actuator)

The injectors operate in exactly the same way as those on the LE2 system (section 3.2.7). However, on the M1.5 system, the injectors are connected in groups of two on four-cylinder engines, but are still all opened and closed at the same time.

Idle speed control valve (actuator)

(Also see section 3.1.6). The air valve used on the M1.5 system is referred to as a 'rotary idle valve'. The valve is operated by a type of electric motor that has its rotation limited by mechanical stops; the motor is therefore able to rotate only partially. Connected to the motor is a flap or valve that is placed in a bypass port through which air flows around (bypasses) the throttle butterfly to the intake system.

Figure 3.37 Signal produced by crankshaft speed/position sensor: Bosch Motronic M1.5 system

1 Electrical connection, 2 Housing, 3 Permanent magnet, 4 Armature, 5 Air passage as bypass around throttle valve, 6 Rotary slide.

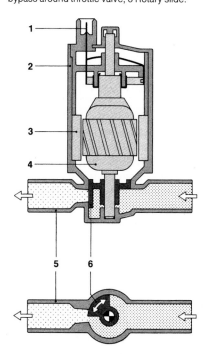

Figure 3.38 ECU controlled air valve controlling the airflow through a bypass port

The electric motor is spring loaded in one direction of rotation, and current flowing through the motor windings will tend to rotate the motor in the opposite direction. By varying the current, it is possible to rotate the motor against the spring to achieve different angles of rotation or positioning; this allows varying volumes of air to flow through the port (Figure 3.38).

Control signal

The ECU provides the earth path for the idle valve circuit. However, the earth path passes through a power stage in the ECU, which rapidly switches *on* and *off* the earth circuit. The result is that a digital control signal is produced with an on/off frequency of around 100 Hz (100 times a second). The ECU alters the duty cycle (on/off ratio) of the control signal, which alters the average current in the circuit; this in turn alters the position of the motor and valve (see section 1.8 for information about altering duty cycles to control actuators). Figure 3.39 shows the typical control signal.

Maintaining and increasing idle speed

The idle control system can control the idle speed in two ways. First, when the engine is at normal operating temperature, if certain loads are applied to the engine, such as an electrical load (headlights, heated rear window, etc.), the additional load would normally cause the idle speed to reduce. The ECU, which is receiving the speed signal from the crankshaft sensor, will immediately detect a minor drop in engine speed, and will change the control signal so that the valve opens slightly, thus restoring the idle speed to the specified value. This process is effectively continuous and ensures that any minor change in engine idle speed is corrected.

The second process for controlling the idle speed relies on information from other sensors. For example, when the engine is cold, the ECU assesses the engine temperature from the coolant temperature sensor information and opens the idle air valve slightly to increase the engine speed and overcome the additional friction and drag that exist in the engine at low temperatures.

Other information can also be used by the ECU to alter the idle speed: for example, when the air conditioning system is switched on, the load of the air conditioning compressor would slow the engine down, but to drive the compressor also requires considerable power that may not be available from the engine at the normal idle speed. The ECU therefore opens the air valve an increased amount which increases the idle speed. Note that the air conditioning system is connected to the ECU so, when the ECU receives an appropriate signal from the air conditioning system, the ECU can implement a faster idle.

Ignition coil (actuator)

The ignition coil is not part of the fuel system, but the same ECU controls the fuelling and ignition systems. The ignition module effectively forms part of the ECU, so the ECU can use the same information from the various sensors to calculate the ignition timing, and then switch the ignition module, which in turn switches the ignition coil. See section 2.3 for information on computer controlled ignition systems.

Electrical systems and wiring (M1.5)

Figure 3.33 shows the wiring of the M1.5 system.

Although some functions of the M1.5 system are similar to the LE2 system, there are many significant differences, as explained below.

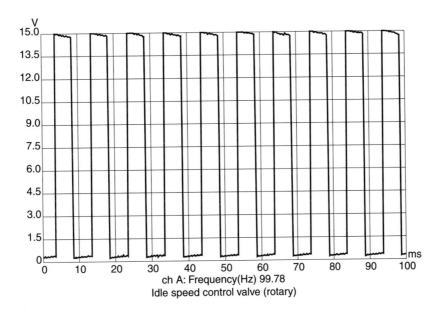

Figure 3.39 Control signals for rotary idle valve

Power supply and relay

The power supply to the M1.5 system is split into two categories: the first category is the supply to the actuators, which operate using full battery voltage; the second category is the reference voltage for many of the sensors, which is usually 5 volts.

The actuator supply is therefore via the system relay, but the reference voltage is provided by the ECU, which has a voltage stabiliser system to reduce the battery voltage down to a stabilised 5 volts for the sensors.

Relay operation

The relay has two sets of contacts: one set switches the power supply to the fuel pump and Lambda sensor heater (where fitted); the second set switches the power supply to the system actuators.

Compared with the LE2 system previously covered, the relay on the M1.5 system operates slightly differently. Each of the energising windings within the relay is earthed via the ECU; therefore, the ECU controls when the energising windings are able to close the contacts.

- The relay receives full battery voltage direct from the battery to relay terminals 30 and 86. When the ignition is switched on, the ECU receives battery voltage via the ignition switch (to ECU terminal 27), which indicates that the driver intends to start the engine. The ECU then completes the earth path for the relay energising windings at ECU terminals 3 and 36 (connecting to relay terminals 85b and 85). Both of the relay contacts will then close, providing a power supply to the fuel pump (relay terminal 87b) and to the rest of the actuators (relay terminal 87). The fuel pump will run briefly to ensure that there is fuel pressure.
- If the engine is then not started, the ECU will switch off the earth path to relay terminal 85b, thus causing the pump contacts to open and switch off the fuel pump.
- When the engine is cranked over for starting, the crankshaft position sensor will provide a signal to the ECU, which will now have an indication that the engine is being started; the ECU will then reconnect the earth path for the energising winding (at relay terminal 85b), thus causing the fuel pump contacts to close again and provide power to the fuel pump.
- The relay will continue to provide power supplies to all components so long as the ECU is receiving the ignition 'on' voltage and a signal from the crankshaft position sensor.
- If the engine were to stop, the signal from the crankshaft position sensor would disappear and the ECU would switch off the earth paths for the relay energising windings. The relay contacts would then open, causing all actuators to switch off.

Injectors

All injectors will receive battery voltage from relay terminal 87 during starting and engine running. Note that the injectors are then connected to the ECU at terminals 16 and 17; these are the earth paths for the injectors. From terminals 17 and 18 the circuit passes through the power stages of the ECU to earth. Therefore, when the ECU switches on the injectors, the power stages will complete the earth circuit for the injectors. Although there are two groups of injectors, for this application the injectors are still switched at the same time.

Idle speed control valve

The idle control valve receives power from relay terminal 87. The earth path for the valve is via ECU terminal 4; this is the circuit within the ECU that connects to the power stage and therefore provides the control signal.

Ignition coil

The ignition coil receives a power supply from the ignition switch, and the coil is switched to earth via ECU terminal 1.

Fuel pump

The fuel pump receives power from relay terminal 87b while the engine is starting and running.

Other actuators

There are some other actuators fitted, including a Lambda sensor heater and an EVAP canister purge valve. Although not all applications of M1.5 had these components, they are emissions control components fitted to many vehicles and are therefore covered in section 3.5.

Coolant temperature sensor

The coolant temperature sensor is connected to the ECU at terminals 45 and 26. Terminal 26 is an earth path that is shared with other components. The reference voltage (5 volts) is applied to the sensor from terminal 45. Because the sensor is part of a series resistance circuit, the voltage at terminal 45 will then reduce, depending on the temperature, and therefore also the resistance value at the sensor.

Airflow sensor

The airflow sensor receives a 5 volt supply at terminal 3 from ECU terminal 12. The voltage is applied across the airflow sensor potentiometer and when the wiper on the potentiometer moves (as the airflow sensing flap moves), the voltage on the wiper contact will change. This changing voltage level is transmitted from terminal 2 of the airflow sensor to terminal 7 of the ECU.

The supply voltage is also applied to the CO adjustment potentiometer (within the airflow sensor). The wiper position on the CO potentiometer resistance track depends on the adjuster screw position, and therefore the voltage at the wiper also depends on the adjuster screw position. However, the voltage at the wiper is applied back to the ECU from airflow sensor terminal 1 to ECU terminal 43. The voltage at these terminals is used by the ECU to adjust the fuelling at idle speed.

The air temperature sensor (located within the airflow sensor) operates in the same way as the coolant sensor described above. The air temperature sensor has a separate 5 volt supply (which is the reference voltage) at sensor terminal 5. As with the coolant sensor, when the air temperature sensor is connected in the circuit, the resistance of the sensor alters the voltage in the circuit. Therefore the voltage at airflow sensor terminal 5 or at ECU terminal 44 depends on the air temperature.

All sensing elements within the airflow sensor assembly connect through to earth via sensor terminal 4 to ECU terminal 26.

Throttle position sensor

The throttle position sensor or potentiometer receives a 5 volt supply to the potentiometer resistance at sensor terminal 2 (supplied from ECU terminal 12). The earth for the potentiometer resistance is via sensor terminal 1 to ECU terminal 26. The potentiometer wiper connection passes to sensor terminal 3 and to the ECU at terminal 53. Therefore, when the throttle is opened and closed, the voltage at sensor terminal 3 and ECU terminal 53 will increase and decrease, thus providing an indication of throttle angle to the ECU.

Crankshaft position sensor

The crankshaft position sensor (or engine speed sensor) is an inductive sensor that produces its own signal. The two main connections from sensor terminals 1 and 2 connect to ECU terminals 48 and 49. These two connections provide a complete circuit for the sensor winding. The signal is transmitted via terminal 1 of the sensor to ECU terminal 48; the other connection is therefore the return or earth path.

Note that a third connection to sensor terminal 3 connects to ECU terminal 19 and to earth; this circuit forms a screen or shield around the sensor wiring to shield out other electrical interference.

ECU

The following list indicates the function of each connection at the ECU terminals. Note that not all terminals are used.

Terminal 1 Switched earth path for the ignition coil
Terminal 2 Earth connection
Terminal 3 Switched earth path for fuel pump relay energising winding
Terminal 4 Switched earth path for the idle speed control valve
Terminal 5 Switched earth path for the EVAP canister purge valve (covered in section 3.5.1)
Terminal 6 Connection to automatic transmission ECU
Terminal 7 Airflow sensor signal
Terminal 9 Signal from vehicle speed sensor
Terminal 10 Earth connection
Terminal 12 5 volt supply to airflow sensor and throttle position sensor
Terminal 13 Connection to diagnostic plug (covered in section 3.7.3)

Terminal 14 Earth connection
Terminal 16 Switched earth path for a group of injectors
Terminal 17 Switched earth path for a group of injectors
Terminal 19 Earth connection
Terminal 20 Earth connection (only connected if the engine does not have a catalytic converter, this connection effectively 'programs' the ECU to control fuelling and ignition applicable to a vehicle without a catalytic converter)
Terminal 21 Earth connection (only connected if the vehicle has automatic transmission, this effectively 'programs' the ECU to perform certain functions differently)
Terminal 22 Connection to dashboard warning light (illuminates the light if there is an engine management system fault)
Terminal 24 Earth connection
Terminal 26 Earth circuit for various sensors
Terminal 27 Ignition on supply from ignition switch
Terminal 28 Signal from lambda/oxygen sensor (covered in section 3.5.7)
Terminal 32 Signal to trip computer (to enable the trip computer to calculate fuel consumption, etc.)
Terminal 34 Connection to automatic transmission ECU
Terminal 36 Switched earth path for relay energising winding (to close main contacts)
Terminal 37 Battery voltage power supply from relay main contacts
Terminal 40 Connection to air conditioning system
Terminal 41 Connection to air conditioning system
Terminal 43 Signal from CO adjuster (in airflow sensor)
Terminal 44 Air temperature sensor signal
Terminal 45 Coolant temperature sensor signal
Terminal 46 Connection to octane adjust plug (connector plugs with different resistance values are connected across this circuit; this indicates to the ECU the octane grade of fuel being used; the ignition timing and fuelling may alter depending on which octane plug is used)
Terminal 47 Earth connection (used on specific applications if the vehicle has four-wheel drive)
Terminal 48 Connection to crankshaft speed/position sensor
Terminal 49 Connection to crankshaft speed/position sensor
Terminal 51 Connection to automatic transmission system
Terminal 53 Signal from throttle position sensor
Terminal 55 Connection to diagnostic plug (covered in section 3.7.3).

3.2.3 Example 3: Multi-point systems with hotwire air mass sensors

This section should be studied in conjunction with Example 2 (section 3.2.2).

System components

The major difference between the system detailed in Example 2 and the examples in this section is the use of a hotwire air mass sensor instead of a vane or flap airflow sensor. The rest of the system is similar to, or the same as, Example 2 and is therefore not repeated.

Injection system wiring differs between manufacturers and applications in each vehicle, so additional wiring diagrams are not included in this section, apart from the wiring for hotwire sensors. However, the wiring of many systems will be similar to that for the Bosch Motronic M1.5 system shown in Figure 3.33, with the obvious exception that terminal numbers at the ECU, sensors, actuators and relays, etc. will be different. Most injection systems are designed to perform the same basic tasks, so the components and wiring requirements are generally similar.

Hotwire air mass sensor (see also section 1.5.5)

Hotwire air mass sensors perform a similar task to vane or flap mechanical airflow sensors, except that air mass sensors measure the mass of air as opposed to the volume of air. Additionally, air mass sensors do not use mechanical means of measurement, but rely totally on electronic measurement of the air mass. The mass of air measured changes with density and temperature (both of which change with altitude). The mass of a given volume of air therefore varies, and the volume of fuel provided should be dependent on the mass of air rather than its volume; this means that mechanical airflow sensors (which measure the volume of air) do not provide sufficient information to the ECU. Any change in altitude, or any other factor that affects the air density, is not accounted for by mechanical airflow sensors.

Sensor operation

Hotwire air mass sensors use the cooling effect of the air flowing through the intake system; the greater the mass or density of that air, the greater the cooling effect. Cooling changes the resistance of a heated wire element; this resistance change is used to produce the output signal from the sensor. A temperature sensing element is also used.

Hotwire air mass sensors generally provide an analogue signal, where the voltage rises and falls with the change in air mass (increase and decrease of air drawn into the engine). Some air mass sensors provide a digital signal.

Some designs of hotwire air mass sensor use an additional heating process to burn off contamination that could build up on the sensing wire; this 'burn off' function is implemented after the engine is switched off and lasts for a short period of around one second.

Figure 3.40 shows the typical appearance of a hotwire air mass sensor and the sensing element, as well as a wiring diagram for a sensor.

Typical wiring connections for this sensor would be:

- a battery voltage supply connection via the injection relay
- a battery voltage supply connection from the ECU when burn off sequence is required

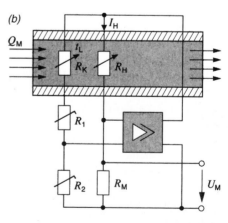

(a)

Q_M
R_M
R_H
R_M

1   Temperature compensation resistor R_K
2   Sensor ring with hot wire R_H
3   Precision measuring resistor (R_M)
Q_M Air mass flow

(b)

Q_M
I_H
I_L
R_K
R_H
R_1
R_2
R_M
U_M

R_K Temperature compensation resistor
R_H Hotwire heater resistor
R_M Measuring resistor
$R_{1,2}$ Bridge balance resistors

U_M Measurement voltage
I_H Heating current
I_L Air temperature
Q_M Air mass flow

Figure 3.40 Example of hotwire mass airflow sensor
a Hotwire air mass meter
b Wiring for hotwire air mass sensor

- an output voltage terminal giving mass air flow as an analogue voltage
- earth connection for burn off
- sensor earth connection
- spare terminal (used for CO adjustment when available).

Hot film air mass sensors

A development of the hotwire sensor is the 'hot film' sensor. Instead of using a heated wire, the hot film type has a thin metallic film sensing element. The operation and general appearance are similar to the hotwire system, although the construction eliminates the need for the 'burn off' process.

3.2.4 Example 4: Multi-point systems with map sensors

This section should be studied in conjunction with Example 2 (section 3.2.2).

System components and layout

The major difference between the system detailed in Example 2 and the examples in this section is the use of a MAP sensor instead of an airflow sensor. The rest of the system is similar to, or the same as, Example 2 and is therefore not repeated.

Map sensor

See also section 1.5.4.

Principle of operation

MAP sensors (Figure 3.41) are used as an alternative to airflow sensors to enable the ECU to calculate the mass of air entering the engine. The MAP sensor information is used in conjunction with the engine speed information to enable the ECU to make the appropriate calculations. MAP sensor systems will therefore usually have a crankshaft speed/position sensor with a large number of reference teeth on the reluctor disc, to provide very accurate engine speed information to the ECU.

The MAP sensor measures the pressure (or depression) in the intake manifold; the pressure depends on engine load and throttle position, as well as engine speed. However, intake pressure can be at a certain value for many combinations of engine speed and throttle position. For example, the pressure or depression at idle speed with a closed throttle can be similar to the depression when the engine is operating at light load with a partially open throttle. Therefore the engine speed and throttle position information are provided separately to the ECU, so that different operating conditions can be allowed for.

Modern MAP sensors use a pressure sensitive component such as a piezo crystal that changes its electrical resistance with presssure. The pressure sensitive components form part of an electronic circuit which then produces an electrical signal that will vary with any variation in pressure.

The MAP sensors are connected to the intake manifold via a pipe, although, for many applications, the sensor is connected directly to the intake manifold or plenum chamber. When the intake system pressure changes, the signal produced by the MAP sensor also changes. MAP sensors can provide digital or analogue signals.

Analogue signal MAP sensor

Any analogue signal MAP sensor provides a voltage that rises and falls with changes in intake pressure. Modern MAP sensors are provided with a 5 volt supply or reference voltage, and the output from the sensor therefore generally varies between approximately 0.25 to 4.75 volts (depending on the intake pressure). Refer to section 1.6.3.

An analogue MAP sensor will typically have a low output at low pressure (i.e. high manifold vacuum), with increasing voltage output as manifold pressure increases.

Figure 3.41 Examples of MAP sensors
a Remotely mounted MAP sensor
b MAP sensor located on intake manifold

In the example shown in Figure 3.42, the 5 volt supply is provided by the ECU to terminal 1 of the sensor. Terminal 3 is the earth connection (via the ECU) and terminal 2 provides the analogue signal. Note that different sensors will have different terminal numbers.

Digital signal MAP sensors

A digital MAP sensor operates in a similar way to an analogue sensor, but it produces a digital signal instead of an analogue signal.

The sensor produces a simple on/off signal. However, when the intake pressure changes, the signal frequency changes, i.e. the number of pulses produced in a second will increase or decrease. As an example, at idle speed where the manifold pressure is low (high depression), the frequency could be around 90 Hz, but when the throttle is opened and the intake pressure rises, the frequency could rise to approximately 150 Hz.

The sensor power supply (typically 5 volts) is a stabilised voltage supplied by the ECU and connected via a terminal on the sensor. Additionally an earth (0 volt) connection terminal as well as a signal output terminal will be available.

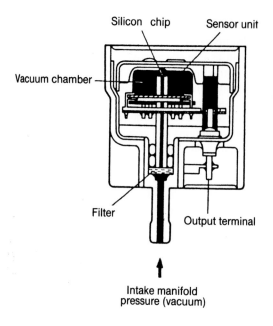

Figure 3.42 *Analogue MAP sensor*

> **Key Points**
>
> Air mass or volume flow meters measure the air consumption of the engine directly as they are mounted in the inlet tract
>
> Manifold pressure sensors are used in conjunction with the throttle position signal and engine speed to calculate engine air consumption indirectly

---

3.3   SINGLE-POINT (THROTTLE BODY) PETROL INJECTION

3.3.1 Simplified injection system

Compromise between a carburettor and multi-point injection

Single-point injection systems have a cost advantage over multi-point injections systems, but they have many of the features of multi-point injection systems that allow them to provide much better fuel delivery and mixture control than carburettors. However, there are several limitations with single-point systems, including certain limitations on emissions control and in the types of engine that can efficiently operate with single-point injection. These limitations are explained below.

A single-point injection system is in many ways similar to a carburettor, because the fuel enters the engine intake system from a single point in the throttle body (Figure 3.43). However, whereas a carburettor relies on the creation of a lower pressure area within the venturi to draw in fuel from a reservoir, single-point injection makes use of a single injector that injects fuel (under pressure) directly above the throttle butterfly (throttle valve or plate). Although the fuel pressure for a single-point system is not as high as for multi-point systems, the pressure is higher than that in the intake system. Typical injection pressures for single-point systems are around 1 bar or slightly less.

With single-point injection, all cylinders receive fuel from the single injector. However, because the injector is controlled by an ECU in the same way as on a multi-point injection system, it is possible to use sensors to provide information to the ECU; this therefore provides better control of fuel quantity than a carburettor, but with reduced cost compared with a multi-point injection system.

Disadvantages

The disadvantages of a single-point system are in fact not dissimilar to those of a carburettor; for example, fuel/air separation when the air and fuel mixture flows around corners in the intake system. Additionally, fuel can still condense against the cold manifold walls during cold running.

Single-point injection was quite widely used on four-cylinder engines but these systems were not

Mono-Jetronic schematic diagram
1 Fuel tank, **2** Electric fuel pump, **3** Fuel filter, **4** Fuel pressure regulator, **5** Solenoid operated fuel
injector, **6** Air temperature sensor, **7** ECU, **8** Throttle valve actuator, **9** Throttle valve potentiometer,
10 Canister purge valve, **11** Carbon canister, **12** Lambda oxygen sensor, **13** Engine temperature sensor
14 Ignition distributor, **15** Battery, **16** Ignition start switch, **17** Relay, **18** Diagnosis connection,
19 Central injection unit.

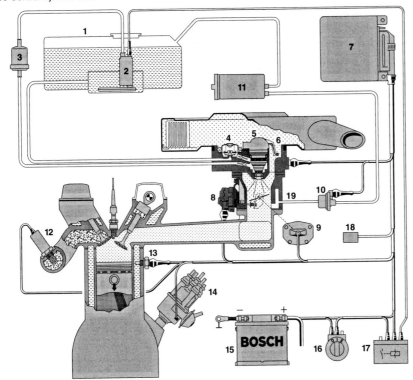

Figure 3.43 Single-point injection system

suitable on longer engines, such as straight six-cylinder engines, because the different intake manifold lengths result in uneven distribution of fuel. This is the same problem that affected many carburettor engines where the length of the intake pipe from the carburettor or single injector to outer cylinders was much greater than to the central cylinders; this resulted in the outer cylinders running more weakly than the inner cylinders. A rich mixture was therefore provided to ensure that all cylinders developed reasonable power and could run reasonably efficiently. However, the central cylinders then operated with a slightly rich mixture, which causes high emissions. Single-point injection is therefore suitable for vehicles with smaller engines, although some V8 engines were fitted with a single-point system; this was possible because the location of the injector within the centre of the V resulted in similar intake pipe lengths to all cylinders.

One other major disadvantage relates to emissions control and emissions control regulations. It is now necessary on modern systems to stop delivery of fuel to a cylinder if that cylinder is operating very inefficiently. If the spark at the plug were very inefficient or failed completely, unburned fuel would flow through the cylinder and into the atmosphere as pollution. Modern multi-point injection systems, can

detect which cylinder is operating inefficiently and switch off the injector to that cylinder. This is not possible on single-point systems where the injector supplies fuel to all cylinders.

3.3.2 Operation of a single-point injection system

Injector (actuator)
The injector (Figure 3.44) operates in much the same way as an injector for a multi-point system. The injector is a solenoid that, when energised, causes the needle to lift off the seat (the typical needle lift is approximately 0.06 mm). A control signal from the ECU opens and closes the injector for a calculated period of time (typically 1.25 ms to 8 ms, depending on operating conditions). It is usual for the injector to be opened at every ignition spark; i.e. on a four-cylinder engine, the injector would be opened each time a spark occurred, which equates to four times for every engine cycle.

Idle speed control (actuator)
As with multi-point injection systems, some form of automated idle speed control is provided. A common

method is to use a stepper motor (see section 3.1.6), which acts on the throttle butterfly via some form of linkage. The ECU controls the stepper motor to either maintain or increase the idle speed for cold running or when load is applied to the engine at idle.

Alternatively, the stepper motor can control a valve, which alters the aperture in a bypass port. The port allows air to bypass the throttle butterfly; therefore, when the valve allows more air to flow through the port, the idle speed increases. Bypass port systems are covered in section 3.1.6.

Sensors

The main information required for a single-point injection system to calculate the required fuel quantity is engine speed and throttle position (throttle opening angle). These two signals provide sufficient information for the ECU to calculate the required quantity of fuel to suit the engine load. In effect, the ECU has an indication of 'air charge' per cylinder from the engine speed and throttle opening signals. Some systems have a MAP sensor to provide additional information relating to engine load.

Ignition trigger or speed signal

On earlier systems, a speed signal was received direct from the ignition system (ignition coil or ignition module). Later when injection and ignition were combined, a signal was provided by a crankshaft speed/position sensor.

Throttle position

A throttle position sensor (usually a potentiometer) provides information relating to throttle angle opening and the rate at which the throttle is being opened or

1 Electrical connection, 2 Fuel return,
3 Fuel inlet, 4 Solenoid winding,
5 Solenoid armature, 6 Valve needle, 7 Pintle.

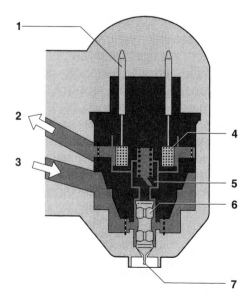

Figure 3.44 Injector for a single-point system

closed. The throttle position sensor operates in the same way as those previously described for multi-point injection systems (sections 3.1 and 3.2). It was, however, common practice to use a set of contacts in the throttle sensor to indicate the closed or idle throttle position.

Air temperature

An air temperature sensor is located in the throttle body (Figure 3.43). Because air density changes with temperature, the information from the sensor assists in calculating the required fuel quantity to match the air density. An air temperature sensor operates in an identical way to air temperature sensors previously covered under multi-point systems (sections 3.1 and 3.2).

Coolant temperature

The operation and function of coolant temperature sensors is the same as for multi-point injection systems (sections 3.1 and 3.2). As with all fuelling systems, enrichment (excess fuel) is needed during cold running, and minor fuelling adjustments can be made for minor changes in engine temperature: the coolant temperature sensor provides the relevant information.

Other sensors

Figure 3.43 shows a lambda (oxygen) sensor and other components that are applicable to emissions control. These components are covered in section 3.5.

Fuel system

The fuel system of a single-point injection system is similar to that of a multi-point system (Figure 3.43). A fuel pump filter and regulator assembly are used, which operate in much the same way as on a multi-point system (see section 3.1.5). However there are two major differences between single-point and multi-point fuel systems. First, single-point systems operate at lower fuel pressures, typically 1 bar.

The second difference is that, because the fuel is injected ahead of (or upstream) of the throttle butterfly, the fuel is injected into a pressure zone that does not change significantly with throttle opening. In section 3.1.5 it was explained that, because a multi-point injector injects fuel into the intake port, the injection pressure is regulated so that it is always at a constant pressure 'above the pressure in the intake port'. The pressure regulator is therefore connected to the intake system pressure so that the regulator can 'sense' intake system pressure.

On a single-point injector, the fuel is injected into a relatively constant pressure zone above the throttle butterfly (which is at atmospheric pressure) and therefore the injection pressure does not need to be altered when the intake pressure changes. The pressure regulator therefore has no connection to the intake pressure.

The fuel supply system and pressure regulator are shown in Figure 3.45.

1 Fuel tank, 2 Electric fuel pump, 3 Fuel filter, 4 Fuel pressure regulator, 5 Fuel injector, 6 Throttle valve.

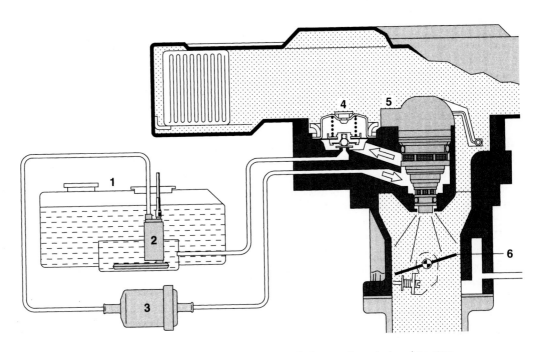

Figure 3.45 Fuel system for a single-point system

Manifold heating

If atomised petrol condenses on cold surfaces, problems can occur when the air:fuel mixture flows through the intake manifold when the engine is cold. On some applications, therefore, an electric heater is located at the base of the intake manifold (Figure 3.46) to help prevent the petrol from condensing.

The heater is switched on when the ignition is initially switched on and during starting; the heater can remain switched on for a number of minutes after starting. During cold running, therefore, the air:fuel mixture flowing from the throttle body is heated, which helps to ensure that the fuel remains atomised.

alternative hot spot
(hedgehog type)

Figure 3.46 Manifold heater on a single-point injection system

3.4   DIRECT PETROL INJECTION

This section covers the basic principles of direct petrol injection (also called gasoline direct injection or GDI). Direct injection systems help to achieve overall combustion efficiencies by operating in conjunction with special combustion chamber designs and with electronic throttle control. In addition, emissions control for direct petrol injection systems is slightly different from that for engines with multi-point port injection. For these reasons, additional information about direct petrol injection is provided in the emissions section (section 3.5).

3.4.1 Benefits of direct injection

Direct injection into the cylinder

Section 3.1.1 mentions older generations of petrol injection systems which used injection pumps to deliver petrol to injectors that were directly injecting into the cylinders. This type of injection was used with considerable success on aircraft engines during the 1930s and 1940s, but the requirements for injection on aircraft engines were slightly different from those for the modern automobile. However, while diesel engines have relied on direct injection through almost the whole life of this type of engine, petrol delivery systems for automobiles were able to be much less sophisticated (i.e. to use carburettors) until emissions regulations forced better control of fuel delivery.

While cost was inevitably a major factor in using relatively inexpensive petrol delivery systems, the technologies and materials that were available at the time also restricted the mass production of what we would now consider to be the ideal fuel system. Modern electronic control and materials have enabled designers to develop fuel injection systems that can efficiently deliver fuel direct to the cylinder, rather than to the intake system.

Figure 3.47 compares multi-point port type injection, single-point (throttle body) injection and direct injection systems.

It is claimed that direct injection, when compared with an equivalent engine with port injection, provides a decrease in fuel consumption in the region of 15% to 20%, while engine power is slightly improved. The details within this section provide an understanding of how these benefits are achieved.

One other benefit is that direct injection systems require very rapid vaporisation of the petrol to enable it to mix quickly with the air. This rapid vaporisation is achieved through the use of high fuel pressures and a special injector nozzle design. Importantly, when a liquid vaporises, it has the effect of drawing heat from the surrounding air, i.e. it cools the surrounding air. Therefore, when fuel is injected into the cylinder, the vaporisation process reduces the temperature of the air in the cylinder, reducing the potential for combustion knock (which can occur if temperatures are too high).

This reduced tendency for combustion knock enables higher compression ratios of around 12:1 to be used (which would otherwise raise cylinder temperatures and cause combustion knock). Thus combustion efficiency is improved, giving more power as well as improved fuel consumption and emissions. In addition, the cooling effect on the air in the cylinder causes the air to become denser; the greater the air density or mass within the cylinder, the greater the power produced.

(a)

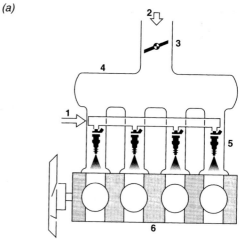

(b)

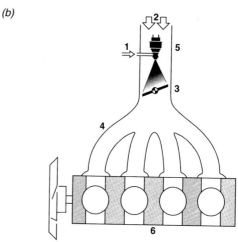

(c)

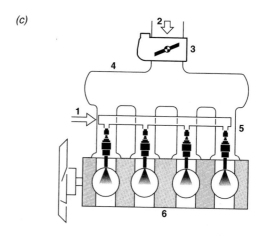

1 Fuel	4 Intake manifold
2 Air	5 Injector
3 Throttle valve	6 Engine

Figure 3.47 Comparison of different types of petrol injection
a Multi-point fuel injection (MPI)
b Throttle body fuel injection (TBI)
c Direct fuel injection (DI)

Mixture formation

Until very recently, the vast majority of petrol engines operated with the air and petrol mixed outside the cylinder (e.g. port type injection); the air and petrol mixture was then drawn into the cylinder during the intake stroke. Although mixing can continue after the air and petrol are inside the cylinder, the initial mixing process starts in the intake manifold (carburettors and single-point injection) or in the intake ports (port injection). With direct injection, the air is still drawn into the cylinder in the conventional manner, but the petrol is injected directly into the cylinder, so mixing occurs only within the cylinder.

> **Key Points**
>
> Gasoline direct injection engines inject fuel directly into the combustion chamber, in a similar way to a diesel engine
>
> These engines have two distinct operating modes for combustion: one is similar to a standard gasoline engine where increased power is needed; the other is similar to diesel engine where economy is most important (e.g. part-load)

One main advantage of mixing the air and petrol in the cylinder is that different mixture formation processes can be achieved using different injection timing. Essentially, there are two types of mixture formation used with direct injection systems: 'homogenous' and 'stratified'.

Homogenous mixture formation

A homogenous mixture is one where the fuel mixes with the air in such a way that the mix is uniform or unvarying throughout the whole volume of air/petrol mix (Figure 3.48a). This means that the whole volume of mixture will have the same air:fuel ratio (no weak or rich pockets of mixture). Therefore, when ignition occurs, all of the mixture will ignite and burn (combust) with equal efficiency and the flame created by initial combustion will therefore spread through the whole mixture (flame prorogation).

In general, a homogenous mixture will operate at or around the stoichiometric air:fuel ratio of 14.7 parts of air to 1 part of petrol (by weight). This is the theoretical ideal ratio which will also provide low emissions of most pollutants. It is possible to operate with weak mixtures of up to 20:1 (or slightly higher) before misfiring occurs. These weaker mixtures provide good economy and low emissions of most pollutants. In practice, maximum torque and power are usually achieved with slightly richer air:fuel ratios of around 12:1 but with higher emissions of some pollutants.

Since the early 1990s in Europe (earlier in the USA), emissions regulations have resulted in engines operating with air:fuel ratios that are generally close to the stoichiometric value for most operating conditions. This allowed catalytic converters to convert most of the pollutants into harmless gases (refer to emissions in section 3.5). Operating at stoichiometric air:fuel ratios

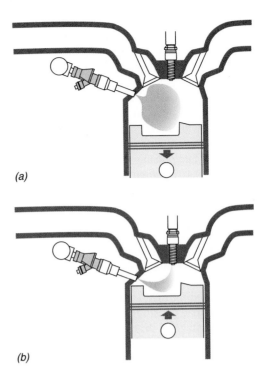

(a)

(b)

Figure 3.48 Homogenous and stratified mixture formation
a Homogenous mixture formation
b Stratified mixture formation

throughout the mixture effectively means that the mixture should be homogenous under all engine operating conditions.

Stratified mixture formation

With stratified mixture formation, a small isolated pocket or cloud of air:fuel mixture is created within the cylinder; the remainder of the air is effectively pure (Figure 3.48b). In reality, it is possible to have a pocket of mixture with a stoichiometric air:fuel ratio (which therefore burns normally), while the remaining air is either completely free of any petrol or has a very small amount of petrol mixed in, i.e. it is very weak.

The small pocket of mixture is directed by the airflow within the combustion chamber so that it is directly exposed to the spark plug. When the spark occurs, therefore, it is only this pocket or cloud of mixture that ignites and combusts. The combustion of this isolated cloud of mixture is used to heat up all of the remaining air, thus producing expansion of the gas within the cylinder. If the remaining 'fresh air' does in fact contain a small quantity of petrol (forming a very weak mixture), it will combust slowly, which will in fact assist in the expansion of the gases.

It should, however, be noted that a stratified mixture formation will not produce as much energy or force within the cylinder as a fully homogenous mix of air and petrol, because only a small percentage of the full charge of air in the cylinder is used to generate the heat. With homogenous mixtures, the full charge of air is mixed with petrol, and therefore all of the mix combusts. It is also possible to alter the air:fuel ratio for the small pocket of mixture so that this pocket also operates on a weaker mixture, but the mixture must be rich enough to achieve good combustion.

The important point to remember is that, although the small localised pocket of mixture has an air:fuel ratio that is rich enough to achieve combustion, the overall mixture within the cylinder has an excess of air because of the large volume of pure air in the rest of the cylinder. It is in fact possible to achieve a total air:fuel ratio of up to 40:1 (the total quantity of air compared with the total quantity of petrol).

The obvious advantage of stratified mixture formation is that the amount of fuel required is much smaller than for homogenous mixtures and therefore fuel consumption is much lower. However, a stratified mixture formation cannot produce the same power as a homogenous mixture, which means that stratified mixes can be used for light engine load operation (idle speed and light load cruising).

One disadvantage of stratified mixture formation is that, at higher engine speeds, excessive turbulence is created, which does not allow the formation of the cloud or pocket of gas to localise around the spark plug tip. This results in poor combustion. Additionally, if an increase in power or torque is required, the air:fuel ratio provided to the pocket of mixture must be richer. This can lead to very small, but very rich, zones of mixture (within the cloud) which result in soot being produced.

Stratified mixture formation is therefore ideal for light load conditions and lower engine speeds, but, when engine speeds increase above mid-range (typically around 3000 rev/min) or increased engine torque and power are required, the engine must operate with a homogenous mixture.

Injection timing

Most direct injection petrol engines operate with stratified and homogenous mixture formations depending on operating conditions. This is achieved by controlling the injection timing. Direct injection systems generally have two distinct timing periods, which provide different characteristics for mixing the air and fuel. One timing period is during the induction (intake) stroke; the other is at the end of the compression stroke.

Intake stroke injection timing

When petrol is injected during the intake stroke (while the air is being drawn into the cylinder), the fuel will mix with all of the air in the cylinder, resulting in complete mixing or homogenous mixture formation. Note that the intake ports can be designed to create swirl or controlled turbulence of the air entering the cylinder, which assists in mixing the petrol with the air. The mixture is typically at or close to the stoichiometric air:fuel ratio, thus enabling good power to be produced with reasonably low emission of pollutants. The high fuel injection pressures used and the design of the injector nozzle create good atomisation of the petrol,

improving the mixing process, which continues during the intake and compression strokes. Figure 3.48 shows the injection of fuel during the intake stroke.

Compression stroke injection timing

A relatively small amount of petrol is injected at the end of the compression stroke, just prior to ignition (Figure 3.48). The design of the combustion chamber includes an area (usually in the top of the piston crown) which promotes swirl or turbulence in a small, localised region. This allows the injected fuel to mix with a small pocket of air, forming a small pocket or cloud of mixed air and petrol. The small pocket of mixture is then directed to the spark plug tip, ensuring ignition of the mixture.

To create the small localised pocket of air:fuel mixture requires special piston and combustion chamber design. In addition, the location of the spark plug and injector in the cylinder are critical. One specific design features an additional flap in the intake tract (known as a charge motion valve). This is used in conjunction with a specially shaped piston crown and inlet manifold design to provide the required gas behaviour in stratified operation mode. This characteristic behaviour is known as 'tumble'. The flap valve is actuated electronically via a stepper motor and is controlled by the ECU. The angle of this valve reduces the cross sectional area of the inlet manifold, thus increasing gas velocity and tumble imparted to the incoming air charge during stratified operation. During homogeneous operation this valve is fully open and has no effect.

Using both timing periods

Direct injection systems in petrol engines generally use both timing periods (intake stroke and compression stroke timing) independently, depending on the operating conditions. For light load driving and at idle, compression stroke injection timing means that very lean mixtures can be used (stratified mixture formation), which provides low power but good economy. When higher engine power is required or when the engine is operating at higher speeds, the injection timing changes to the intake stroke, providing a full charge of mixed air and petrol to the cylinder (homogenous mixture formation).

Because the injector timing is entirely controlled by the ECU, it is possible to time the injection to any point in the engine operating cycle. The exact time of injection during the intake stroke period and the compression stroke period can therefore be adjusted to suit the exact operating conditions, such as speed, temperature, etc.

There are also certain conditions under which injection takes place on both the intake and the compression strokes. A small quantity of fuel is delivered on the intake stroke, which produces a homogenous but weak mixture. Injection occurs again on the compression stroke to produce a normal stratified charge (which will have an air:fuel ratio that is close to stoichiometric). With this dual injection process, the stratified charge ignites and combusts normally which then creates combustion in the rest of the air (which has a weak homogenous mixture). This process produces more power or torque than when the system is operating with only a stratified mixture formation. This is used when the system is changing from stratified to homogenous operation to provide a smooth transition.

Throttle control and mixture control to regulate power and torque

While direct injection has a number of advantages that on their own help to improve engine efficiency and reduce emissions, it is the fact that direct injection allows 'stratified mixture formation' to be used that provides the greatest benefit. With direct injection, there are effectively two types of mixture formation and combustion process that can be used at different times (see injection timing above). However, getting the full benefit of both these processes, especially the stratified mixture formation, requires additional changes to engine design and engine control.

Filling the cylinder with air

Ideally, a cylinder should be fully charged with air at the end of the intake stroke (the largest possible volume of air), causing higher pressures at the end of the compression stroke. When combustion occurs, the heat produced causes the air to expand, but when a higher volume of air is compressed into the small combustion chamber, the expansion will be greater.

Ideally therefore there should be no restrictions that could prevent the cylinder from filling with air during the intake stroke. Unfortunately, petrol engines have traditionally had a throttle butterfly to regulate airflow into the cylinder as a means of controlling engine torque and power: when the engine is operating at light loads the throttle is almost fully closed, restricting the airflow into the cylinder. The cylinder is therefore only partially filled with air, resulting in low efficiency (low volumetric efficiency). Additionally, power is wasted by the pumping action of the piston on the intake stroke, which is trying to draw air through the restriction.

To avoid this, the throttle should remain as far open as possible to enable improved volumetric efficiency with subsequent improvements during the combustion and expansion phases. This is in fact achievable with direct injection by holding the throttle open during light

load conditions and then using an alternative means of controlling torque and power. The throttle is electrically operated using a stepper motor or similar device, which is in turn controlled by the system ECU (see engine management systems, section 3.1.6).

Controlling power by altering the air:fuel ratio

As explained earlier in this section, when an engine has direct fuel injection, the stratified mixture formation process is used during light load operation. It is possible to alter the air:fuel ratio of the stratified charge (the small pocket of mixture), which will alter the energy produced during the combustion and expansion phases. So, if a weak stratified charge mixture is used, less energy will be produced compared with when the mixture is at the ideal air:fuel ratio (or slightly richer).

Therefore if the throttle is held in the open position (by controlling the stepper motor), a full charge of air will fill the cylinder on each intake stroke, but the energy produced on the power stroke will be regulated by the air:fuel ratio in the small pocket of mixture.

Note that when the engine is required to produce more power because the load is increasing (when accelerating), it must operate with a homogenous mixture formation. The stratified mixture formation process operates with air:fuel ratios that are much too weak to enable good torque and power to be produced. Air:fuel ratios must be controlled within a fairly tight tolerance for homogenous operation, so it is not possible to use changes in air:fuel ratio to control torque and power: the throttle must be used to control the torque and power.

Different processes for different operating conditions

Depending on the driving conditions, the engine therefore operates with different processes as shown in Figure 3.49.

3.4.2 Operation and components

Evolution from port injection systems

Direct injection systems have many similarities to the port injection systems described earlier, so many of the components (sensors and actuators) are identical or

Figure 3.49 Using the different operating processes for different operating conditions

Condition	Stratified or homogenous	Intake or compression stroke injection	Power regulation: throttle or air:fuel ratio
Light load and idle (above mid-range engine speeds, the system reverts to homogenous operation)	Stratified	Compression	air:fuel ratio
Load (torque and power)	Homogenous	Intake	Throttle
Transition from stratified to homogenous	Stratified and homogenous	Intake and compression	Throttle
Cold running (warm-up phase)	Homogenous	Intake	Throttle

very similar. In effect, direct injection is an evolution from port injection. The main physical differences are the fuel system pressures, fuel pumps and the location of the injectors.

While the injectors are inevitably more robust to cope with the harsh environment within the cylinder (high pressure and temperatures), the principle of operation is the same as for port type injectors.

The ECU is in principle the same as those used on port type systems, but inevitably, different programming is used to control the slightly different operating processes. In this section, therefore, detailed descriptions will be provided only for those components, sub-systems and processes that are significantly different from those of port injection systems.

Injectors

Injectors used in direct injection systems operate in much the same way as for those in port injection systems: the injector is constructed with a solenoid that opens the injector valve by moving the needle off a seat, thus allowing fuel to flow through the valve. The opening time and opening duration of the solenoid are controlled by the ECU so that the required quantity of fuel is injected at exactly the correct time. Figure 3.50 shows an injector used on a direct injection system.

Vaporising the fuel

To provide a good mixture of air and fuel in both stratified and homogenous mixture formations requires finely vaporised petrol. The high pressures (typically up to 5 bar) used by direct injection systems, in

conjunction with the injector nozzle design, cause the petrol to be delivered from the injector in very fine droplets that can vaporise rapidly before they contact the cylinder or piston surfaces, which could then cause the fuel to return to a liquid state. The rapid vaporisation provides much quicker mixing with the air. However, an additional benefit is that, when vaporisation occurs, it has a cooling effect on the air, which lowers the potential for combustion knock.

High voltage for rapid opening

The injectors have a very limited time in which to deliver the fuel to the cylinders. On port injection systems, the whole of one engine cycle is available for injecting fuel, i.e. two crankshaft revolutions (where each cylinder can pass through the four strokes and fuel can be injected at almost any time or all the time if necessary). With direct injection, there is only limited time on the induction stroke or on the compression stroke to inject the fuel; the injectors must therefore open as quickly as possible to maximise the time available to be used for injecting fuel.

While the ECU produces the control signal in the same way as on a port injection system, the control signal is then transmitted to a driver module which is usually separate from the ECU. The driver module contains capacitors that are charged up while the injector is switched off (closed). When the 'on' section of the control signal is received by the driver module (indicating the start of injection), the capacitor rapidly discharges at between 50 and 100 volts (depending on system design); this high voltage is discharged through the injector circuit. This short high voltage discharge from the capacitor causes a very rapid and strong build-up of the magnetic field in the injector solenoid winding, which in turn causes the injector needle to quickly lift off the nozzle seating. Once the injector is open, current flow through the injector solenoid winding is reduced and a 'hold on' voltage of around 7 volts is used to hold the injector open until it is time to close the injector.

Injection pressure

In direct injection systems, fuel can be injected at the end of the compression stroke, when cylinder pressures can reach 20 bar. To obtain the required atomisation of the fuel in this high pressure environment and to deliver the required quantity of fuel quickly, it is necessary to use a high fuel injection pressure. The pressure in the fuel rail (to which all the injectors are connected), is typically around 120 bar (see fuel delivery system later in this section).

Throttle control

Section 3.4.1 explained that, when the engine is operating with the stratified mixture formation process, the throttle is held open and engine torque is controlled using changes in the air:fuel ratio. The throttle must therefore not be directly connected to the throttle pedal, and is in fact controlled by the ECU, which sends

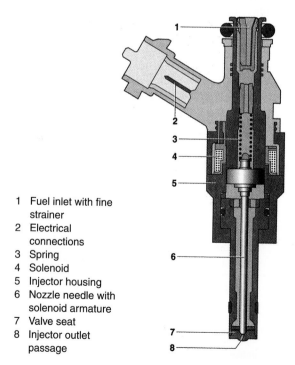

1 Fuel inlet with fine strainer
2 Electrical connections
3 Spring
4 Solenoid
5 Injector housing
6 Nozzle needle with solenoid armature
7 Valve seat
8 Injector outlet passage

Figure 3.50 Direct injection high pressure injector

control signals to a motor (usually a stepper motor), making the throttle open and close as required.

In effect, the driver selects a desired level of performance or engine operation in the usual way by moving the throttle pedal. The throttle pedal is connected to a potentiometer and, as the throttle pedal is moved, an analogue signal is sent to the ECU. The ECU can control the opening of the throttle depending on the driver input via the throttle pedal and on other factors such as temperature, engine speed, etc. However, when the system is operating using the stratified mixture formation process, the throttle is held open and engine power is controlled by changes in the air:fuel ratio.

Figure 3.51 shows an electronically controlled throttle assembly.

Sensors

The sensors used for direct injection systems are generally the same as those used for conventional multi-point port injection systems, but an additional sensor measures pressure in the fuel delivery rail. A direct injection system forms part of a complete engine management system, which also controls ignition, emissions systems and other engine related systems, so reference should be made to section 3.6, as well as Chapter 1, which covers sensors used in modern fuel injection systems.

Although the sensors used are generally the same as those previously described for port injection systems, there are slight differences relating to measurement of the mass of air entering the cylinders.

Mass airflow measurement

It is important to note that, when the engine is operating with an open throttle and engine power is controlled by the air:fuel ratio, there is effectively little restriction in airflow through the intake system, so there is little reduction in pressure in the intake manifold and ports. Remember that the low pressure or depression in a throttled engine is caused by the restriction of the throttle butterfly. Changes in manifold depression are therefore not as significant as with a throttled engine, but it is more difficult to calculate the mass of airflow.

Many direct injection systems use a hot film airflow sensor (see sections 1.5.5 and 3.2.3), which can be used in conjunction with an intake manifold pressure sensor (section 1.5.4). An air temperature sensor is integrated with the hot film sensor assembly. The combined information from the sensors enables the ECU to make appropriate adjustments for the mass of air entering the system.

Other systems use two pressure sensors: one measures the atmospheric or ambient air pressure; the second measures the intake manifold pressure. An air temperature sensor is also used. The ECU uses the information to make the appropriate air mass calculations.

The ECU uses its calculations about the mass of air induced into the engine to provide the appropriate signals to control the amount of fuel to be injected, and also other functions such as ignition timing.

Fuel delivery system

The fuel delivery system has to provide fuel at much higher pressures than on normal, port injection systems, to enable fuel to be injected into the cylinder when cylinder pressures are high (on the compression stroke). Additionally, higher injection pressures help to create better fuel atomisation and vaporisation.

Low pressure pumping system

A conventional low pressure electric pump (the same as that on a port injection system) is used to move the petrol from the tank to a high pressure pump. The low pressure system operates at around 3 bar to 5 bar, depending on the system design. A high pressure pump is driven by the engine (usually from the camshaft) and delivers fuel to the fuel rail at pressures up to 120 bar.

The low pressure system has a pressure regulator, which is usually located in the fuel tank with the fuel pump. When the fuel pressure exceeds the required value, excess fuel is released from the regulator and is allowed to flow back into the tank. A normal fuel filter is also usually located in the tank. Figure 3.52 shows the basic layout of a low pressure system which feeds fuel to the high pressure pump.

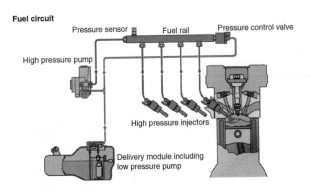

Figure 3.52 Low and high pressure fuel pumping system for direct petrol injection

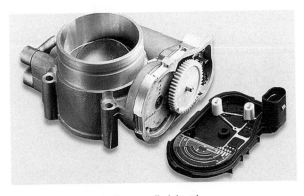

Figure 3.51 Electronically controlled throttle

High pressure pumping system

There are two main types of high pressure pumping system, shown in Figures 3.53 and 3.54.

The example in Figure 3.53 is referred to as a 'continuous delivery' system. The engine driven pump provides an excess of fuel to the fuel rail; i.e. it supplies a greater quantity of fuel than is consumed by the engine. The pump volume will increase with engine speed, which will result in excessively high fuel pressures. However, a pressure control valve (or regulator valve) is fitted at the end of the fuel rail, which allows excess fuel to flow back to the low pressure system. The pressure control valve is electrically operated (usually a solenoid type) and controlled by the ECU, which provides a control signal to the valve.

The ECU receives information from a pressure sensor, which is also located on the fuel rail. In response to the signal from the pressure sensor, the ECU controls the regulator valve, adjusting the pressure to the required value. The control valve also acts as a mechanical safety valve in case fuel pressure exceeds safe limits. The excess fuel flowing from the control valve then flows back to the low pressure side of the system.

The example shown in Figure 3.54 is referred to as a 'demand controlled' system. The fuel pump contains a fuel quantity control valve which regulates the flow of fuel from the pumping element. In effect, the control valve performs a similar function to the pressure control valve described in the previous section, except that, in this example, when the quantity control valve opens it allows excess fuel to flow directly from the pump back to the return line. In this system, it is therefore possible

to control the quantity of fuel delivered by the pump to match engine requirements.

The ECU uses the pressure sensor signal to identify fuel pressure and then control the 'quantity control valve' to regulate pressure to the required value.

Three barrel pump

The three barrel pump shown in Figure 3.55 has three pumping plungers which are forced to move along the barrel through the rotation of a cam ring located on the main pump shaft (an eccentric element). The pump is usually mounted on the engine, with the pump shaft driven by the engine camshaft. While the engine is turning, the three plungers will move up the barrels due to the action of the cam ring, and a return spring forces the plungers to return down the barrels. This movement of the plungers forces fuel (delivered by the low pressure pump to the high pressure pump) to be pumped out to the fuel rail at high volume and pressure. A separate pressure control valve then regulates fuel pressure.

The use of three plungers and the shape of the cam ring ensure that the pumping action from the three plungers overlaps; this reduces the pressure pulsations and fluctuations produced by the individual plungers.

Single barrel pump

The single barrel pump is mounted so that a cam lobe on the engine camshaft can act against a single plunger. Fuel flows from the low pressure system into the high pressure plunger, and, in the example shown in Figure 3.56, the pump uses the integral ECU controlled quantity control valve to control the quantity of fuel that is able to flow back to the return line. When the valve is fully open, all of the fuel pumped by the

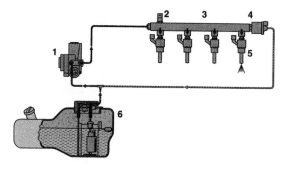

Figure 3.53 Continuous fuel delivery system

1 High pressure pump HDP1
2 High pressure sensor
3 Fuel rail
4 Pressure control valve
5 High pressure fuel injectors
6 Fuel tank with pump module, including pre-supply pump

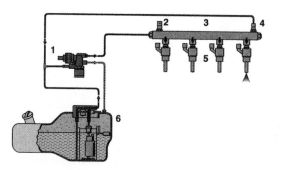

Figure 3.54 Demand controlled fuel delivery system

1 High pressure pump HDP2
2 High pressure sensor
3 Fuel rail
4 Pressure limiter
5 High pressure fuel injectors
6 Fuel tank with pump module, including pre-supply pump

plunger flows back to the return line, but when the valve is closed, all the fuel flows to the fuel rail. By continuously moving the control valve between the open and closed positions, the amount of fuel flowing to the fuel rail can be controlled as required by the injectors.

A pulsation damper or pressure attenuator is used to dampen the pressure pulses produced by the single plunger. The damper has a diaphragm that is forced against the fuel pressure by a spring. When pressure pulses occur, the diaphragm moves against the spring, creating a larger volume above the plunger which slightly reduces the pressure. As the plunger rises and falls, creating pressure pulses, the diaphragm also moves to create larger and smaller volumes above the plunger, thus damping the pressure pulses. In addition, the fuel rail contains a large volume of fuel, which also helps to reduce pressure fluctuations.

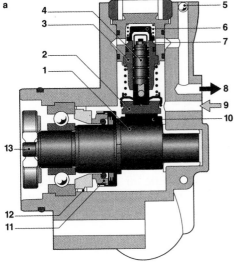

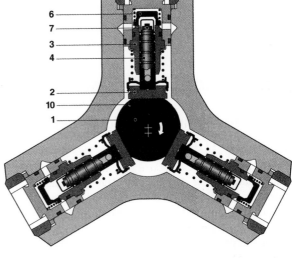

1	Eccentric element	8	High pressure
2	Slipper		connection to rail
3	Pump barrel	9	Fuel inlet (low pressure)
4	Pump plunger (hollow	10	Cam ring
	piston, fuel inlet)	11	Axial seal (sleeve seal)
5	Sealing ball	12	Static seal
6	Outlet valve	13	Input shaft
7	Inlet valve		

Figure 3.55 Three barrel high pressure pump
a Longitudinal section
b Cross-section

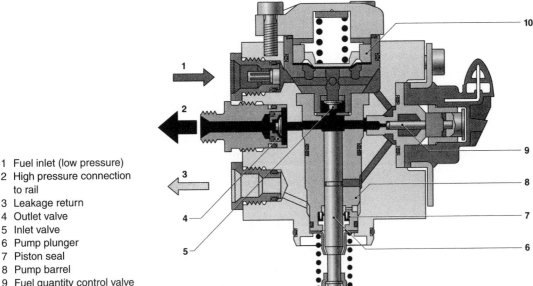

1 Fuel inlet (low pressure)
2 High pressure connection to rail
3 Leakage return
4 Outlet valve
5 Inlet valve
6 Pump plunger
7 Piston seal
8 Pump barrel
9 Fuel quantity control valve
10 Fuel pressure attenuator

Figure 3.56 Single barrel high pressure pump

Injection system pressure during starting

When the engine is being cranked for starting, there is little or no residual pressure in the high pressure system. Full pressure is not produced by the high pressure pump until the engine is turning over at higher speeds. During starting, the injectors are timed to inject during the intake stroke when the cylinder pressure is low; it is therefore possible to use low pressure fuel (that is flowing out of the high pressure pump) for starting. When the engine is turning at a sufficient speed, so the pump is delivering high pressures, the pressure sensor signal indicates the higher pressure value to the ECU, which can then alter the injection timing to the compression stroke, provided, of course, that this is appropriate for the operating conditions.

Injection pressure in a gasoline direct injection engine is much higher than a port injected gasoline engine. This pressure is monitored and controlled by the ECU

The fuel supply system consists of a low pressure pump to lift the fuel from the tank as well as a high pressure pump to raise the pressure to injection pressure levels. The high pressure pump is engine driven; the low pressure pump is electrical

3.5   EMISSIONS AND EMISSION CONTROL (PETROL ENGINES)

3.5.1 Lambda and the stoichiometric air:fuel ratio

The excess air factor

References have been made here and in *Hillier's Fundamentals of Motor Vehicle Technology: Book 1* to the stoichiometric air:fuel ratio, i.e. the ratio of air and fuel that would in theory provide complete combustion. It is usually quoted as 14.7 parts of air to 1 part of fuel by weight (e.g. 14.7 grams of air for 1 gram of petrol). In reality, it is oxygen contained within the air which is required for the combustion process. To obtain the appropriate quantity of oxygen, it is necessary to mix the air and petrol in the stoichiometric ratio. It is interesting to note that the quoted ratio is 14.7:1 by weight, but if the volumes of the two elements are compared, the volume of air is approximately 9500 times larger than the volume of petrol. Therefore every litre of petrol burned in an engine requires 9500 litres of air to be drawn in (assuming the stoichiometric ratio is used).

There has been a tendency in recent years to refer to the correct ratio of petrol and air as the 'air factor' or more precisely the 'excess air factor'. The stoichiometric air:fuel ratio should provide the correct amount of oxygen, which can be regarded as 1. The Greek symbol lambda (λ) is used to indicate the excess air factor as shown below:

1 If the mixture is correct, then the excess air factor is correct, which is expressed as $\lambda = 1$ (lambda = 1).

2 If there is too much air (a weak mixture) then the excess air factor is greater than 1, which is expressed as $\lambda > 1$ (lambda is greater than 1).

3 If there is too little air (a rich mixture) then the excess air factor is less than 1, which is expressed as $\lambda < 1$ (lambda is less than 1).

Emissions control systems often function efficiently only when there is the appropriate amount of oxygen in the exhaust gas (see section 3.5.6 and other parts of section 3.5).

Comparison of lambda and air:fuel ratios

Figure 3.57 shows a comparison between the air:fuel ratio scale and the lambda scale. Note that the stoichiometric value of 14.7:1 relates to lambda = 1 ($\lambda =1$). When the air/fuel mixture is weaker, the lambda value increases, i.e. lambda is greater than 1 ($\lambda > 1$). When the air/fuel mixture is rich, lambda is less than 1 ($\lambda < 1$).

Lambda window

Although the ideal air:fuel ratio is 14.7:1 ($\lambda = 1$), there is a small tolerance or window for an air:fuel ratio that results in low emissions and good combustion. The amount of oxygen contained within the exhaust gas is critical to the operation of catalytic converters (section 3.5.6) and some other emission reducing devices. To ensure the correct amount of oxygen is contained within the exhaust (for efficient catalytic converter operation) it is necessary to operate the engine at the stoichiometric air:fuel ratio (i.e. $\lambda = 1$). At this ratio,

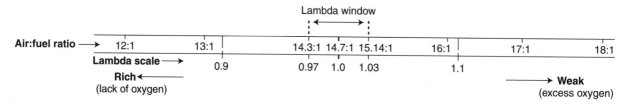

Figure 3.57 Lambda (excess air factor) compared with the air:fuel ratio scale

the CO, HC and O_2 are in a balance so the catalytic converter can function at its most efficient and reduce pollutant levels. However, as mentioned above, there is a window of tolerance for the air:fuel ratio, within which the catalytic converter can still function efficiently; this tolerance is referred to as the lambda window.

The lambda window range is generally quoted at a lambda value of 0.97 to 1.03. Figure 3.57 provides an indication of the air:fuel ratio corresponding to the lambda window.

If the air:fuel ratio is controlled accurately so that the excess air factor is always within the lambda window, the catalytic converter will operate at optimum efficiency at all times. However, section 3.5.4 explains that under certain engine operating conditions, it is necessary to operate with air:fuel ratios that are outside the lambda window.

3.5.2 Pollutants and the environment

Worldwide problem

Environmental considerations have forced many countries to introduce regulations to limit the pollution caused by motor vehicles. Emissions from motor vehicles damage human health, plant life and the environment. Problems are particularly severe in areas where the geographic and climatic conditions create an atmospheric envelope which traps the pollutants.

The first countries of the world to introduce stringent emission controls were the USA, Australia, Japan and Sweden. The EU has for many years enforced strict emission regulations, especially since the early 1990s. This has resulted in very significant changes in automotive technology and design. Each time new emission standards are introduced, the limits are reduced. Manufacturers have to continually update their vehicles to meet requirements adopted in the country in which they are to be sold.

Although most industrial nations now recognise the problems of pollution from vehicles, and therefore impose legislation, not all countries or regions impose the same standards. However, the main vehicle producing nations have to manufacture vehicles that comply with the tougher regulations imposed in the countries where their vehicles are sold in volume, so emissions control systems are still reasonably effective even for those vehicles sold into countries where legislation is weaker.

Pollutants and the petrol engine

With vehicles powered by petrol engines, there are specific areas of the vehicle's operation that cause pollution:

- *exhaust gas* – can contain unburned fuel (HC), partially burned fuel (CO), dangerous nitrogen oxides (NO_x) from combustion, and lead (Pb) from

petrol additives (leaded fuel is no longer widely used on most modern vehicles)
- *crankcase* – during engine operation, emissions are passed into the crankcase, including some combustion gases which pass the piston, vaporised lubrication oil (HC) and corrosive acid compounds
- *fuel system including the fuel tank* – the petrol that is stored in the fuel tank gives off a vapour (HC).

Devices used to 'clean up' vehicle pollutants are costly, and their use has often resulted in a lower power output and higher fuel consumption. Consequently, the trend has been for manufacturers to fit emission control devices only if they are required to meet local country regulations. However, modern technologies are changing this situation, because most emission control technologies are not as restrictive to engine power or as 'fuel thirsty' as older emission control systems. Emission control is therefore becoming more consistent across most regions of the world.

Conflicting requirements

Emission control and emissions reduction systems are often complex in their operation, and frequently rely on chemical and thermal reactions to achieve the desired results. However, there have been, and still are, many systems or designs which reduce one or more pollutants but which increase the emission of other pollutants. When this happens, it is necessary to treat the increased pollutant, so, emission control systems must work together to reduce the levels of all the various pollutants.

It is also true that some emission reduction systems reduce power or increase fuel consumption, but this is becoming less of a problem owing to the technologies available, and the philosophy of 'reducing pollution at source'; i.e. engines are now designed to be more efficient or 'pollution conscious'. This is a reversal of the trend from the early days of emission control when existing engine designs produced high emissions levels, and treatment of the pollution occurred after the pollutants had been created by the engine. However, even the latest engines with exceptional combustion efficiencies still produce pollutants that must be reduced by subsequent means. This method of pollutant reduction is often referred to as 'after treatment'.

One conflicting area of emission control that is increasingly becoming a focus of attention is the improved efficiency of converting the pollutants into the so-called harmless gases. Within the exhaust gas, the three largest components are in fact not normally regarded as pollutants:

- *nitrogen (N_2)* – approximately 71.5% of the exhaust gas (but note that nitrogen forms almost 78% of the atmosphere, and is not regarded as a pollutant)
- *water (H_2O)* – approximately 13.1% of the exhaust gas (again, not regarded as a pollutant)
- *carbon dioxide (CO_2)* – a product of complete or efficient combustion, representing approximately

13.7% of the exhaust gas (not regarded as a harmful pollutant but is now of concern, as explained below).

The primary concern with regard to the harmless gases is carbon dioxide (CO_2), which is not a toxic or directly harmful pollutant but which does have an influence on global warming. Unfortunately, the more complete the combustion of fuel, the greater the level of CO_2.

Note that CO_2 naturally exists in the atmosphere; animals breathe out CO_2, and it is absorbed by plants. The problem is that the level of CO_2 in the atmosphere has increased (due to the burning and combustion of fossil fuels), which is upsetting the natural balance of atmospheric gases. This is added to by the destruction of plant life (especially the rainforests). The overall increase in CO_2 is a significant factor in the greenhouse effect which leads to global warming.

The problem is that increased efficiency of combustion leads to an increase of CO_2. Furthermore, when some of the true pollutants are treated, they are also converted to CO_2. In effect, during combustion, the hydrocarbons in the petrol mix combine with oxygen in the air to form CO_2, and any unburned or partially burned fuel emitted from the combustion chamber is then treated in a catalytic converter and also turned into CO_2.

The only effective way of reducing production of CO_2 is to reduce the consumption of fuel. This can be achieved by operating on leaner (weaker) air:fuel ratios, such as are achieved with direct injection systems.

Composition of the exhaust gas

Figure 3.58 shows the composition of exhaust gas when the combustion process takes place with a stoichiometric air:fuel ratio ($\lambda = 1$).

Emission regulations for petrol engines
Test programme

Before any new vehicle can be sold in the EU, and many other countries, a number of examples of the vehicle must be submitted to the regulating body of a member state for tests to be carried out. This is to test whether the vehicle type meets current legislated standards.

Each vehicle has to complete a test cycle which reflects the vehicle being driven in an urban environment. The process is similar in most countries where emissions legislation is in force.

The vehicle is started from cold and subjected to various speeds, including motorway type driving. To monitor the emissions accurately the tests are carried out with a vehicle dynamometer. The tests involve a standardised driving procedure, including engine at idle, as well as gear changing and braking, to simulate driving conditions in a reasonably sized town.

Previous emission regulations limits were determined on the cubic capacity of the engine. However in 1992 the EU introduced EU Stage I emission regulations with which all new vehicles had to comply (Figure 3.59). In January 1996, the EU imposed stricter emission limits with EU Stage II. In 2000, vehicle manufacturers had to ensure that vehicles met EU Stage III emission standards before they could be sold. In 2005 all new vehicles had to comply with EU Stage IV.

So far we have described engine combustion related emissions. Vehicles are also subject to evaporative emission testing, i.e. emissions that are emitted through the vaporisation of fuel stored in the fuel tank and contained in the fuel pipes. These tests are carried out in a gas-tight chamber at various ambient temperatures, with the engine stationary and running.

Engines submitted for test must also be designed to run on unleaded petrol, to reduce lead based additives in fuels. In addition the petrol tank filler pipe must be designed to prevent the tank from being filled from a petrol pump delivery nozzle with an external diameter of 23.6 mm or greater. This regulation means that nozzles of pumps supplying lead free petrol have to be smaller than those used with pumps dispensing leaded fuel.

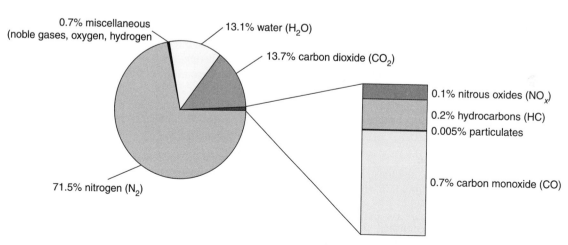

Figure 3.58 Composition of exhaust gas

Figure 3.59 EU Emissions regulations

Standard	Year of introduction	CO g/km	HC g/km	NO_x g/km	NO_x + HC g/km
EU Stage I	July 1992	2.72	N/A	N/A	0.97
EU Stage II	January 1996	2.2	N/A	N/A	0.5
EU Stage III	January 2000	2.3	0.2	0.15	N/A
EU Stage IV	January 2005	1.0	0.1	0.08	N/A

Different emissions reduction technologies

The method adopted by an engine designer to meet the emission limits depends on the technology available to a manufacturer. When it appeared likely that one option to reduce emissions would involve the fitting of a catalytic converter and its accompanying fuel mixture control system, the likely cost for use on small and medium sized cars would be relatively high compared with the cost of the vehicle. This encouraged many manufacturers to develop lean burn engines. Tests show that this type of engine gives a good fuel economy and a much lower emission level than conventional engines. It was expected that the lean burn engine would meet the expected future emission requirements, but the introduction in 1989 of a more stringent standard that was based on a new European extra-urban driving cycle (EUDC) meant that to attain the new limits, even the lean burn engine would need to be fitted with an exhaust catalyst.

It is only recently that developments in direct petrol injection systems met with the requirements to use less fuel (for CO_2 reductions), so lean burn processes are again becoming viable. The use of stratified mixture formation (see section 3.4) and different types of catalytic converter design now enable very lean mixtures to be used under light load and at lower engine speeds.

3.5.3 The pollutants

Creation of pollutants

As noted earlier, when complete combustion occurs, the fuel and oxygen combine to form carbon dioxide (CO_2). Put simply, one carbon atom combines with two oxygen atoms. The thermal reaction within the cylinder (the combustion process) is most efficient when the air:fuel ratio is stoichiometric. In theory, if this ratio is used all the time, all of the fuel and oxygen combust and produce carbon dioxide. Therefore, in theory there should be no unburned fuel or unburned oxygen. Carbon dioxide is a product of complete combustion. Water (H_2O) and nitrogen (N_2) are also emitted. With the carbon dioxide they form just over 98% of the exhaust gas. However the remaining gases include oxygen and hydrogen but also include pollutants, which represent around 1% of the total exhaust gas.

The 1% of exhaust gas that is regarded as pollution can be broken down into three main pollutants (see Figure 3.60): carbon monoxide (CO), hydrocarbons (HC), and oxides of nitrogen (NO_x). In addition, very small percentages of 'particulates' exist which are effectively soot, but for petrol engines the percentage is exceptionally low and generally not of concern. Diesel engines produce much more soot, which is regarded as a diesel engine pollutant that must be treated.

Figure 3.60 Main pollutants from internal combustion engines

Pollutant	Origin	Effects
Carbon monoxide (CO)	Incomplete combustion or partially burned fuel	Poisonous to human beings when inhaled, CO adheres to haemoglobin in the blood and prevents oxygen being carried to body cells
Hydrocarbons (HC)	Unburned fuel, vaporised fuel escaping from fuel system	Irritates eyes and nose. Cancer risk. Odour
Carbon (C)	Partially burned fuel	Smoke – restriction in visibility. Can carry carcinogens (cancer causing agents). Odour
NO_x (oxides of nitrogen – NO and NO_2)	Very high combustion temperatures cause nitrogen to combine with oxygen. Highest when air:fuel ratio is just slightly weaker than stoichiometric ratio	Toxic to humans. NO_2 combines with water to form nitrous acid, which causes lung disorders. It combines with other exhaust products to give eye and nose irritants; it also affects the nervous system. Component of smog
Lead (Pb)	Added to petrol to raise octane rating. Lead is no longer allowed as an additive in fuel in most regions; it also damages catalytic converters	Toxic to humans, causing blood poisoning and nervous disorders

The exhaust gas also includes sulphur compounds in very small quantities and these are not regulated by legislation. However, the compounds (primarily sulphur dioxide (SO_2)) are produced because of sulphates in the fuel. The amount of sulphate in the fuel is subject to legislation which has progressively restricted the level from 1000 ppm (parts per million) down to 50 ppm.

Figure 3.60 shows the main pollutants that are subject to emissions legislation and therefore subject to reduction processes. Those pollutants that occur during combustion are referred to as byproducts of combustion.

Treating or reducing the pollutants

There are effectively two main routes to reducing pollutants.

1   The first route is to design the engine, fuel system and ignition system so that lower levels of pollutants are produced during combustion. Much progress has been made in these areas in recent years and modern designs of combustion chambers, fuel systems and ignition systems have all contributed to substantial reductions in pollutants.

Importantly, providing the correct air:fuel ratio has a major influence on the levels of pollutants. Figure 3.61 shows how CO, HC and NO_x emissions are affected when the air:fuel ratio changes. Other factors affect the levels of pollutants produced (such as high temperatures) but the chart indicates the changes in pollutants assuming other factors remain the same. Note that the chart indicates the trend in the gas values and not the actual values.

2   The second route to reducing pollutants is to change the pollutants chemically once they have left the combustion chamber (after treatment). There are a number of ways in which this is achieved, described in section 3.5.5 through to section 3.5.10.

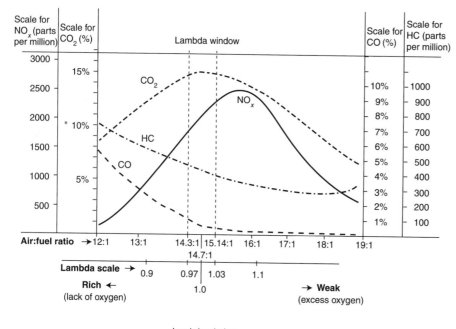

1. It can be seen from the graphs that when all the relevant gases are taken into consideration, the best compromise is when the air:fuel ratio is at or around 14.7:1 (lambda =1).

2. When the excess air factor is around lambda = 1 (within the lambda window) the CO_2 is at its highest, indicating relatively complete combustion.

3. It is only the NO_x emissions that are high when the excess air factor is in the region of lambda = 1 (theoretically correct air:fuel ratio). Note that the NO_x peaks when the mixture is slightly weak of 14.7:1 air:fuel ratio (lambda = 1.05 approximately).

4. When the excess air factor is less than lambda = 1, there is virtually no O_2. When the air:fuel ratio is weaker (lambda greater than 1), the O_2 level rises significantly.

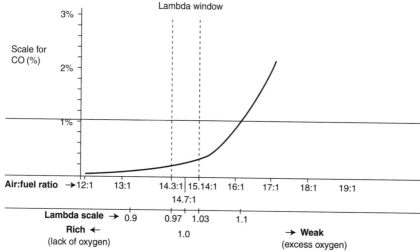

Note. The values shown for all of the gases are typical for an engine operating at medium load conditions. The values will change with load, engine design, fuel and ignition system designs.

Figure 3.61 The influence of air:fuel ratio (lambda/value) on pollutant levels

Carbon monoxide (CO)

Carbon monoxide (CO) is formed when fuel is only partially burned (incomplete combustion). A carbon atom from hydrocarbons (fuel) combines with a single oxygen atom (from the inducted air) in the cylinder to form CO. Compared with CO_2, CO lacks one oxygen atom, due to a deficiency of oxygen in the combustion mixture (or a pocket of mixture). Carbon monoxide is therefore formed when a cylinder receives either a rich or poor mixture of fuel and air, which leads to isolated pockets of rich mixture. Carbon monoxide can also form when the mixture is excessively weak, when fuel droplets do not vaporise; however, formation of CO in a weak mixture is not at the same level as in a rich mixture. Carbon monoxide measurement is therefore a good indicator of a rich mixture, but not of a weak mixture.

Methods of reducing CO include:

- *Control of mixture strength* – control of the air:fuel ratio by the fuel system, especially under slow running and cold starting conditions. Engine management control has improved this under all conditions.
- *Improved fuel distribution* – multi-point fuel injection has largely overcome this problem, with direct injection providing further improvement. Good distribution was difficult to achieve with a carburettor or single-point injection system.
- *More precise engine tuning* – engine management systems ensure that the correct air/fuel mixture is supplied to the engine during all operating conditions; therefore no manual adjustment is possible to alter the mixture strength.
- *Compact combustion chamber* – modern engine designs incorporate very compact combustion chambers. Long narrow chambers associated with an 'over-square' engine often gave a high CO content.
- *Improved mixing of air and fuel* – intake port and combustion chamber design (including piston crown shape) can help to promote good mixing; this is especially true for engines using direct injection.
- *Leaner air/fuel mixtures* – the recent trend towards lean mixture operation (stratified mixture formation) has helped reduce CO levels.
- *Throttle positioner system* – these open the throttle slightly when the engine is at idle or when decelerating.
- *Precise ignition timing* – ensures that the spark occurs at the correct time and remains constant between servicing intervals. Computer controlled ignition and engine management systems achieve this.
- *After treatment* – catalytic converters and other systems help to convert CO into CO_2 (covered later in this section).

Hydrocarbons (HC)

Hydrocarbons in the exhaust gas represent unburned fuel from incomplete combustion. A rich mixture (lack of oxygen or excess fuel), results in high levels of hydrocarbons, because there is insufficient oxygen to combine with the fuel during the combustion process. Any reduction in combustion efficiency will result in high levels of hydrocarbons, e.g. a cylinder misfire caused through an ignition fault or reduced compression (a mechanical fault). Excessively weak mixtures can also result in high levels of hydrocarbons, because excessively weak mixtures cannot support complete combustion within the combustion chamber. However, careful design of the engine and fuel systems reduces this problem to a level where weak mixtures produce very low levels of hydrocarbons.

Methods of reducing hydrocarbon emissions include:

- *Control of mixture strength* – control of the air:fuel ratio by the fuel system, especially under slow running and cold starting conditions. Engine management control has improved this under all conditions.
- *Improved distribution of the fuel* – multi-point fuel injection has largely overcome this problem, with direct injection providing further improvement. Good distribution was difficult to achieve with a carburettor or single-point injection fuel system.
- *More precise engine tuning* – engine management systems ensure that the correct air/fuel mixture is supplied to the engine during all operating conditions; therefore no manual adjustment is possible to alter the mixture strength.
- *Improved mixing of air and fuel* – intake port and combustion chamber design (including piston crown shape) can help to promote good mixing; this is especially true for engines using direct injection systems.
- *Leaner air/fuel mixtures* – the recent trend towards lean mixture operation (stratified mixture formation) helps reduce HC levels.
- *Mixture adjustment during deceleration* – fuel injection systems provide precise metering of the fuel during deceleration (decel fuel cut off or reduction).
- *Precise ignition timing* – ensures that the spark occurs at the correct time and remains constant between servicing intervals. The ignition timing is retarded when the engine is slow running or decelerating. Computer controlled ignition and engine management systems achieve this.
- *After treatment* – catalytic converters and other systems help to convert HC into CO_2 (this is covered later in this section).

Hydrocarbons are also formed when fuel vaporises and escapes into the atmosphere from the fuel system, and when unburned fuel passes the pistons into the crankcase. These problems can be reduced in the following ways:

- **Closed crankcase ventilation system** – unburned fuel passing the pistons and entering the crankcase is prevented from escaping to the atmosphere by a positive crankcase ventilation (PCV) system. The unburned fuel is returned to the induction system.
- **Sealed fuel system** – a fuel evaporative emission control (EVAP) system seals the fuel tank, collects the vaporised fuel, passes it through a charcoal filled canister and delivers it to the induction manifold for combustion in the engine cylinders (this is covered later in this section).

Oxides of nitrogen (NO_x)

Nitric oxide (NO) and nitrogen dioxide (NO_2) are grouped together under the term oxides of nitrogen (NO_x). The atmosphere consists of approximately 78% nitrogen and 21% oxygen. The air drawn into the combustion chamber is heated during combustion; under certain conditions the oxygen and nitrogen can combine to form harmful NO_x. The formation of NO_x occurs with combustion temperatures above approximately 1300°C. However, combustion temperatures can easily exceed 2500°C during full load conditions when the production of NO_x reaches a critical limit. Formation of NO_x is also accelerated when the air:fuel ratio is slightly weaker than stoichiometric.

Methods of reducing NO_x include:

- **Combustion chamber shape** – the shape of the combustion chamber can be designed to increase flame speed. Used in conjunction with lower compression ratios, such chambers reduce NO_x formation, but normally only at the expense of fuel economy and engine power.
- **Increase in air:fuel ratio** – the highest flame speed and NO_x content occurs when the mixture is about 12% richer than the stoichiometric value. An engine designed to operate on a weak mixture has reduced emissions, but vehicle driveability suffers unless the ignition timing and air/fuel mixture are set correctly. However, direct injection systems with stratified mixture formation help to overcome this problem.
- **Ignition timing** – computer controlled ignition systems can control the ignition timing to prevent sudden advance in ignition timing (for a given brief time period) when the throttle is snapped open.
- **Valve timing** – by changing the inlet and exhaust valve timing (i.e. the overlap period), the combustion temperature can be lowered by inducing exhaust gas into the intake port (the process of using exhaust gases to reduce combustion temperatures is covered later in this section). Variable valve timing can optimise the overlap period during engine operation.

- **Intake air temperature** – reducing the intake air temperature can lower the combustion temperature and therefore lower NO_x production. If the engine is fitted with a turbocharger, the fitting of an intercooler can reduce NO_x emissions significantly.
- **Decrease in flame speed** – exhaust gas recirculation (EGR) systems direct some exhaust gas back to the induction manifold to slow down the combustion when the engine is under certain load conditions. The EGR system does however reduce the maximum power of the engine.
- **After treatments** – the fitting of a three-way catalyst in the exhaust system reduces the level of NO_x. More recent designs of catalytic converter include NO_x storage catalysts, covered later in this section.

'Catalyst' is the name given to a material that produces or hastens a chemical action without undergoing any change itself.

Carbon dioxide (CO_2)

In theory, if the correct amount of air combines with the correct amount of fuel during perfect combustion, this results in carbon dioxide (CO_2), water (H_2O) and nitrogen (N_2). Carbon dioxide is therefore a product of complete combustion. Although it is not possible for perfect combustion to occur in the 'real world', the more efficient the combustion process, the higher the CO_2 content in the exhaust. It is therefore necessary to provide the correct air:fuel ratio to produce as perfect combustion as possible. Any fault in the ignition system, fuel system or combustion efficiency will lower the CO_2 content in the exhaust gas.

Carbon dioxide is not directly harmful to humans and is not regarded as a pollutant, but it is harmful in the long term to the environment, and contributes to global warming. Therefore, if the combustion process is efficient and can be operated with weak mixtures, less fuel should be used, reducing CO_2 emissions.

Oxygen (O_2)

Oxygen is an essential element to the combustion process. During the combustion process the oxygen should combine with hydrocarbons to form carbon dioxide and water, leaving no oxygen or hydrocarbons in the exhaust gas. Although not a harmful emission, the exhaust gas contains a very small percentage of oxygen (which is effectively unburned during the combustion process). A rich mixture will result in no oxygen in the exhaust gas whilst a weak mixture (whether intended or caused through insufficient fuel or an air leak in the inlet manifold) will result in high oxygen content in the exhaust gas.

A reduction in combustion efficiency (e.g. a misfire) will result in some of the fuel and oxygen not being burned, which will increase the oxygen content in the exhaust. Excess oxygen can combine with additional gases to form other pollutants such as NO. If the air:fuel ratio is chemically correct and the combustion process is efficient, oxygen emissions should be almost zero.

3.5.4 Influences of engine operation on the pollutants

In theory, a petrol engine should operate at the stoichiometric air:fuel ratio at all times, because this ratio should result in complete combustion of the oxygen and petrol: harmful emissions should be low and power should be at its optimum level. However, an engine is not a perfect machine. Other requirements, such as reduced fuel consumption, dictate a need to use air:fuel ratios that are either slightly richer or slightly weaker than the stoichiometric value.

Although there are many factors dictating the exact air:fuel ratio used in an engine, the following list provides an understanding of the different requirements. Note that inefficiencies in older engine designs and older type fuel ignition systems exaggerated many of the problems, such as poor mixing of the air and fuel. Therefore some of the problems are not as severe as in the past, although in most cases they still occur to a limited extent.

Light load/part load

In general, under these conditions, an engine can operate on mixtures where there is excess air, i.e. with weak mixtures. With the modern generation of direct fuel injection and stratified mixture formation, mixtures can now be used with excess air ratios as weak as 40:1 during light load conditions. Note however that if an engine is not operating with stratified mixture formation and the emissions control includes a standard three-way catalytic converter, it is necessary to operate at around the stoichiometric ratio to enable the converter to convert the pollutants into harmless gases.

Full load

To achieve maximum power, the stoichiometric ratio should in theory be suitable; however, the air and fuel do not completely or perfectly mix (especially on carburettor systems) which results in some fuel not mixing with the air; i.e. a weak mixture can exist in the combustion chamber with any unmixed fuel unable to burn efficiently. Therefore, a slightly richer mixture must initially be provided so that enough fuel is able to mix with the air and form a good combustible mixture. Any excess fuel will cause some rich pockets of mixture to exist. In addition, there are conditions where fuel will condense on the intake manifold and cylinder walls, which again will require additional fuel to ensure that sufficient is available to form a good mixture.

For older engines with a less efficient design of intake manifold and intake port, poor mixing of air and fuel was a major problem. Excessively rich mixtures were provided by the fuel system to ensure that sufficient correctly mixed fuel was available during combustion. Modern intake and fuel systems have improved the mixing process. It is therefore possible to reduce the amount of excess fuel for full load operation.

Cold starting/cold running

The problems associated with cold engine operation are similar to the problems of operating at full load conditions, i.e. poor mixing and fuel condensing on cold surfaces. When the fuel is cold, it is more difficult to vaporise and therefore does not mix as easily with the cold air. In addition, the intake manifold and intake port walls are cold, which causes atomised fuel to condense. This problem is repeated when the fuel contacts the cold cylinder walls. It is therefore necessary to provide an excessively rich mixture to ensure that sufficient fuel can mix with the air and achieve combustion.

Using port type fuel injection (as opposed to a carburettor or single-point injection system) reduces the problem of fuel condensing on the intake system walls. A further improvement is gained by injecting directly into the cylinder. However, cold cylinder walls still cause condensation of fuel; therefore a rich mixture is still required during cold starting.

When the engine has started, heat is passed to the cylinder walls so it is possible to reduce the amount of enrichment. On older engines, it was necessary to maintain a rich mixture immediately after starting, but the use of fuel injection into the ports or into the cylinder reduces condensation problems so it is now possible to operate using air:fuel ratios that are at or close to stoichiometric immediately after cold starting.

It is also general practice to provide a slightly fast idle speed after cold starting; this enables the engine to overcome power losses caused by increased friction and oil drag on cold engines. A fast idle also enables some loads to be applied to the engine (e.g. electrical or auto-transmission loads) which could otherwise cause the engine to stall. During the warm-up period, the increasing temperature of the engine allows progressively weaker mixtures to be used and idle speeds to be reduced.

Idle speed (normal operating temperatures)

Modern engines generally operate using air:fuel ratios around the stoichiometric value or slightly weaker. Most engines are relatively inefficient at idle speed, especially engines with carburettors, where low air speeds contribute to poor mixing of air and fuel. It is therefore necessary to provide relatively rich mixtures to ensure that there is sufficient fuel available to mix with the air.

Modern engines are very efficient. Injection systems and other design features improve the mixing of air and fuel at idle speed. However, valve timing and other design features are generally compromised so that an engine is more efficient at normal operating speeds, i.e. at mid-engine speeds where most driving takes place. There is still a theoretical requirement for a slightly richer mixture to be provided at idle speed. In reality, the use of idle speed control systems and improved efficiencies enable engines to operate at stoichiometric (or close to stoichiometric), which is essential where conventional three-way catalytic converters are used.

Transition

When a driver changes the operating conditions of the engine, e.g. from light load to full load, this is referred to as a transition. One major problem with older engines that used a carburettor was that air would respond to a transition much more rapidly than petrol. Because air is less dense than petrol, when the throttle is suddenly opened, the volume of air flowing to the engine increases rapidly but the petrol takes longer to respond. It should also be remembered that the increased flow of air created an increased depression in the carburettor venturi which in turn caused additional fuel to be drawn from the float chamber (fuel reservoir). There was, however, a small but important time delay in this process. Therefore, with most carburettor systems, when the throttle is initially opened, a momentarily weak mixture results. Carburettors were fitted with different devices that caused additional fuel to be delivered when the throttle was opened, e.g. small pumps, directly operated by the throttle linkage.

With injection systems, it is much easier to ensure that the appropriate amount of fuel is injected at exactly the same time the throttle is opened and the air volume increases. It is possible, so sensitive is the control system, to detect the rate at which the throttle is being opened, so that the fuel can be increased in anticipation of the air volume increasing.

During deceleration, when the load on the engine is reduced by the driver closing the throttle, it is possible to provide a weak mixture or to cut off fuel delivery completely. Although this function was difficult to achieve with carburettors, injection systems can control the amount of fuel injected so that a progressive reduction (or cessation) in fuel supply is achieved which results in lower fuel consumption and reduced emissions.

3.5.5   Processes and devices for emissions control and reduction

Engine and engine control systems

As noted earlier, modern engine design and control systems have been continuously improved with the result that the whole fuel delivery, ignition and combustion process is considerably more efficient than in older engines. The overall effect is that engines now produce far lower levels of pollutants. The use of computer controlled fuel injection and ignition systems has had a dramatic effect on overall efficiencies, but further improvements have been achieved through improved engine design and electronic control of mechanical systems. Examples include changes to combustion chamber and intake port design as well as electronic control of valve timing (variable valve timing). Higher compression ratios and four valve per

cylinder designs also help to reduce the levels of most pollutants, although in some cases there is a risk of increasing some pollutants, which then have to be treated separately.

Most of the significant changes and improvements, such as fuel injection and ignition systems, are dealt with individually within this book, however, many changes go almost unnoticed and simply form an evolutionary part of general engine development. In fact, many small changes or features might only be applicable to one particular engine design and do not necessarily justify individual explanation or coverage. However, technicians will encounter many individual design features when working on particular vehicles, so reference should always be made to specific vehicle information wherever possible.

Although engines now produce far less pollution than in the past, even the low levels now produced are regarded as excessive. Additional means are needed to further reduce pollutant levels. Sections 3.5.6 to 3.5.10 cover the main pollutant reduction and control systems which are referred to as 'after treatment' systems.

Lean burn technology

Lean burn technologies have been developed and applied for many years, although there have been certain limitations in the past, due to the control of NO_x emissions.

Lean burn engines use very weak mixtures (excess air) which is viable for light load engine operation. For an engine to produce power or torque, a more enriched mixture is required, closer to the stoichiometric air:fuel ratio. Lean burn engines do, however, produce low emissions of CO and HC, and use less fuel than engines that have to operate around the stoichiometric ratio for most of the time.

Lean burn engines generally use stratified mixture formation (see section 3.4), whereby a small pocket of rich mixture is created adjacent to the spark plug, but the rest of the cylinder is filled with a weak mixture or with air containing no petrol. The stratified mixture principle results in the rich mixture pocket igniting easily; the combustion of this pocket then spreads through to the rest of the weak mixture or simply heats the remaining air, thus causing gas expansion. The overall mixture is weak which results in low consumption of petrol and low CO and HC emissions.

The use of mixtures slightly weaker than stoichiometric can cause high NO_x emissions; however, when the mixture is further weakened (by a large excess of oxygen) such as on lean burn engines, NO_x levels reduce owing to lower combustion temperatures. The problem is that the NO_x does still exist in the exhaust gas of a lean burn engine, so a catalytic converter is needed for further reduction. However, since there is an excess of oxygen in the exhaust gas when the CO and HC are catalytically converted to CO_2, the oxygen molecules are taken from the excess oxygen and not from the NO_x. This means that the NO_x does not lose its oxygen and is therefore not reduced to nitrogen. More recent developments have enabled direct injection systems to provide a high level of control over mixture formation (see section 3.4), because direct injection can switch from stratified mixture operation (an overall weak mixture with a rich pocket) to homogeneous mixture operation (a normal air:fuel ratio, close to stoichiometric throughout). Additionally, recently developed NO_x accumulator catalytic converters overcome the problem of untreated NO_x escaping to the atmosphere (see section 3.5.6).

After treatment systems

In many after treatment systems, a process of chemical or thermal reaction is used to convert harmful gases into less harmful or harmless gases. Whilst an in-depth understanding of chemistry would be an advantage, you need only to appreciate the basic process by which chemical conversions take place.

For those systems that do not directly use chemical or thermal reactions, individual explanations are provided in the following sections.

Chemical change and thermal reactions

In very simple terms, a thermal reaction uses heat to create a change in a substance, e.g. the change of water into steam. However, thermal reactions can promote a more fundamental change in substances and can cause or assist different substances to combine (chemical change); this phenomenon is used to reduce harmful emissions.

With exhaust gases, it is of interest to note that much of the chemical change occurs by moving oxygen atoms from one gas to another. Carbon monoxide (CO) has one oxygen atom (hence 'monoxide'); by adding another oxygen atom the monoxide changes to dioxide. A similar process occurs with hydrocarbons (HC). Two oxygen atoms can combine with each carbon atom to form CO_2. Although oxygen atoms can be extracted from the small amount of unburned oxygen in the exhaust gas, there are also oxygen atoms contained within the oxides of nitrogen (NO_x). The chemical changes that occur include removing oxygen from NO_x; the oxygen can then combine with CO and carbon from the HC to form CO_2. The advantage is that the NO_x now loses oxygen molecules to leave just nitrogen which is not a pollutant. In reality, NO_x in exhaust gas is generally made up of nitric oxide (NO) and nitrogen dioxide (NO_2), of which the latter is the most harmful. When oxygen atoms are removed some NO can remain, which is relatively harmless unless it later meets with more oxygen (usually when the gases leave the exhaust pipe and enter the atmosphere).

The above brief explanation provides a very basic understanding of the process of chemical change, which in reality is much more complex. It is sufficient to appreciate that such chemical changes occur, which result in harmful gases being converted into relatively harmless gases.

Oxidation process and catalysts

It has been mentioned previously that heat helps to promote chemical change; this includes oxidation processes (the reaction of oxygen with the gases). An initial oxidation process occurs within the engine itself – the combustion process in the cylinder. During this process, oxidation of the fuel occurs and CO_2 is formed. In reality, perfect oxidation or combustion does not occur, so partially or completely unburned fuel (CO and HC) is produced.

By creating a secondary combustion or oxidation process, it is possible to convert most of the remaining CO and HC into CO_2. Although various devices can create a secondary oxidation, the most commonly used type on modern vehicles is the three-way catalytic converter; this is discussed in section 3.5.6. It should be remembered that a catalyst is a substance that helps to promote chemical change without actually changing itself. So, making use of heat and a catalyst, a secondary oxidation process converts the harmful gases into harmless ones.

The important point to remember is that for an oxidation process to be effective, spare oxygen must be available.

Other processes for treating pollutants

A number of other devices are used to convert or reduce emissions of harmful gases.

- *Thermal afterburning* – this process relies on injection of air into the exhaust ports, which results in continued combustion when the gases have left the cylinder. It was used in the past to convert CO and HC, and has been used in conjunction with catalytic converters, the thermal afterburning being effective during the warm-up phase, before the catalytic converter has reached operating temperature.
- *Other thermal devices* – some engines have in the past been fitted with 'hot spots' in the exhaust system. In effect a glow plug device is located in the exhaust manifold or down pipe. The device can be electrically heated but can also rely on exhaust heat. When the device is at high temperature, it causes secondary or continued combustion of the exhaust gases, thus converting CO and HC to CO_2. This type of thermal device is no longer widely used.
- *Exhaust gas recirculation (EGR)* – this is a process whereby a controlled amount of the exhaust gas is fed back into the intake system. The air drawn into the cylinder therefore contains a percentage of exhaust gas, which has the effect of reducing the combustion temperature. Because the levels of NO_x increase with high combustion temperatures, the use of EGR to lower the combustion temperatures causes a reduction in the amount of NO_x produced. EGR is covered in detail in section 3.5.8.

- *Evaporative emission control (EVAP control)* –
  evaporative emissions can be released into the
  atmosphere from the fuel tank and fuel system.
  Petrol vapour (HC) occurs naturally, so methods are
  used to prevent its escape. The main system in use
  relies on creating a sealed fuel system. Fuel vapours
  are fed through to the engine intake system.
  However, when the engine is not running, vapours
  are collected in a charcoal canister, which releases
  the vapour to the engine when it is running. EVAP
  systems are covered in section 3.5.10.

- *Valve and ignition timing* – although not strictly
  regarded as after treatment, control of valve and
  ignition timing can help to reduce pollutants. Valve
  timing can be arranged so that the intake valve
  opens before the exhaust valve closes (valve timing
  overlap). In this way, during the induction stroke
  some of the exhaust gas that has not been expelled
  from the cylinder will mix with the fresh intake air.
  As with controlled exhaust gas recirculation, the
  exhaust gas helps to reduce the combustion
  temperature and the formation of NO_x. Variable
  valve timing allows different overlap periods to be
  used at different engine speeds. Although this
  facility is aimed at producing improved torque and
  power throughout the engine speed range, it also
  assists in maintaining lower emissions.

    Ignition timing can be altered to help improve
  some emission levels. An appropriate example is
  when ignition timing is retarded, so that the
  combustion process is retarded, which means that
  combustion continues when the exhaust valve
  opens. The result is that excess oxygen in the exhaust
  system can now combine with the CO and HC during
  a combustion process that continues within the
  exhaust ports. This process is very effective for cold
  engines where a rich mixture is required (an excess
  of CO and HC). The additional heat created by the
  late combustion process also helps to heat up the
  catalytic converter. The disadvantage is that the high
  temperatures produced when the gases enter the
  exhaust ports (where there is oxygen) increase the
  formation of NO_x.

3.5.6 Catalytic converters

Principle of operation

Catalytic converters are the most commonly used
devices for after treatment for CO, HC and NO_x
reduction. As the name implies, catalytic converters
convert some of the exhaust gases, primarily the
pollutants, into harmless gases. Converters use heat to
change the gases, but a catalyst is used to accelerate the
process.

  During the 1970s, oxidation catalysts were fitted
(primarily for the US market) as a means of converting
CO and HC into CO_2 (see the previous section). This
type of catalyst was also referred to as a 'single-bed'

converter. The catalytic converter was located in the
exhaust system; the exhaust gases flowing through heat
the converter, enabling it to carry out the oxidation
process. However, the subsequent requirement to also
reduce levels of NO_x resulted in an additional catalyst
being used, ahead (upstream) of the oxidation catalyst.
The two catalysts were often combined into a single
assembly, referred to as a 'dual-bed' catalyst because the
conversion processes still remained separate.

  One problem with the oxidation catalytic converter
was that, if the system were fitted to an older engine
that operated with a relatively rich mixture, there was
insufficient oxygen in the exhaust gas to allow
oxidation to take place. This was also true if the NO_x
reduction catalyst were fitted ahead of the oxidation
catalyst, because the NO_x catalyst operated with a
relatively rich mixture. It was therefore necessary to use
an air injection system to ensure that the oxidation
catalyst had sufficient oxygen (Figure 3.62).

  A significant development was the introduction of
the three-way catalytic converter which was able to
reduce the three main pollutants (CO, HC and NO_x)
within one converter. The three-way converter became
the most widely used across the US, Europe and
elsewhere.

Correct air:fuel ratios for different converter processes

As discussed in the previous section, there is a need for
free oxygen to enable CO and HC to be converted to
CO_2. However, oxidation catalysts (and dual-bed
catalysts) were fitted to earlier vehicles with engines
that operated with relatively rich mixtures (a lack of
oxygen). These vehicles were often fitted with
carburettors as opposed to the more efficient fuel
injection systems, resulting in relatively poor mixture
formation. There was therefore insufficient spare
oxygen to allow the oxidation process to take place. To
provide the oxygen required by the catalytic converter
an air injection pump was usually fitted to pump air
into the exhaust system just ahead of the oxidation
catalyst.

  However, NO_x reduction operates more efficiently
with a lack of oxygen (a slightly rich mixture or $\lambda < 1$).
When the NO_x flows through the NO_x reduction catalyst,
the oxygen will readily separate from the NO_x, owing to
the lack of free oxygen in the exhaust gas, thus leaving
just nitrogen (N_2). However, if there is already an excess
of oxygen in the exhaust gas, there is a reduced
tendency for oxygen to separate from the NO_x. The NO_x
reduction process is therefore more suited to engines
operating on relatively rich mixtures in which oxygen is
lacking in the exhaust gas.

  With the three-way catalytic converter, the process
of NO_x reduction and CO/HC conversion takes place in
the combined assembly. Although some spare oxygen is
available in the exhaust gas, the oxygen required for CO
and HC conversion is also taken from NO_x. The
important factor for the efficiency of a three-way

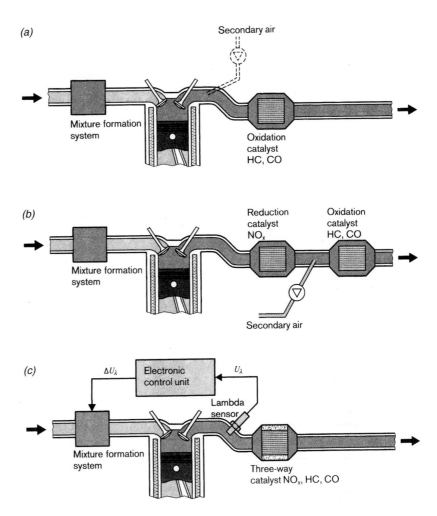

Figure 3.62 Catalytic converter systems
a Single-bed oxidation catalyst
b Dual-bed catalyst
c Single-bed three-way catalyst

converter is the balance of the gases; i.e. the oxygen content must not be excessive, otherwise NO_x reduction will not take place. At the other extreme, too little oxygen in the exhaust gas will prevent the oxidation of CO and HC (the CO and HC will not combust and convert into CO_2). Additionally, too much CO and HC in the exhaust gas will mean that there will be insufficient oxygen to facilitate full conversion to CO_2. It is essential that the balance of the gases is correct, which means that the air:fuel ratio must also be correct. The correct oxygen level in the exhaust gas is achieved by operating the engine at the stoichiometric air:fuel ratio ($\lambda = 1$).

Figure 3.62 shows the three most commonly used types of catalytic converter. A fourth type of converter is now gaining popularity – an NO_x accumulator converter. This type is now being used on vehicles operating with stratified mixture formation and direct fuel injection. NO_x accumulator converters are covered later in this section.

Operating temperatures

To enable this chemical change in the gases, the catalytic converter must operate at relatively high temperatures. Because the conversion of CO and HC is based on an oxidation process (in effect a second

combustion process), the temperature must be sufficient to allow ignition of the gases. A typical ideal temperature is between 400°C and 800°C for most types of oxidation converter.

Heat is provided by the flow of exhaust gas through the converter, but the oxidation process creates additional heat. So long as the air:fuel ratio is correct, the oxidation process maintains the heat to continue the process.

For most types of catalytic converter, excessive heat will cause either loss of efficiency or permanent damage. Consistent temperatures of 1000°C or more will permanently damage the converter, and long periods of operation at between 800 and 1000°C will accelerate the ageing process of the converter. The location of the converter is therefore critical to prevent excessive heat being passed from the exhaust gases as they exit the exhaust ports. Exhaust gases lose heat as they flow through the exhaust system, so a location further from the exhaust port is more suitable.

However, there is a need to heat up the converter immediately after starting the engine. The closer the converter is to the exhaust ports, the quicker this happens. There has therefore been a tendency to use a small 'pre-cat' located very close to the exhaust ports, and a larger conventional converter in the exhaust system under the vehicle. The pre-cat is designed for higher temperature operation and stability, whilst the larger converter is designed for lower temperature operation. Note, however, that many vehicles are fitted with a single high temperature converter located close to the exhaust ports (usually just after the exhaust manifold), as shown in Figure 3.63.

Construction of catalytic converters

Although there are a few variations in the construction of catalytic converters, the majority of the three-way types are constructed as detailed below and shown in Figure 3.64. Note that the illustration also shows a lambda sensor, which is discussed in section 3.5.7.

Maximum surface area

The objective is to expose the exhaust gases to the catalyst material. To enable as much of the exhaust gas as possible to be exposed to the catalyst, it is necessary to use a series of small tubes that, together, have a large surface area. If there is not enough surface area, the conversion process will not treat sufficient amounts of gas. It must be remembered that the exhaust gases flow through the converter at high speed, so a large number of small tubes ensures that the gas flow is not restricted, but at the same time the large number of tubes allows the maximum amount of surface area.

It is common practice to construct the converter using a monolith or substrate that is a honeycomb made of ceramic material (typically a magnesium aluminium silicate). Note that some monoliths are produced using a finely corrugated, thin metal foil.

The surfaces of the tubes formed by the honeycomb are thinly coated with aluminium oxide (referred to as a washcoat). The coating provides a rougher surface, with a much larger surface area than a smooth surface (imagine a smooth surface, such as a mirror, covered in very small bumps or hills). The aluminium oxide can increase the surface area by as much as 7000 times.

Coating of precious or noble metals

The active material, the catalyst material, is then added to the washcoat. Active materials vary, but for the oxidation catalysts (CO and HC conversion), platinum and/or palladium are used. These two materials accelerate the oxidation of CO and HC. In a three-way converter, rhodium is also used to accelerate the reduction of NO_x.

These active materials are expensive and are referred to as noble or precious metals. However, only around 2 to 3 grams of these materials are used to coat the surface areas of the converter, as the coating is exceptionally thin.

Casing

The honeycomb or monolith is contained within a steel casing. To protect the honeycomb from damage caused by vibration, etc., it is mounted in matting that swells when initially heated. The matting therefore forms a protective layer around the honeycomb and also forms a gas seal.

Potential faults and problems with catalytic converters

High temperatures and misfires

As was mentioned, catalytic converters operate ideally between 400°C and 800°C, with temperatures much higher than this causing accelerated ageing or permanent damage.

One major factor that can increase the temperature within the catalytic converter is an engine misfire. When a misfire occurs, a quantity of petrol and air remain unburned, and these flow out of the cylinder and through the exhaust system into the catalytic converter. The heat in the exhaust system and existing combustion process within the converter will cause the unburned air and fuel to ignite and combust and this additional fuelling of the combustion process within the converter creates excessive heat that can lead to temperatures in excess of 1400°C. Such temperatures

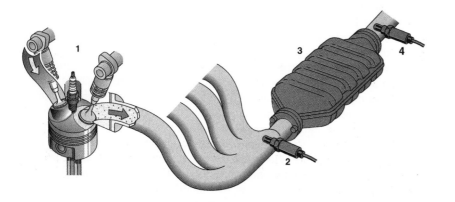

1 Engine
2 Lambda oxygen sensor upstream of the catalytic converter (two-step sensor or broadband sensor, depending on system)
3 Three-way catalytic converter
4 Two-step lambda oxygen sensor downstream of the catalytic converter (only on systems with lambda dual-sensor control)

Figure 3.63 Location of catalytic converters

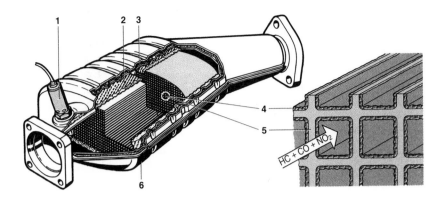

1 Lambda oxygen sensor
2 Swell matting
3 Thermally insulated double shell
4 Washcoat (Al_2O_3 substrate
   coating) with noble metal coating
5 Substrate (monolith)
6 Housing

Figure 3.64 Catalytic converter construction (three-way type)

will quickly melt the substrate or monolith in the converter, causing permanent damage. Note, however, that even brief misfires will accelerate the ageing process of the converter.

Modern engine management systems can detect a misfire using the various sensors. One indicator of a misfire is a high oxygen level in the exhaust gas, which is detected by the oxygen sensor (section 3.5.7). In addition, the engine management ECU can check the acceleration rate of the crankshaft using information provided by the crankshaft speed/position sensor. When the power stroke occurs within each cylinder, it causes an acceleration of the crankshaft, but a misfire by one cylinder will cause reduced acceleration compared with the 'good' cylinders. The ECU can assess which cylinder is misfiring and cut off the fuel supply to the affected cylinder. Without delivery of fuel, there will be no unburned fuel passing through to the catalytic converter, although unburned oxygen will remain.

Leaded fuel and other contaminants

Lead compounds restrict the ability of human cells to absorb oxygen. Leaded petrol has been banned in the EU since 2000. The amount of lead allowed in petrol was previously subject to progressive reductions. Many other countries have also banned leaded petrol.

With regard to leaded fuel and catalytic converters, lead compounds clog the pores of the active materials, reducing their efficiency. Excessive build-up of lead stops the conversion processes from taking place. Therefore, vehicles fitted with catalytic converters must not be operated with leaded fuel.

It is also possible for the active materials in catalytic converters to be affected by other contaminants, such as deposits from the engine oil that pass by the piston rings into the combustion chambers. A worn engine, producing high emissions, can also contribute to the rapid deterioration of its catalytic converter.

NO_x accumulator converters

The increased use of lean burn technologies (primarily stratified mixture formation with direct fuel injection), results in an excess of oxygen in the exhaust gases when very weak air/fuel mixtures are used. The excess oxygen prevents effective reduction of NO_x by the three-way catalytic converter (see lean burn technologies in section 3.5.5). It is therefore necessary to find alternative methods of reducing the amount of NO_x.

NO_x accumulator catalytic converters are now being fitted to many vehicles with lean burn engines. The accumulator type converter is not dissimilar to the standard three-way converter in construction, but other active materials are included, such as oxides of potassium, calcium and barium. The converter can operate in the same way as a three-way converter when the air:fuel ratio is around the stoichiometric value.

However, when the engine is operating with very weak mixtures (i.e. with excess oxygen in the exhaust gas), the accumulator converter operates in a different manner. The oxidation process causes the nitrogen and NO to attract excess oxygen thus producing NO_2. However, the additional active materials cause a further change which results in nitrates being formed. The nitrates are then stored (accumulated).

Accumulation and conversion

As described above, the accumulator converter stores NO_x as nitrates, but at some stage the stored NO_x must be released; otherwise the converter will eventually become over-saturated (its maximum storage capacity will be reached). As the amount of NO_x stored in the accumulator converter increases, it impairs the device's ability to store more NO_x so a means of assessing when the stored NO_x must be released is required. Two methods can be used.

1 An NO_x sensor downstream of the converter indicates to the ECU when higher levels of NO_x are

flowing out of the converter because the converter is no longer storing the NO_x in sufficient quantities as it is almost full to capacity. At this stage the NO_x is released from the converter.

2 A mathematical process is used (ECU programming), which calculates the likely amount of NO_x that is stored (based on operating conditions and temperature). At the calculated time the process for NO_x release is implemented.

When the accumulator converter is assessed to be full, the engine is briefly operated using a rich mixture (typically with an air:fuel ratio of 12:1 or richer), resulting in an excess of CO, HC and H_2 in the exhaust gas. In simple terms, the oxygen in the NO_x is lost, leaving nitrogen. The oxygen combines with CO and HC to give CO_2 and H_2O (water).

The end of the conversion process can be assessed either using another ECU calculation (again using conditions and time), or with an oxygen sensor located after the converter: the end of the process will be when the oxygen in the exhaust gas (after the converter) has fallen to a predefined level.

An NO_x accumulator converter can be used in conjunction with a three-way converter. Figure 3.65 shows an arrangement where both converters are fitted into an exhaust system. Note that the three-way converter is fitted close to the exhaust manifold (in the pre-cat location) with the NO_x accumulator further downstream. The NO_x accumulator converter operates at lower temperatures than the three-way converter (ideally around 300–400°C, compared with 400–800°C for the three-way type). This means that the two converters must be separate.

3.5.7 Oxygen/lambda sensing (controlling the air:fuel ratio)

Oxygen content: the critical factor

It has been highlighted a number of times within this chapter that the oxygen content of the exhaust gas is critical to the operation of the catalytic converter (as well as to other emission control devices). Achieving the correct oxygen content very much depends on the air:fuel ratio, which should be stoichiometric ($\lambda = 1$).

Modern engine management systems are able to provide very accurate control of the air:fuel ratio. However, to attain the highest possible accuracy, it is necessary to monitor the oxygen levels in the exhaust gas.

An oxygen sensor (as shown in Figure 3.66) is used to measure the oxygen content; this device then transmits a signal to the ECU. If the oxygen content in the exhaust gas is too high or low, the ECU is able to change rapidly the fuelling as necessary, ensuring that the oxygen level is restored to the correct value. When the oxygen level is correct, $\lambda = 1$. The sensor is often referred to as a 'lambda sensor'.

When the oxygen content is at $\lambda = 1$ (or within the lambda window described in 3.5.1), the catalytic converter is able to convert CO and HC efficiently into CO_2 and also reduce NO_x levels.

Figure 3.66 Oxygen/lambda sensor

Closed and open loop operation

Section 3.5.3 provides details of the air:fuel ratios used for different engine operating and driving conditions. Older engines operated using a wide range of air:fuel ratios often far beyond the lambda window. For light load conditions an air:fuel ratio of 17:1 or weaker was not uncommon, and under full load 13:1 or richer would have been used. However, such extreme ratios are not suited to vehicles fitted with catalytic converters, because they would dramatically reduce the converter efficiency (which relies on the excess air factor being $\lambda = 1$).

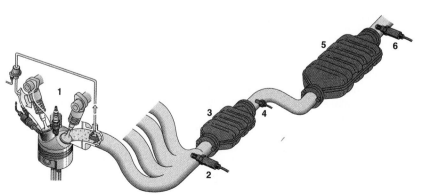

1 Engine with EGR system
2 Lambda oxygen sensor upstream of the catalytic converter
3 Three-way catalytic converter (pre-cat)
4 Temperature sensor
5 NO_x accumulator type catalytic converter (main cat)
6 Two-step lambda oxygen sensor, optionally available with integral NO_x sensor

Figure 3.65 Location for an NO_x accumulator converter and three-way converter

For most engines since the early 1990s air:fuel ratios are controlled as closely as possible within the lambda window (ideally at λ = 1). It is not always possible to avoid slight enrichment for full load conditions, and for cold running it is also often necessary to briefly provide some enrichment. However, light load conditions are generally achieved using air:fuel ratios within the lambda window. In general, every new or modified version of an engine or an engine control system allows increased operation within the lambda window, enabling more efficient catalytic converter operation and a greater reduction in pollutants.

Engines with stratified charge mixture formation and direct fuel injection operate with exceptionally weak mixtures under light load conditions; for further information, see section 3.4 (direct fuel injection) and also lean burn technology in section 3.5.5.

Closed loop

When an engine is operating under conditions where the mixture is at or close to λ = 1, the oxygen or lambda sensor monitors the oxygen content in the exhaust gas, and the ECU responds to the sensor signal as necessary. The process is referred to as 'closed loop' because there is a continuous loop or repeat of the necessary actions, i.e. monitoring and correction, as shown below and in Figure 3.67.

Action 1   Oxygen/lambda sensor measures the oxygen.
Action 2   Signal sent by sensor to ECU.
Action 3   ECU alters fuel quantity if necessary to change the oxygen level.
Action 1   Oxygen/lambda sensor measures the oxygen.

In a closed loop operation, the ECU calculates the required fuel quantity based on information from the various sensors (air mass, throttle position, temperature, etc.) but the oxygen/lambda sensor checks the actual oxygen content and provides the

appropriate signal to the ECU. If the oxygen content is incorrect, the ECU makes a fine adjustment to the fuel supply to enable the correct oxygen content to be achieved.

Open loop

When engine operating conditions or driving conditions dictate that the air:fuel ratio should be outside the lambda window (usually a rich mixture for full load or cold running conditions), the lambda sensor signal is effectively ignored. The fuel quantity will therefore depend entirely on the ECU calculations from other sensor information. The ECU will, however, revert back to closed loop operation as soon as the operating and driving conditions dictate.

Lambda/oxygen sensor operation (step type)
General principles

Although there are a few variants of lambda sensor, the general principle of operation relies on comparing the oxygen content in the exhaust gas to the oxygen content in the air. In effect the oxygen content in the air acts as a reference level against which the oxygen content in the exhaust gas is compared.

In all types of lambda sensor in common use, an electrical signal is produced by the sensor, depending on the amount of oxygen within the exhaust gas. The signal voltage changes with changes in oxygen level. A signal is therefore transmitted to the fuel injection or engine management ECU, which alters the fuel quantity as necessary, until the oxygen content of the exhaust gas is correct for efficient catalytic converter operation.

Step type sensor operation

The more commonly used early generation of lambda sensor is referred to as the step type or 'narrow band' sensor. The name originates from the characteristics of the signal voltage produced by the sensor as explained in the following paragraphs.

Figure 3.68 shows a schematic view of a simple step type lambda sensor located in the exhaust pipe. In the

1 Fuel, 2 Air, 3 Central injection unit,
4 Fuel injector, 5 Engine, 6 Lambda oxygen sensor, 7 Catalytic converter, 8 ECU with Lambda closed-loop control, 9 Exhaust gas.
U_λ Sensor voltage, U_v Injector triggering pulse.

1. Sensor ceramic
2. Electrodes
3. Inner electrical contacts
4. Outer (housing) electrical contacts
5. Exhaust pipe
6. Porous ceramic protective layer
7. Exhaust gas
8. Air

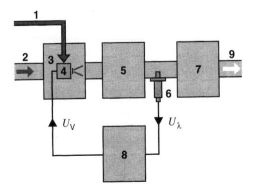

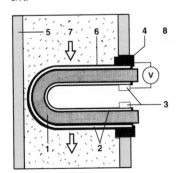

Figure 3.67 Closed loop operation

Figure 3.68 Schematic view of a step type lambda sensor

illustration, the sensor ceramic (item 1) is coated on both sides with a layer of platinum that acts as electrodes (items 2). The inner electrode is exposed to the atmosphere, whilst the outer electrode is exposed to the exhaust gas. The outer electrode has an additional layer of porous ceramic (item 6) to protect it against the exhaust gases that would eventually erode the platinum layer.

At higher temperatures, the main ceramic (item 1) allows oxygen ions through if there is a difference in the oxygen content either side of the ceramic. When this occurs it causes a small voltage to be produced across the two platinum electrodes (shown as the small meter connected across the electrodes in the illustration). The voltage produced depends on the difference in oxygen content on either side of the ceramic. Because one side of the ceramic is exposed to the atmosphere (with an oxygen content of around 20.8%) and the other to the exhaust gas (with an oxygen content of around 0.2% to 0.3% in the region of $\lambda = 1$), there is a large difference in oxygen content either side of the ceramic. The large difference causes ions to be conducted through the ceramic, which in turn results in a small voltage being produced across the electrodes.

Figure 3.69 shows the voltage output from a step type lambda sensor. An important point to note is that when the air:fuel ratio is weaker than stoichiometric ($\lambda > 1$), the voltage produced is typically lower than 100 mV (0.1 volts); in fact, the voltage may be as low as 50 mV and increase only very slightly as the mixture becomes a little richer. When the air:fuel ratio is richer than stoichiometric ($\lambda < 1$), the voltage produced is around 950 mV (0.95 volts). The voltage only decreases slightly as the mixture becomes weaker. However, when the mixture changes to just slightly weaker or richer than stoichiometric (just either side of $\lambda = 1$) the voltage suddenly jumps from the weak mixture value of approximately 100 mV to the rich mixture value of approximately 950 mV.

In effect, the voltage produced by the sensor changes little as a weak mixture becomes richer (i.e. lambda is still greater than approximately 1.03). However, when lambda reaches approximately 1.03, the voltage suddenly jumps in a large step to a lambda of approximately 0.97. If the mixture continues to become richer (i.e. $\lambda < 0.97$), the voltage change is once again very small.

The large step in voltage that occurs between about $\lambda = 0.97$ and $\lambda = 1.03$ provides a very distinct signal that enables the ECU to detect the change in oxygen when the air:fuel ratio alters slightly away from $\lambda = 1$. Conveniently, the lambda values of 0.97 and 1.03 effectively define the lambda window (this is covered in section 3.5.1 and shown in Figure 3.57).

The signal voltage shown in Figure 3.69 is obtained at a temperature of approximately 600°C. The voltage produced also varies with temperature, so it is essential that the ECU responds only to the sensor signal when the sensor is at a defined operating temperature. The

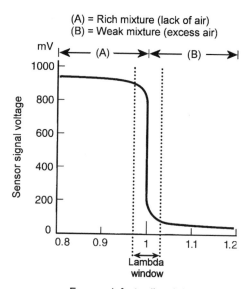

Figure 3.69 Voltage output from a step type lambda sensor

sensor starts to function reliably when the temperature reaches approximately 300–350°C. An ideal temperature is around 600°C. Because the sensor response to changes in oxygen content is very slow at lower temperatures, the ECU is able to ignore these slow responses and operate in 'open loop' mode. When the sensor is at the required temperature and the response time is quicker, the ECU then operates in 'closed loop' mode. Response times to changes in oxygen level are around 50 ms for a fully hot sensor, whilst for a cold sensor the response can take much longer than 1 second, which is not suitable for operating in closed loop because of the time delay.

The standard step sensor relies on heat from the exhaust gas to reach operating temperature. Immediately after starting and during warm-up from cold the system will operate in open loop until the sensor is at operating temperature. The sensor should ideally be located close to the exhaust manifold to obtain as much heat as possible after starting; however, because of the potential for overheating and premature deterioration, sensors are generally located some distance from the manifold.

Heated step type lambda sensor

To overcome the problems of temperature variation, which can change the accuracy and reliability of the lambda sensor signal, heated sensors were developed. There are two main types of heated sensor (step type), as shown in Figure 3.70.

Figure 3.70a shows a direct development of the step sensor described above. This type has an electrical heater located in the sensing element of the sensor assembly. When the engine is started and is running, battery power is supplied via a relay to the heater. The heater rapidly raises the temperature of the sensor so that closed loop operation can start as little as 20 or 30 seconds after a cold start.

Figure 3.70b shows a later type of heated step type lambda sensor. Although this type operates in a similar manner to the first type, the sensing element and heater assembly are layered. The illustration shows this layered construction.

Limitations of step type sensors

Step type sensors (heated and unheated) provide a signal change that can only be effectively detected by the ECU when the air:fuel ratio alters at the rich or weak extremes of the lambda window. The sensor can only clearly indicate when the lambda factor is at these points, i.e. when there is a stepped change in the voltage (as illustrated in Figure 3.69). These easily identifiable stepped changes are easily detected by the ECU, but it is not easy to measure the exact signal corresponding to $\lambda = 1$ (which occurs at around 450 mV) because the voltage rise or fall is too rapid when the value is close to $\lambda = 1$.

Whilst the step type sensor signal is very effective for vehicles fitted with three-way catalytic converters, this narrow band of operation does not allow the sensors to be effective when engines operate with a wider range of air:fuel ratios. This is especially relevant to the modern generation of direct injection engines that operate with a stratified charge and air:fuel ratios that may be as weak as 30:1 or 40:1. A sensor is therefore required that can measure oxygen levels over a broader range of air:fuel ratios; such sensors are covered later in this section.

Operating signals for step type lambda sensors

It was highlighted earlier in this section that a significant change in voltage is produced by the sensor by changes around $\lambda = 1$. The approximate lambda value range that causes the jump in voltage is $\lambda = 0.97$ to $\lambda = 1.03$ (see Figure 3.69).

If we assume that the engine and lambda sensor are at full operating temperatures, the ECU will provide the appropriate fuelling that should in theory result in an air:fuel ratio of $\lambda = 1$. In reality, minor variations will always occur; and the lambda sensor signal provides the reference to the ECU regarding such deviations.

The measuring and correction process then passes through the following phases (this is closed loop operation, also referred to as 'feedback control').

1 If we assume that a very slightly rich mixture exists, the lambda factor will be slightly low ($\lambda < 1$). The sensor signal voltage will therefore rise to approximately 950 mV, and the ECU will reduce the fuel quantity slightly, which will cause a weakening of the mixture and a reduction in the sensor voltage.

2 The sensor will now detect the weakening of the mixture, which will produce a slightly increased oxygen level. The lambda factor will increase ($\lambda > 1$), which will cause the sensor voltage to fall to approximately 100 mV. The ECU will detect the reduced voltage and again alter the fuel quantity, this time to provide a slight enrichment.

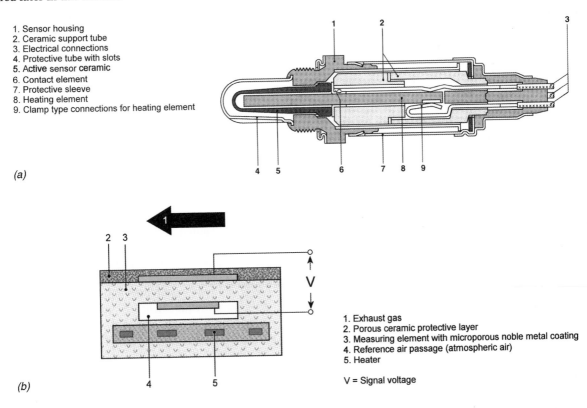

1. Sensor housing
2. Ceramic support tube
3. Electrical connections
4. Protective tube with slots
5. Active sensor ceramic
6. Contact element
7. Protective sleeve
8. Heating element
9. Clamp type connections for heating element

(a)

1. Exhaust gas
2. Porous ceramic protective layer
3. Measuring element with microporous noble metal coating
4. Reference air passage (atmospheric air)
5. Heater

V = Signal voltage

(b)

Figure 3.70 Heated lambda sensors
a An example of a heated lambda sensor
b Alternative type of sensor element with combined heater

3 The process will now start again, resulting in a continuous increase and decrease (oscillation) in the sensor voltage, as shown in Figure 3.71.

The frequency of the oscillations of the lambda sensor signal depends on the speed of response for the sensor, i.e. how quickly the sensor registers the change in oxygen, which can be as rapidly as within 50 ms. However, the fuelling change leads to an inevitable delay in the alteration of the oxygen content, as this change passes through the exhaust system to the sensor. It is common to find that the frequency of change for the sensor signal is around 1–3 Hz, depending on engine speed, temperature and other factors.

The sensor signal in Figure 3.71 shows a very consistent and regular oscillation which is seldom seen in practice owing to minor variations that occur in the oxygen content of the exhaust gas sample. The hash that exists around the signal is typical of a lambda sensor signal.

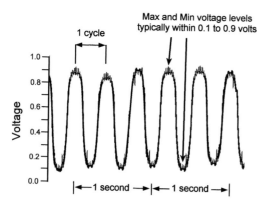

Figure 3.71 Continuous signal produced by a step type lambda sensor

Broadband sensor

As mentioned earlier, the broadband sensor can be used to measure the oxygen content over a very broad range of air:fuel ratios, i.e. across a wide range of lambda values from approximately 0.7 to 4. The broadband sensor is therefore suitable for lean burn engines, such as those using a stratified mixture formation (typically on modern direct injection engines). In addition, the broadband sensor can be used on diesel engines and engines operating on gaseous fuels.

As well as offering a capability of measuring over a wider lambda range, the broadband sensor provides a progressive voltage change across the range of operation, as opposed to the stepped voltage jump that occurs with a narrow band step sensor.

Operating principles

Figure 3.72 shows the construction of the sensing elements in a broadband sensor. The construction is similar to the later type step sensors, with the different materials arranged in layers.

Item 7 in the illustration is effectively a step type sensor element or cell; however there is an additional cell, referred to as the 'oxygen pump cell' (item 8). An extremely small diffusion gap (item 6) separates the pump cell from the step type sensing cell. There is however a barrier (a porous diffusion barrier, item 11) through which the oxygen from the exhaust gas must flow before it reaches the diffusion gap. Once in the diffusion gap the oxygen affects one electrode on the step type sensing cell. The other electrode of the step type cell is exposed to the reference air (oxygen in the atmosphere), just as with a standard type step sensor. The step type cell is measuring the oxygen content in the diffusion gap, which would be lower than the oxygen content in the air, thus causing a voltage to be produced by the step type cell; this voltage is transmitted to the control unit.

However, exhaust gas must flow through the pump cell before it can reach the diffusion gap. The pump cell also has the capacity to pump oxygen through the diffusion barrier in either direction, so it can increase or decrease the oxygen content in the diffusion gap. The pumping action is created by providing a small controlled voltage to the pump cell's platinum electrodes; the way the current flows dictates whether oxygen is pumped in or out of the diffusion gap. The objective is to use the pump cell to maintain the oxygen content in the diffusion gap at a value of $\lambda = 1$. If the diffusion gap contains too much or too little oxygen (weaker or richer than $\lambda = 1$) because of high or low oxygen levels in the exhaust gas, the pump cell then decreases or increases the oxygen in the diffusion gap to achieve $\lambda = 1$.

The process starts with the step type cell measuring the oxygen content in the diffusion gap, creating a voltage signal that is assessed by the electronic control unit. Note that the initial oxygen level and oxygen level for normal operation will depend on the oxygen content in the exhaust gas, which will have flowed into the diffusion gap. If the oxygen level in the diffusion gap is too high or too low (higher or lower than $\lambda = 1$), the electronic control applies the appropriate current at the pump cell electrodes to pump oxygen in or out of the diffusion gap as required to achieve $\lambda = 1$. The level of current required is an indicator of the oxygen being pumped in or out of the diffusion gap, and is therefore also an indication of the oxygen content of the exhaust gas.

If the oxygen content in the diffusion gap is at $\lambda = 1$, there is no requirement for pumping oxygen, and the current will be zero. However, if the oxygen content is high ($\lambda > 1$) a negative current is used to pump oxygen out of the diffusion gap; if the oxygen content is low ($\lambda < 1$) a positive current is used to pump oxygen into the diffusion gap. The electronic control unit produces a sensor signal (voltage change) that is dependent on the current level required to maintain the oxygen content in the diffusion chamber at $\lambda = 1$.

1. Exhaust gas
2. Exhaust pipe
3. Heater element
4. Electronic control (combined within ECU)
5. Reference cell containing air (atmospheric)
6. Diffusion gap

7. Step type measuring element with measuring electrode on side adjacent to diffusion gap, and reference electrode adjacent to the reference cell
8. Oxygen pump cell with pump electrode
9. Porous protective layer
10. Gas access passage
11. Porous diffusion barrier

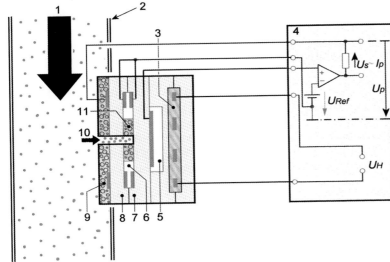

Ip = Pump current
Up = Pump voltage
UH = Heater voltage
URef = Reference voltage (450 mV corresponds to Lambda 1)
Us = Sensor voltage

Figure 3.72 Broadband sensor (sensing element construction)

Sensor heating

Within the sensing unit assembly, a heater element is constructed to heat the sensor rapidly and maintain a relatively constant temperature that is not greatly influenced by exhaust gas temperature. The function and operation of the heater are the same as described for the step type sensor. Broadband sensors generally operate in the range 650–900°C.

Sensor output signal

Sensors produced by different manufacturers might provide slightly different output signals to be monitored by the engine management ECU. An example of a broadband sensor signal is shown in Figure 3.73. Note that the voltage change is progressive across a wide lambda range; the illustration shows the voltage change within the range of λ = 0.7–1.5, although higher lambda values are measured and provide slightly higher voltage values.

Other types of lambda sensor

Some lambda sensors rely on a special semiconductor device that responds to changes in oxygen content by altering its resistance. When a voltage is applied across this device, the resistance change affects the current in the circuit (a series resistance circuit). This change is an indicator of oxygen content. Thus it is possible to apply a 5 volt reference voltage to the sensor, obtaining a signal voltage that ranges from 1 to 4 volts, depending on the oxygen content in the exhaust gas.

3.5.8 Exhaust gas recirculation

A method of reducing NO_x

NO_x formation

Within section 3.5, and in other sections of Chapter 3, many references were made to oxides of nitrogen (NO_x). These are regarded as a pollutant and are formed by the combination of oxygen molecules and nitrogen molecules (both of which exist naturally in the air.

Whilst NO_x formation increases when the air:fuel ratio is very slightly weaker than the stoichiometric value (i.e. λ = 1.05–1.1; see Figure 3.61), it is also true that NO_x formation increases significantly when combustion temperatures rise. NO_x formation occurs because of the heat of the combustion process, which enables a chemical change to take place. For NO_x this

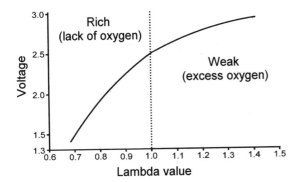

Figure 3.73 Output signal voltage for one type of broadband sensor

can start when combustion temperatures are around 1300°C, but the formation of NO_x increases at around 1800°C and accelerates if temperatures exceed around 2500°C.

When an engine is operating under load conditions, especially when the air:fuel ratio is close to $\lambda = 1.05$–1.1 (which can exist during part load conditions), combustion temperatures will rise. However, high load conditions, where a full charge of air enters the cylinder (with the throttle fully open), will inevitably cause higher combustion temperatures, but under high load conditions the mixture is usually slightly richer, which helps to reduce NO_x formation.

When an engine is operating under part or medium load conditions with an air:fuel ratio slightly weaker than $\lambda = 1$, combustion temperatures are high and the oxygen content of the exhaust gas enables high levels of NO_x to be formed. Although catalytic converters can be used to reduce NO_x levels after it has been formed during combustion, it is often also necessary to use other means to reduce the production of NO_x during the combustion process. In general, these devices or processes are designed to reduce combustion temperatures.

Using the exhaust gas

A very effective and well established method of reducing combustion temperatures is to pass a percentage of the exhaust gas back into the intake system where the exhaust gas mixes with the new charge of air entering the cylinder.

Exhaust gas is made up of a high percentage of inert gases, such as water vapour (H_2O) and carbon dioxide (CO_2). An inert gas does not combust, so when these gases mix with the air flowing into the cylinder, they cause a lowering of the combustion temperature and a reduction in the formation of NO_x.

A widely used method of enabling exhaust gas to mix with the fresh intake air is to recirculate some of the exhaust gas back into the intake manifold (Figure 3.74). This process is referred to as exhaust gas recirculation (EGR).

Note that a similar but less effective result can be achieved when the valve timing is arranged so that there is valve overlap, i.e. the intake valve opens before the exhaust valve closes (at the end of the exhaust stroke). The result is that some exhaust gas mixes with the incoming fresh charge of air. The amount of valve overlap on most engines was fixed, until recently. However, variable valve timing mechanisms are now used for many engines so that different overlap periods can be used at different engine speeds. In reality, variable valve timing systems are used to enable good power or torque to be achieved over the whole engine speed range, but the added benefit of valve overlap is to facilitate the mixing of some exhaust gas with the fresh charge of air, thus reducing combustion temperatures and NO_x.

Controlling the quantity of recirculated exhaust gas

For those engines operating with homogeneous mixture formation (all of the air drawn into the engine is mixed with fuel), it is possible to introduce around 10–15% of the exhaust gas back into the fresh charge of air that is drawn into the cylinder. This percentage does not dramatically affect fuel consumption and power, but is usually sufficient to reduce the NO_x by a significant amount. Slightly higher levels of exhaust gas recirculation can be used on engines operating with a stratified mixture formation (direct injection engines).

Importantly, the amount of exhaust passing through to the intake system will depend on the exhaust gas pressure and the intake manifold pressure (or

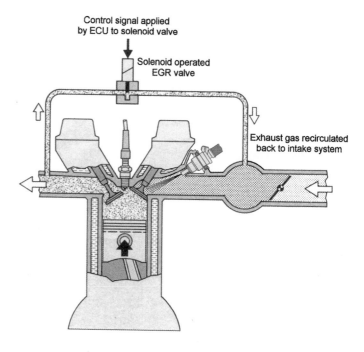

Figure 3.74 Exhaust gas recirculation system (EGR)

depression). If the exhaust gas pressure is high, such as when the engine is under high load (when the throttle is fully open, high volumes of air are drawn into the cylinder which results in high volumes of exhaust gas, increasing the pressure in the exhaust system), a higher flow of exhaust gas into the intake system will result. It is therefore necessary to control the flow of exhaust gas into the intake system to ensure that excessive quantities of exhaust gas do not enter the intake system and combustion chamber, which would cause poor combustion.

In general, the exhaust gas is recirculated during part/medium load conditions but not when the engine is at idle or at full throttle (when a richer mixture might be used which would cause a reduction in NO_x).

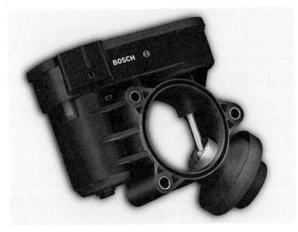

Figure 3.75 EGR valve with integrated solenoid

EGR valve

An EGR valve (Figure 3.75) is used to control the flow of recirculated gas. Figure 3.74 shows an EGR valve located in the pipe that feeds the exhaust gas to the intake system. In this example, the valve is directly opened and closed by a solenoid which is controlled by the ECU. The ECU, which is receiving information from various sensors, (e.g. engine speed, throttle position, temperature, etc.) opens the valve the appropriate amount to allow the required amount of exhaust gas to be recirculated to suit engine operating conditions.

The EGR solenoid may be supplied with a digital control signal that allows the gas valve to be accurately positioned. The control signal duty cycle is altered to provide an increased or decreased current/voltage to the solenoid, which causes the valve to open or close to a greater or lesser extent (see section 1.9).

Different types of EGR control system

The simplest type of system to control the flow of gases in an EGR system is shown in Figure 3.74. This relies on a single valve, directly controlled by the ECU. However, other systems have been used, requiring additional valves and sensors, that ensure that recirculated exhaust gas is passed to the intake system.

Figure 3.76 shows a system where the main EGR valve is opened and closed by 'vacuum' (low pressure or depression) which is taken from the intake system. The vacuum level applied to the EGR valve is in turn regulated by an ECU controlled vacuum valve. On this type of system, it is the vacuum control valve that receives the digital control signal from the ECU.

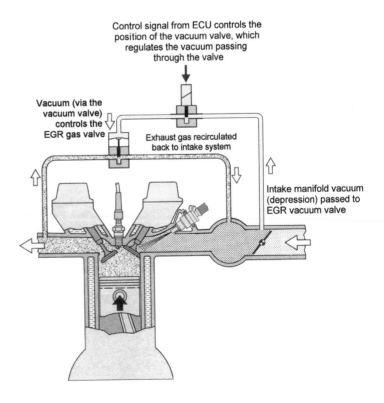

Figure 3.76 EGR system with vacuum valve control

In some systems, the EGR valve is fitted with a sensor that tells the ECU the amount the valve is open. Other systems use a pressure sensor to detect the pressure in the exhaust recirculation pipe. With these sensors, the ECU is able to assess the amount of exhaust gas flowing in the EGR system.

3.5.9 Secondary air injection

Previous parts of section 3.5 have highlighted the problems of high emission levels during cold running. Even modern engines require some enrichment during the early phases of the warm-up period. Enrichment is required to overcome condensing of the fuel on cylinder walls and intake system walls, and to ensure that sufficient fuel is able to vaporise in what is initially a relatively cold environment.

However, a rich mixture will have insufficient oxygen (λ of around 0.9 or less) which will result in high levels of CO and HC. In many cases, these CO and HC levels exceed what is permitted and must therefore be reduced. Because the levels are so high, there is too much CO and HC, and insufficient oxygen for the catalytic converter to change the CO and HC into CO_2. Furthermore, in the early phases of engine start-up, the catalytic converter is not at working temperature.

It is possible to inject air into the exhaust ports or exhaust manifold, which enables oxygen to combine with the CO and HC, owing to the temperature of the exhaust gas. In effect, a combustion or oxidation process occurs in the exhaust manifold. The secondary air injection process is used only for short periods after the engine is started from cold, but is sufficient to reduce the CO and HC levels during this period. In addition, the combustion of gases in the exhaust manifold or ports adds additional heat to the exhaust gas, which assists in quickly raising the temperature of the catalytic converter, so it is able to function sooner.

Air pump injection

Figure 3.77 shows a layout for an air pump based air injection system. The electrically driven air pump draws air from the atmosphere (via the air filter) and pumps it into the exhaust manifold through a control valve which regulates the amount of air depending on operating conditions. The control valve is connected to the intake manifold (position A on the diagram) and intake vacuum (depression) can therefore be passed to the secondary air valve via a control valve. The vacuum passing to the secondary air valve is regulated by a control valve, which is controlled by the ECU.

When the engine is able to operate without mixture enrichment and the catalytic converter is at working temperature, the air pump is switched off.

Pulse air sysdems

Operating in much the same way as air pump injection systems, the pulse air system relies on pressure pulses in the exhaust pipe to draw in air, rather than using a pump (Figure 3.78). The exhaust system is subject to positive and negative pressure pulses when the engine is running. Positive pulses occur when an exhaust valve opens; negative pulses occur when the valve closes but exhaust gases continue to move through the exhaust system.

A valve (one-way valve in the diagram) is used to let the air into the exhaust manifold. It opens when the pressure pulse in the exhaust system is low, and closes when pulse pressure is high. The pulse pressure in each exhaust port changes when the exhaust valve opens and closes, so the valve opens and closes continuously and rapidly during the warm period.

Vacuum from the intake manifold is fed to the pulse air solenoid valve, which is controlled by the ECU. When the ECU control signal opens the valve, vacuum is passed to the 'vacuum controlled valve' which in turn also opens, thus allowing air to flow to the one-way valves and the exhaust manifold. The ECU can control

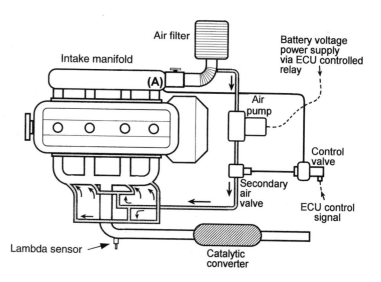

Figure 3.77 Secondary air injection system (with air pump)

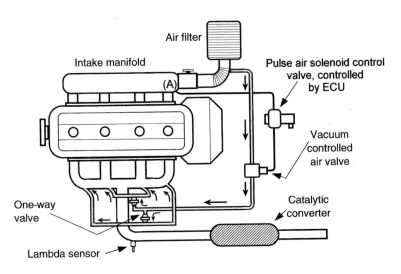

Figure 3.78 Pulse air injection system

the pulse air solenoid valve so that the vacuum affecting the control valve is regulated, thus enabling regulation of the air flowing into the exhaust manifold.

3.5.10 Evaporative emission control

Evaporative emission control systems (EVAP) are used to prevent vapour from the fuel tank and fuel system from escaping into the atmosphere. Figure 3.79 shows a basic EVAP system.

A charcoal (carbon) canister is connected to the fuel tank. The canister collects the fuel vapour which is stored by the charcoal. When the engine is running, vacuum (depression) in the intake system draws the vapour from the canister and into the engine where it mixes with the intake air. A 'canister purge valve' is controlled by the ECU using a digital control signal (section 1.9), to ensure that the flow of vapour to the intake system is regulated. This allows a controlled amount of vapour to enter the intake system for different operating conditions. Typically, the vapour will be drawn from the canister during light/medium load engine conditions.

When the vapour mixes with the intake air, there will be a slight enrichment of the air/fuel mixture. The ECU will therefore adjust the injected fuel quantity to compensate. However, because the process of drawing vapour from the canister usually occurs only when the lambda control system is operating in a 'closed loop', the lambda sensor transmits an appropriate signal to the ECU if the mixture is too rich, thus enabling the ECU to make any corrections.

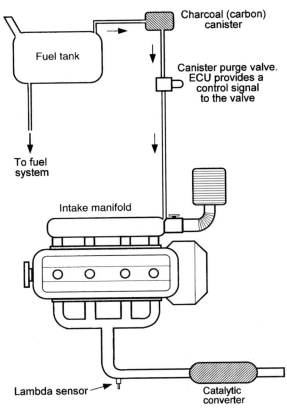

Figure 3.79 Evaporative emission control system (EVAP)

Key Points

EGR reduces cylinder combustion temperature, which in turn reduces NO_x emission

The main way that emissions are reduced is by maintaining accurate ignition and mixture strength

Evaporative emissions are reduced by storing them in charcoal canisters and then burning them in the engine

3.6 ENGINE MANAGEMENT (THE CONCLUSION)

3.6.1 Combining the various systems

The requirement for integrated control

Each of the individual engine systems so far covered within Chapter 3 (ignition, injection and emission) have been subject to continuous development and improvement. In isolation, there have been improvements in engine power, fuel consumption and lowering emission levels. However, the control of each system needs to be integrated with the control of the other systems to achieve the optimum results.

An example of integrated or combined control is the need sometimes to alter ignition timing and fuel quantity at exactly the same time to suit a change in engine operating conditions. To achieve the best results, communication between the ignition ECU and the fuel system ECU is essential. Another example is the need to alter timing and fuelling when certain emission control functions are implemented: again, communication between the different engine systems is essential to achieve optimum system and engine efficiencies.

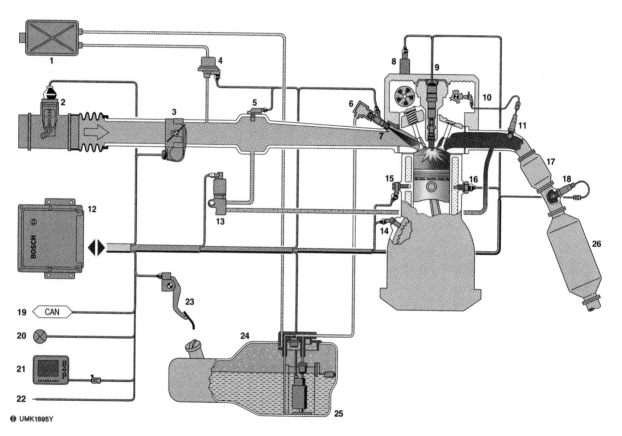

UMK1895Y

Key

1 Activated charcoal canister
2 Hot film air mass sensor with integrated temperature sensor
3 Throttle device (electronic throttle control)
4 Regeneration valve
5 Intake manifold pressure sensor
6 Fuel rail
7 Fuel injector
8 Actuators and sensors for variable valve timing
9 Ignition coil and spark plug
10 Camshaft phase sensor
11 Lambda sensor upstream of primary catalytic converter
12 Engine ECU
13 Exhaust gas recirculation valve
14 Speed sensor
15 Knock sensor
16 Engine temperature sensor
17 Primary catalytic converter (three-way catalytic converter)
18 Lambda sensor downstream of primary catalytic converter
19 CAN interface
20 Fault indicator lamp
21 Diagnostics interface
22 Interface with immobiliser ECU
23 Accelerator pedal module with pedal travel sensor
24 Fuel tank
25 In-tank unit comprising electric fuel pump, fuel filter and fuel pressure regulator
26 Main catalytic converter (three-way)

The on-board diagnostics system configuration illustrated by the diagram reflects the requirements of EOBD

Figure 3.80 Bosch ME Motronic engine management system

On early generations of engine management system, ignition and fuel injection ECUs were separate, but they communicated so that control functions were harmonised. In addition, it was possible to share the information from the various sensors. One temperature sensor could be used to transmit a signal to one of the ECUs, which in turn would transmit a signal to another ECU. This approach reduced the need to duplicate sensors and wiring, which inevitably reduced cost.

Single ECU

During the late 1970s, some engine management systems were produced with a single ECU. This type of system became much more widely produced during the 1980s. Currently, nearly all light vehicle petrol engines are fitted with a single ECU that controls most of the functions. In effect, all of the engine related systems are managed by a single ECU.

The next stage of integrated control systems would be to control all vehicle functions from a single ECU: for example, the engine and chassis systems (including features such as anti-lock brakes), could all be controlled from a single ECU. Although some attempts have been made to produce a single 'vehicle' control unit, the trend is to use high speed communication networks that enable all of the vehicle system ECUs to communicate and share information.

3.6.2 Modern engine management systems

Apart from the diagnostic functions, almost all of the individual systems that make up a modern engine management system have been covered in the previous sections of Chapter 3. The following two examples of modern engine management systems illustrate the way in which all of the previously discussed systems are integrated using a single ECU.

Figure 3.80 shows a Bosch ME Motronic engine management system which uses port type fuel injection along with direct ignition and various emission control devices.

Figure 3.81 shows a modern direct injection engine management system (Bosch MED Motronic). This system is similar to the example shown in Figure 3.80, but note the differences in the fuel injection and emission control systems.

Both systems feature European on-board diagnostics (EOBD) connections which are covered in section 3.7.

> **Key Points**
>
> Full engine management systems combine ignition and fuel control as well as controlling many other aspects such as EGR
>
> Most modern engine management ECUs are linked by CAN to other systems such as transmission management

---

MED 7 Motronic system for direct fuel injection on spark ignition (SI) engines

1 Air mass meter with temperature sensor,	**5** Pressure control valve	**10** Lambda oxygen sensor (LSF)
2 Throttle valve (ETC)	**6** Fuel distributor/Fuel rail	**11** Fuel supply module including presupply pump
3 Intake manifold pressure sensor	**7** Ignition coil	**12** Fuel injector
4 High pressure pump	**8** Lambda oxygen sensor (LSU)	**13** Pressure sensor
	9 NO$_X$ catalytic converter	**14** EGR valve
		15 ECU

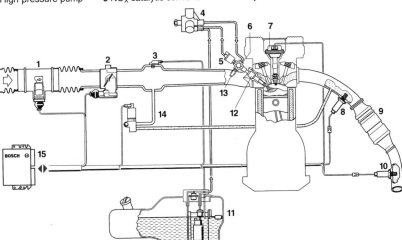

Figure 3.81 Bosch MED (direct fuel injection) Motronic engine management system

3.7 ENGINE SYSTEM SELF-DIAGNOSIS (ON-BOARD DIAGNOSTICS) AND EOBD

3.7.1 Self-diagnosis of system faults

Reasons for self-diagnosis (on-board diagnostics)

Since the mid-1980s, an increasing number of European market vehicles have been equipped with some form of self-diagnosis. Self-diagnosis systems were in use earlier, but mainly on American market products.

Self-diagnosis is the capacity of a vehicle system (or more precisely the system ECU) to detect system operating faults, and provide an indication that a specific fault exists.

Self-diagnosis was initially fitted to fuel and ignition systems, but it has become increasingly fitted to most vehicle systems with electronic control. Self-diagnosis is now found on vehicle systems such as ABS (and other vehicle stability control systems), automatic gearboxes, air conditioning, airbags and other safety systems. Self-diagnosis is a function of the system computer or ECU, which monitors and assesses all the input signals (from sensors) as well as providing the output control signals. The system ECU is able to distinguish correct from incorrect signals (and operation) for much of the system that is being controlled.

Self-diagnosis was introduced to overcome a number of potential problems.

1 One aim of self-diagnosis is to overcome the problems of working and diagnosing faults associated with 'new technology'. This is especially important as each new vehicle system is introduced. Repair technicians need to be able to identify faults relatively quickly and easily.

2 Fast and accurate diagnosis should help to reduce warranty costs, while retaining customer loyalty and satisfaction.

3 The self-diagnosis system can be used during vehicle assembly to ensure that each vehicle leaves the assembly plant without detectable faults.

4 Importantly, modern engine management systems and emission control systems are fitted to vehicles to ensure that emission levels remain low and within legislated limits. Many faults that would result in unacceptable emissions can remain undetected by the driver. With a self-diagnostic system, it is possible to provide a warning to the driver or the workshop technician, along with an indication of what the fault is.

5 Modern vehicle systems rely on complex software programs within the ECU as well as electrical and electronic systems. In a high percentage of cases, technicians are not familiar with these 'new' technologies. Self-diagnostic systems are designed to support technicians on unfamiliar aspects of a new motor vehicle.

Self-diagnostic facilities should help to reduce the length of time that faults remain undetected.

Self-diagnosis systems form only a small part of the whole facility. The next section highlights other functions that can be implemented by the system computer to further assist in reducing emissions when faults occur, and to assist a technician to test or check vehicle system operation. The self-diagnosis facility is often referred to as OBD (on-board diagnostics).

Vehicle manufacturers appoint authorised dealers or repair workshops to sell and maintain vehicles. These usually have very sophisticated, dedicated equipment containing code reading or scan tools as part of the overall equipment package. However, independent repair workshops usually purchase general purpose code reading equipment, designed to function on many makes and models of vehicle. The general purpose equipment is usually designed so that cartridges or pods can be inserted into the code reader; the different cartridges contain different software programs that enable the code reader to communicate and operate with different vehicles.

Fault codes, blink codes and fault related messages

Once the ECU has recognised that a fault exists on a vehicle system, it is able to implement other functions.

The following list covers the common functions performed by the ECU when a fault is recognised.

1 The ECU can illuminate a dashboard warning light to indicate to the driver that a fault exists.

2 A system failure, such as a sensor fault, could cause the engine to run poorly and generate high emissions. Under these conditions, the ECU might be able to control the engine management system so that it operates in a 'limp home' or 'fail safe' mode. When the ECU implements limp home operation, it normally substitutes a preset value for the failed sensor, which should ensure reasonable engine operation.

3 The ECU can provide some form of coded output (fault code) which is accessed or retrieved by a 'fault code reader' or through other means such as a 'blink code' transmitted via the dashboard warning light or via an LED based test tool. A fault code usually consists of a number (or series of numbers), although some systems provide a series of letters or even a short message. As explained later in this section, some standardisation has been adopted across all vehicles for fault code systems, whereby specific faults are allocated a dedicated code number. This standardisation generally only applies to emissions related faults, but inevitably embraces the engine management system.

Methods of retrieving fault codes

As mentioned above, fault codes can be retrieved from the vehicle ECU using a fault code reader which, when connected to the ECU, displays a code number related to the fault.

Many systems, however (especially older systems and non-engine management systems), provide what is often referred to as a 'blink code'. A blink code can be output by the ECU to the dashboard warning light, and the number of flashes on the warning light corresponds to the relevant code number. Some systems use an LED light (often located on the ECU) or codes might be accessed by connecting a separate LED tester (or a volt or dwell meter). When a fault code number has been retrieved, the technician refers to the appropriate information source to look up the code number and establish the nature of the fault. Most code readers indicate the messages within the code reader software.

To access a blink code, it is normally necessary to perform a set procedure which effectively 'instructs' the ECU to output the code. The procedure may involve linking two terminals on a connector plug or other similar procedures which will then cause the ECU to output the code.

When a code reader is connected to the appropriate connector plug, it communicates with the vehicle ECU, and by following the instructions supplied with the code reader (or the instructions on the code reader screen display), the technician can make the code reader transmit an instruction to the ECU which causes the ECU to output the codes. The instruction from the code reader may take the form of a password; when the instruction or password is sent to the ECU, the ECU provides the coded output, thus allowing the code reader to display the code number.

Although some inexpensive code readers effectively act as a means of accessing the simple blink code (i.e. they simply provide a code number), most elaborate readers also display a message which details the nature of the fault associated with the displayed code.

When a blink code is read via a warning light or LED, it is normal practice to count the number of times the light flashes. When more than one code exists, different systems will use slightly different methods of separating the different codes. There are different methods of displaying a code number. For instance, code 12 could simply be displayed by 12 flashes, but alternatively could be displayed by providing one flash, a pause, then two flashes.

The example in Figure 3.82 shows how two codes might be displayed (i.e. code 12 and then code 23). A brief pause is provided between the 'tens and units' as is the case between the 1 and the 2 of code 12, and between the 2 and the 1 of code 23. However, a longer pause (in this case 2 seconds) is provided between the two different codes, as is the case between codes for 12 and 23.

Some inexpensive code readers simply provide a flashing LED; the flashes are counted in the same way as a normal blink code. Most code readers provide a display screen that indicates the code as a number. A code reader might provide a relevant message in addition to the code number.

Two-digit code

One-digit code

Normal

T or TE₁ terminal ON

Normal

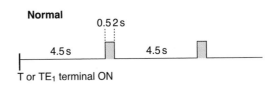

T or TE₁ terminal ON

Abnormal
(Trouble codes 12 and 23 shown)

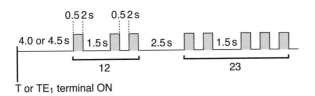

T or TE₁ terminal ON

Abnormal
(Trouble codes 2 and 3 shown)

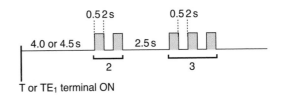

T or TE₁ terminal ON

Figure 3.82 Example of a blink code (code 12 followed by code 21)

3.7.2 How the ECU recognises and overcomes system faults

Expected operating values

Virtually all the circuits connected to the system computer (ECU) carry a voltage or signal that should lie within certain operating values. These values are programmed into the ECU, which can compare actual signal values with expected or programmed values.

For example, the power supply for the ECU might be expected to fall between lower and upper limits of 9 volts and 15 volts. If the voltage is above or below the expected limits, this would be recorded as a fault by the ECU – the starting point for self-diagnosis.

Many sensors on computer controlled vehicle systems operate by providing a voltage or signal voltage that should normally lie within certain easily defined limits. The ECU can thus recognise that a fault exists, assuming that the fault causes the signal voltage to fall outside the expected limits or tolerance.

Example of fault detection using a simple temperature sensor circuit

One example of a sensor circuit that should usually provide a voltage within defined limits is the engine coolant temperature sensor. It functions by changing its resistance as the coolant temperature changes. The sensor forms part of a series resistance circuit, which means that when the resistance of the sensor changes, it affects the voltage in the circuit (Figure 3.83).

The ECU provides a reference voltage to the temperature sensor circuit which, on modern systems, is normally 5 volts. When the circuit is complete (sensor plug connected) the voltage on the section of the circuit between the ECU and the sensor is reduced (by the action of the resistances). The exact voltage depends on the value of the resistances and, although the ECU resistance remains the same, the sensor resistance changes, thus affecting the voltage in the circuit.

On nearly all temperature sensor circuits, a typical operating value is around 3.0–3.5 volts when the coolant temperature is low (a cold engine). The voltage then falls to around 0.3–0.7 volts when the engine is hot. It is possible for the voltage to reach higher or lower values, but this would mean an extremely cold or hot engine.

Assuming that the sensor and associated wiring are in good condition, and that extreme cold and hot temperatures are reached, it is possible (although very unlikely) for the voltage in the circuit to reach as high as 4.5 volts or as low as 0.2 volts. These values can be used by the ECU as maximum and minimum values, and the only likely situation that would cause the voltage to lie outside this range would be a fault in the wiring, sensor or ECU itself. In reality, a tolerance must be allowed slightly outside of the expected maximum and minimum values: in our example we will use 0.1 volts as the minimum and 4.8 volts as the maximum. Figure 3.84 shows typical values for normal operation and for detecting a fault.

There are two main faults that the ECU will easily identify: a break in the circuit and a short in the circuit. Figures 3.85 and 3.86 show a circuit break (open circuit) and a short circuit. In both cases the fault is shown as a wiring problem. However, any part of the circuit, including the sensor resistance itself, could suffer a short circuit or a circuit break, which would provide the same results.

Figure 3.84 Example of temperature sensor circuit operating voltages and voltages that would be regarded as a fault condition

Condition	Sensor signal voltage
Extremely hot (engine running at very high temperature but this condition must be allowed for)	minimum value may be as low as 0.2 volts
Extremely cold (engine running at very low temperature but this condition must be allowed for)	maximum value may be as high as 4.5 volts
Fault condition (ECU detects voltage values that are outside normal expected values)	less than 0.1 volt or greater than 4.8 volts

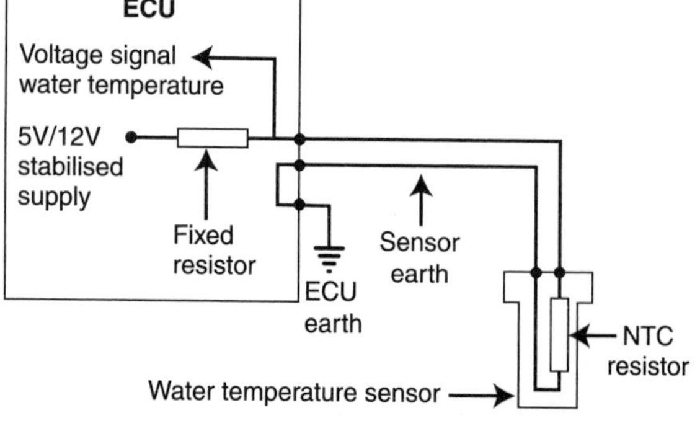

Figure 3.83 Schematic layout of temperature sensor circuit

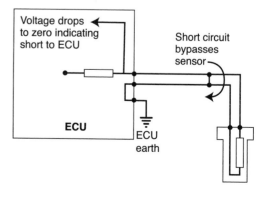

Figure 3.85 Temperature sensor circuit with a short to earth

Short circuit

When there is a short circuit (Figure 3.85) that results in the signal wire shorting through to earth, the 5 volt reference supplied by the ECU is connected directly to earth. The current has already flowed through the resistance in the ECU, so, when the circuit is connected to earth, the voltage falls to zero.

The circuit is now the same as a light circuit in which a voltage is applied to a bulb and then from the bulb to earth. The voltage on the earth side of the bulb is zero. The resistance in the ECU acts in the same way as the light bulb.

The ECU monitors the voltage in the signal circuit, which would normally sit within acceptable operating limits of 0.2–4.5 volts. Because the voltage detected is now zero, the ECU recognises this as a fault. The ECU is able to allocate a fault code to this particular fault.

Note that the ECU might provide a fault code for a fault on the sensor circuit. However, many systems will provide a code that states: 'the voltage level in the temperature sensor circuit is too LOW'.

The ECU cannot determine the exact nature of the fault; it can only establish that a fault exists causing a low voltage. Therefore the technician must still carry out a detailed investigation of the circuit.

Open or broken circuit

A broken or open circuit (Figure 3.86) prevents the flow of current through the circuit. Without a current flow, a resistance does not have any effect on the voltage level in the circuit. Therefore, the 5 volts, applied as a reference voltage by the ECU, remains at 5 volts.

The ECU is again monitoring the voltage at point A (this is the voltage in the signal circuit which would normally be within the acceptable operating limits of 0.2–4.5 volts). Because 5 volts is now detected at point A, the ECU recognises this as a fault, and allocates an appropriate fault code.

Note that the ECU might provide a fault code which indicates that a fault exists on the sensor circuit. However, many systems will provide a code that states: 'the voltage level in the temperature sensor circuit is too HIGH'.

The ECU cannot determine the exact nature of the fault: it can only establish that a fault exists, causing a high voltage. Therefore the technician must still carry out a detailed investigation of the circuit.

Self-diagnosis on other types of sensor or circuit

The system ECU is able to monitor any of the circuits connected to it. The ECU is effectively pre-programmed with the acceptable values for the various circuits, and is therefore able to identify a fault when values lie outside acceptable limits.

Many sensors on a system provide a digital signal, i.e. a signal that consists of on/off pulses, such as the signal from a Hall effect trigger used for vehicle speed sensors, ignition triggers, etc. The ECU can monitor the pulses and detect the correct operating voltage for the signal, or whether the pulse is acceptable or unavailable.

Other sensors provide analogue signals, which again might consist of a series of pulses. A crankshaft speed/position sensor usually provides a series of pulses which the ECU is able to detect as being at a certain voltage. Again, the ECU can detect whether the signal is acceptable or unavailable.

The ECU also provides operating signals to actuators such as injectors or idle speed control valves. If the actuator and associated circuits are good, an electric current will flow through the ECU in order to control the actuator. The ECU is therefore able to recognise many of the faults owing to the fact that, if there is a fault, the current flow might be incorrect, or there might be no current flow at all if the circuit is broken.

In all cases where a fault is identified by the ECU, the technician should attempt to gain as much information as possible about the operation of the system. Knowledge of the way in which the ECU detects particular faults and provides substitute values can assist in accurate diagnosis.

Limp home/emergency operation

In a large number of cases when a fault is detected by the ECU in a sensor circuit the ECU might be able to substitute a value for the failed circuit. If the temperature sensor signal voltage is outside the expected values, the ECU will detect the fault. The ECU has programmed substitution values for certain faults, which can be used to ensure that the engine can still run. With a temperature sensor fault, the ECU could substitute a temperature value, such as a warm running value, that enables the car to be driven to a repair workshop. However, the engine would be difficult to start from cold because the substituted value is for a warm engine.

Modern systems can implement a more complex substitution process. Again using the temperature sensor fault as the example, the ECU timer facility enables it to calculate the length of time the engine has been running, and then internally substitute a temperature value depending on that time period (e.g. if the engine has been running for an hour, the substitution value would be equivalent to normal

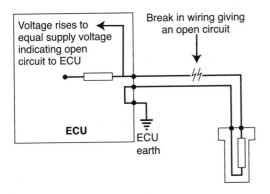

Figure 3.86 Temperature sensor circuit with a break in the wiring (open circuit)

engine temperature). When the engine is switched off for a long period, the ECU would calculate that the engine was cold, and provide a cold running temperature value. At various time intervals, the ECU can substitute progressively warmer temperature values until the engine is assumed to be at normal operating temperature.

It is possible for the ECU to use substitution values for many of the sensors. It is often the case that the substitution process allows the engine to operate without any indications that there is a fault. The driver would often be unaware that a fault exists, except that the warning light on the dashboard illuminates.

There are however a number of faults that will not allow a substitute value to be used. An obvious example is a power supply or earth circuit fault. Another sensor that cannot be easily substituted is the main crankshaft position/speed sensor. Without the signal from this sensor, the ECU has no reference to engine speed or exact crankshaft position, but if additional position sensors are fitted to the engine (such as a camshaft or cylinder identification sensor) these can allow the ECU to provide a limited means of operating the engine systems.

There are a number of terms used to describe the process whereby an ECU substitutes operating values; examples include:

- limp home
- limited operating strategy (LOS)
- emergency operating strategy.

Faulty signal values that are within expected limits

Basic self-diagnosis and fault code systems (including many of the systems produced before the end of the 1990s) have certain limitations, because they only define a fault when the signal is outside expected or acceptable limits. This method of diagnosis can lead to situations where a fault does exist, but the ECU cannot recognise it.

Again, using the temperature sensor circuit as an example, if the sensor itself failed in such a way that the sensor resistance remained at a value corresponding to a normal engine temperature, the voltage in the sensor circuit would also be at an acceptable value. The ECU would not then recognise this failure.

If, for example, the sensor failed, so that the resistance of the sensor (and therefore the voltage in the circuit) corresponded to 40°C (a warm engine) the ECU would only detect this value, and provide a slightly rich fuel mixture which is applicable to the warm engine temperature. That the voltage in the circuit is 'stuck' at this value will not be registered as a fault by these older systems.

However, as described in the previous paragraphs dealing with limp home/emergency operation, most modern systems now have a facility to recognise that the value is unchanging: the ECU can then provide a substitute value.

Many systems up until the late 1990s (and possibly later) did not have the facility to recognise faults for which the value remained within acceptable limits. Therefore technicians should always be prepared for self-diagnosis and fault code systems that do not indicate a fault, even if a fault exists in the system.

Overcoming the limitations of less sophisticated self-diagnosis systems

The previous paragraphs highlighted the fact that less sophisticated systems have certain limitations that must be accounted for when carrying out diagnosis. However, most of these limitations have now been overcome by the system manufacturers, by increasing the capability of the self-diagnostic section of the computer.

More capable systems operate on what is sometimes referred to as 'improbable or implausible'. In effect, the ECU is programmed with a degree of 'intelligence', which enables it to judge whether a signal or value on a circuit is probable or plausible.

For example, a temperature sensor value not altering from a cold value when the engine has been running for a considerable amount of time would be regarded as improbable or implausible. The ECU can use more than one item of information from the other sensors or from programmed logic to make a judgment. An example of programmed logic would be: 'a cold temperature value cannot be correct when the engine has been running for a long time'.

A signal would not be plausible if:

1 the throttle position sensor indicates that the throttle has just opened fully
2 the engine speed has increased
3 the airflow sensor indicates that there has been no change in the air being drawn into the engine.

The above situation would indicate a likely airflow sensor fault, which could in fact be overridden by the ECU; in this case, it could ignore the airflow sensor fault and rely on throttle position and engine speed as a means of calculating the fuelling and ignition requirements. Therefore, the ECU on a modern system has far better ability to diagnose a fault and, where necessary, override the faulty inputs.

Adaptive strategy

Adaptive strategy provides the ECU with the ability to relearn the values provided by the sensor circuits.

A simple example is the signal voltage provided by a throttle position sensor when the throttle is in the idle or closed position. The ECU might initially be programmed to expect a certain voltage, e.g. 0.5 volts (with a small tolerance or range), when the throttle is closed or in the idle position.

However, wear in the linkage and other changes that can occur over a period of time, can result in a change in the voltage when the throttle is closed. If, over a period of time or at a set time during the system operation, the ECU is able to detect that this voltage is now different, it can replace the original expected value with the new value.

Although not directly related to fault code reading, it is worth noting that an adaptive strategy can have a major effect on the way the system identifies or deals with a fault. Additionally, it will have a direct effect on the success of rectification work. The particular example of the throttle position sensor voltage (and many other examples of the ECU being able to relearn values) may not have a direct effect on the self-diagnostic process but if a sensor or a circuit does fail on the vehicle and a new sensor or component is fitted, the ECU must go through a period of 'relearning' the new values in order to be able to provide the correct control over the engine.

It is worth noting that, after rectification work is carried out, or even if a battery has been disconnected, the ECU might need to relearn the values of the sensors, etc. For example, some engine management systems can take more than 16 km (10 miles) to relearn sensor values. It is also a common requirement that an engine must go through a full cycle of operation, such as cold start, load and cruise conditions, etc., before it can fully relearn the system signals. The engine may therefore not perform properly until the ECU has relearnt and adapted to the new values.

When a vehicle battery is disconnected the ECU might suffer memory loss, so it is advisable to test drive the vehicle after the battery has been reconnected to ensure that the engine is performing normally.

3.7.3 Live data/serial data and other additional functions of self-diagnostic systems

Live data/serial data

In addition to providing fault codes, modern systems can give other information to the technician about the operation of the vehicle system. Engine management systems, for example, are able to provide live data via the fault code reading equipment.

The ECU is already monitoring the circuits of the engine management system in order to control the system. The ECU relies on signals from the sensors, etc. to control fuelling, ignition timing, emissions and other functions. It is relatively easy for the ECU to output or transmit those same signal values to a code reader or similar item of test equipment.

If a capable code reader is connected to the engine management system diagnostic plug, the code reader is able to display a considerable range of measurements relating to the operation of the engine management system. Different systems provide different items of data, but the following list indicates just a few of the sensor measurements that can be accessed via the live data systems, with the use of a suitable code reader or similar equipment:

- battery voltage
- engine speed
- airflow sensor signal voltage
- coolant temperature sensor signal voltage
- throttle position sensor voltage
- lambda (oxygen) sensor signal voltage
- air temperature sensor signal voltage
- MAP (vacuum) sensor signal.

Additionally, the ECU can also provide control signal values covering:

- ignition timing
- injection control
- EVAP system solenoid control
- idle speed valve control duty cycle (on/off ratio).

In fact, a wide range of control signal values and sensor signal values can be accessed on modern systems. Additionally, operational information can be accessed, such as whether the system is operating in closed or open loop for emission control (see section 3.5.7).

With the live data information, it is possible for the technician to check on ECU operation and ensure that the system is operating as intended.

Note that some of the values may be converted by the code reader into a more acceptable form. The coolant temperature sensor voltage could be displayed in the normal way, as a voltage, but can be converted to give the coolant temperature in degrees, e.g. 0.9 volts = 85°C.

Live data allows the technician to view a considerable range of readings that would otherwise need to be accessed by more traditional measurement tools, such as multimeters or oscilloscopes.

In addition to the examples of live data shown above, the ECU can also output information about computer or ECU calculations. This can include the calculated load and other values which are usually displayed in a format that does not assist technicians unless they have access to dedicated data.

The live data output and other information delivered by the ECU is often referred to as 'serial data' or 'data stream information'. These terms simply refer to the way in which a code reader or other test equipment communicates with the ECU. As with personal computers, data communication (such as between the PC and a printer) is achieved by transferring information in series along a wire, i.e. with one piece of information following another.

Using live data for diagnosis

There is no doubt that live data is an aid to diagnosis. In previous sections we have noted that fault codes are primarily of use if the fault causes the signal values to lie outside acceptable limits. However, if a fault results in signal voltages or values that are within acceptable limits, it may not be recognised by the ECU. Therefore, if an engine management system has an undetected or unrecognised fault, but the engine is obviously not running properly, it is possible to examine the live data to see if the signal values are correct for the engine operating conditions.

Again referring to the coolant temperature sensor as an example, the sensor signal voltage might indicate '0.9 volts = 85°C', but this could not be correct if the engine had not been run for some hours. In other words, the engine is cold but the temperature sensor is indicating that the coolant is almost up to the hot operating temperature. The values would not be recognised as a fault on many systems, but the live data display allows the technician to compare values against what should be expected for the conditions.

As another example, if the ECU detects a signal that is not plausible or probable, such as the airflow sensor signal discussed previously (see section 3.7.2), the ECU might not provide a fault code that indicates the exact fault. However, reference to the live data should enable an experienced technician to identify that the airflow sensor signal is incorrect under certain operating conditions.

Snapshot or playback mode

Various terms are used to describe the snapshot or playback facility. This facility enables the fault code reader to display fault codes, or in some cases live data that were recorded earlier.

The exact capability varies depending on the system; however, it is possible for the code reader (in conjunction with the ECU) to capture codes or data at a time when a fault occurred. This facility is extremely useful when trying to trace intermittent faults that do not necessarily show up during workshop tests. The test equipment can be connected to the vehicle, which is driven until the intermittent fault occurs.

It is often the case that the code reader/ECU combination can record a range of measurements or live data at the time a fault occurs. The measurements and data are monitored while the vehicle is being driven or the engine is running. It may be necessary for someone to press a start button on the code reader when the fault occurs (such as a noticeable misfire). The measurements received from just prior to the fault until just after it are stored.

Some vehicle systems might have already registered a fault code relating to an intermittent fault. The code reader/ECU combination can be programmed to capture and store the data next time the particular intermittent fault occurs. In some cases, the ECU will automatically store applicable data when a fault occurs, and it is then simply a matter of connecting the test equipment at some later stage to obtain the data that was stored at the time the fault occurred.

The final result is that the data can be analysed after an intermittent fault has been noticed, thus enabling the technician to perform an accurate diagnosis.

Not all vehicle systems and not all code readers allow the snapshot or playback facility to function.

Service adjust mode

Some vehicle systems, notably engine management systems, have a service adjust mode which can be used for some basic service set procedures. On some older systems, idle speed and other operating values could be set or adjusted, but with most modern systems this facility is not required.

There are occasions, however, when some basic settings can be altered, such as in a country with low quality fuel. It is possible on some vehicles to effectively reprogram the ECU so that it alters the timing and fuelling characteristics to suit different fuel qualities. In reality, the ECU has a number of programmed characteristics already located in its memory: it is simply a matter of selecting the appropriate program by using the code reader or other suitable equipment.

Actuator simulation tests

It is becoming increasingly common for systems to incorporate an actuator test facility. As well as monitoring the electrical circuits for an actuator such as an injector, modern ECUs are able to provide a control signal to the actuator (in effect a simulation of the actuator signal). This control signal has a known value, so that the operation of the actuator can be checked. It is usual to implement this facility using the code reader: the technician selects the appropriate function, which causes the actuator signal to be transmitted from the ECU to the actuator, which then operates.

With modern systems, the ECU can provide a control signal to a number of components or actuators in the system. In engine management systems, for example, the ECU can control the injectors, the idle valve, the EVAP canister purge valve and possibly other items (such as the exhaust gas recirculation system valve). During an actuator test, the ECU is instructed to operate these components independently and normally, when the engine is not running.

In this way it is possible for the technician to hear or observe operation of the various actuators, which helps to establish whether these components are functioning correctly, and that the associated wiring is good.

When an actuator test is carried out on the injectors, it is likely that fuel will be injected into the intake manifold or into some cylinders. It is advisable that the fuel pump is disconnected to prevent excessive fuel entering the engine. As a minimum precaution, the spark plugs should be removed and the engine cranked over to evacuate excess fuel.

'Set procedure' testing

Several engine management systems rely on the technician following a set procedure or test routine that requires a number of actions to be performed by the technician. These set procedures are usually dictated to the technician via the code reader. In effect, instructions are provided for the actions that the technician must perform.

When the code reader is connected to a diagnostic plug, various messages displayed on the code reader provide the technician with relevant instruction to perform a certain task, before going on to the next phase of testing. On some systems, the whole self-diagnostic routine is based around the need for the technician to perform certain procedures all the way through the test sequence.

Typical procedures that need to be carried out include altering the engine speed, turning the steering (to check power steering pressure switch operation) and depressing the brake pedal (to check brake switch operation).

If the procedures are not carried out as instructed, the test results will be incorrect, and the ECU might diagnose a fault that does not in fact exist. In other cases, the ECU will not proceed to the next set of tests until the correct responses or readings have occurred or been recorded.

Clearing codes

It is important that, when a fault has been rectified, the original fault codes are removed from the ECU memory. The process for clearing codes varies with each make and model of vehicle, and will also depend on whether blink codes are being accessed or a code reader is being used.

Reference should always be made to the specific information on each vehicle to ensure that the correct process is used to clear old fault codes.

Common problems with the use of code reading equipment

Although self-diagnostic systems, code reading and retrieval of live data are generally reliable facilities, a number of problems can arise which are often blamed on the code reader, but may in fact be due to common problems such as operator error or system faults that prevent good test results being obtained.

The following lists those common faults that often result from what are termed 'communication errors' between the code reader and the system ECU.

1 All instructions provided by the equipment manufacturer might not have been followed exactly. When certain procedures are not performed in the correct order or as instructed, the ECU might not allow further tests to continue or might provide incorrect results.

2 Instructions provided on the code reader display might not be followed accurately. If any procedure is carried out incorrectly or not at the correct time, the ECU might not allow tests to continue or incorrect results might be obtained.

Minor changes are often made to systems because of modifications that occur throughout the production life of a vehicle. This can result in small changes to the procedures that have to be carried out by the technician when accessing fault codes, etc. Although the technician might be conversant

with a particular system, a variant of that system might require slightly different procedures or even use different fault codes.

3 All connections between the code reader and the diagnostic plug must be checked. Some systems and code readers require a separate power supply or earth connection to be made (usually an adapter lead or harness is provided to connect the equipment to the battery). Check whether the system being tested requires the use of a separate harness.

4 The code reader or the application cartridge/card must be correct for the system being tested. It is unfortunately not uncommon for a code reader (or the application cartridge) to be designed to operate with a particular range of systems, and for the vehicle manufacturer to then modify the system in production, which can prevent communication with the original code reader or cartridge.

5 All wiring between the code reading equipment and the diagnostic plug, and between the plug and the ECU must be checked. It is also necessary to check for poor earth connections to the ECU and check the power supply to the ECU and to the code reader.

A reduced power supply (flat battery) can cause communication to cease if the voltage level falls below a certain limit.

Different terminology for code reading equipment

A scanner or scan tool is another term (often used to describe American equipment) applied to code reading equipment. In general, the term code reader is applied to something that simply extracts codes from the vehicle system. A scanner is an item of equipment which effectively scans the ECU memory for information.

However, the terms code reader and scanner are loosely used by the industry as product names, as well as being general terms to identify equipment that communicates with a vehicle system ECU.

3.7.4 Use of test equipment to access fault codes

The test equipment (code reader or scan tool) provides specific instructions about equipment operation and the connection processes. It is useful to understand some typical processes for equipment use and for accessing blink codes, fault codes and live data.

Blink codes via the dashboard warning lights

A blink code is the simplest form of fault code reading, especially when displayed via the dashboard warning light. Dashboard warning lights are now fitted to virtually all passenger vehicles, with a typical appearance as shown in Figure 3.87.

Figure 3.87 Dashboard warning light

It is necessary to refer to the specific vehicle information to find out how its blink codes can be retrieved, but the following example shows how blink codes are retrievable on one particular range of vehicles.

Example of blink code retrieval
In this example, it is necessary to instruct the ECU to provide a blink code output to the dashboard warning light. Here the instruction to the ECU is provided by linking two terminals on the diagnostic harness plug (Figure 3.88). When the two terminals are linked and the ignition is switched on, the ECU causes the warning light to flash an appropriate number of times, depending on whether there is a fault code stored in the ECU memory.

As discussed in section 3.7.1, the number of flashes of the warning light represents the fault code: counting the flashes enables the technician to read the code.

There are many other methods used by vehicle manufacturers for instructing the ECU to output fault codes via the warning light, so refer to specific instructions for each vehicle.

Retrieving blink codes via a vehicle system LED
Some vehicles use an LED located on the ECU (or in other locations on the vehicle) to enable a blink code to be read by the technician. As with the warning light blink codes, a specific procedure needs to be performed to instruct the ECU to output the code to the LED light.

Accessing blink codes using an LED probe
On some vehicles (mainly older models), it is possible to access the blink code using an LED probe (Figure 3.89). The process usually involves connecting the probe tip to a terminal or connection of the ECU, or to a terminal of a wiring harness plug, while the other connection for the probe (the crocodile clip in Figure 3.89) remains connected to earth.

As with blink code retrieval using the warning light, it is usually necessary to instruct the ECU to output the codes. Refer to specific vehicle information for the correct procedure and to establish where the LED probe tip should be connected.

One example of a procedure for instructing the ECU to output a blink code using an LED probe is where two terminals on a connector or harness plug are linked using a switch. This process was used in some older generation Audi models.

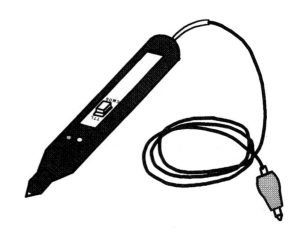

Figure 3.89 An LED probe for accessing the blink code

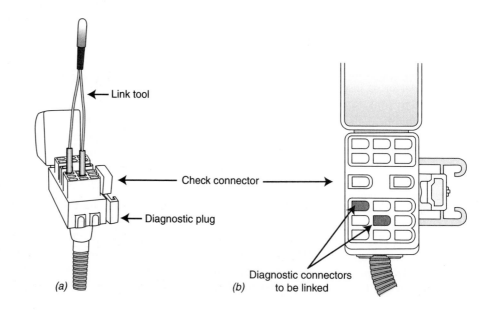

Figure 3.88 Example of linking terminals on the diagnostic plug to instruct the ECU to provide blink code output
a Link tool inserted into connector to initiate diagnostic sequence
b Plan view of connector terminals

← Link tool

← Check connector →

← Diagnostic plug

Diagnostic connectors to be linked

(a)   *(b)*

A switch is connected across the two specified terminals, and then the LED probe connected across two other terminals of the harness plug. The specific instructions will indicate when the switch should be closed or open. This action makes or breaks the circuit across the two terminals. If the switch is opened and closed at the appropriate times, the ECU will output the fault codes as a blink code on the LED probe.

Obtaining codes and fault related information using a code reader/scan tool

Using a code reader/scan tool is the most informative method of retrieving fault related information from the ECU.

A code reader/scan tool must be connected to the ECU to obtain the information; connection is made to a diagnostic plug (Figure 3.90), which in most modern vehicles (with engine management systems) is located inside the passenger compartment. However, some other vehicle systems, such as ABS, have a diagnostic plug located in the engine compartment or elsewhere.

Note that European regulations now specify that the engine management diagnostic plug is to be located within a defined region of the passenger compartment; this is explained more fully in section 3.7.5.

Appropriate vehicle application software

Many code readers can use different cartridges, pods or software to enable them to function on different makes and models of vehicle and on different makes of vehicle system. Although some code readers are designed to operate on only one (or a few) makes and models, most have the facility to use different application software, which can be purchased from the code reader manufacturer. Depending on the equipment design, the software is contained within replaceable pods or cartridges. In some cases new software can be downloaded via the Internet.

Most code readers are capable of operating with many different makes and models of vehicle. Software upgrades enable newer models to be covered without necessarily requiring a complete new code reader.

Starting the communication

For almost all vehicle systems, the ECU requires some form of password before it will output the fault codes or live data to the code reader. The password is usually an electronic code that is transmitted from the code reader to the ECU. In most cases, the appropriate software cartridge is installed in the code reader, or the appropriate vehicle is selected from the menu on the code reader, causing the correct password to be sent to the ECU. When the ECU has received the password, the ECU and the code reader can then communicate.

Retrieving fault codes and data

Once communication has been established between the code reader and ECU, the capacity to retrieve codes and information will depend on the equipment being used and the system being tested. In general, however, instructions are provided on the code reader display, or are included in an operator manual.

Following the correct procedures will then allow fault codes, messages or live data to be retrieved, as well as enabling other functions to be performed, such as actuator tests and intermittent fault detection.

Figure 3.90 Connection of a code reader to the vehicle diagnostic plug

Different vehicle systems will provide different levels of information. Some may provide only simple fault codes, whilst modern engine management systems provide a considerable depth of live data, etc. Additionally, lower cost code readers might not be able to display all of the information available from the ECU, and may not be able to initiate many of the other ECU test functions, such as actuator testing.

3.7.5 EOBD (European on-board diagnostics)

Emissions related legislation affecting on-board diagnostics

The term on-board diagnostics refers in general to the facilities already described relating to self-diagnosis. However, originally in America and more recently in Europe, legislation has imposed certain standards for on-board diagnostic systems, with particular regard to emission control systems. In reality, because emission systems are now under the control of the engine management system, the operation of the engine management system is influenced by the legislation.

The American market has had on-board diagnostic legislation for some years (OBD 1 and OBD 2). In Europe, legislation was introduced in January 2000 that applied to new models (subsequently embracing diesel engines as well as petrol engines). In Europe, the on-board diagnostic legislation is referred to as EOBD (European on-board diagnostics) and is an adaptation of the American OBD 2, which was originally introduced in 1996. EOBD is part of a range of regulations introduced by the EC aimed at controlling or reducing the emissions from motor vehicles. There are many aspects to EOBD regulations, but the relevant issues are discussed within this section.

Whilst the regulations are primarily aimed at emissions control systems/engine management systems, other vehicle systems also affect emission levels, such as the air conditioning. The air conditioning system may be operating at idle speed, thus causing the idle speed to reduce as well as demanding engine power. An engine management system must ensure that the idle speed is maintained, and also ensure the air:fuel ratio is controlled, so power can be developed without increasing emissions significantly. It is common to find fault codes on modern systems that embrace air conditioning functions, automatic transmission functions, and also codes for other vehicle systems that communicate or co-operate with the engine management system.

Long term monitoring of emissions from the vehicle

One objective of the regulations is to ensure that emissions levels from motor vehicles are maintained at acceptable levels for the operating life of the vehicle, and also that, when the emissions levels are unacceptable because of a fault, vehicle systems are able to detect the incorrect emissions and identify the fault. In effect, the regulations impose a requirement for monitoring emissions and emissions control systems (including the engine management system). This requirement effectively defines the technical functions of the engine management system and some of the ECU diagnosis software. EOBD regulations resulted in the introduction of post-cat monitoring, i.e. an oxygen or lambda sensor located after the catalytic converter (section 3.5.7). This additional lambda sensor allowed the ECU to monitor the efficiency of the catalytic converter process. A second lambda sensor signal indicates the oxygen content of the exhaust gas in the catalytic converter.

The self-monitoring and self-diagnostic capability of the modern engine management ECU is highly complex, and the software program embraces many variables that can occur during engine management system operation. As a simple example, if the signal voltage from a temperature sensor exceeds the maximum programmed limit (e.g. 4.8 volts, as used in earlier examples in section 3.7.2), this would be regarded as a fault on older systems. However, EOBD systems must have a built-in tolerance that allows the signal voltage to exceed the maximum limit for a very brief period of time.

ECU programming must therefore permit an occasionally faulty signal, so long as it occurs only for an exceptionally short period and on a limited number of occasions; under these specified conditions, the ECU would not regard the fault as permanent, so no fault code would be stored and the warning light would not be illuminated.

Standardisation of fault codes, communication and diagnostic plugs
Standardised codes

Another significant aspect of EOBD is the standardisation of many engine system related fault codes. Prior to EOBD, vehicle manufacturers used their own coding system to indicate faults – there was no consistency across makes or models. Whilst vehicle manufacturers are still allowed to use their own fault code system and codes (which can be used in their authorised repair workshops in conjunction with the dedicated vehicle test equipment), there is a standardised list of codes and messages that apply to emissions related system faults. The standardised system of codes must be accessible to general purpose code reading equipment, so that equipment manufacturers can produce code reading equipment that provides the same fault codes and messages irrespective of the vehicle being tested.

The standardised codes, which number in excess of 500, are referred to as P Zero or P0 codes. Vehicle manufacturers' own coding systems are referred to as P1 codes. The P0 codes must still be accessible even if a vehicle manufacturer uses its own P1 coding system.

The letter P denotes the power train (effectively the engine and emission systems). Other code letters refer to different aspects of the vehicle, as shown below:

P = power train (standardised EOBD codes)
C = chassis system codes
B = body system codes
U = network system codes (this relates to the communication networks where different computers or ECUs communicate with each other).

A zero (0) following a letter (as in P0) indicates a standardised code such as EOBD, or a code established by the Society of Automotive Engineers (SAE) or other organisations. A number 1 or 2 following a letter (as in P1 or P2) indicates a manufacturer's own code. Note that EOBD does not at this time embrace standardisation or access to live data, but only fault codes and fault messages.

Figure 3.91 shows the structure of the standardised P0 fault codes and messages.

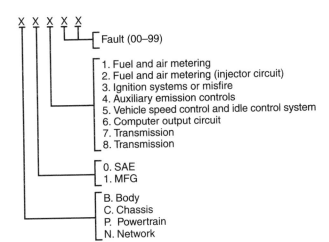

Figure 3.91 Examples of EOBD standard P0 fault codes

Standardised communication

EOBD rules identify a common 'language' that should be used in the computer system, so that it communicates with a standard type or general purpose code reader. The standardised language is in fact referring to the computer protocol used when the code reader and ECU communicate. Included in the standardisation are the passwords to enable the code readers to gain access to the information and data within the ECU.

Standardised diagnostic connector plug

EOBD specifies a standard diagnostic plug which has 16 terminals or connector pins (Figure 3.92). The function of the pins is also standardised, i.e. some of the 16 pins are designated as part of the EOBD system and are allocated specific functions such as battery voltage, power supply and earth connection for the code reader communication terminals (the terminals through which the codes and data are transmitted from the ECU to the code reader). This allows a single code reader to connect to any modern vehicle with a single connector harness and plug. The result is that vehicle testing stations, police forces and workshops can have a standard code reader to retrieve EOBD information from any vehicle.

The location of the diagnostic plug has also been defined within EOBD regulations. In general, it is sited close to the driver's seat, approximately between the centre line of the vehicle and the steering column. The connector plug is found on many vehicles just under the dashboard, adjacent to the driver's leg, although in some vehicles it is on the centre console.

Malfunction indicator lamp

The malfunction indicator lamp (MIL) is another term for the engine warning light. The MIL is intended for use when emissions/engine management system faults occur, or emissions are outside predefined limits. The MIL must be positioned on the dashboard and must not be red when illuminated. When the MIL is illuminated, it indicates that a system fault exists, and that the engine management system might be operating using the 'limp home' function. There are two main operating strategies for the MIL.

1 If the MIL illuminates permanently (no flashing) when the engine is running, it indicates that the ECU has detected a fault that could allow excessive emissions to be produced. It also indicates that a fault code or message is stored in the ECU memory. The fault code can be accessed using a code reader or scan tool.

2 If the MIL flashes continuously when the engine is running, it indicates the ECU has detected an engine misfire. In such cases, it is possible for excess oxygen and fuel to ignite in the catalytic converter, causing permanent damage, or at least to accelerate its ageing. If the MIL is flashing, the driver should ideally reduce engine speed and load, and take the vehicle to a repair workshop as soon as possible.

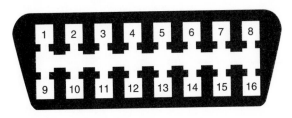

Figure 3.92 16-pin diagnostic connector plug

Misfire detection

Another feature of EOBD systems is the facility to detect misfires. There is a strong possibility that the catalytic converter might be damaged because of a misfire, and high emissions of HC are produced when misfires occur, so the engine management system must be able to detect misfires and, in some cases, cut off fuel to the affected cylinder.

Misfires can be detected using several methods as listed below.

1 **Monitoring the crankshaft speed and acceleration** – when the combustion process occurs in a cylinder, it produces power that forces the crankshaft to accelerate. If the combustion process in a cylinder is not efficient, or produces less power than the other cylinders, the acceleration at the crankshaft will not be as great as for the other cylinders. This difference enables the ECU to establish which cylinder is misfiring or running less efficiently.

2 **Spark detection** is a method whereby the ECU monitors the voltage in the ignition coil. When a misfire occurs, the changes in secondary circuit firing and spark voltage can also affect the voltage in the primary circuit. The process is not dissimilar to examining the ignition circuit voltages using an oscilloscope or test meter. By comparing voltages across the different cylinders, and referencing expected or previous voltages for that cylinder, the ECU can identify which cylinder is misfiring.

3 **A misfire** causes an increase in the unburned oxygen content of the exhaust gas. The lambda/oxygen sensor will detect the high levels of oxygen, and the ECU will register this as a fault. This process alone does not identify *which* cylinder is misfiring, but by analysing the misfire detection information provided by other methods such as in (1) or (2), the ECU can assess which cylinder is at fault.

Cylinder isolation

If exhaust oxygen levels are excessively high, which will usually be accompanied by high levels of unburned fuel (HC), it is possible for the ECU on many modern systems to cut off fuel delivery to the affected cylinder. As well as reducing the high HC emissions, cutting off the fuel supply to the affected cylinder reduces the risk of excessive combustion of fuel and oxygen in the exhaust system and catalytic converter, combustion which could create high temperatures and damage the catalytic converter.

Web links

Engine systems information

www.bosch.com
www.sae.org
www.imeche.org.uk
www.picotech.com
www.autotap.com
www.visteon.com
www.infineon.com
www.kvaser.com (follow CAN Education links)

Teaching/learning resources

Online learning material relating to powertrain systems:

www.auto-training.co.uk

Chapter 4

ENGINE MANAGEMENT – DIESEL INJECTION

what is covered in this chapter . . .

- ■ Development of modern diesel fuel systems
- ■ Development and electronic control of the rotary type diesel injection pump
- ■ Cold-start pre-heating systems
- ■ Electronic control of diesel injection (common rail systems)

4.1 MODERN DIESEL FUEL SYSTEMS

4.1.1 Emissions, economy and engine performance

As with the petrol engine, legislation has forced designers of diesel engines to reduce emissions of pollutants, whilst at the same time consumer demand for improved engine performance and economy has potentially conflicted with emission requirements. However, again as with petrol engines, improved engine design and the development of the fuel systems has resulted in improvements in almost all areas.

Emissions

In comparison with most petrol engines, the diesel engine operates with very weak air:fuel ratios. Apart from some modern direct petrol injection engines operating at light load, a petrol engine generally operates with a lambda value (excess air factor) of close to 1. Diesel engines, however, always operate with a lambda value greater than 1 and as high as lambda 1.4.

Because of this high excess of air, carbon monoxide (CO) emissions are exceptionally low, with values as low as 0.01% at idle and with a typical maximum of around 0.2% (200 parts per million) at full load. Hydrocarbon (HC) emissions are also low at less than 50 parts per million (ppm) at full load, but this can rise to approximately 500 ppm at idle speed, which is in fact higher than emissions from petrol engines.

Emissions of oxides of nitrogen (NO_x) are high with diesel engines and, as with petrol engines, levels can reach 2500 ppm.

The diesel engine does not generally use any form of air volume or air mass control, i.e. there is normally no throttle control to regulate the volume/mass of air entering the cylinder. The volume of air drawn into the cylinders is entirely dependent on engine speed, load and design; therefore power or torque control is totally dependent on fuel quantity (air:fuel ratio). Engine torque and power are therefore controlled by the quantity of fuel injected into the cylinder. Exceptionally weak mixtures will result in low power and torque levels, suitable for light load operation. However, when it is necessary for the engine to produce higher levels of torque and power, the quantity of fuel must be increased (a richer air:fuel ratio).

Since engine torque and power are dependent on the air:fuel ratio, when power or torque are required a rich mixture (reduced oxygen content) is provided which results in an increase in CO and also in NO_x emissions (due to combustion temperature increase). Additionally, the levels of soot emitted increase with richer mixtures (soot can be regarded as fuel droplets that have not vaporised, compared with HC emissions, which are vaporised fuel).

In recent years, legislation has imposed progressively tougher emissions limits, with the Euro 4 legislation for 2005 dictating further reductions in emissions. Various emissions reduction techniques are therefore used on modern diesel engines with particular focus on electronic control of diesel injection systems. In fact, the introduction of 'common rail' diesel injection systems is an interesting development, with their similarity to direct injection petrol systems that have also been relatively recently introduced.

The subject of diesel emissions is frequently debated by the politicians and scientists, with the result that there is a continuously changing view as to whether diesel or petrol engines produce the more harmful emissions.

Economy and engine performance

Traditionally, because diesel engines operate with relatively weak air:fuel ratios (compared with petrol engines), fuel consumption is generally much lower than an equivalent petrol engine. However, diesel engines have generally produced less power than an equivalent size of petrol engine, although torque levels are usually higher. The diesel engine is, however, ideally suited to turbocharging, which can enable the diesel to produce high torque and high power outputs.

Many modern passenger car diesel engines with turbocharging can in fact match the performance of their petrol equivalents (even in the sportier models). Equivalent performance with reduced fuel consumption is a major consumer benefit.

Another significant factor for the consumer is the cost of diesel fuel. In general, in Europe, diesel fuel is less costly than petrol (with the notable exception of the UK). For this reason, many European countries have high percentages of diesel cars, with in excess of 50% being normal in some countries. In the UK, there has been a trend towards a higher percentage of vehicle sales being diesel (beginning around 2000), with up to 30% of the total cars sold now being diesel engine vehicles (especially for smaller cars).

One other factor that has noticeably changed with the diesel engine is noise. Modern injection systems and engine designs have resulted in a considerable reduction in the traditional diesel knock, an important factor for the consumer. The intrusion of diesel engine noise into passenger compartments is much lower and there is also a significant reduction in noise outside the vehicle.

> **Key Points**
>
> In comparison with petrol/gasoline engines, diesels operate with very weak mixtures. This results in very low carbon monoxide emissions
>
> Diesel engine performance was generally inferior to that of petrol/gasoline engines but the addition of a turbocharger makes the performance similar. However, diesel economy is still better

4.1.2 Diesel engine developments

As with the petrol engine, fundamental diesel engine design has improved. General improvements embrace the combustion chamber and the use of four valves per cylinder, as well as improved intake port designs. However, it is fuel systems that have provided the greatest change to the diesel engine. With the progressive introduction of electronic control, which was initially used to enhance the operation of traditional diesel injection pumps (in-line as well as rotary), through to fully electronic common rail systems, electronic control has made some very significant improvements to the diesel engine.

Inevitably, the improvements have been very much forced by environmental considerations (emissions legislation), but with the addition of consumer benefits, the diesel engine has become a much more accepted engine type, especially in countries where the petrol engine was traditionally the preferred option for passenger vehicles.

4.1.3 Decline of in-line pump and rotary pump injection systems

Electronic control for in-line diesel injection pumps is generally used only on large engines in heavy commercial vehicles. Passenger cars and light commercial vehicles increasingly used rotary type pumps through the 1980s and 1990s. With legislation forcing further emissions reductions, the trend has more recently been towards electronic control for unit injectors and more frequently, common rail injection systems which are similar in layout and operation to a modern petrol injection system.

Figure 4.1 shows an in-line type pump (for a six-cylinder engine), which has electronic control to take care of functions that were previously mechanically or hydraulically/pneumatically controlled. Injection timing (start of delivery) and fuel quantity are controlled by the ECU which passes a control signal to solenoids or other actuators that then alter the position of the mechanical devices within the pump. In effect, the pump operates in much the same way as older designs but electronic systems enhance its capability and accuracy. The in-line pump is not covered in this book because of its lack of use in passenger and light vehicles. For an understanding of the operation of in-line pumps, see Chapter 2 in *Hillier's Fundamentals of Motor Vehicle Technology Book 1*.

*1 Pump cylinder, 2 Control sleeve, 3 Control rod,
4 Pump plunger, 5 Camshaft, 6 Port-closing actuator solenoid,
7 Control-sleeve setting shaft, 8 Rod-travel actuator solenoid,
9 Inductive rod-travel sensor, 10 Connector,
11 Inductive speed sensor.*

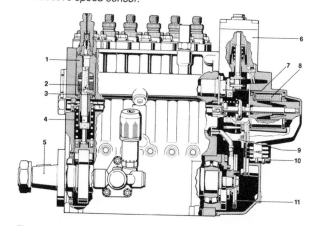

Figure 4.1 Bosch in-line diesel injection pump

4.2   THE ROTARY DIESEL INJECTION PUMP

4.2.1 Rotary pumps 'without' electronic control

This section covers just one type of rotary pump. See Chapter 2 in *Hillier's Fundamentals of Motor Vehicle Technology Book 1* for additional information on the operation of diesel injection pumps.

Figure 4.2 shows a VE pump fitted in a self-bleeding fuel system layout similar to that used on light vehicles. As with other rotary pumps, this type has one pumping element and a number of high pressure outlets, one for each engine cylinder.

1 Fuel tank, 2 Fuel filter, 3 Distributor-type fuel-injection pump, 4 Nozzle-and-holder assembly, 5 Fuel return line, 6 Sheathed-element glow plug, 7 Battery, 8 Glow-plug and starter switch, 9 Glow control unit.

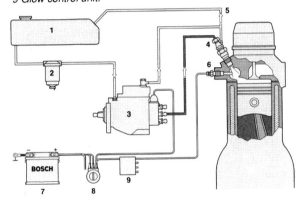

Figure 4.2 Bosch distributor pump fuel system

In addition to the basic features associated with modern distributor rotary pumps, various add-on modules can be fitted to the VE pump; these include:

- a solenoid operated fuel cut-off to give the driver a key start/stop operation
- an automatic cold starting module to advance the injection
- a fast idle facility to give even running during warm-up
- torque control for matching the fuel output with the fuel requirement.

The section through the pump (Figure 4.3) shows the layout of the basic sub-systems; these include:

- a low pressure fuel supply
- a high pressure fuel supply and distributor
- a fuel shut-off solenoid
- a distributor plunger drive
- an automatic injection advance unit
- a pressure valve
- a mechanical governor.

Low pressure fuel supply

Driven at half crankshaft speed by a drive shaft, a transfer pump with four vanes delivers fuel to the pumping chamber at a pressure set by the regulating valve.

This fuel pressure, which rises with engine speed, is used to operate the automatic advance unit. It also gives an overflow through the pump body, which aids cooling and provides the self-bleeding feature. After

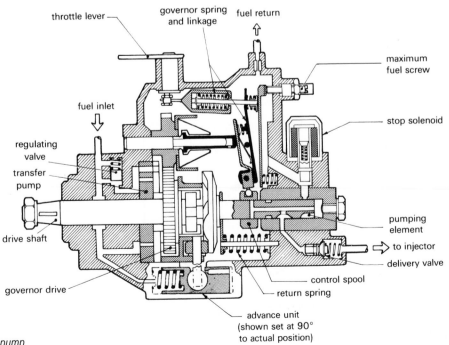

Figure 4.3 Bosch VE distributor pump

passing through a small restriction at the top of the pump the surplus fuel is returned to the fuel tank.

High pressure fuel supply

Figure 4.4 is a simplified view of the pumping chamber with part of the distributor head cut away to show the pump plunger. Besides rotating in the head to give a valve action, the plunger is reciprocated through a constant stroke to produce the high pressure. The axial movement is provided by a cam plate moving over a roller ring. The quantity of high pressure fuel delivered to the injector via the outlet bore is controlled by the position of the control spool. The control spool varies the effective pumping stroke: the stroke increases as the spool is moved towards the distributor head and therefore increases the quantity of fuel delivered.

In the position shown in Figure 4.4a the rotation of the plunger has caused one of the metering slits to open the inlet passage. At this point all outlet ports are closed. Prior to this, the plunger had moved down the chamber to create a condition for the fuel to enter and fill the high pressure chamber.

Slight rotation of the plunger closes the inlet port and causes the single distributor slit in the plunger to open one of the outlet ports. Whilst in this position the plunger is moved up the chamber to pressurise the fuel and deliver it through the outlet bore to the injector.

The position of the plunger at the end of the injection period is shown in Figure 4.4b. At this point, the control spool has already allowed a considerable movement of the plunger before the cut-off bore in the plunger has been uncovered. The exposure of this port

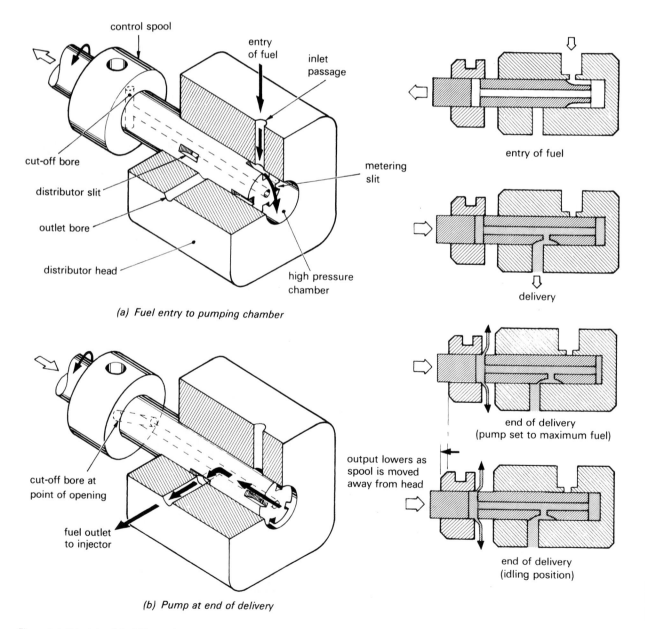

(a) Fuel entry to pumping chamber

(b) Pump at end of delivery

Figure 4.4 Principle of the VE pumping unit

instantly reduces the pressure and terminates the injection. Further pumping movement of the plunger causes the fuel in the pumping chamber to be returned to the pump cavity. With the spool set in this maximum fuel position, which corresponds to the fuel requirement for starting, a movement of the control spool to an extreme position away from the distributor head reduces the output to a minimum; this is the spool setting for slow running.

Fuel shut-off

The 'no fuel' or 'stop' position is provided by a solenoid operated valve. The solenoid cuts off the fuel supply to the inlet passage when the 'ignition' key is switched off.

Distributor plunger drive

The plunger must be rotated and reciprocated. Figure 4.5 illustrates how this is done.

port stops; when the pump element ceases to supply fuel to the outlet port, the delivery valve closes which immediately causes the pressure to drop in the high pressure line which, in turn, causes immediate closure of the injector. However, pressure remains sealed in the high pressure line.

Automatic injection advance unit

The roller ring assembly is not fixed rigidly to the casing; instead it can be partially rotated through an angle of up to 12° to allow the automatic advance mechanism shown in Figure 4.6 to vary the injection timing.

When the pump is rotated, fuel under *pressure* from the transfer pump is delivered to the timing advance chamber via the pump cavity. A rise in the pump speed causes the transfer pump pressure and flow to increase. The increase in pressure moves the timing advance

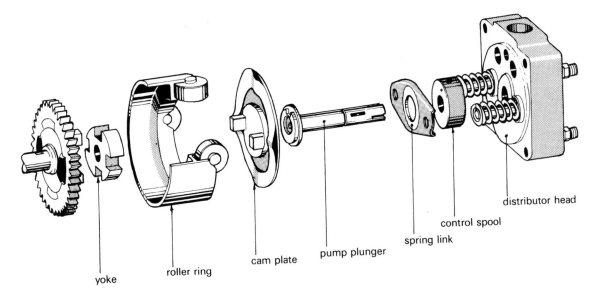

Figure 4.5 Plunger drive

The distributor pump driveshaft is rotated at half crankshaft speed (for a four-stroke engine), and is transmitted via a yoke and cam plate to provide rotary motion to the pump plunger.

Reciprocating motion is provided by the rotation of a cam plate as it moves over four roller followers fixed to a roller ring. In a pump suitable for a four-cylinder engine, four lobes are formed on the cam plate and contact between the plate and rollers is maintained by two strong plunger return springs. A yoke positioned between the driveshaft and the cam plate allows the plate to move axially whilst still maintaining a drive.

Pressure valve

A delivery valve is fitted in the distributor head at the connection point to the high pressure fuel lines (see 4.3). The valve is used to seal the pressure in the high pressure line when the fuel delivery to the fuel outlet

piston against its spring, which in turn, causes the actuating pin to rotate the roller ring in a direction opposite to the direction of rotation of the driveshaft. The rotation of the roller ring advances the injection timing.

Governor

The VE pump is fitted with either a two-speed or an all speed governor. The layouts of these types of governor are similar, but differ in the arrangement of the control springs.

Figure 4.7 shows the main construction of a two-speed governor, which controls the engine during the idling and maximum speed operation. At other times the driver has near direct control of the quantity of fuel delivered and hence the power output of the engine.

The centrifugal governor, which consists of a series of flyweights, is driven from the driveshaft through

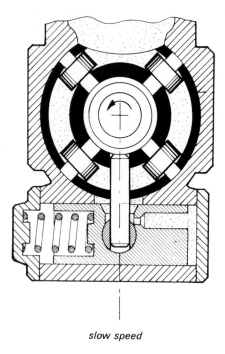

slow speed

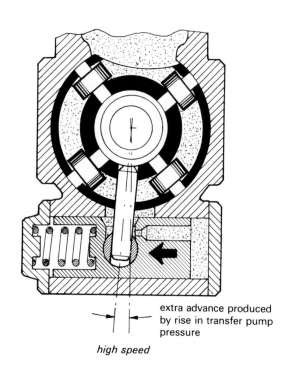

extra advance produced
by rise in transfer pump
pressure

high speed

Figure 4.6 Principle of the automatic advance

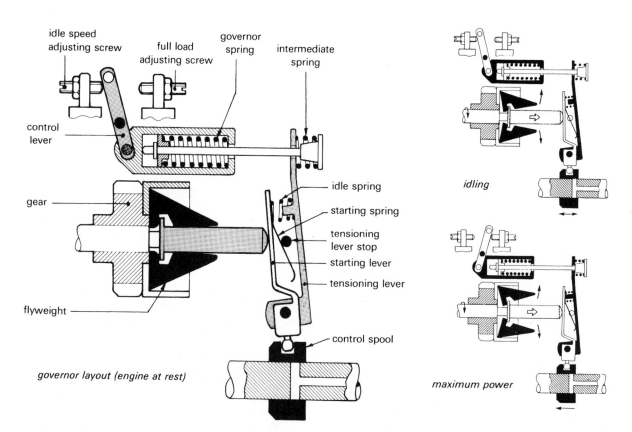

Figure 4.7 Governor – mechanical type

gears with a ratio that steps up the speed. The high speed flyweight rotation given by this ratio ensures good sensitivity of the governor, especially during the idling phase.

An increase in engine speed, and the associated centrifugal action on the flyweights, produces an outward force that pushes a sliding sleeve against a control lever system. This lever, which is connected at its lower end to the control spool on the pumping plunger, can move only when the sliding sleeve is able to overcome the reaction of the spring that is in use at that time.

Starting

With the accelerator pedal half depressed and the governor stationary, the starting spring pushes the sliding sleeve towards the flyweights and moves the control spool to the maximum fuel position.

Idling

When the engine starts, the release of the accelerator, combined with the outward movement of the flyweights, causes the lever to move the control spool to the minimum fuel position. When the engine is operating in this phase, smooth idling is obtained through the interaction of the flyweights and idling spring.

With the accelerator pedal lever against the adjustable idling stop, any small speed increase causes the flyweights to exert a larger force on the sliding sleeve. This slightly compresses the idling spring and, as a result, the spool control lever moves the spool and reduces the fuel delivery.

Any slight drop in engine speed produces the opposite action, so smooth idling under governor control is obtained.

Mid-range operation

Once the idling range has been exceeded, the larger governor force puts the idling and starting springs out of action. At this stage the intermediate spring comes into use to extend the idle control range and so smooth the transition from idle to mid-range operation. The intermediate spring is stronger and provides a flexible link between the driver's pedal and the control spool lever, so that, when the accelerator pedal is depressed, a slight delay in engine response is introduced.

Beyond this phase any movement of the accelerator produces a direct action on the control spool.

Maximum speed

During mid-range operation, the pre-load of the main governor spring causes the spring assembly to act as a solid block. However, when the engine reaches its predetermined maximum speed, the force given by the flyweights equals the spring pre-load. Any further speed increase allows the flyweights to move the spool control lever. This reduces the quantity of fuel being delivered and so keeps the engine speed within safe limits.

4.2.2 Injectors

The purpose of the injector is to break up the fuel to the required degree (i.e. to atomise it) and deliver it to the combustion region in the chamber. This atomisation and penetration is achieved by using a high pressure to force the fuel through a small orifice.

Many vehicles use a type of injector that incorporates a valve. The *closed* system is responsive to pump pressure; raising the pressure above a predetermined point allows the valve to open, and stay open until the pressure has dropped to a lower value. The 'snap' opening and closing of the valve gives advantages, which make this system popular.

The complete injector, shown in Fig. 4.8a, consists of a nozzle and holder, which is clamped to form a gas-tight seal in the cylinder head. A spring, compressed by an adjusting screw to give the correct breaking (opening) pressure, thrusts the needle on to its conical seat. Fuel flows from the inlet nipple through a drilling to an annular groove about the seat of the needle. A thrust, caused by fuel acting on the conical face X, will overcome the spring and lift the needle when the pressure exceeds the breaking pressure. The opening of the valve permits discharge of fuel until the pressure drops to the lower limit. Any fuel which flows between the needle and body acts as a lubricant for the needle before being carried away by a leak-off pipe.

4.2.3 Injector nozzle types

There are three main types of nozzle:

- single hole
- multi-hole
- pintle.

Single hole nozzle

See Figure 4.8b. A single orifice, which may be as small as 0.2 mm (0.008 in), is drifted in the nozzle to give a single jet form of spray. When this nozzle is used with indirect injection systems, a comparatively low injection pressure of 80–100 bar is used.

Multi-hole nozzle

See Figure 4.8c. Two or more small orifices, drilled at various angles to suit the combustion chamber, produce a highly atomised spray form. Many engines with direct injection systems use a four-hole nozzle with a high operating pressure of 150–250 bar. A long stem version of this type makes it easier to fit the injector in the head.

Pintle nozzle

See Figure 4.8d. Swirl chambers can accept a soft form of spray, which is the form given by a pintle nozzle when it is set to operate at a low injection pressure of 110–135 bar.

A small cone extension on the end of the needle produces a conical spray pattern and increases the velocity of the fuel as it leaves the injector. This type tends to be self-cleaning.

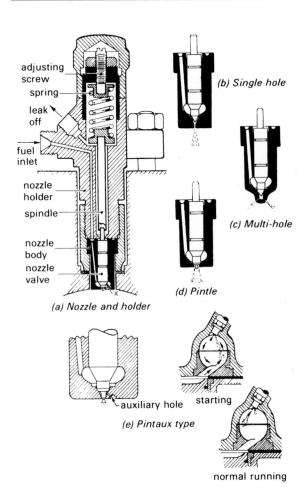

adjusting screw
spring
leak off
fuel inlet
nozzle holder
spindle
nozzle body
nozzle valve

(a) Nozzle and holder

(b) Single hole

(c) Multi-hole

(d) Pintle

auxiliary hole
(e) Pintaux type

starting

normal running

Figure 4.8 Injectors

The elimination of heater plugs on some small indirect injection engines has been made possible by the invention of a special pintle nozzle known as the 'pintaux' type, as shown in Figure 4.8e. Starting conditions produce a small needle lift, and so fuel passes through the small auxiliary hole and is directed to the hottest part of the chamber. Under normal running pressures, the full lift of the needle discharges the fuel through the main orifice.

4.2.4 Rotary pumps with electronic control

With an ever increasing demand on the compression ignition engine to develop more power with lower emissions, together with an increase in fuel economy, electronic control of the diesel fuel system has now become the standard for passenger vehicles with diesel engines.

Although the very latest generations of electronic diesel systems are in fact very similar to petrol injection systems, i.e. the injectors are directly controlled by the system ECU (section 4.3), technicians may still encounter early generations of electronic diesel systems

where the electronic control influenced the operation of a rotary pump. One example of this type of electronic control is therefore detailed below and illustrated in Figure 4.9. The general term used to describe these systems is electronic diesel control (EDC).

An electronic diesel control system can give the following advantages:

- lower emissions
- lower soot emissions
- increased engine output.

The non EDC Bosch VE pump accurately controls the quantity of fuel delivered by the injectors with the use of the control spool as well as a governor and an automatic advance unit. However, external influences, such as engine temperature and air density, will affect the engine performance and also the emissions. Precise control of the fuel system can be achieved with the use of electronic diesel control.

The EDC electronic control unit (ECU) controls the fuel system by using two actuators, a solenoid operated control spool and a solenoid operated timing advance unit, which are located in the distributor pump (Figure 4.9). The pump uses many of the components that are fitted to the VE-type distributor pump, including the fuel shut-off valve and the fuel delivery plunger.

The ECU monitors the engine operating conditions from information supplied by sensors and provides the correct control signals to the actuators, giving precise control of the fuel delivered to the injectors. The EDC system uses sensors very similar in operation to those used with petrol fuel injection systems (see Figure 4.10).

An accelerator cable between the throttle pedal and the distributor pump is no longer required to control the fuel volume. The position of the throttle pedal is monitored by the EDC ECU with the use of a throttle position sensor fitted to the throttle pedal linkage. The ECU controls the volume of fuel delivered to the injectors by using a solenoid operated control spool.

The engine speed is monitored by a sensor fitted to the engine crankshaft; the sensor is usually of the inductive type. An additional sensor is fitted to the distributor pump, which monitors the speed and position of the fuel control spool in relation to crankshaft position. The ECU uses the information from these sensors, together with additional sensor information to determine the volume of fuel and fuel injection timing.

A manifold absolute pressure (MAP) sensor enables the ECU to monitor the volume of air entering the engine. The ECU calculates the air density from the MAP sensor signal in conjunction with the intake air temperature sensor signal. The MAP sensor signal is also used to monitor and control the turbo boost pressure. The ECU controls the turbo boost pressure with a waste gate actuator solenoid.

Two temperature sensors are used: an engine coolant temperature sensor to monitor engine temperature and an intake air temperature sensor. The ECU uses

Distributor injection pump for electronic diesel control

1 Control collar position sensor, **2** Solenoid actuator for the injected fuel quantity, **3** Electromagnetic shut-off valve, **4** Delivery plunger, **5** Solenoid valve for start-of-injection timing, **6** Control collar.

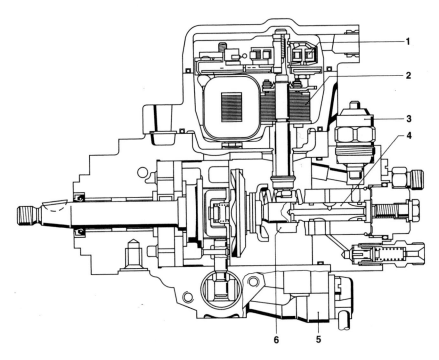

Figure 4.9 An electronically controlled diesel rotary pump (EDC)

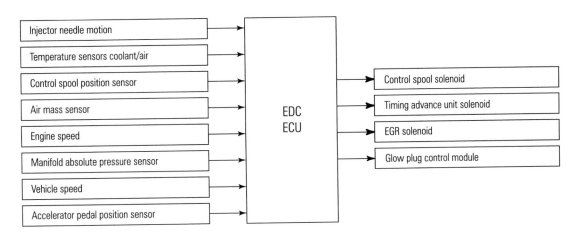

Figure 4.10 Inputs and outputs for an EDC system

temperature information for fuel volume control. This information is also used to control the length of time that the glow plugs operate during starting.

An injector motion sensor is fitted to one of the injectors (Figure 4.11), usually to number 1 cylinder. At the start of fuel injection, when the fuel pressure increases and lifts the injector valve from the seat, the sensor produces a signal. The start of injection influences engine starting, combustion noise, fuel consumption and emissions. The ECU monitors the sensor signal and determines, in conjunction with the

engine speed sensor information, the fuel injection timing control.

To enable the modern diesel engine to meet emission regulations, many engines are fitted with an exhaust gas recirculation (EGR) system. During certain engine operating conditions, the exhaust gases are mixed with the fresh air in the induction system, which lowers the combustion temperature, thus reducing the harmful emissions produced by the engine. The volume of EGR is measured with a mass air flow sensor, either a hot wire or a hot film type. The ECU controls the EGR

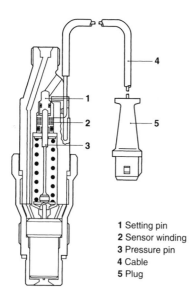

1 Setting pin
2 Sensor winding
3 Pressure pin
4 Cable
5 Plug

Figure 4.11 An injector with a motion sensor

valve actuator accordingly to ensure the correct volume of exhaust gases are recirculated to provide the correct emission levels.

The position of the control spool in relation to the distributor plunger determines the volume of fuel delivered to each injector, in the same manner as previously described with the Bosch VE pump. The volume of fuel delivered dictates the engine speed and engine power. A mechanical governor is no longer fitted to the distributor pump; the position of the control spool is electronically controlled by the EDC ECU with a solenoid. Depending on the position of the spool, the volume of fuel is either increased or decreased. The position of the spool can be altered to provide maximum fuel for full load through to zero fuel to prevent fuel from being supplied to the injectors. The exact position of the control spool is monitored by the ECU with a position sensor.

As with the VE pump, the fuel pressure inside the pump is relative to engine speed. The timing advance unit functions in a similar manner to that of the VE pump, except that the fuel pressure applied to the advance unit is controlled by the EDC ECU with the use of the timing advance unit solenoid. The fuel injection timing can either be advanced or retarded by altering the control signal to the solenoid.

The EDC ECU controls the engine idle speed by controlling the volume of fuel delivered. To ensure that the engine idle is as smooth as possible, the ECU will slightly vary the volume of fuel to each cylinder by the corresponding amount.

The EDC ECU also incorporates a diagnostic function similar in operation to that of a petrol engine management system. If a fault occurs with the system, the ECU will if possible operate with a limited operating strategy (LOS). If a sensor circuit fails, the ECU will substitute the value of the sensor circuit, to provide limited emergency operation of the system. If the ECU detects a system fault, it illuminates a warning lamp in the instrument panel to alert the driver that a fault has occurred; the fault will also be stored in the memory of the ECU in the form of a code. To diagnose the system fault, the fault information can be retrieved from the EDC ECU memory with the appropriate diagnostic test equipment.

Many modern vehicles are prevented from being driven by the fitting of an engine immobiliser system. Early immobiliser systems prevented diesel engines from being started by isolating the power supply to the distributor pump stop solenoid, preventing fuel from entering the plunger. Modern electronically controlled diesel fuel systems are immobilised within the ECU. If the ECU receives an incorrect immobiliser code from the driver, it prevents fuel from being supplied to the injectors by isolating the control signals to the distributor pump solenoids.

> **Key Points**
>
> Electronic diesel control (EDC) systems can vary timing and fuel quantity by acting on the automatic advance unit and the control spool
>
> Inputs to an EDC system are similar to those used for petrol/gasoline engine management

---

4.3 COLD-START PRE-HEATING SYSTEMS

4.3.1 Cold starting

Direct injection engines

All compression ignition engines require some special provision for cold starting, although modern direct injection engines (injecting directly into the main combustion chamber, as opposed to into a pre-chamber) may require cold-start assistance only at low ambient temperatures. The heat generated during compression, even under cranking conditions, is usually sufficient to cause ignition of the vaporised fuel.

For most cold-start conditions, the direct injection engines used in most modern passenger cars are able to start relatively easily: the injection of a larger quantity of fuel (a rich mixture), and the greater amount of easily ignitable fractions contained in the injected charge, are generally sufficient to start a cold direct injection engine. However, with many modern direct injection engines, assistance during cold starting is needed to reduce harmful emissions when the engine is initially started.

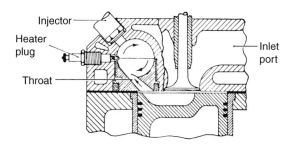

Figure 4.12 Indirect diesel injection into a pre-chamber

Indirect injection engines

With indirect injection (Figure 4.12), the pre-chamber is not exposed to the same amount of heat as the main combustion chamber (heat is lost to the cylinder walls and combustion chamber walls). These greater heat losses therefore dictate that indirect injection engines have extra provision to ensure ignition of the fuel during cold starting. A significant design difference is that higher compression ratios are used for indirect injection engines: ratios of about 16:1 are used with direct injection engines, while indirect injection engines use higher ratios of the order of 22:1, and in some cases a ratio as high as 30:1 is used. These higher compression ratios increase the heat produced during compression, which aids cold starting. A high compression ratio is also used in indirect injection engines to raise their thermal efficiency, and hence economy, unlike direct injection engines; this tends to counteract the greater heat loss caused by the larger surface areas of an indirect injection combustion chamber.

4.3.2 Cold-start assistance

Manifold heaters

Seldom used on modern passenger car engines, manifold heaters are electrical units fitted to pre-heat the air as it passes through the inlet manifold to the cylinder.

Pintaux injector

A Pintaux injector is a pintle injector which has an auxiliary hole to direct fuel down the throat of the pre-chamber during the cranking period (see Figure 4.8e). This type of injector is suitable for indirect injection engines.

Heater plug

Still the most widely used form of cold-start assistance on diesel engines, the 'glow plug' or 'heater plug' is fitted in the combustion chamber and is effectively an electric heater that can be used during cold starting and in the early phases of cold running. When the air is cold, the air in the combustion chamber is heated by an electrical heating element for a few seconds prior to starting a cold engine. The time that the glow plugs

operate for is usually dependent on engine temperature: the colder the engine, the longer the glow plugs function.

The glow plugs are usually controlled automatically by a timer relay or an electronic control unit (ECU). When the ignition is switched on, the controller usually illuminates a glow plug warning light in the instrument panel to warn the driver when the glow plugs are operating. Modern direct injection engines have a glow plug fitted to each cylinder. The glow plugs used on many modern diesel engines can remain switched on for a few minutes after the engine has started, 'post-glow', normally with a reduced electrical current to prevent the glow plugs from overheating and burning out. This provides additional heat in the combustion chamber to improve the combustion process and therefore lower emissions when the engine is started from cold.

Modern diesel injection systems are electronically controlled, so it is convenient and more effective for the diesel fuel system ECU also to control the glow plug operation. The ECU is already receiving information from the temperature sensors and other sensors so it can control the glow plug operating time, the current flow (reduced current and heating after starting), and the warning light (the indication to the driver when the engine can be started).

Modern glow plugs have heating elements that are effectively resistances with a positive temperature coefficient or PTC; the PTC increases the resistance of the heating element as the element temperature rises, thus progressively reducing the current flow. In effect, the current flow is self-regulated to prevent overheating of the heating element, while still allowing an initial high current to heat up the element for the cold start.

Figure 4.13 shows a glow plug in a combustion chamber of a direct injection engine. Figure 4.14 shows the construction of a modern glow plug and Figure 4.15 shows the arrangement for controlling the operation of

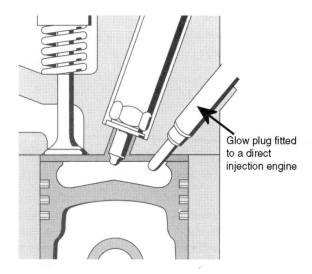

Glow plug fitted to a direct injection engine

Figure 4.13 Glow plug location on a direct injection engine combustion chamber

the glow plug. Note that in the example (Figure 4.15), the ECU (which is receiving information from the temperature sensors) is effectively controlling the 'glow plug control unit'; the control unit regulates the high current passing to the glow plugs.

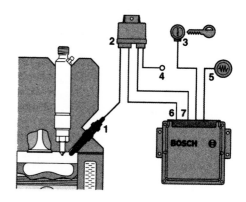

1 Sheathed-element glow plug
2 Glow control unit
3 Glow-plug and starter switch
4 To battery
5 Indicator lamp
6 Control line to the engine ECU
7 Diagnosis line

Figure 4.15 Glow plug control

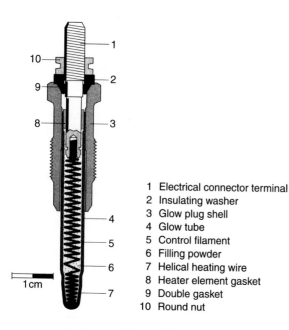

1 Electrical connector terminal
2 Insulating washer
3 Glow plug shell
4 Glow tube
5 Control filament
6 Filling powder
7 Helical heating wire
8 Heater element gasket
9 Double gasket
10 Round nut

Figure 4.14 Glow plug construction

Key Points

Most diesel systems use a glow plug in the combustion chamber to help increase the temperature of the injected fuel

Glow plugs are controlled by a timer relay or an ECU so that the optimum heat time is used depending on the engine temperature

4.4   ELECTRONIC CONTROL OF DIESEL INJECTION (COMMON RAIL SYSTEMS)

Note: Modern electronic diesel systems operate in a very similar way to electronic petrol injection systems, especially direct petrol injection. See sections 3.1 to 3.4 for information on sensors, actuators and control signals for electronic injection systems. Chapters 1 and 2 include additional information about sensor and actuator operation.

4.4.1 Advantages and disadvantages of direct injection

Direct injection systems have been used on larger diesel engines for many years, especially for heavy commercial applications. Since the 1980s, light passenger cars have also increasingly been fitted with smaller direct injection engines. Direct injection is a more efficient method of fuel delivery: it develops more power and has a lower fuel consumption than indirect injection (where the fuel is delivered into a pre-combustion chamber). Direct injection does, however, have one major disadvantage: the combustion noise is higher than that of indirect injection, which is undesirable in passenger motor vehicles.

The combustion noise is generally referred to as combustion knock and is caused by ignition of the fuel after injection has initially started. The short delay between 'start of injection' and the ignition of the fuel means that there is a relatively large quantity of fuel that initially ignites; this causes a rapid combustion and pressure rise in the early phases of the combustion process, which causes an audible knock. On most fuel injection systems used up until the late 1990s, which were relying on mechanical pumps to generate the pressure for injection, it was relatively difficult to precisely control the fuel quantity delivered during the early injection phase. If the initial quantity of fuel injected is too large, ignition is rapid and initial gas expansion is rapid, thus causing the combustion knock.

Therefore an objective with the modern direct injection diesel fuel system is to control the initial injection quantity in what is termed the 'pilot injection phase', which is when a small quantity of fuel is injected, ahead of the main injection period. This small quantity of fuel causes a small rise in pressure during the pilot phase, thus reducing the rapid speed of combustion, which in turn reduces combustion knock.

4.4.2 Common rail

Common rail diesel fuel systems have been widely used in commercial vehicle and large diesel engine applications for many years. Common rail refers to a system whereby the injectors receive fuel from a common supply rail, which is fed fuel under pressure by an engine driven pump. On early common rail systems the pump provided fuel at a relatively low pressure; the fuel was then passed to the injectors through a pipe (or even through holes or tubes built into the cylinder head). The injectors contained a pumping element (usually driven from the engine camshaft via a rocker system), which produced the high pressure necessary for injecting the diesel fuel. Some common rail systems delivered fuel to a separate pumping element which then passed the fuel at high pressure to the injector.

One advantage of using a common delivery rail is that the high pressure pumping element is located in or close to the injector, so the high pressure created by the pumping element does not have to pass through a long delivery pipe, which is the case for traditional diesel fuel pump systems, where the pump is a considerable distance from the injectors. With a long delivery pipe carrying high pressure, when the pump delivers the fuel it causes a pressure wave to travel along the delivery pipe (which is full of fuel); the time delay in the high pressure wave reaching the injector causes timing inaccuracies of injector opening and closing. With the short or non-existent high pressure delivery pipe on common rail systems, this delayed pressure wave problem is eliminated or reduced: see the following paragraphs dealing with unit pumps and unit injectors.

Unit pumps and unit injectors

Figure 4.16 shows a relatively recent type of 'unit injector', where the fuel injector contains a pumping element that is driven by a cam and rocker system. The cam lobe can be part of the normal camshaft used to operate the inlet and exhaust valves. The injector is fed with fuel at a relatively low pressure from a common supply rail (feeding all injectors). The high pressure is then created by the pumping element in the injector itself. Unit injectors can deliver fuel at typical pressures of 2000 bar.

With this type of unit injector, a solenoid attached to the injector controls a valve arrangement that opens or closes an outlet or spill port. When the outlet port is open, the pumping element will still function and build up pressure, but the fuel will pass straight out of the outlet port back to the low pressure fuel system. When the outlet port is closed by the solenoid, this will cause pressure to build up above the injector nozzle (due to the action of the pumping element). The pressure build-up will then cause the injector nozzle to open and deliver fuel. At the appropriate time, the solenoid will open the outlet port again, which will cause an immediate drop in pressure above the nozzle. This will then allow the spring in the injector nozzle to return to

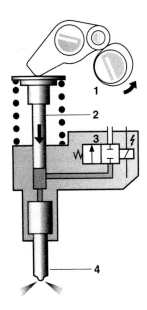

| 1 Actuating cam | 3 High pressure solenoid valve |
| 2 Pump plunger | 4 Injection nozzle |

Figure 4.16 Unit injector with combined pumping element for a common rail system

the closed position (a closing spring is located in the nozzle, as in older injectors – see Figure 4.8).

The solenoid is controlled by an ECU, which functions in much the same way as a petrol injection system ECU: i.e. the ECU receives information from sensors and is therefore able to control the opening and closing of the injector, thus controlling fuel quantity (the injection duration).

Figure 4.17 shows a similar arrangement to that of the unit injector but the pumping element is separate

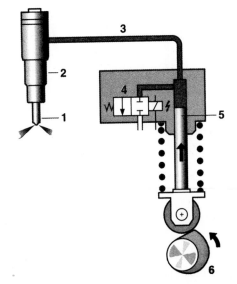

1 Injection nozzle	4 High pressure solenoid valve
2 Nozzle holder	5 Pump plunger
3 High pressure line	6 Actuating cam

Figure 4.17 Unit pump system for a common rail system

from the injector; a short delivery pipe is therefore required to deliver the high pressure fuel from the pumping element to the injector. This type of system is generally referred to as a 'unit pump' system and is suited to engines where the camshaft location may not allow a combined unit injector and pumping element to be used.

For both the unit injector and the unit pump systems, the common rail supply (from the low pressure pump) can be via a low pressure delivery pipe or through a hole or port system built into the cylinder head.

4.4.3 Electronically controlled common rail systems using a single high pressure pump

The logical evolution of the common rail system is to use a single high pressure pump feeding the common supply rail. The injectors will therefore not contain a pumping element (or require separate individual pumping elements), but can still be controlled using a solenoid which regulates the outlet port of the injector. Figure 4.18 shows the general layout of this type of system. Note that this type of system is virtually identical in principle to a 'direct injection' petrol injection system (section 3.4). Although fuel at high pressure will pass from the common fuel rail to the injectors, the opening and closing of the injectors is not dependent on pressure waves passing through the pipe: it is totally dependent on the solenoid action, which causes the injector outlet port to open or close (as on the unit injector).

With this type of common rail system, as well as controlling the injector timing and injector duration (fuel quantity control), the pressure at which the fuel is

injected into the combustion chamber can also be altered to suit the engine operating conditions and cylinder pressure. The fuel delivered to the common fuel supply rail (by the engine driven high pressure pump) can be monitored by a pressure sensor and controlled using a pressure regulator. The pressure of the fuel delivered to the injectors can therefore be controlled so that it is always at the desired value. Typical injection pressures are around 1600 bar.

With electronic control, the injection timing can be accurately controlled to allow the fuel to ignite and burn correctly within the combustion chamber. Conventional diesel fuel systems inject the total volume of fuel required by the cylinder during one injector opening. For this type of common rail system with higher fuel pressure, the volume of fuel can be injected into the combustion chamber in stages: a pilot injection, main injection and sometimes a post injection. The pilot injection period can be controlled, so that only very small quantities of fuel are injected, thus reducing combustion knock. Post injection can be used to aid the control of emissions: a small quantity of fuel is injected at the end of the power stroke or even on the start of the exhaust stroke, the fuel vaporises and passes through to an NO_x catalyst which then reduces NO_x emissons.

Using the information from the various system sensors, the ECU determines the volume of fuel and the point in time at which the fuel is to be injected to provide the required power from the engine. Figure 4.19 shows a typical single high pressure pump common rail system (sometimes referred to as a common rail accumulator system), whilst Figure 4.20 shows a complete system with sensors and actuators; note that the illustration shows a turbocharged engine, where the boost pressures are also controlled by the ECU.

4.4.4 Fuel pressure system

Low pressure system

With a low pressure system, the fuel pressure is produced by a low pressure pump that supplies fuel from the fuel tank via a fuel filter to a high pressure pump. The ECU controls the operation of the low pressure pump. The pump location and design are very similar to those of a petrol fuel injection system. Figure 4.21a shows the layout of the fuel system. Figure 4.21b shows a typical low pressure fuel pump. Figures 4.21c and 4.21d show roller cell and gear type low pressure pump elements. Note that a conventional fuel filter is fitted in the low pressure system (Figure 4.22).

High pressure system

The high pressure pump, normally driven at half crankshaft speed by the camshaft, generates the high fuel pressure which is stored in the common fuel rail, hence the name 'common rail' (Figure 4.23). The ECU varies the pressure produced by the high pressure pump

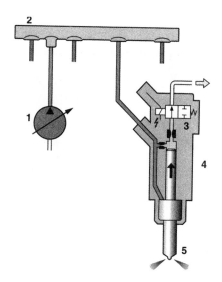

1 High pressure pump
2 Rail (high pressure fuel acccumulator)
3 High pressure solenoid valve
4 Injector
5 Injection nozzle

Figure 4.18 Electronically controlled common rail system using a single high pressure pump

Common rail accumulator injection system on a 4-cylinder diesel engine

1 Air mass meter, **2** ECU, **3** High pressure pump, **4** High pressure accumulator (rail), **5** Injectors, **6** Crankshaft speed sensor, **7** Coolant temperature sensor, **8** Fuel filter, **9** Accelerator pedal sensor.

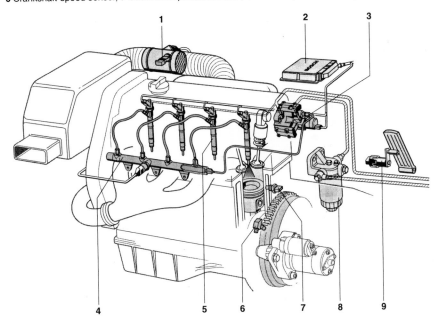

Figure 4.19 Common rail accumulator injection system

up to a maximum pressure of typically 1300 to 1600 bar with electrically operated solenoid valves within the pump assembly. The ECU varies the fuel pressure according to engine operating conditions; the fuel pressure is not relative to engine speed (apart from during engine cranking). The diesel fuel lubricates the internal cams and plungers of the high pressure pump.

The high pressure pump (Figure 4.24) is driven by the engine and is usually located in the same position as a traditional diesel pump. The fuel pressure is monitored by the ECU with a fuel pressure sensor situated in the common rail (Figure 4.23), so the fuel is always delivered at the correct pressure to suit the engine operating conditions. The fuel passes from the fuel rail to the injectors through metal fuel pipes. These pipes are approximately the same in length and manufactured without excessively sharp bends which might restrict fuel flow. Note that if any of the fuel pipes are disconnected during service or repair, they should be renewed. The pipes are made from steel which deforms thus providing some flexibility for fitting and to allow for vibration as well as small movements that will occur due to engine expansion caused by heat. The high pressure pump connections, when tightened, ensure a fuel tight seal.

The common rail acts as an accumulator or reservoir of fuel, damping pressure fluctuations in the high pressure system due to the pumping action and injection. The fuel rail is also fitted with a fuel pressure regulator (Figure 4.25), so if the fuel pressure becomes abnormally high, the excess pressure will pass through

the pressure limiting valve and return to the fuel tank. A mechanical fuel pressure limiting valve was used on early common rail fuel systems. With later systems, the ECU controls the fuel rail pressure with an electrically operated solenoid valve. Note that the ECU monitors the fuel pressure in the fuel rail and controls the pressure with a solenoid valve on the side of the high pressure pump.

4.4.5 Fuel injection system

(See Chapters 1 and 2 for information on electronic system sensors and actuators, and on electronic actuator control signals.)

The ECU controls the injectors by making use of a similar principle to that of petrol fuel injection. The common rail fuel system uses many of the sensors that provide information for electronically controlled distributor pump diesel fuel systems and for petrol injection systems. These include:

- an engine speed sensor fitted to the crankshaft
- a camshaft position sensor
- an accelerator pedal position sensor
- a MAP sensor
- an engine coolant and intake air temperature sensor
- an air mass sensor.

These sensors are used to monitor engine operating conditions. The accelerator sensor provides the ECU with driver requirements: whether the driver wishes to

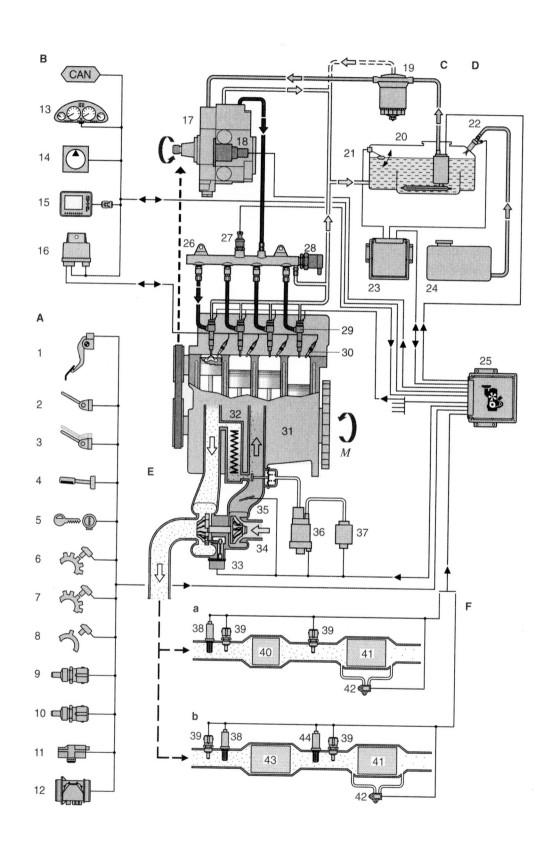

Figure 4.20 A complete common rail injection system (single high pressure pump system)

Key to Figure 4.20

Engine, engine management, and high pressure fuel injection components
17 High pressure pump
18 Metering unit
25 Engine ECU
26 Fuel rail
27 Rail pressure sensor
28 Pressure control valve (DRV 2)
29 Injector
30 Glow plug
31 Diesel engine (01)
M Torque

A Sensors and setpoint generators
1 Pedal-travel sensor
2 Clutch switch
3 Brake contacts (2)
4 Operator unit for vehicle speed controller (cruise control)
5 Glow-plug and starter switch ('ignition switch')
6 Road speed sensor
7 Crankshaft speed sensor (inductive)
8 Camshaft speed sensor (inductive or Hall sensor)
9 Engine temperature sensor (in coolant circuit)
10 Intake air temperature sensor
11 Boost pressure sensor
12 Hot-film air mass meter (intake air)

B Interfaces
13 Instrument cluster with displays for fuel consumption, engine speed, etc.
14 Air-conditioner compressor with operator unit
15 Diagnosis interface
16 Glow control unit
CAN Controller Area Network
(on-board serial data bus)

C Fuel-supply system (low-pressure stage)
19 Fuel filter with overflow valve
20 Fuel tank with pre-filter and Electric Fuel Pump, EFP (presupply pump)
21 Fuel-level sensor

D Additive system
22 Additive metering unit
23 Additive control unit
24 Additive tank

E Air supply
32 Exhaust gas recirculation cooler
33 Boost pressure actuator
34 Turbocharger (in this case with variable turbine geometry (VTG))
35 Control flap
36 Exhaust gas recirculation actuator
37 Vacuum pump

F Exhaust-gas treatment
38 Broadband lambda oxygen sensor, type LSU
39 Exhaust gas temperature sensor
40 Oxidation type catalytic converter
41 Particulate filter
42 Differential pressure sensor
43 NO_x accumulator type catalytic converter
44 Broadband lambda oxygen sensor, optional NO_x sensor

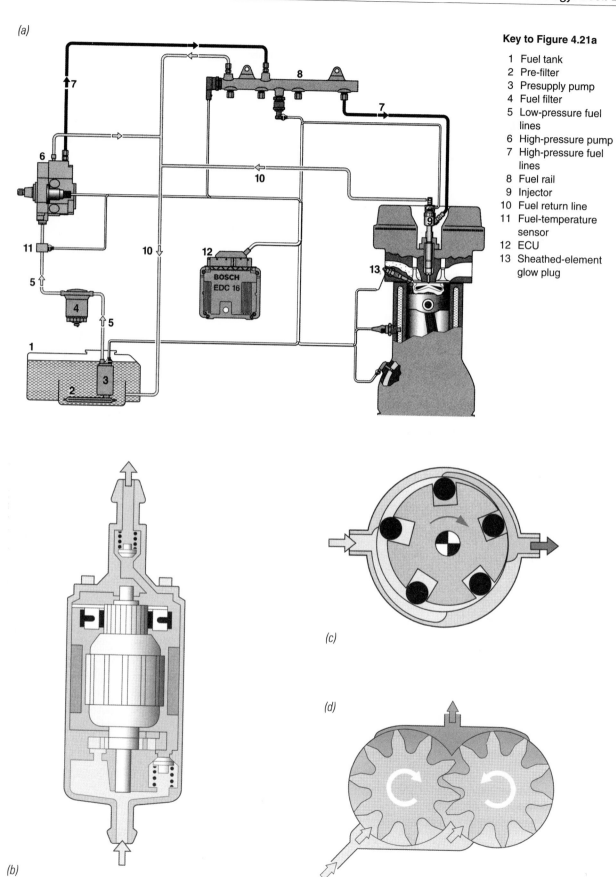

(a)

Key to Figure 4.21a

1   Fuel tank
2   Pre-filter
3   Presupply pump
4   Fuel filter
5   Low-pressure fuel
    lines
6   High-pressure pump
7   High-pressure fuel
    lines
8   Fuel rail
9   Injector
10 Fuel return line
11 Fuel-temperature
    sensor
12 ECU
13 Sheathed-element
    glow plug

(b)

(c)

(d)

Figure 4.21 Low pressure fuel system and low pressure pumps

Figure 4.22 Fuel filter

accelerate, decelerate or allow the engine to idle whilst stationary. The ECU uses the sensor information to calculate the desired fuel pressure, injection volume and duration to produce the required engine power and torque.

The fuel within the common rail is at a constant pressure during injection and therefore the volume of fuel injected is also constant during the injector opening period. Therefore a precise volume of fuel can be delivered during the injector opening period.

The EDC ECU determines the injector opening time period (injector duration) from sensor information and provides a control signal to the injector accordingly. The high fuel pressure exerts a great force at the injector needle valve, and therefore a very high voltage and current are required to initially open the injector. The injector driver control module provides the necessary high voltage control signal to the injector. The module might be located within the ECU, or in some cases fitted as a separate unit. The ECU uses the engine speed sensor to provide the timing control for each injector. Additional information is required to synchronise each injector with the cylinder cycle. A cylinder recognition sensor monitors the camshaft position, which provides the ECU with the information necessary to control the phasing of the injectors. The injectors are situated in the cylinder head and spray fuel into the swirling air within the combustion chamber, which is normally integrated into the crown of the piston.

If the current is switched off to the solenoid circuit the injector is not energised and the injector needle valve is closed, which prevents the pressurised fuel leaving the injector nozzle (Figure 4.26). The high pressure fuel is applied to the needle valve at the lower section of the injector and also a control chamber which is located on top of the injector needle valve within the top section of the injector. The pressure of the solenoid spring and the needle valve spring is higher than the fuel pressure applied and therefore the needle valve remains closed.

The ECU determines the injection period during which the injector opens and injects a volume of fuel into the combustion chamber. The ECU provides the injector with a control signal that energises the injector solenoid (Figure 4.26). The solenoid valve lifts, allowing the fuel pressure to escape from the control chamber into the chamber above. The fuel passing to the chamber returns to the tank via the fuel return system. The initial current required to lift the solenoid is high, because of the pressure of the spring. Once the solenoid is open, a smaller current is required to maintain the solenoid position: the ECU applies a holding current.

An orifice restriction prevents the high pressure fuel from rapidly re-entering the control chamber; the control chamber pressure is lower than the fuel pressure

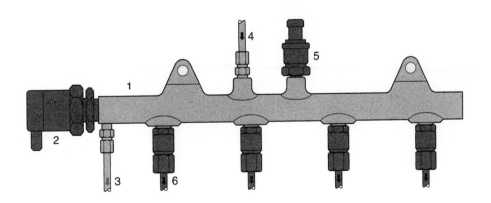

1 Fuel rail
2 Pressure control valve
3 Return line from fuel rail to fuel tank
4 Inlet from high pressure pump
5 Rail pressure sensor
6 Fuel line to injector

Figure 4.23 High pressure fuel system

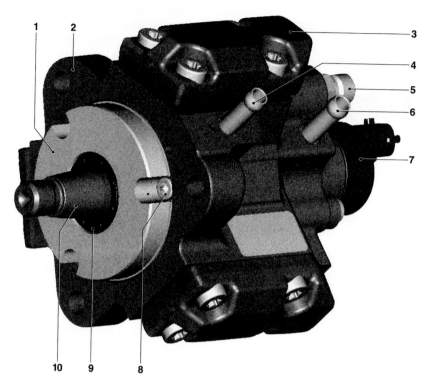

1 Flange
2 Pump housing
3 Engine cylinder head
4 Inlet connection
5 High pressure inlet

6 Return connection
7 Pressure control valve
8 Barrel bolt
9 Shaft seal
10 Eccentric shaft

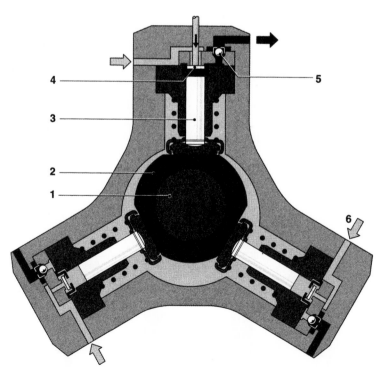

1 Drive shaft
2 Eccenter
3 Pump element with pump plunger
4 Inlet valve
5 Outlet valve
6 Fuel inlet

Figure 4.24 High pressure pump

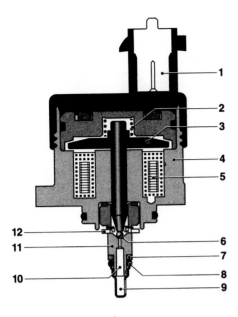

1 Electrical connections
2 Valve spring
3 Armature
4 Valve housing
5 Solenoid coil
6 Valve ball
7 Support ring
8 O-ring
9 Filter
10 High pressure fuel supply
11 Valve body
12 Drain to low pressure circuit

Figure 4.25 Fuel pressure regulator

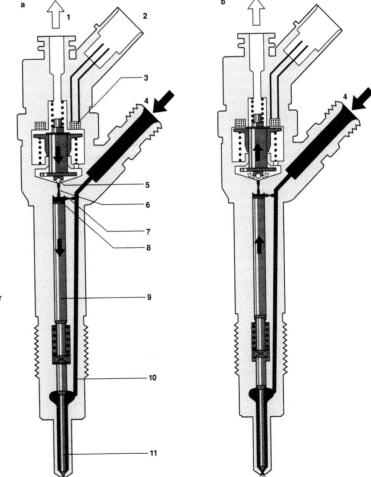

Injector (schematic)

a Injector closed
   (at rest status)
b Injector opened
   (injection)
1 Fuel return
2 Electrical connection
3 Triggering element
   (solenoid valve)
4 Fuel inlet (high pressure)
   from the rail

5 Valve ball
6 Bleed orifice
7 Feed orifice
8 Valve control chamber
9 Valve control plunger
10 Feed passage
    to the nozzle
11 Nozzle needle

Figure 4.26 Common rail injector

applied to the needle valve. The difference in fuel pressure between the control chamber and at the needle valve causes the valve to lift from the seat and fuel is expelled through the injector nozzle into the combustion chamber. The pressure of the injected fuel is equal to the pressure in the fuel rail. The high fuel pressure, together with the design of the injector nozzle, allows excellent atomisation of the fuel injected, which promotes good mixing of the air and fuel within the combustion chamber. Thoroughly mixing the air and fuel reduces hydrocarbon and soot emissions.

To end the injection of fuel, the ECU switches off the current flow through the injector solenoid circuit, allowing the solenoid plunger and valve to return to its seat. The closing of the solenoid valve allows the control chamber to refill with high pressure fuel from the fuel rail. The high fuel pressure in the control chamber, together with the force of the needle valve spring, exerts a greater force than that of the high fuel pressure at the base of the needle valve, so the needle valve returns to its seat and injection ceases.

Pilot injection

Earlier designs of diesel fuel systems (in-line and rotary pump systems) generally inject the total volume of fuel during one injector opening period for one cylinder cycle. There is a time period between the start of injection and the start of ignition of the fuel. When the fuel ignites, the cylinder pressure rapidly increases, which pushes the piston down the cylinder. The sharp rise in cylinder pressure is heard and referred to as diesel or combustion knock.

The common rail fuel system normally injects the total volume of fuel (for the combustion process) in two injection stages, often referred to as pilot injection and main injection.

A small volume of fuel is injected before the piston reaches TDC. This small volume of fuel, typically between 1 and 4 mm^3 is used to condition the cylinder before the main volume of fuel is injected. The pilot injection raises the cylinder pressure slightly due to the combustion of the fuel: therefore the temperature within the cylinder also rises. If the pilot injection occurs too early in the compression stroke, the fuel will adhere to the cold cylinder walls and the crown of the piston, increasing the hydrocarbons and soot in the exhaust gases.

Figure 4.27 shows the difference in the combustion chamber pressure rise when pilot injection is used compared with when there is no pilot injection. Note the steeper rise in pressure that occurs just after TDC when there in no pilot injection; it is this steep pressure rise that is creating the diesel or combustion knock.

Main injection

The time delay between the points at which the fuel is injected and ignited is reduced because the pilot injection provides a slightly higher cylinder temperature and pressure. The rate at which the combustion

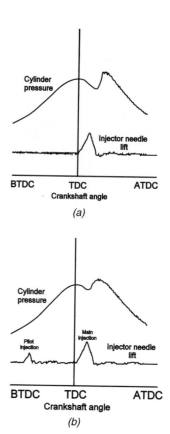

Figure 4.27 Combustion pressures
a without pilot injection
b with pilot injection

pressure increases is less severe, resulting in a reduction in combustion noise, lower fuel consumption and lower emission levels.

The length of time that the injector is opened (injector duration), together with the pressure at which the fuel is injected, dictates the volume of fuel delivered to the cylinder. It should be noted that although changing the duration of injector opening time would affect the volume of fuel delivered, an increase in the fuel pressure is generally used as the primary means to increase the volume of fuel delivered to a cylinder. At high engine speeds, insufficient time exists between the stages of injection and it is not possible to provide pilot injection. The ECU combines both pilot and main stages of injection and uses a single injector opening period to inject the volume of fuel required.

The ECU monitors any imbalance between the torque generated between cylinders. After each injection period, the power stroke occurs, which accelerates the speed of the crankshaft. The ECU monitors the acceleration speed of the crankshaft through the engine speed sensor signal. If all cylinders are producing an equal amount of power, the acceleration of the crankshaft between each cylinder power stroke should also be equal. Engine wear will affect the power produced by each cylinder, and the

ECU can alter the fuel volume and injection timing to cylinders to equalise the power each cylinder produces at low engine speeds. Unequal power between cylinders is very apparent at idle, but the ECU stabilises the engine speed, ensuring a smooth engine idle.

Turbocharger boost pressure control

If a turbocharger is fitted, the ECU controls the turbocharger boost pressure. The ECU monitors the inlet manifold pressure with a pressure sensor. If the pressure is too high (over-boost) the ECU regulates the pressure by using a waste gate in the exhaust manifold. Some later vehicles are fitted with a variable geometry turbocharger, where the ECU alters the geometry inside the exhaust turbine to vary the boost.

Exhaust gas recirculation

The ECU controls exhaust gas recirculation (EGR). This returns some of the exhaust gases into the induction system to reduce the harmful emissions emitted from the exhaust, i.e. oxides of nitrogen or NO_x (see section 3.5). The ECU monitors the air mass sensor signal situated in the air induction system, and the sensor provides an indication of the volume of exhaust gas recirculated.

Unlike earlier generations of diesel engine, many induction systems are fitted with a throttle plate in the induction system. When the throttle plate (butterfly) is used in a petrol engine, it alters the air volume entering the engine and therefore alters engine power. However, a throttle plate in a diesel engine is used to alter the rate of EGR. At low engine speeds, the angle of the throttle plate is adjusted to provide a depression in the manifold, which induces the rate of EGR. At high engine speeds and loads the throttle plate is fully open

to prevent restriction to the flow of air into the engine. The throttle plate is either operated by a stepper motor or by the modulation of a vacuum switching valve.

Key Points

Sensors used in common rail injection systems are very similar to those used for petrol/gasoline injection

A high pressure engine-driven pump supplies fuel to electronically controlled injectors

Common rail systems can operate at pressures up to 1600 bar

Web links

Engine systems information

www.bosch.com
www.sae.org
www.imeche.org.uk
www.picotech.com
www.autotap.com
www.visteon.com
www.infineon.com
www.kvaser.com (follow CAN Education links)

Teaching/learning resources

Online learning material relating to powertrain systems:

www.auto-training.co.uk

TRANSMISSION

what is covered in this chapter . . .

5.1 PURPOSE OF THE TRANSMISSION SYSTEM

Any vehicle equipped with a combustion engine as its prime mover requires a transmission system to transmit torque at an appropriate speed to the driving wheels. Fundamentally, the transmission system is needed because internal combustion engines have quite a limited speed range at which useable torque is produced (this varies, but generally lies in the range 1500–5000 rev/min). Operation within this speed range is also important for the engine to achieve maximum efficiency. This is clearly beneficial for fuel economy and to minimise exhaust emissions. There are several other reasons why a transmission system must be incorporated in the powertrain:

• to provide variable torque at varying speeds selectable by the driver for the appropriate condition, such as low speeds, overcoming gradients, comfortable cruising speeds

• to provide a 'neutral' state, i.e. a situation where the engine can run without being connected to the driving wheels, for example, when a vehicle is stationary

• so that the vehicle can be driven backwards (in reverse), for manoeuvring, parking, etc.

• to provide torque multiplication: the internal combustion engine cannot produce any torque at zero speed. Therefore a transmission (including a clutch of some sort) is needed to overcome vehicle inertia (resistance to change of speed) at standstill. This provides a smooth application of tractive force in a manner that can be controlled by the driver, and consequent movement of the vehicle from zero speed.

5.2 TRANSMISSION TYPES

The various types of vehicle powertrain transmissions can be classified according to their operating principles.

- **Multi-stage transmissions** have a number of fixed gear ratios which can be selected manually by the driver, or automatically by a mechanical or electrical control system according to the vehicle operating status.
- **Continuously variable transmissions** (CVTs) are infinitely variable between certain boundary limits achieved through hydraulic or mechanical means.

They can also be classified by their construction.

- **In-line transmissions** have an input shaft on one end and an output shaft at the other. They are predominantly used in front engine, rear wheel drive applications.
- **Dual shaft transmissions** have their input and output shafts misaligned or eccentric, typically for front wheel drive applications.

Multi-stage transmissions rely on fixed, geometrically locked elements (i.e. gears), whereas CVTs use friction locking principles to achieve the necessary ratios. This friction locking function needs an additional energy input (for example, from the oil pump used to generate hydraulic pressure for gearbox operation in an automatic gearbox or CVT), which reduces the overall efficiency of the gearbox itself. This inefficiency is offset by the fact that, because of the infinitely variable transmission ratios, the engine can operate closer to its maximum efficiency, which increases the efficiency of the powertrain as a complete unit.

Another factor that differentiates transmissions systems is their level of automation. In Europe, traditional manual transmissions are dominant, whereas in America or Asia, automatic shifting hydraulic, or electrohydraulic, transmissions have the largest share of the market. These traditional transmissions are now being displaced by modern transmissions that incorporate the latest developments in mechatronics and software such that they have the efficiency of traditional manual transmissions with all the benefits of an automatic shifting transmission. In addition, they can operate in manual or semi-automatic mode according to driver preference and it is possible to integrate the shifting of transmission ratios with other vehicle control or safety systems for maximum driver benefit.

Table 5.1 summarises the common transmission types and their characteristic features.

Key Points

All vehicles with an internal combustion engine require a clutch and gearbox for reasons of performance and efficiency

The main types of gearbox are manual or automatic and both types can be electronically controlled

Table 5.1 Transmission types

Transmission type	Transmission ratio via	Comparative mass	Comparative noise	Comparative efficiency[a]	Gearshift comfort factor[b]
Manual, synchromesh	Fixed gears	Low	Low	+10%	–
Automatic, hydraulic shift	Planetary gears and torque converter	Medium	Low	0%	0.90
CVT	Belt/chain type drive	High	Medium	+5%	0.95
Toroidal variator drive (Torotrack)	Friction wheel variator	Very High	Low	+7%	0.95
Automatic shifting manual transmission	Fixed gears, electro-mechanical actuation	Low	Low	+15%	0.63
Dual clutch transmission	Fixed gears, electro-hydraulic actuation	Medium	Low	+8%	0.87

[a] Efficiency when compared to an automatic, multistage transmission at given operating point with a petrol/gasoline engine
[b] Measure of the quality of the change of transmission ratio: 1 = completely smooth, 0.1 = rough transition

5.3 HISTORY OF ELECTRONIC CONTROL

5.3.1 First developments in electrical control for transmissions

Traditionally, transmissions and powertrains in vehicles were purely mechanical systems. One of the first developments to incorporate an electrical control element was the overdrive system. This system was fitted to many sporting or GT cars in the 1950s and 1960s and was also available as an option on many other car models during that period.

The overdrive was a self-contained unit, fitted to the existing gearbox casing, providing an additional gear ratio which could be engaged in third or fourth gear. The extra gear ratio was less than one, giving the output shaft a higher speed than the input shaft. (Usually, transmissions fitted at that time had a top gear ratio of 1:1, known as 'straight through drive'). Thus, with overdrive selected, for a given road speed, engine speed was reduced and this provided more relaxed cruising and better economy. An inhibitor switch on the gearbox prevented engagement of overdrive in first and second gears.

The heart of the overdrive system was a single epicyclic gear set (as used in many automatic gearboxes) with engagement effected via a hydraulically actuated cone clutch (Figure 5.1). This provided the most redeeming feature of the system: even though the system provided an extra gear, it was not necessary to declutch (i.e. disconnect the engine torque from the gearbox input shaft) in order to engage or disengage the extra gear. This provided improved drivability and a sporty overtone to the vehicle. The driver could just 'flick' a switch to engage or disengage the extra gear.

The engagement of the gear was implemented hydraulically via an oil pump to generate pressure, which caused an actuator to engage or disengage the clutch. The control of the hydraulic circuit was implemented electrically via a simple solenoid valve and

this is where the electrical control begins. The system allowed the driver to engage overdrive via a switch on the gear knob. This was a simple circuit, with an interlocking switch, to ensure that overdrive could be selected only in third or fourth (top) gear.

This is a very simple control circuit (Figure 5.2) to ensure that the overdrive operates only when the correct conditions exist. This was only the start of the integration of electrical control into vehicle transmissions: from this point, the growth in sophistication developed rapidly.

5.3.2 Integration of electronics for transmission control

In the 1980s the next major step forward for transmission system control was the integration of electronic control for automatic gearboxes. This was a logical progression which allowed greater degrees of freedom and flexibility, such as adapting shift control to driving style, simplified hydraulics in the gearbox and reduced costs.

A further advantage of this system, exploited during the late 1980s and 1990s, was the integration of transmission control with engine control. Control units could share information from common sensors, reducing costs. Strategies to improve gear shifts by using engine control parameters (such as ignition timing) could also be used to improve drivability and performance.

These systems have been developed in combination, even further in more recent years. Tighter integration between transmission/engine control and management, brought about by increasingly stringent emission regulations, means that complete control of the powertrain is essential for modern vehicles. No longer can the engine and transmission be considered as separate units. Current developments in vehicle

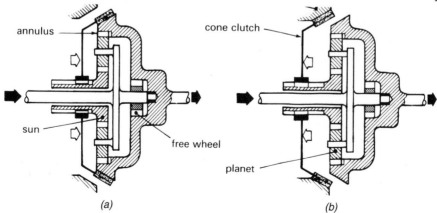

(a)   (b)

Figure 5.1 An early overdrive assembly
a Direct drive
b Overdrive

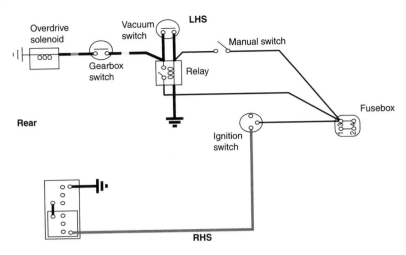

Figure 5.2 Basic overdrive circuit diagram

dynamic control systems require open, fast communication between control elements (steering, braking, transmission, engine, etc.) and tightly integrated systems to achieve high levels of vehicle safety and performance.

5.3.3 Future developments

Future developments will involve improvements in control performance. One of the latest engine technologies under development (homogeneous charge compression ignition, or HCCI) requires dynamic real time control to achieve the required performance and to operate within, for example, emissions limits. This level of control performance, in combination with fast communication between electronic control units, allows further refinement of transmission and powertrain control.

Transmissions for hybrid engine technologies require special consideration. Electric motors can produce maximum torque at zero speed and hence do not need a gearbox as such. When these motors are used in conjunction with a combustion engine, a sophisticated powertrain control system must be used. This uses the appropriate prime mover according to the driving conditions and operates the whole system as efficiently as possible (the control system needs to provide energy recovery, battery management, switch over from electric to IC engine power and vice versa, etc.)

There is no doubt that this technology will evolve and change shape as powertrains are developed to produce more efficient, cleaner vehicles with increasingly higher performance and drivability.

> **Key Points**
>
> Engine and transmission electronic systems must communicate to improve efficiency
>
> Powertrains are constantly evolving

5.4 MULTIPLEXING

5.4.1 Integrated electronic control units

The transmission system can be improved and made more sophisticated by integrating the transmission control unit (TCU) with the engine control unit (ECU). This is a purely electronic control/software development. The transmission, engine and equipment remain unchanged.

Linking together the operation of these two units (Figure 5.3) provides integrated powertrain management. This is now common practice with modern vehicles and it is a logical step forward to improve the vehicle powertrain system as a whole unit rather than considering engine and transmission as separate systems. Some vehicle manufacturers are now

opting to produce a single electronic control unit for engine and transmission called a PCU, or powertrain control unit. This represents the ultimate step in harmonisation and physical integration of the control systems.

Typical technology adopted by most manufacturers for this type of integration and communication is via the controller area network (CAN) bus. Most electronic control units have inbuilt CAN capability and the level of system integration and interaction is chosen by the manufacturer but not limited. Integration of the vehicle control systems can provide a number of advantages.

- Maximum efficiency and performance can be fully realised through integrated control of the engine, transmission and powertrain components. For example, the gearbox shift function can be incorporated with the engine torque control and this can be adjusted during the shift to optimise drivability.

- Sensor information can be shared and used for transmission operation and optimisation as well as engine functions (for example, engine speed, throttle position and engine temperature). Overall sensor count is minimised (reducing manufacturing costs) and wiring system complexity is reduced.

- Vehicle control systems can be harmonised to work together such that their function and operation can be complementary. This is particularly important with safety systems. Operation of transmission components such as four-wheel drive, active differential locks and torque distribution can be fully integrated with safety systems such as stability control, traction control, anti-lock braking and brake force distribution, and engine control functions such as throttle position and torque.

For more detailed information about the technology for interfacing ECUs, see *Hillier's Fundamentals of Motor Vehicle Technology Book 3.*

5.4.2 Electronic transmission control as a black box

Electronic control of the transmission is an inevitable step forward for motor manufacturers, who have already implemented full electronic control and management of the engine fuel, ignition and control systems. This step is necessary to optimise the overall efficiency of the vehicle power unit. No longer can engine and vehicle be considered separately, so full

integration and overall electronic control of the complete powertrain is a reality today. This enables manufacturers to achieve the levels of performance, drivability and economy that the market demands.

It is important to remember though that the powertrain or transmission control is a simple system! It is similar to any other system on the vehicle. As such, understanding of its operation can be broken down into manageable elements. This is particularly important with fault diagnosis.

The powertrain or transmission control ECU can be considered as the central component in this system. It is supplied information about the powertrain status from a number of strategically placed sensors. This information would typically include pressure, temperatures, rotational speeds (wheels or gearbox shafts), linear speeds (vehicle speed) and driver requirements (throttle position or gear lever position). The ECU processor runs a software program in real time which responds to these inputs and calculates corresponding actions to be taken. These actions are implemented by actuators connected to and driven by the ECU. For example, these could be solenoid valves to supply pressurised oil to brake bands or clutches in the gearbox, or signals to other engine systems to implement some required action (for example, to retard the ignition during a gear shift).

Sophistication in transmission and powertrain technology is shifting from mechanical to electronic technology or mechatronics. Sophisticated mechanically based control systems (such as a hydraulic valve block for an automatic transmission) are being replaced with software and electronics with much higher degrees of freedom and flexibility. The consequence of this is that the remaining mechanical

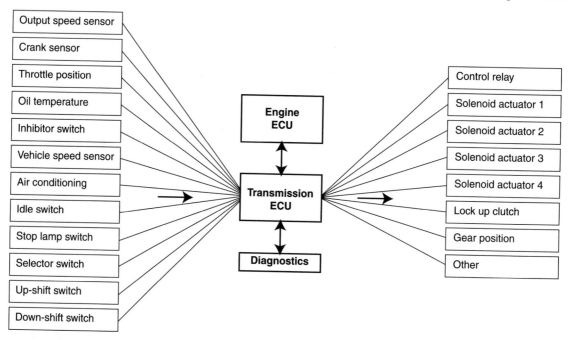

Figure 5.3 Powertrain control unit showing inputs and outputs

parts become simpler, since there is less intelligence needed within them. This means that the skills of the motor vehicle technician or engineer must also shift in the same direction. These days it is not possible to avoid the prospect of facing electronic or electrical faults on vehicle powertrain or transmission systems. This does not need to be a problem! A logical thought process in conjunction with simple functional decomposition or breakdown of the system will overcome any fault that could occur.

Figure 5.4 shows a simple functional breakdown of a powertrain control system.

5.4.3 General comments

The above developments in electronic control systems have reduced the mechanical complexity of the gearbox design itself. The distinction between automatic and manual gearbox construction is becoming less clear. For example, in the 1970s, the construction of an automatic gearbox was completely different from that of a manual, constant mesh gearbox. The automatic gearbox was expensive to manufacture. In place of the manual gearbox's clutch there was a torque converter. In place of the gears and synchromesh there were planetary gears and in place of a gear lever there was a simple selector lever connected to an extremely sophisticated and complex all hydraulic system of valves to control gear shifting and selection.

Developments in electronics, sensors and actuators have simplified the mechanical construction of gearboxes to the point where a modern, automatic gearbox is very similar to a manual gearbox, except that

clutch operation and gear selection can be implemented using electroactuators. A system like this uses all electronic control and therefore offers many possibilities for the use of advanced control methodology and communication with other vehicle systems.

The first developments in electronic control of transmissions consisted of replacing hydraulic control with electronic control, but still using planetary gears, brake bands and clutches; so the mechanical automatic gearbox was still of conventional construction. After this step, integration with engine control and management systems became usual to increase efficiency and drivability. Current technology is such that less direct control is given to the driver in many vehicle systems. Brakes and dynamic stability are electronically controlled and monitored. Throttle and traction control are fully electronic. In line with this trend, gear selection and clutch control of a manual gearbox can be implemented and greatly improved with the addition of electronic control and monitoring (for example, a Tiptronic or a direct shift gearbox (DSG)). We are now reaching the point where the difference between an automatic gearbox and a manual gearbox is just in software function rather than hardware or construction.

Key Points

All complex systems can be broken down and represented in a diagram showing inputs and outputs

Some systems use a single ECU for engine and transmission control. Others allow the ECUs to communicate using a CAN system

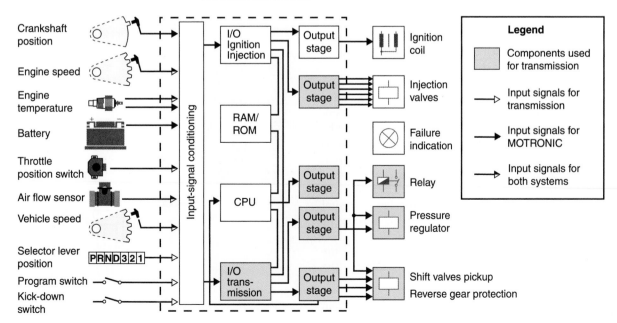

Figure 5.4 Electronic control of transmission shown as a block diagram

5.5 SENSORS AND ACTUATORS USED IN TRANSMISSION SYSTEMS

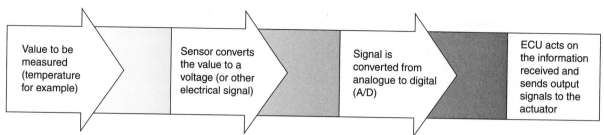

| Value to be measured (temperature for example) | Sensor converts the value to a voltage (or other electrical signal) | Signal is converted from analogue to digital (A/D) | ECU acts on the information received and sends output signals to the actuator |

Figure 5.5 Representation of sensor operation

The sensors and actuators provide the essential data and control elements of the powertrain control system (Figure 5.5).

5.5.1 Sensors

Most of the sensors used in powertrain or transmission systems are similar in technology to the equipment used for engine management or engine control systems, so they are subjected to a similar harsh operating environment. They have to work reliably in extremes of temperatures and pressures and perform their required task for as much of the life of the vehicle as possible.

Normally the sensor has a simple transfer function relating or converting the measured value to an output signal. In most cases, for an automotive system, the output signal would be a voltage. This voltage would be connected to the ECU input. An analogue to digital converter inside the ECU digitises this signal ready for processing by the central processing unit (CPU). The process for driving the actuator is similar but reversed. The CPU outputs the demand value digitally to a digital to analogue converter, and then the analogue signal output will operate the actuator or actuator controller to move the actuator to the required position (note that the actuator controller could be inside the ECU; for example, it could be a stepper motor driver circuit).

An important point to consider is the development of smart sensor technology. Sensors fitting this description are being developed and implemented more frequently in modern vehicles. A smart sensor could be described as one that has 'local intelligence'. This means that, rather than just being essentially a converter, converting some physical quantity into an electrical quantity, this sensor can have additional functions, such as analogue to digital conversion, digital communication with the driver, self monitoring, a plausibility check, etc. The development of this technology has only been possible because of the dramatic miniaturisation of CPU technology. The advantages are that:

- there is distributed intelligence in the powertrain control system; a greater overall intelligence in the system; and less load on the ECU CPU

- signal transmission can be digital, with a vastly improved signal quality and reliability, and is less susceptible to interference
- the bus system can be standardised; sensors can be daisy chained on the bus; and there is a significant reduction in cabling/wiring.

Powertrain sensors are similar in their technology to sensors used for engine control (for example, speed of rotation sensors). Below, there is a brief overview of the specific technology.

Speed (rotation) sensor

Speed sensors are used in engine control. For example, all ECUs need a crankshaft position sensor and most need a camshaft position sensor as well. Speed sensing of gearbox shafts is important for auto shift functionality and to provide closed loop feedback for shift quality control. The two main technologies used are inductive analogue sensors and digital Hall effect sensors. Both of these, when used as rotation sensors, measure relative velocity and form part of an incremental rotation sensing system. They are used in conjunction with an encoder or toothed wheel. A typical inductive sensor's cross section is shown in Figure 5.6.

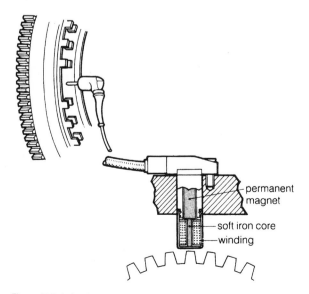

permanent magnet

soft iron core

winding

Figure 5.6 Inductive type speed sensor

The inductive sensor is simple and reliable; it works on the principle that a moving magnetic flux will induce a voltage into an adjacent conductor. The construction shown includes a permanent magnet and soft iron core, around which an induction coil is wound. The sensor is mounted in close proximity to an encoder wheel or a gear wheel with a tooth profile. When this gear wheel is rotated, the movement (passing) of the teeth in close proximity to the sensor disturbs the magnetic flux and hence induces a small voltage in the coil. The voltage approximates a sine wave; its amplitude increases as the speed increases (up to a saturation point). The frequency is a function of the number of teeth on the wheel (which is fixed) and the speed of the wheel. Thus the frequency of the signal is proportional to the instantaneous speed of the encoder or gear wheel. The air gap and tooth profile dictate the overall output signal profile and a reference mark can be provided with a missing tooth or teeth. Through special pulse configuration and teeth profiles, the shaft position and direction of rotation, as well as speed, can be measured. One limitation of this sensor is that it is passive in nature: it cannot detect zero movement or position.

The Hall effect sensor (Figure 5.7) is similar in outward appearance and use to the inductive sensor. The main difference is the fundamental operating principle. The Hall effect is widely used in industrial sensing technology as well as automotive sensing applications and can be described simply as a voltage produced by the interaction between the current flowing and the magnetic field around a current carrying conductor. This voltage is a function of the magnitude (size and direction) of the current and magnetic flux strength, but also of the material of the current carrying conductor. In all automotive sensor applications the sensing element (the current carrying conductor) is a semiconductor and hence optimised to provide a high quality output signal (normally a voltage).

Hall effect sensors are also used for current sensing applications, where they can sense the current flowing in a cable via the magnetic field around it. The main advantages of a Hall effect sensor when used as an incremental rotation sensor are that:

- the output signal it produces has a fixed amplitude; only the frequency varies
- the signal is normally a square wave, which is easily processed with simple electronic circuitry in the ECU
- the sensor is active and can be used for position sensing: it can sense zero position, because the encoder wheel does not have to be moving to generate a signal.

One example of the use of these sensors in transmissions is to provide information about torque converter turbine speed. This would be used in the control strategy for shifting, for torque converter lock up control and also for determining the correct line pressure during shifts. Additionally these sensors would be used in CVT applications for determining actual gear ratios.

Gearbox RPM sensors comply with two main protocols:

- the signal frequency is proportional to the speed
- the frequency and pulse width modulated (PWM) signals give information about speed (including zero speed, i.e. standstill) and direction of rotation.

Temperature sensors

Powertrain or transmission control systems need to monitor the temperature of the transmission. A sophisticated system will be calibrated to adjust system pressures and responses as the temperature changes to achieve the optimum drivability under all engine conditions. Such a system will also act to prevent failure of the transmission from excessive temperatures in extreme working conditions.

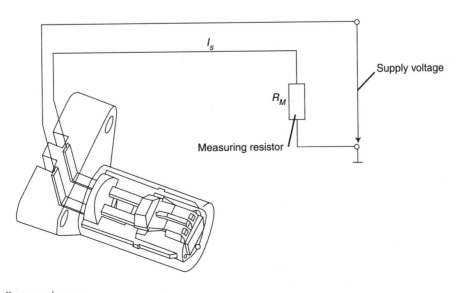

Figure 5.7 Hall effect speed sensor

The sensing technology is similar to that used in engine temperature sensors (Figure 5.8). The sensors are continuous function devices that change resistance with temperature (they are resistive elements with a negative temperature coefficient or thermistors). A temperature sensor would typically be mounted near the torque converter, or the oil sump of the transmission, or both in automatic transmission applications. For automated manual transmission (such as Tiptronic or DSG) there is a mechatronic assembly mounted on the gearbox. This unit houses an electrohydraulic control assembly as well as the transmission ECU itself. This is a harsh environment, so temperature sensors are mounted not only to sense oil temperature but also to sense ECU control unit temperature. The latter is integrated within the assembly.

Transmission temperature sensing will become more commonplace as engine and transmission controllers become more tightly integrated (with full powertrain control), and also, as emission legislation and onboard diagnostic legislation become more comprehensive.

Driver's lever position sensor
The lever position sensor is the main user interface to the driver (Figure 5.9). Depending on the manufacturer and the vehicle, it will have a number of functions:

- mode selection for the desired gear (park, reverse, neutral, etc.)
- reversing light operation
- selection of overdrive
- shift up and down for sequential gearboxes.

Additional switches (Figure 5.10) can be incorporated for the driver to select different shift modes to suit driving styles or conditions. These will change the shift strategy, line pressure and torque converter control according to the selected mode. For example, winter

driving mode could set the transmission in third gear and disable torque converter lock up. For driving in slippery conditions this mode reduces torque at the wheels to prevent wheel spin. Another typical selection is 'sport' mode, which changes the shift point selection and kick down trigger point to optimise acceleration and give a sporty feel to gear shifting.

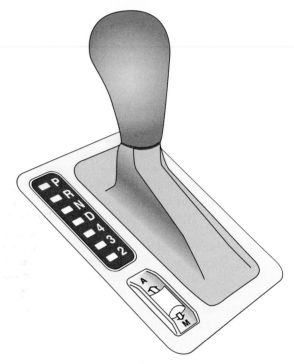

Figure 5.9 Transmission gear selection lever

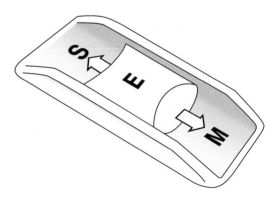

Figure 5.10 Selection switch

Pressure sensor
It is important to control pressure in the transmission system, particularly in traditional automatic transmissions, to ensure good performance of the control and actuator system. The valves and actuators all need the hydraulic pressure to be correct to maintain optimum system performance under all conditions. As temperature changes, the viscosity of the lubricant can change, which in turn can affect the system pressure.

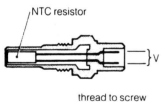

thread to screw
into engine block

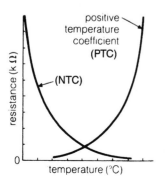

Figure 5.8 Temperature sensor

The technology used is similar to that used for engine control (Figure 5.11): a pressure sensing element (a thick film or semiconductor) is mounted in a housing and exposed to the system pressure via a channel in a fitting or mounting screw. With this sensor technology additional circuitry can be included for linearisation and temperature compensation of the raw signal. This signal can be amplified to provide an appropriate output voltage signal level.

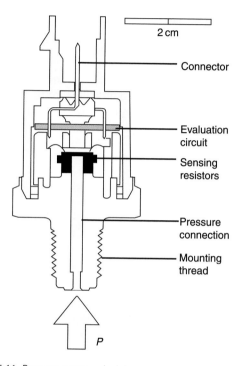

Figure 5.11 Pressure sensor principle

Drivetrain torque sensor

A recent development is a sensor to measure drivetrain torque in production vehicles. This is particularly useful, since it could provide true closed loop feedback and control of drivetrain torque distribution under operational conditions. Additionally, real time limit monitoring of transmission torque throughput could help prevent damage to any transmission or powertrain components. Such a sensor is also useful for monitoring the efficiency of the powertrain. The sensor technology used is non-contact magnetoresistive. Sensor units have been developed that can be integrated into existing installations with minimal design changes.

Torque sensing can use one of two principles: measurement of stress in the shaft material (this is a function of the shaft torque); or measurement of angular displacement due to torsion between two points on the shaft. Torque sensors for powertrain applications use the former method and measure this stress via a magnetoelastic principle.

The ability of the shaft material to concentrate magnetic flux (i.e. its magnetic permeability) varies with torque: a magnetoelastic torque sensor detects

changes in permeability by measuring changes in its own magnetic field.

One design of magnetoelastic sensor is constructed as a thin ring of steel tightly coupled to a stainless steel shaft. This assembly acts as a permanent magnet whose magnetic field is proportional to the torque applied to the shaft. A magnetometer converts the generated magnetic field into an electrical output signal that is proportional to the torque being applied. In another proposed design (Figure 5.12), a portion of the shaft is magnetised and the non-contact sensor measures changes in the magnetic field caused by the torsional forces in the shaft.

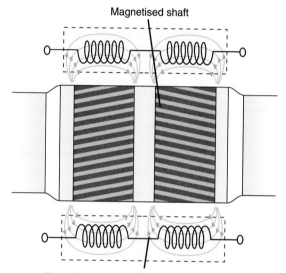

Flux gates measure the axial magnetic field
generated by the shaft under torsional load
based on the magnetoelastic principle

Figure 5.12 Magnetoelastic torque sensor measurement principle

Position sensors

For certain applications a number of sensors could be mounted in strategic positions to confirm that an action has taken place, or to provide an input signal. For example, sensors could detect gear lever movement for sequential shift application, or travel sensors could detect movement of shift forks in an electronically automated manual gearbox. For these applications small Hall sensors are commonly used for their robustness and reliable operation (Figure 5.13).

Indirect sensor signals for transmission/powertrain control

A number of sensor inputs to the transmission or powertrain control are necessary to fully integrate and harmonise the operation of the engine and transmission. Even though these signals may not be obviously linked to operation of a gearbox, the current trend to close integration of engine and transmission to provide an integrated powertrain unit means that this type of integration becomes essential to support overall targets of low fuel consumption, good drivability and optimum performance. Typical inputs appropriate for an electronically controlled automatic gearbox are as follows.

- **Engine coolant temperature** – This is sensed via a negative temperature coefficient (NTC) sensor for engine management functions. With the transmission system certain functions, such as the torque converter lock-up clutch, are disabled until the engine reaches operating temperature.
- **Engine speed (rev/min) via crank position sensor** – A fundamental input to the transmission controller, as well as to the engine control system, this signal is the transmission input speed. The signal is a conditioned version of the ECU crankshaft position sensor signal. It is needed to optimise the transmission strategy for the various engine operating states.
- **Brake on/off** – This simple digital state signal is derived from the brake pedal in a similar way to the brake light switch. It is normally provided via a separate switch mounted on the brake pedal or via a double pole brake light switch, for safety reasons. This signal is used to disengage the torque converter clutch under braking conditions.

- **Air conditioning status** – This signal is used by the powertrain control to compensate for the additional load placed on the engine by the air conditioning system. It is derived from the compressor clutch signal. The transmission control line pressure is trimmed slightly according to the additional load.
- **Mass air flow/manifold pressure** – This signal is used as a fundamental indication of engine load. It is measured by an air mass flow sensor. Certain manufacturers prefer to derive engine load from manifold pressure and throttle position. In either case, this load signal is a parameter used in the control of line pressure and lock up clutch function.
- **Throttle position** – Another fundamental input to the engine and transmission control, this signal is important not only for absolute throttle position but also for rate of change during fast changing driver demand (e.g. tip in or WOT). The signal will be used to control shift scheduling, and to control the line pressure and torque converter.
- **Vehicle speed** – The vehicle speed is one of the main powertrain outputs (in addition to torque) and hence is a critical parameter to monitor and feed back. The existing vehicle speed sensor is used for this purpose to determine shift scheduling and line pressure control.

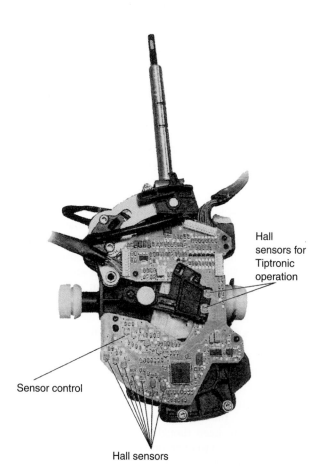

Hall sensors for Tiptronic operation

Sensor control

Hall sensors

Figure 5.13 Gear lever sensor control unit

Key Points

Most sensors convert a physical variable to an electrical signal

The main types of sensor used in transmission are: speed, temperature, pressure and position

Torque sensors are under development for use with transmission control systems

Indirect sensors supply information from other vehicle systems

5.5.2 Actuators

Actuators are devices that convert the low level electrical signal from the ECU into actual, physical movement. This could be continuous, cyclic movement or movement to a set position in accordance with a demand value. With the current trend towards indirect operation of powertrain components (drive by wire), actuators form an important element of the powertrain control system. Clearly, an actuator needs to activate a physical output to the required position, in the required time. The sensor must be able to repeat this as and when desired, reliably, for many operating cycles throughout the life of the vehicle. The actuator must also be capable of operating at the extremes of temperature that could be encountered around the globe.

The current trend is towards totally electrical actuation as opposed to electrical servo operation. For example, rather than having an electrical solenoid open a hydraulic valve to provide oil pressure to a hydraulic actuator for physical movement, the actuator is totally electrical/electronic, with an electrical mechanism providing the physical movement (i.e. direct rather than indirect electrical actuation). The reason for this is that, as electronics and electrical technology has developed, it has become possible to produce reliable highly efficient electroactuators cheaply, with the required performance. These do not need large amounts of electrical power, yet can still provide the required force.

These actuators are compact and self-contained (they need only electrical signal and power cables: no additional power source (such as oil pressure) is needed for the necessary force to be generated). Hence integrating these units into existing powertrain installations or new installations where space is at a premium (always the case for modern vehicles) is less of an issue for manufacturers. Another important benefit, becoming increasingly significant, is that these actuators can have 'local intelligence'. The benefits of this are clear: the actuator can provide reliable feedback to the control system about its performance. An actuator can provide not just positional feedback (which is important for closed loop control) but also status monitoring, such as temperature or a signal plausibility check. This allows complex safety and redundancy to be integrated in the overall control system. For example, a clutch actuator could monitor the system for wear of the clutch and inform the driver when clutch replacement will soon be needed. Such actuator intelligence can be used by the control system to provide real time monitoring of the powertrain components, checking for faults and efficiency of operation. This technology will become essential as requirements for on board diagnostics and system monitoring become more sophisticated and as legislation becomes tighter.

The following section discusses the different types and basic operating principles of commonly found powertrain actuators.

Electrohydraulic actuators
Simple on/off actuator
Simple solenoid actuators (Figure 5.14) are commonly used within the transmission system to direct flow of oil into and out of components as required, typically to implement gear shifting and for torque converter control. Their basic construction consists of a spool valve to control fluid flow connected to a simple solenoid arrangement. Current supply to the solenoid changes the valve state. They can be constructed for use as on/off or change over valve (normally open or closed). They are usually switched at battery voltage because they demand a high current at initial actuation (pull in of the solenoid). The benefits of these actuators include their simple, robust construction.

Variable position bleed actuator
The variable position bleed actuator is used in applications where a variable movement and position

Figure 5.14 Solenoid actuator

are required for fluid control (see Figure 5.15). For transmission applications, such an actuator would be used in a gearbox as a bleed valve, for example in pressure control applications where the output pressure from the valve would be a function of the supply current. An important design criterion is to reduce 'stiction' or static friction in the valve to allow precise positioning with minimal error. This can be achieved through careful port design. An electronic control circuit with pulse width modulation would typically be used to operate this valve by supplying the appropriate varying current according to demand. An important feature of the circuit is that it should be able to provide an appropriate current to activate the valve quickly and then supply sufficient current to hold the valve position without overheating (different currents for pull in and holding are provided by an intelligent driver circuit). This is similar to a fuel injector driver circuit in the engine ECU.

It is very common to find all the required electrohydraulic actuators mounted in a complete assembly on or in the gearbox casing. This has a number of advantages:

- interconnecting hydraulic paths between the valves are short, minimising pressure drop
- one casting contains all the valves, reducing manufacturing costs
- the system is easier to integrate into the gearbox assembly or design
- its single interface point is easier to integrate into the system electronics.

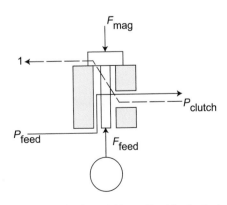

Figure 5.15 Schematic of a variable position bleed actuator

Another recent development is to combine within the electrohydraulic assembly, the electrical and electronic parts, including the ECU! This creates a complete, self-contained mechatronic unit for control and management of the transmission. Very close interfacing of hydraulics and electronics gives greater reliability and reduces the installation space needed. In addition, the complete transmission assembly forms a compact, modular unit that can be easily integrated into current or new vehicle designs. A typical example is shown in Figure 5.16.

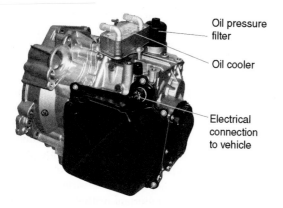

Figure 5.16 Mechatronic unit

Electroactuators
Clutch actuator

There are several designs for electronic control and electrical actuation of the clutch. The type chosen by each manufacturer depends greatly on whether an existing gearbox design is being adapted, or whether the gearbox design is new and will integrate electrical clutch operation from inception.

Figure 5.17 shows a current design used in a production vehicle. This basically consists of a package containing a brushless DC motor with feedback of position. The rotary motion is converted to linear

1 Actuator motor
2 ECU
3 Worm
4 Worm gear
5 Worm gear shaft
6 Pin
7 Position sensor
8 Compensation spring
9 Push rod
10 Master cylinder

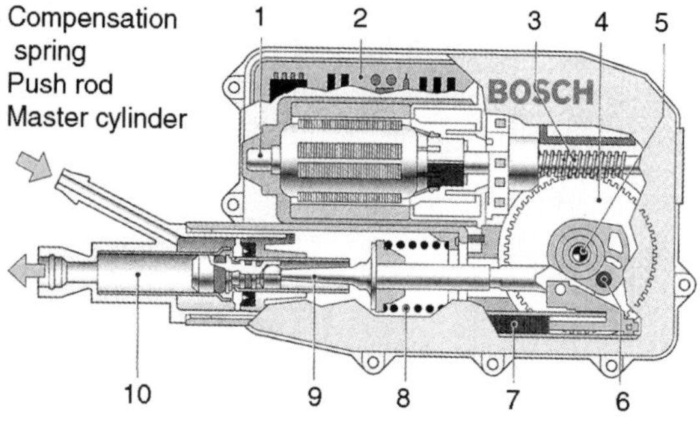

Figure 5.17 Worm gear drive actuator

motion via a worm driven crank assembly. This in turn operates a piston inside the unit which provides hydraulic pressure to a clutch slave cylinder assembly. In this case, therefore, the existing clutch actuator (a hydraulic slave cylinder) remains and the electroactuator replaces the master cylinder assembly. Clearly this system also incorporates an ECU and a clutch pedal position sensor. The main advantage of such a system is that it can be (and has been) introduced in a production vehicle. Minimal changes or adaptations are needed in the vehicle design to incorporate this system.

The disadvantage is that retaining an existing hydraulic system means that this system still needs to be maintained. In addition, the dynamic response of such a system is reduced because there is more inertia in the system due to the increased component count and the interfaces between the actuator and the clutch itself.

An improvement is to dispense with the existing actuator system and mount the electroactuator as close as possible to the clutch itself. This is feasible for a completely new design of gearbox or powertrain. Design of the actuation mechanism can also improved with greater operating force and higher efficiency. One design applies the force directly at the release bearing via a concentric release mechanism (Figure 5.18). It uses an axial screw ball bearing track (a helix) with a rotating collar such that, as the collar turns, an axial force is applied to the clutch release bearing via the ball bearings. The collar is rotated by a brushless DC motor with a position feedback signal. This motor drives a lead screw assembly to convert rotary to linear motion. This linear force is applied to the collar via a Bowden cable (shown in Figure 5.19).

An alternative mechanism is to apply the force to the release bearing via a lever mechanism (Figure 5.20). In this case the actuator can also be mounted close to the clutch on the bell housing. The actuator uses a brushless DC motor with positional feedback. This provides a high level of reliability and longevity. The rotary motion is converted to linear movement via a lead screw or spring band system incorporated in the

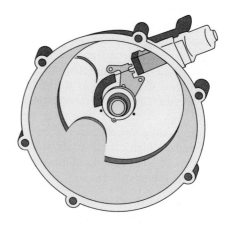

Figure 5.18 Direct acting clutch actuator

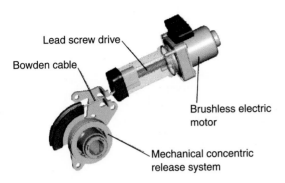

Figure 5.19 Mechanical concentric clutch release system for clutch actuator

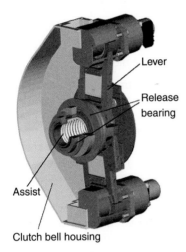

Figure 5.20 Dual clutch actuation system

actuator. This is transmitted by a simple lever arrangement as a force at the release bearing. This system is capable of transmitting high forces (for clutches transmitting up to 900 Nm) and can also be used in dual clutch applications.

Gear shift actuator

Clearly, with a normal automatic transmission, gears are changed via a number of actuators and a combination of brake bands and clutches, which operate hydraulically. For electronic control applications, they are activated by gearbox system oil pressure which is switched via solenoid type valves as described above. Therefore the actuators are hydraulic but controlled electrically. In this section we will focus specifically on electroactuators: actuators where the force is generated by some electrical means and controlled electronically.

Actuators of this type are used in the latest generation of highly efficient automatic shifting transmissions. These transmissions are generally, in construction, similar to a manual gearbox, except that the driver has only indirect control of the gear shift process. Most vehicles using this system receive driver input from switches on the steering wheel (typically

flipper controls as in racing cars). The driver tells the ECU that a shift is required; the ECU then calculates the best time to do this and therefore has the ultimate control over the process, taking into account other factors, such as vehicle stability, braking, steering and other dynamic factors.

There are a number of methods of gear shift actuation depending on the gearbox type. The main differentiating factors are whether the transmission is retrofitted with actuators or is a new design where this technology will be used. Another factor is whether the transmission is an auto shift gearbox (a manual transmission with electroactuation of the shifting process) or is a parallel shift gearbox (such as the Volkswagen direct shift gearbox (DSG), where the next gear is engaged while the vehicle is in the existing gear; this requires a twin clutch arrangement).

The system shown in Figure 5.21 is a retrofit unit used with an existing gearbox design for a small front wheel drive vehicle. In this particular application gear selection is via a push pull and twist rod. This rod enters the gearbox and has a selector 'finger' attached which pushes forward and backward the appropriate selector rail for the required gear (Figure 5.22).

The actuator unit consists of two brushless DC motors, one to provide forward and backwards movement (for gear selection) via a quadrant gear. The other provides movement side to side (across the gearbox 'gate') via a rack mechanism. The existing gear interlock mechanism is employed to prevent selection of two gears at the same time. It is important to note that this actuator assembly was designed for the first generation of automatic shift gearboxes, where modularity (i.e. the ability to reuse existing components in gearbox designs) was the most important factor.

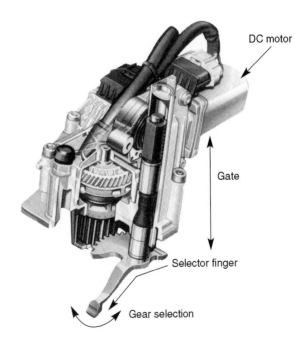

Figure 5.21 Retrofit gear shift actuator

Current designs of actuation mechanism are in line with current trends in transmission and powertrain design: manual constant mesh gearboxes are used, but with electrical actuation of clutch and gear selection. Hence the housings for these actuators will be designed in from concept. The choice of whether the gearbox behaves as a manual or automatic transmission (or both) will simply be controlled via software and perhaps the driver interface (such as whether or not there is a clutch pedal; whether the gear lever is one with a manual style gate, or is an auto-style selector lever, a sequential selector lever or a steering wheel paddle change).

Figure 5.23 shows a shift drum with an integral motor which could be installed directly into a gearbox housing.

This selection mechanism is similar to those used in most motor cycles, in that the drum has grooves forming tracks into which the gear selector forks engage. The tracks are designed such that, as the drum rotates, the appropriate selectors move the synchromesh hubs in and out of engagement to select the appropriate gear. A brushless DC motor is used, integrated within the drum, complete with a planetary gearbox to provide the required operating speed and force. The advantage of this design is its compactness and ease of installation into the gearbox housing. If a single motor is used to drive the assembly the system can be relatively low in cost but there are some points to consider:

- the gearbox design has to accommodate the arrangement from concept; it cannot be retrofitted
- the shift drum arrangement means that gear shifts have to be sequential; arbitrary shifts cannot be made (for example, from fourth to second gear)

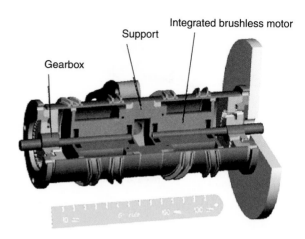

Figure 5.23 Double shift drum with internal drive

- the latter can be avoided by using a double shift drum arrangement: Figure 5.24 shows an example with external drive motors.

Reduction and torque multiplication are provided by a spur gear. For these systems both motors must be capable of sufficient force to provide gear selection reliably, compared with the previous retrofit design, where only one motor needs to be capable of generating this force (the other just moves across the gearbox 'gate'). This factor increases the overall cost of the assembly. Another important point is that interlocking of the gear selection must be prevented: in theory, both actuators could engage a gear at the same time. Interlocking can be implemented with a mechanical arrangement as well as through software.

A double shift actuator arrangement is currently more appropriate for parallel shift gearboxes or DSG systems where maximum advantage can be gained from an optimised shift process. By using two actuators, with active interlocks, reduced gear change times can significantly improve vehicle performance and acceleration. This provides a clear sales argument to the customer for the additional cost of this technology.

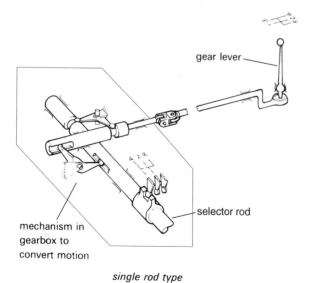

single rod type

Figure 5.22 Manual gear shift actuator for front-wheel drive

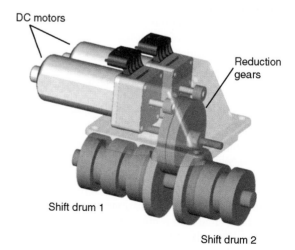

Figure 5.24 Double shift drum with external drive

These actuators are becoming increasingly commonplace on modern vehicles and will certainly be more common in the future. Current actuator drive units, brushless DC motors, provide reliable technology that can last the life of the vehicle, and they are suitable for use in safety critical applications (as above). The compact design of the motors means that the actuators require no greater space than the manual mechanisms they replace. Additional technology can be integrated in the actuator design, such as:

- incremental travel measurement
- electronic commutation
- position sensing.

This means that additional sensor mounting to support operation of these actuators is not specifically required because it is built in.

Key Points

Actuators (most of them) convert an electrical signal into a physical action

A common transmission actuator is a solenoid operated valve that controls fluid pressure

The current trend is towards full electrical operation, so that the actuator, for example, acts directly on the component and no fluid pressure is required

Smart actuators are being developed that contain local intelligence

DC motors are popular as they can even be used to retrofit for 'manual' gear shifts

5.6 CLUTCH ELECTRONIC CONTROL

5.6.1 Introduction

The clutch is a simple device which can be employed in any rotating drive system where it is necessary to disengage or re-engage the transmission of torque. A friction clutch is used for vehicle transmission systems.

The clutch system consists of a driven and a driving member (Figure 5.25). In a transmission, the driving member is usually also the engine flywheel. The driven member is a friction disc which connects via a spline to the gearbox input shaft. The friction disc is clamped by a spring disc in the rest position, and hence drive and torque can be transmitted from driving to driven member. The spring clamping can be relaxed as required by the operator (in a vehicle transmission, via the clutch pedal); this allows the friction disc to spin freely and hence no torque is transmitted. If the spring pressure is gradually released, the clamping force can be gradually applied to the friction disc and hence torque can be progressively transferred between the driving and driven members as required. This allows the smooth take up of drive and transfer of torque between the engine and gearbox. The clutch in a vehicle transmission allows the effective disconnection of the engine and gearbox as required by the driver. This is needed for three main reasons:

- as mentioned, it allows the smooth application of torque from the engine to the gearbox, which is necessary for the vehicle to start from stationary, because a combustion engine has to be running at a minimum speed to produce power and torque
- to allow disconnection of the engine, so that no torque is transmitted through the gearbox; this

allows the driver to shift from one gear to another in a fixed ratio manual gearbox
- to provide a temporary neutral condition for stop and start driving, for example, in traffic.

5.6.2 Electronic clutch management

For many years, mechanical friction clutches, operated directly via a foot pedal (mechanically or hydraulically) have remained completely unchanged. As the clutch forms such a critical part of the transmission/powertrain system, simple mechanical operation directly by the driver leaves much room for improvement. Electronic control of the clutch, in combination with full integration of clutch operation with the overall powertrain control system provides several possible benefits:

- improved drivability, with more comfortable and smoother clutch and gear shift action, and with anti-stall protection in automatic mode
- effortless operation, particularly when fitted to vehicles with high engine torque
- improved pedal feel for the driver, with reduced leg pressure required
- improved reliability, which is achieved through reduced driveline wear and tear, and the total absence of mechanical linkages for clutch actuation
- an automatic shifting mode when used with a suitable gearbox
- improved crash protection for occupants because the pedal box is less intrusive
- data acquisition of clutch use for maintenance scheduling.

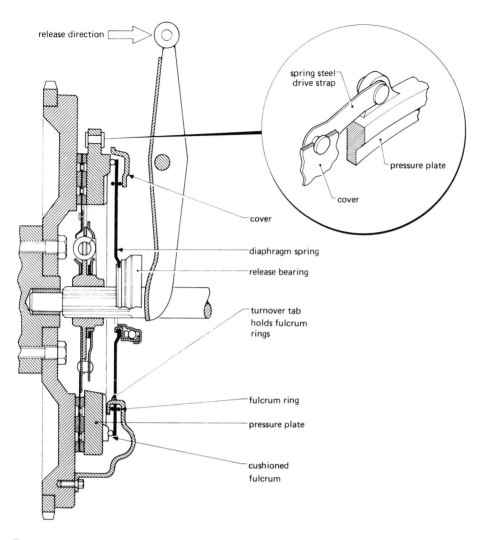

Figure 5.25 Standard vehicle manual clutch

Such a system has been developed and can be fitted to existing production models as well as to new designs of powertrain systems for road vehicles. Such a system replaces the existing hydraulic or mechanical actuation assembly with an electromechanical actuator (see Figure 5.26). A pedal position sensor is attached to the clutch pedal for driver input and the whole system is controlled by an ECU integrated in the powertrain control system, which takes additional information on vehicle behaviour from the engine and powertrain ECUs and sensors. The ECU controls the clutch actuator directly and thus the mechanical link between the clutch pedal and clutch is completely eliminated.

The basic functions of this unit are exactly the same as those of a manual transmission: to accelerate the vehicle from rest and stop it. Movement from rest requires precise control of clutch engagement and this can vary according to the operating conditions (a hill start will require different control from a start on the level). Changing gear is a highly dynamic process and requires precise control for the gears to change

smoothly and seamlessly. Stopping (declutching) is a simple process when carried out manually, but adding electronic control opens up possibilities during extreme conditions for clutch operation to be more controlled and fully integrated with the other vehicle safety systems (such as stability control, ABS and traction control) to improve vehicle safety.

Additional functions can be added to the system according to the application: for example, one could add:

- drivetrain condition monitoring
- creep control for accurate slow speed movement
- active vibration damping for powertrains without a dual mass flywheel.

The system can implement clutch operation in less than one-tenth of a second to optimise safety and driver comfort. Additionally, it operates seamlessly to correct driver errors. The pedal stroke and resistance are fully adjustable to suit the driver and the vehicle type. The system's compact design can save weight and offers greater flexibility of installation in a vehicle.

Powertrain efficiency
Enhanced driver comfort using a mechatronic clutch

CBW transmission system

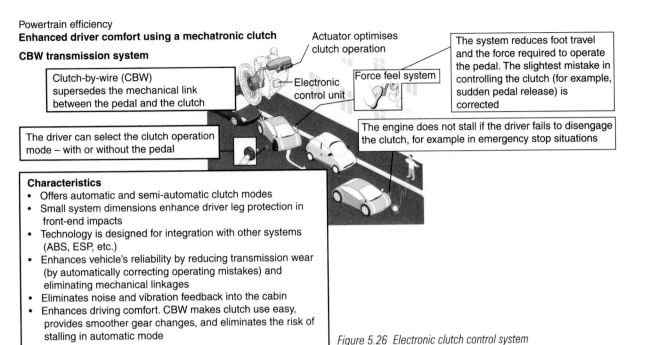

Clutch-by-wire (CBW) supersedes the mechanical link between the pedal and the clutch

Actuator optimises clutch operation

Electronic control unit

Force feel system

The system reduces foot travel and the force required to operate the pedal. The slightest mistake in controlling the clutch (for example, sudden pedal release) is corrected

The driver can select the clutch operation mode – with or without the pedal

The engine does not stall if the driver fails to disengage the clutch, for example in emergency stop situations

Characteristics
- Offers automatic and semi-automatic clutch modes
- Small system dimensions enhance driver leg protection in front-end impacts
- Technology is designed for integration with other systems (ABS, ESP, etc.)
- Enhances vehicle's reliability by reducing transmission wear (by automatically correcting operating mistakes) and eliminating mechanical linkages
- Eliminates noise and vibration feedback into the cabin
- Enhances driving comfort. CBW makes clutch use easy, provides smoother gear changes, and eliminates the risk of stalling in automatic mode

Figure 5.26 Electronic clutch control system

5.6.3 Twin clutch arrangements

The latest developments in gearbox automation (DSG or parallel-shift gearboxes) require a twin-clutch arrangement (Figure 5.27), because the gearbox is

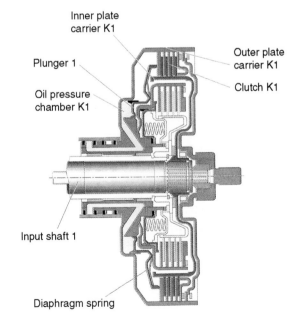

Inner plate carrier K1

Plunger 1

Oil pressure chamber K1

Outer plate carrier K1

Clutch K1

Input shaft 1

Diaphragm spring

Figure 5.27 Twin multiplate clutch in section

effectively spilt into two halves. During operation, i.e. upshift or downshift, an appropriate gear can be pre-selected while the torque is still transmitted through an existing gear. This dramatically reduces the gear shift time, torque transmission to the wheels is practically uninterrupted and acceleration times can be significantly improved. This technology will be discussed in more detail in the appropriate section of this book.

In this application, clutch engagement and disengagement are handled electronically. Normally, wet clutches are used, actuated by hydraulics. The electronic controls are interfaced via VBA valves, driven with a PWM signal which is generated from the ECU according to demand.

DSG technology will be discussed and explained in more detail in a later section of this chapter.

Key Points

Parallel shift boxes pre-select the next gear while an existing gear is still in use

Electronic clutch control improves efficiency and driveability

Clutch control can be fully electrical or an actuator can be used to operate the slave cylinder, for example

5.7   MANUAL GEARBOX ELECTRONIC CONTROL

5.7.1 Introduction

Manual gearboxes (Figure 5.28) have not been dramatically affected by developments in electrical and electronic systems until recently. Early sliding mesh gearboxes with straight cut gears were noisy and harsh, and were difficult to use. Later, constant mesh gearboxes with helical gears were quieter, but still difficult to use (double de-clutching was required). Modern synchromesh gearboxes are quiet and easy to use, but gears cannot be engaged unless they are synchronised. These developments all happened in the early years of the mass produced car industry: since the introduction of the synchromesh gearbox on mass produced vehicles in the 1960s little has changed in manual gearboxes, apart from their increasing number of gears (initially from four to five, and now six gears are commonplace).

Engine electronic systems have developed rapidly over the past 20 years. Now these developments are starting to impact on the transmission, even on a completely mechanical device, the manual gearbox. Drive-by-wire systems are becoming more common within the industry and in production vehicles. The next step with manual transmission (already available at the top end of the market) will be the introduction of electronic shift control and actuation (even if manually controlled by the driver) in conjunction with electronic clutch actuation and monitoring (where the driver controls the clutch position with virtual clutch pedal).

This technology is particularly interesting in applications where improved fuel economy is the main target: for maximum economy, driver behaviour becomes more critical. Therefore, by automating the gear shift process, the powertrain system can be optimised to give the best possible fuel consumption: the system can eliminate some driver errors and driving styles which can compromise performance and fuel economy. Where economy is the ultimate target, it is much better to use automated manual transmissions than other types of transmission, such as CVT or hydraulic automatic transmission. This is because manual transmissions do not suffer from the internal losses (due to the hydraulic power needed for shift actuation) associated with automatic gearboxes and hence offer greater efficiency.

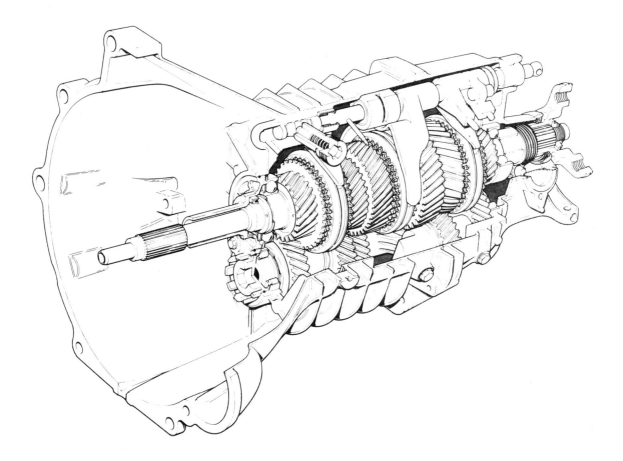

Figure 5.28 Constant mesh gearbox

Contrary to the above reasons of economy, automated manual shift gearboxes are often used in high performance vehicles because the manual gearbox is more efficient than other types! Hence, for ultimate vehicle performance, it is the preferred choice. With electronic control of shifting and clutch actuation, shift times can be optimised and improved considerably compared with manual control by the driver. Advanced strategies for acceleration from rest can be implemented to improve vehicle performance. In addition, as noted previously, the transmission control can be integrated with other vehicle control systems for stability and traction to provide the ultimate in high performance driving. For example, in a critical situation such as downshifting on a slippery surface, the clutch can be released instantaneously if there is excessive engine drag torque, so that the car will not lock the driving wheels and slide.

This technology has been developed and marketed successfully by manufacturers of high-performance vehicles, such as BMW, Ferrari, and Aston Martin, and it is widely used in motor sport, where the goal is ultimate vehicle speed and performance.

Table 5.2 shows gear shift times for different vehicles with automated manual gearboxes.

Table 5.2 Gear shift times

Gearbox/model	Minimum shift time (ms)
BMW SMG 1 (M3 E36)	220
BMW SMG 2 (M3 E46)	80
Ferrari F1 (575M)	220
Ferrari F1 (360 F1)	150
Ferrari F1 (Maserati 4200GT)	80
Bugatti Veyron	200
Aston Martin Vanquish	250
Alfa Romeo Selespeed	700

An important additional feature of electronic control is its 'self-learning' capability. The transmission control software can be designed to be adaptive to a person's driving style, and a driver can select a driving mode, such as sport mode. BMW calls this feature 'Drivelogic', when it is offered with their sequential manual gearbox (SMG) on their high performance M series models. This function allows the driver to choose the transmission shift characteristics from 11 different driving programs. These range from a balanced dynamic program (program S1) to a very sporty program (S5). Finally, the driver can also choose a program (S6) where the system's dynamic stability control (DSC), which comes standard, is deactivated. Here, the transmission will shift and respond with a dynamic performance similar to that of a racing car, thus giving the driver the 'ultimate driving machine' experience!

The highlights of the BMW SMG system are as follows:

- fast and precise gear shifting within 80 milliseconds
- sequential shift actuation via a selector lever or steering wheel buttons
- shift warning lights on the dashboard
- self-learning adaptation of the gearbox over time
- 'Drivelogic' personal settings – 11 driving programs ranging from balanced dynamic to strictly sport
- a sequential shift mode
- a fully automatic shift mode
- special functions – slip recognition, a climb assistant and an acceleration assistant.

5.7.2 Case study: VW electronic manual gearbox

Volkswagen has produced the world's first production 3 litre car! That is, the company has developed a car that uses only 3 litres of fuel every 100 km. The factors affecting fuel economy are many and varied: namely aerodynamics, rolling resistance, powertrain design and vehicle mass. These all have to be optimised to achieve the required efficiency from the vehicle to lower the fuel consumption consistently to this level.

The vehicle used is a VW Lupo, adapted to give greater powertrain efficiency. One of the most important adaptations was to implement electronic switching in the transmission (Figure 5.29). This was done to reduce the possibility of increased fuel consumption caused by drivers' gear shifting habits. This system also ensures that the vehicle is in the correct gear, to give the best fuel consumption, at all times relative to the driving conditions. The system covers three main component areas:

- **Mechanical** – The transmission is the manual system used in current VW production small cars. The gearbox was made lighter via additional drillings in internal components and by reducing the oil capacity. Additional mechanical components in the system include the selector mechanism shaft and levers
- **Hydraulics** – The manual shift mechanism was completely replaced by an electro-hydraulic unit. The clutch is operated through an actuator mechanism. Hydraulic power for the shift and clutch is provided by an electric hydraulic pump and pressure accumulator
- **Electronics** – The driver uses a throttle pedal sensor and selector lever, with the gear shift and clutch operated via electro-hydraulic valves. Information about shift position and selector lever position is fed back through potentiometers and micro switches. At the heart of the system is the transmission ECU.

The system can operate in manual, sequential mode or automatic mode. Pushing the selector lever sends a shift demand signal to the ECU via micro switches, and the lever assembly contains a potentiometer to detect the absolute position of the lever for selection of neutral,

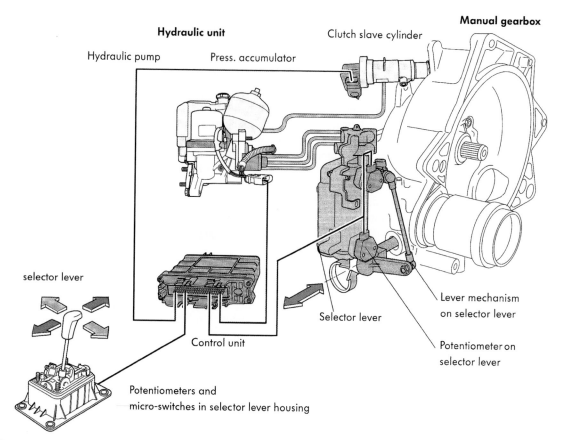

Figure 5.29 VW electronic manual gearbox overview

reverse or automatic shift mode. When a shift is made, the ECU calculates if this is appropriate from a number of input signals. These are:

- engine speed and torque
- throttle position
- brake pedal and pressure
- vehicle speed.

The signals are provided by sensors connected directly to the transmission ECU or via the CAN bus interface to the engine ECU. The process of changing gear is exactly the same as a driver would implement manually. First the clutch is opened via the hydraulic clutch actuator (Figure 5.30); pressure is supplied and controlled at the actuator via a solenoid valve operated by the ECU. The clutch position is fed back to the ECU through a movement sensor mounted on the actuator. The clutch limit positions are monitored by the ECU at regular intervals to compensate for clutch wear.

Once the clutch is open, gears are shifted by the hydraulic pistons in the electro-hydraulic shift actuator (Figure 5.31), and controlled via solenoid valves. There are two pistons for gear selection and two for gate selection (each piston pair provides forward and backward force), each piston has its own controlling solenoid valve to apply or release hydraulic pressure smoothly and progressively. This is essential for smooth synchronisation during gear shifting. Potentiometers

are fitted for gate and gear selector movement and these send the measured position back to the ECU.

Once the next gear is fully engaged the clutch actuator is released and the clutch closes to reinstate torque into the gearbox. During transient operation the clutch is kept approximately 20% open to ensure good response during gear changing and to reduce transition times.

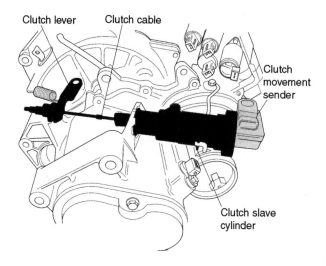

Figure 5.30 Clutch slave cylinder

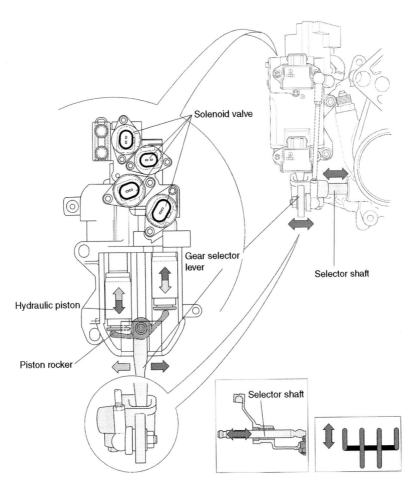

Solenoid valve

Gear selector
lever

Selector shaft

Hydraulic piston

Piston rocker

Selector shaft

Figure 5.31 Selector assembly

An additional feature of the system is the stop/start function. This eliminates fuel wastage when the vehicle is idling. When the vehicle is stationary, the engine stops if the brake pedal is pressed for more than 3 seconds. When the pedal is released, the engine is restarted automatically and first gear is engaged so that, when the driver presses the accelerator pedal, the vehicle accelerates immediately. This feature is managed by the transmission ECU and is an integrated part of the overall fuel consumption reduction strategy for this vehicle.

5.7.3 Case study: Volkswagen direct shift gearbox (DSG)

There are a number of advantages and disadvantages of automatic and manual transmissions.

- **Manual gearbox** – It is the most efficient type of gearbox with minimal power losses; the driver has full control over shifting and hence is provided with sportier driving.
- **Automatic gearbox** – This has the greater level of smoothness and comfort, with no interruption in torque transmission during driving.

The ultimate gearbox would be one that combines the best attributes of both types with the latest in control and system integration technology. VW has proposed this in the form of their direct shift gearbox (DSG); this technology is also known as a parallel shift gearbox (PSG). This attempts to combine the transmission concepts of automatic and manual systems into a completely new generation of gearbox.

The main system highlights are:

- a six speed synchromesh gearbox (plus reverse)
- selectable, pre-programmed driving modes (sports, etc.)
- a sequential shift via a lever or steering wheel buttons
- a completely integrated mechatronic control unit which houses ECU electronics and electro-hydraulic controls, mounted on the gearbox, providing a system with minimal external interface connections
- a hill-holder function and creep regulation, with enhancements for low-speed driving and manoeuvring
- system fault handling, with full electronic diagnostic capability, and a limp home mode.

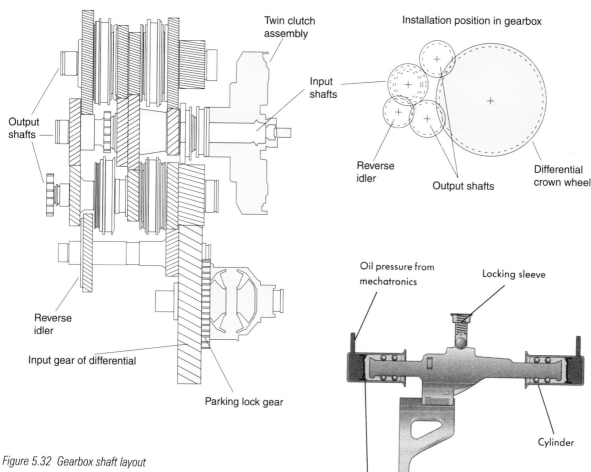

Figure 5.32 Gearbox shaft layout

Mechanical construction

The torque is transmitted into the two transmission units via an integrated twin clutch assembly with hydraulic actuation for both clutches. A dual-mass flywheel is used to insulate the transmission from engine torsional vibrations (see the diagram in the Clutch section). The two input shafts are combined concentrically, each one fitted with a pulse wheel so the ECU can detect rotating speed (Figure 5.32). The two output shafts hold the gear synchromesh units and both transmit torque to the differential gear. The differential also includes a gear wheel for a locking pawl to provide a 'park' position (with the wheels locked by the transmission).

Gear selection is via selector forks (Figure 5.33), in a similar way to a normal, manual gearbox, except that, in this case, the selector forks are hydraulically actuated through oil pressure. A small piston mounted at each end of each selector fork is supplied with pressurised oil according to shift requirements from the control system. A small permanent magnet fitted to each selector fork allows the ECU to detect the precise fork position and hence gear engagement via a sensor in the gearbox. Once the selection is made the pressure is released and the selector fork is held in position by a locking mechanism.

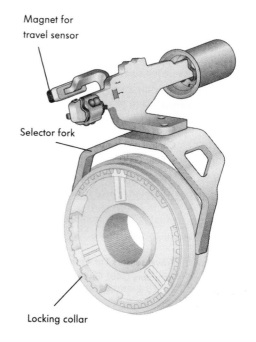

Figure 5.33 Selector mechanism

An important part of the gearbox is the oil lubrication system. This provides not just lubrication and cooling but also hydraulic power for the actuators to shift gears and operate the clutches. The oil pump is driven directly from the engine input through a shaft. The lubrication system also incorporates its own filter and heat exchanger, since it is so critical to correct system operation and performance.

Electronics and control system
At the heart of the system is the mechatronics transmission module (MTM) (see Figure 5.34). The robust construction of modern electronic technology makes it commonplace with electronic transmissions to integrate the electronics, electrics, hydraulics and mechanics into a single module, mounted at the transmission itself. This has the advantage that it provides the highest level of component integration with the minimum number of external interfaces and connections to the vehicle, which greatly improves reliability.

In the DSG system the MTM is at the centre of the system and all sensors and actuators are connected to it, since all actions are initiated and monitored by it. This unit also houses the ECU itself.

The sensors in the system measure the following:

- clutch oil temperature – at this position in the gearbox the lubricant is under the greatest thermal stress, and by monitoring the temperature at this point the control unit can regulate the flow of oil accordingly
- gearbox input speed – this is basically the same as the engine speed
- input shaft speed – a speed sensor on each input shaft monitors the speed input to each half of the gearbox; they are mounted on the opposite side of the clutch to the above sensors, which allows the system to monitor the clutch status and slip ratio
- output shaft speed – two sensors are mounted on a single pulse wheel but with phase shift between

them; they monitor output shaft speed and direction of vehicle travel (by offsetting the two signals)
- clutch pressure – sensors are used in the regulation of clutch operation
- gearbox oil temperature – sensors protect the gearbox from overload and are used to initiate a warm-up function
- control unit temperature – sensors protect the system electronics
- selector fork travel – sensors monitor the actual position of the selector fork for gear selection status
- selector lever – sensors provide information about absolute position (park, reverse, neutral, etc.) and sequential shift (up, down).

The electro-hydraulic part of the control system consists of a number of actuators:

- a pressure control valve – this modulating valve regulates the main system pressure according to engine torque
- clutch pressure control valves – modulating valves control the clutch operation
- an oil pressure control valve – a modulating valve controls cooling oil flow
- gear actuator valves – on/off solenoid valves engage and disengage gears via selector forks
- a multiplexer control valve – an on/off valve controls the position of the so-called multiplexer; this unit is used together with the gear actuator valves for gear selection and reduces the number of gear actuator valves required
- safety valves – modulating valves isolate hydraulic pressure in sections of the gearbox in the event of a safety related fault; they also allow rapid opening of each respective clutch, if necessary, when an overpressure occurs.

Additional interfaces are provided via the CAN to:

- the anti-lock braking system (ABS), the electronic differential lock (EDL) and the traction/stability control (ESP) system
- the diesel or gasoline engine management system
- the selector lever control unit
- the steering column electronic control unit.

Basic principle of operation
The DSG consists in essence of two manual, synchromesh gearboxes in one unit. Each one has its own clutch and torque input from the engine. These clutches are wet, multi-plate clutches that are actuated hydraulically under the control of the transmission ECU. Look at Figure 5.35: the first, third, fifth and reverse gears are within transmission unit 1 and the second, fourth and sixth gears are within transmission unit 2.

The fundamental principle behind splitting the transmission in this way is that one transmission can be engaged (i.e. in gear, transmitting torque) while the other transmission can be in the next gear (i.e. in gear

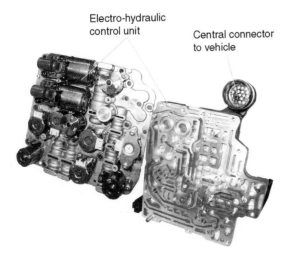

Electro-hydraulic control unit

Central connector to vehicle

Figure 5.34 Mechatronics module

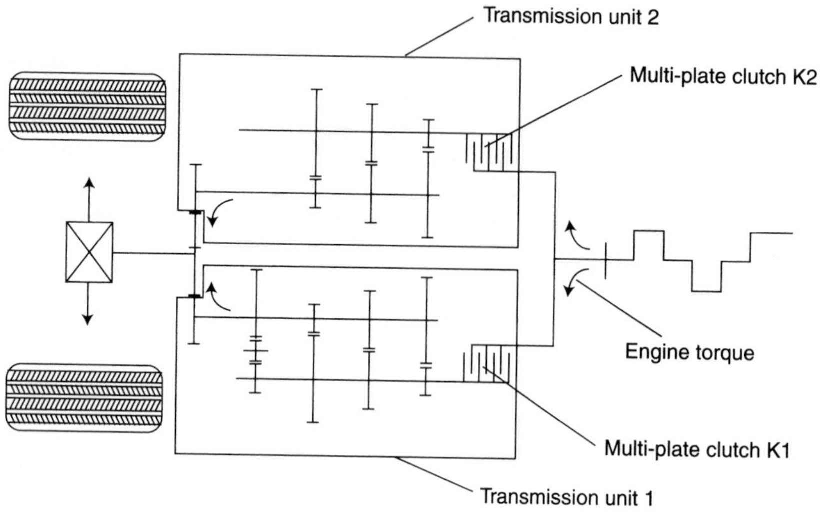

Transmission unit 2

Multi-plate clutch K2

Engine torque

Multi-plate clutch K1

Transmission unit 1

Figure 5.35 DSG basic principle

but not transmitting torque), in preparation for the next gear change. This gear change can be made very rapidly, just by switching torque transmission from one clutch to the other. It can be implemented in a controlled manner, such that there is minimal loss of torque at the road wheels.

With its double-clutch design and sophisticated electronic control, the system is as comfortable to use as an automatic transmission. In addition, its capacity to implement lightning quick gear shifts means no loss of torque transmission at the wheels, so performance driving is particularly rewarding.

One important point to note though is that, because hydraulic power is required to operate the gearbox, there are some small parasitic losses, which reduce the overall efficiency slightly. Parallel shift gearboxes that are currently under development by other manufacturers use twin plate dry clutches with fully electrical actuation of the clutches and gear shifting. This improves efficiency as there are no power requirements if the gearbox is in a quiescent condition (i.e. a gear is fully engaged, with the gearbox transmitting torque).

Key Points

Manual gearboxes under full electronic control are effectively fully automatic – but are more efficient than epicyclic or CVT gearboxes

A clutch actuator is needed to control manual boxes automatically

Most manual systems can operate in manual, sequential mode or automatic mode

Electronic control reduces shift times considerably

5.8   TORQUE CONVERTER ELECTRONIC CONTROL

5.8.1 Introduction

A torque converter (Figure 5.36) is standard in automatic transmissions of all types and basically replaces the clutch. It converts a high speed/low torque input from the engine into high torque/low speed output to drive the transmission and therefore allows the smooth take-up of the vehicle from rest. Also, because of the 'slip' effect, it infinitely multiplies the number of gear ratios available by effectively interpolating between each fixed gear ratio.

A torque converter is basically an opposed pump-turbine unit, enclosed in a casing partially filled with hydraulic oil.

The pump side of a torque converter is directly connected to the prime mover (the combustion engine) and the rotation torque circulates the oil inside the casing. This imparts energy into the fluid in the form of

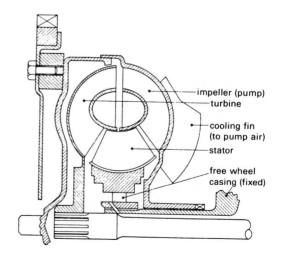

impeller (pump)
turbine

cooling fin
(to pump air)
stator

free wheel
casing (fixed)

Figure 5.36 Torque converter

kinetic energy. The turbine is placed directly in the path of the moving fluid (i.e. directly opposite the pump), so the dynamic energy in the fluid is recovered by the turbine and converted back into torque. This simple system is known as a fluid flywheel. The torque converter (Figure 5.36) has an impeller mounted between the pump and turbine to improve efficiency. The impeller (or stator) is mounted to the casing via a one-way clutch which allows it to rotate in one direction only. The stator redirects the fluid path under certain conditions to ensure that the fluid strikes the turbine at the correct angle and speed under all conditions, thus greatly improving the overall torque output of the unit.

5.8.2 Torque converter lock-up clutch

Most modern automatic transmission systems incorporating a torque converter will use a lock-up clutch across the converter to improve fuel economy. The basic problem with a torque converter is that it relies on a speed difference between the input and output shafts to be able to operate and transfer or multiply torque. If the speeds are the same, hydrodynamic oil circulation will not take place and torque will not be transmitted. Loss of speed in the torque converter is known as slip, and causes some power to be lost as heat.

For overall powertrain efficiency, losses must be minimised so a lock-up clutch is fitted to the converter between the turbine and impeller (on the casing) (Figure 5.37). When required by the control system (for example, when a vehicle is cruising in top gear) the lock-up clutch can be engaged and the converter

bypassed. This clearly prevents slip and the parasitic losses that are unavoidable in the converter itself during normal operation. Integrating operation of this clutch is particularly easy when the control system itself is electronic.

The clutch can be engaged or disengaged by the transmission ECU with an electro-hydraulic control system. This could be a simple on/off arrangement such that the clutch is engaged only in top gear, or it could be engaged in top and second-to-top gears. This would be a relatively simple way of increasing the overall transmission efficiency in cruise conditions only.

5.8.3 Optimisation of lock-up clutch – slip control

A further improvement in efficiency can be gained by activating the torque converter lock-up as often as possible or practical. This would increase the efficiency of the transmission even further but would also create a problem. The torque converter also has a damping function: it isolates the transmission and powertrain components from engine induced vibrations and hence improves the drivability and smoothness of the vehicle. When the torque converter lock-up clutch is engaged, this damping is lost, which could severely affect the driving comfort at low speeds. Therefore, with a simple lock-up clutch on/off arrangement, a compromise between efficiency and economy has to be found.

A recent development, made possible by advances in control electronics, is a provision for the lock-up clutch to operate progressively. This is implemented via PWM VBA valves to control hydraulic pressure to the lock-up clutch, allowing progressive, controlled

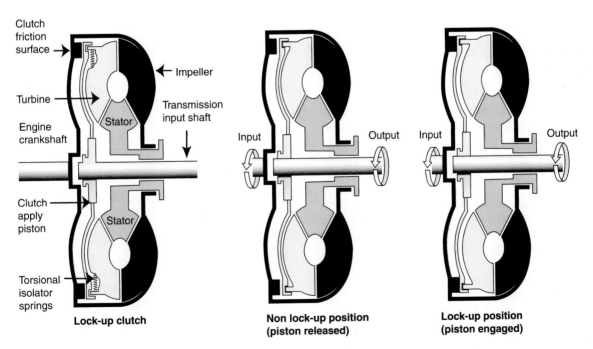

Lock-up clutch

Non lock-up position (piston released)

Lock-up position (piston engaged)

Figure 5.37 Torque converter with lock-up clutch

engagement and disengagement of the clutch. With sophisticated control algorithms and methodologies, a clutch slip control system can be created to optimise converter efficiency, while still providing the superior drivability of an automatic gearbox.

A typical system uses the converter and clutch together and monitors the power distribution via the slip speed. This is established from the speed difference between the engine and torque converter turbine. Hence the power transmission distribution can be controlled and optimised, so that the system can provide a distribution ratio that gives instantaneously the best balance between power loss and noise/vibration. In particular, this feature can improve transmission efficiency at low vehicle speeds, with a consequent reduction in fuel consumption.

5.8.4 Torque converter developments

The torque converter remains an important part of current transmission system developments and its efficiency can be improved further with the integration of electronic control. Using the latest computer modelling techniques at the design stage can increase the basic unit efficiency and specific power capacity considerably by optimising internal fluid flows and flow paths. Further enhancements and developments made possible through the flexibility of electronic control are:

- idle disconnection of the torque converter – an additional clutch controlled via the transmission ECU, mounted between the engine and torque converter, can be designed into the pump housing (it is similar to a lock-up clutch); this allows disconnection of the converter and gearbox internals to reduce drag and friction losses when the engine is idling

- a reverse torque converter – modifying the basic construction of the torque converter to allow the stator to transmit force (rather than being mounted on a one-way clutch fixed to the casing) means that, with the turbine locked, the reaction force against the stator could be used to provide a reverse rotation, which would be useful for CVT applications, where a planetary gear set is still needed within the gearbox to provide this function at significant extra cost

- an integrated torque converter and starter–alternator – a multi-function unit that combines traditional engine starting and electrical power requirements, which, with electronic control, provides additional features, such as traffic start/stop functions, electrical assistance during acceleration, hybrid drive options and power regeneration, improving the overall efficiency and adaptability of the powertrain.

Key Points

Almost all torque converters now contain a lock-up clutch. Using electronics, the slip can be controlled to improve efficiency and drivability

Under electronic control a torque converter can be made to produce a reverse rotation and be disconnected completely at idle

Integrating the torque converter with a starter–alternator provides features such as traffic stop/start and acceleration assistance

5.9 AUTOMATIC GEARBOX TRANSMISSION MANAGEMENT

5.9.1 Introduction

Automatic transmissions have been available in vehicles since the early days of the development and mass production of cars. In the UK, the automatic gearbox has always been seen as a luxury option, while, in the US, the automatic gearbox is standard on most passenger cars.

The basic automatic transmission (see Figure 5.38) consists of a sophisticated hydraulic–mechanical system incorporating a torque converter (a hydrodynamic device) in place of the clutch. A system of planetary (epicyclic) gears provides the various forward and reverse ratios. The whole system is controlled via a sophisticated mechanism of valves supplying pressurised oil to brake bands and clutches for engagement of the appropriate gears. Such systems worked well and were fully adopted by motor manufacturers before the revolution in microelectronics

which brought in sophisticated engine management systems. The additional degrees of freedom provided by electronic control have enabled the shift processes to be optimised and have resulted in improvements in the operation and efficiency of automatic gearboxes.

Where electronic control is implemented the basic mechanical arrangement of the gearbox remains the same as in hydraulically controlled units (Figure 5.39): drive into the gearbox from the engine via a torque converter, planetary gear sets to provide the fixed ratios, with gear changes implemented via brake bands and one-way clutches. With electronic systems, an electronic control unit (ECU) with a central processing unit (CPU) has a number of inputs from the vehicle, engine and driver. The required gear is calculated and then implemented via the electrical actuation of hydraulic valves to provide pressurised oil to the appropriate brake bands or clutches.

Figure 5.38 Exploded view of ZF 6 speed automatic gearbox fitted to some Jaguar models

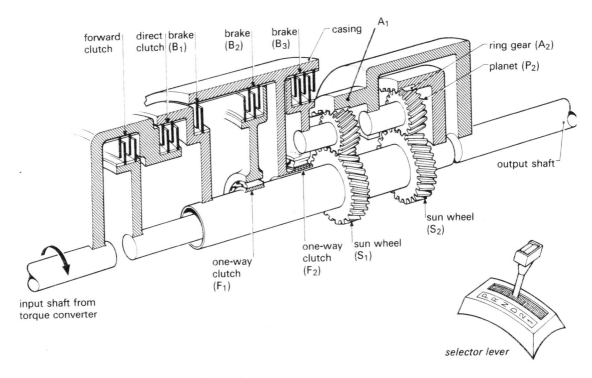

Figure 5.39 Gear train layout in the Borg Warner 55 gearbox
(a previous generation)

The main advantages of using electronic control are:

- multiple shift patterns can be selected by the driver (such as sport, and winter patterns, etc.)
- gear shifting can be made smoother
- systems can be easily adapted to different vehicles, reducing integration costs for manufacturers
- the hydraulic control system is simplified, with no need for one-way clutches.

The main technical features of an electronically controlled transmission (Figure 5.40) are as follows.

- With electro-hydraulic selection and implementation of gearshifts, shift points are determined by the control system according to driver requirements and vehicle conditions. Gears are changed via a number of electro-hydraulic solenoid valves that feed hydraulic pressure to the brake bands and clutches. Electronic control algorithms can optimise the engagement and disengagement of these internal components to allow for inertia, drag, etc. This makes for fast, smooth gear changes. Most recent systems dispense with internal overrunning clutches, since shifts can be performed smoothly and safely purely with electronic control. This reduces the weight and size of the transmission.
- Electronically controlled systems have a sophisticated torque converter lock-up strategy to optimise transmission efficiency yet still provide the high degree of shift quality needed.
- The number of gears has increased to extend the range of gear ratios. With electronic control, shifts are seamless and of high quality, so the number of ratios can be extended to five or more (mechanically controlled transmissions have three or four gears).
- The system pressure is controlled and adapted according to the transmission status via an electro-hydraulic valve. This improves shift quality and transmission efficiency over the life of the vehicle (and with high-load or low-temperature conditions). It ensures that wear of the friction components (clutches and brake bands) does not impair the performance of the transmission.

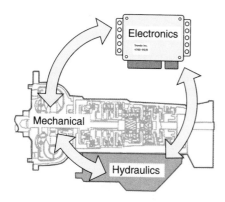

Figure 5.40 Electronically controlled automatic transmission gearbox

Key Points

In some electronic control systems, the basic mechanical arrangement of the gearbox remains the same as with hydraulically controlled units

Electronic control of an automatic box allows different modes to be selected by the driver

Electronics simplify the hydraulic control systems

Converter lock-up strategy can be improved

5.9.2 Automatic transmission management

Basic requirements for electronic transmission control

The control system must be capable of providing the following features:

- **gear selection** – shifting to or selection of the correct gear ratio for the current driving conditions, taking into account the system information from the sensors at all times
- **shift quality** – adapting system pressure control dynamically to provide seamless shifts, and implementing torque converter lock-up for maximum efficiency
- **driver input** – allowing additional input from the driver, such as kick-down or sequential shifts
- **fault handling** – detecting system faults and errors, ensuring all shift operations are plausible, preventing shifts operations that could cause dangerous driving conditions, and providing a limp home capability
- **an adaptive response** – the ability to recognise and adapt to individual driver styles and driving preferences.

The basic control functions of an automatic transmission electronic control are as follows.

Shift point control

Generally, the actual shift point is determined from a number of shift maps stored in the ECU which can be pre-selected by the driver with a manual switch. Typically, these maps would allow for driving modes such as 'sport', 'economy' or 'winter'. The shift points are a function of accelerator position and driving speed and take into account boundary limitations such as engine speed limits (maximum and minimum). They incorporate an element of hysteresis to prevent unnecessary shifting, which could reduce driver comfort.

The shifting operation is time-critical: the finite time taken to release and apply the friction components is an important factor and, in the most sophisticated applications, is taken into account in the software calibration. The latest generation of transmissions with no overrun clutches require overlap control of the hydraulic clutch operation to allow smooth transition from one gear to the next. This is particularly demanding on the control system and requires high CPU capability and real-time performance.

A further, more recent development is adaptive shift point and transmission control. This means that the ECU itself must be capable of adapting the shift points according to driver and vehicle conditions. From evaluation of the driver inputs (kick-down, use of the brake, accelerator and selector lever) the basic shift points can be adapted to suit the current driver style. The driving conditions can be established via interfaces to other control systems (such as the ABS and engine management ECU). The following conditions can easily be recognised and control adapted accordingly:

- gradients are detected by comparing current and requested acceleration with engine torque; the system adapts by moving gear shifts to give higher engine speeds
- cornering is detected through differences in wheel speeds, so requested shifts can be delayed or prevented to optimise vehicle stability
- in winter driving in ice or snow, wheel slip is detected by measuring wheel speeds, so lower gears are avoided to reduce tractive force on surfaces with low friction coefficients
- for traction control the shift strategy is adapted to provide maximum traction.

Torque converter lock-up control

As mentioned previously, the torque converter usually has a lock-up clutch to bypass it under certain conditions. This improves the efficiency of the transmission but must be implemented carefully so that shift quality and drivability are not adversely affected: the torque converter acts as a damping element for torsional vibrations at lower engine speeds. The converter lock-up clutch has three states: open, closed and controlled. These states are defined and determined in a similar manner to the gear shift point control and are a function of engine speed and throttle demand. An optimised characteristic curve for the converter lock-up process is available for each gear and is stored in the ECU calibration. The settings take into account the need to optimise fuel consumption and tractive force.

Engine torque control during shifting

The evolution of automatic transmission with electronic control has resulted in certain developments such as torque converter lock-up and an increased number of gears. These make it possible to design a sophisticated and efficient powertrain system. However, these developments place additional demands on the control system to produce an efficient and smooth shifting process, which can only be realised via a harmonised engine and transmission control system. The shift process can be optimised through engine intervention during shifting using torque control. Of course, this requires an interface between the engine and transmission controls and, as discussed previously, current technology supports this easily (via CAN).

The main aims of engine intervention control are:

- to improve shift smoothness and drivability
- to reduce wear by shortening slip times and forces
- to transmit higher power
- to improve synchronisation during shifts.

Torque can be controlled in one of two ways. Most commonly it has been controlled by retarding the ignition angle from the set position. This can be done easily and has a fast response but clearly can only be applied to gasoline engine vehicles. With more recent technology, where there is a torque based functional structure for engine control, with a CAN interface, torque can be controlled through a torque interface, which would be used with a number of other vehicle control systems, such as ABS and TCS.

Pressure control

System pressure control is an important factor in shift comfort, second only to torque control. It is responsible for controlling the forces in the friction elements in the gearbox during shifts and is a key factor in maintaining consistent performance in shift quality throughout the life of the vehicle. As with shift point control, adaptive algorithms can be used to allow for life cycle variations in the transmission (the wear of friction components) and engine (changing tolerances), as well as changes in response caused by variations in the temperature of the automatic transmission fluid (ATF). The system compares actual shift times with stored reference values and uses this as the basis for making incremental adjustments to the system pressure up to a maximum deviation of $\neq 10\%$. This limit is imposed for reasons of operational reliability. The adjustment values are stored in the ECU memory so that they can be reinstated each time the system powers on when the vehicle starts up.

Safety functions

Several safety related features must be included in the transmission control system; these generally prevent critical driving conditions caused by driver error or failed components. Uncontrolled shifting is particularly undesirable, especially downshifting, which could cause serious problems for the driver, or destruction of the transmission.

Monitoring of the electronics system and components themselves is particularly important. The CPU in the ECU is monitored via internal and external circuits; the software code execution is monitored for plausibility during run time; and sensors and actuators are continuously checked for correct and plausible operation.

If a sensor or actuator fails, in most cases substitute values can be used and the system switched to 'limp home' mode. For example, the transmission output speed signal can be substituted by a wheel speed signal, temperature sensor values can be replaced with fixed values. This would be sufficient to allow the vehicle to be driven home or for repair. These safety enhancements and error handling methods give an increased degree of confidence and acceptance in the marketplace for full electronic control systems.

Diagnostic functions

The diagnostic capability and functionality of current systems now forms approximately 30% of the system software resources. The main reason for this is the requirement for vehicles to comply with on board diagnostics (OBD) in order to meet current and future legislation. The diagnostic function handles the storage of fault information and the communication of this data to the service tester. The fault memory inside the ECU is sub-divided into:

- primary fault memory – non-volatile memory that contains fault code and type, plus a warm-up counter and system flags (an OBD requirement)
- secondary fault memory – one memory slot per fault code, containing filters, time stamps and flags
- back-up memory – optional memory with deleted fault codes from the primary fault memory
- snapshot memory – for use with diagnostic testing.

The most important monitoring functions for the transmission are:

- solenoid valve monitoring
- pressure regulator monitoring
- run-time monitoring of program code.

In the past, access to fault information has been manufacturer specific but, with the introduction of OBD, a standardised protocol for communication to a tester, with standard fault codes, is now in general use.

5.9.3 Case study: Tiptronic gearbox

Introduction

Tiptronic is the name used by Porsche to describe their sequential shift automatic gearbox with intelligent shift strategy adaptation. This technology was a joint development between Porsche, ZF and Bosch. The name 'Tiptronic' is also used by other manufacturers to describe this technology. The system consists of a standard automatic transmission (i.e. torque converter, epicyclic gear sets) with full electronic control. The driver has the choice of driving in automatic mode, or of using the manual lever (Figure 5.41) for sequential shifting. Later versions (Tiptronic-s) also incorporate steering wheel buttons for up and down shifts.

Operation

When the system is driven in automatic mode an intelligent driving program runs. This takes into account basic information about vehicle and engine speed, vehicle acceleration and throttle position, and adapts this according to the dynamics of the vehicle (road resistance) and the ambient conditions (altitude). This information is made available to the Tiptronic control unit, which then decides which shift map to use and what adjustments are necessary to it. This process is carried out continuously and 'steplessly' and is invisible to the driver.

Additional functions are:

- a warm-up map – an optimised transmission operation for fast warm up of the engine and catalyst; upshift points are delayed, and the converter clutch remains open
- an active shift to sports map – rapid movement of the accelerator initiates the sports map; the system shifts back to the economy map automatically
- kick-down – this does not initiate a change of shift map
- downshift during braking – this allows engine braking assistance
- overheat protection – this is automatically initiated by restricting engine torque via the engine ECU

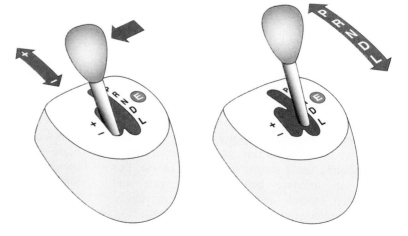

Figure 5.41 Tiptronic gearbox

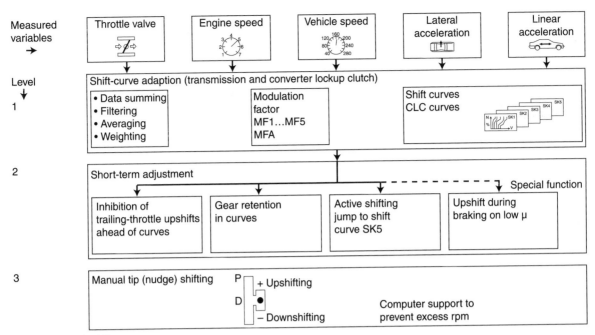

Figure 5.42 Tiptronic shift strategy

- gear hold in manoeuvres – lateral acceleration is detected and the current gear is maintained for maximum stability
- torque reduction during shift – for smooth gearshifts
- torque converter lock-up – from second gear up, depending on engine load and shift characteristic curve.

Figure 5.42 illustrates the shift curve adaptation process for the Tiptronic system.

5.9.4 Case study: Honda's four-speed all clutch-to-clutch system

The Honda clutch-to-clutch automatic transmission system (Figure 5.43) is of particular interest as it is a departure from the usual design of an automatic gearbox. A traditional automatic gearbox has epicyclic gear sets, with brake bands and clutches to provide the appropriate forward and reverse gears. These are all activated by electro-hydraulics and controlled by an ECU. For a traditional front-engine–rear-drive vehicle this can be easily accommodated in the powertrain layout. For transverse front-engine–front-drive vehicles, this arrangement becomes difficult to fit within the engine compartment. Honda's solution is closer to a manual gearbox in form and is specifically designed for use in front-wheel drive Honda cars.

Of particular interest is the gear shifting and selection mechanism. The system does not use epicyclic planetary gears, but is closer in design to a standard constant mesh gearbox. The system provides four forward gears plus reverse. The schematic is shown in Figure 5.44.

The shaft layout consists of an input or mainshaft, which drives a secondary shaft via an intermediate gear. Between these two shafts is the countershaft. The output from this shaft drives the road wheels via the differential. The countershaft has all the fixed, forward gears mounted on it, as well as a servo-operated dog clutch selector for selecting forward or reverse.

The fixed gears on the countershaft mate with corresponding freewheeling gears (of different ratios) mounted on the main and secondary shafts. The freewheeling gearwheels are engaged or disengaged with the shaft via hydraulic, multi-plate clutches, one for each gear. When a gear is required, the appropriate clutch is engaged and torque is transmitted via that gear. Changing gear is simply a matter of disengaging one clutch and engaging another.

A simple analogy is to compare this unit with a normal manual gearbox. The countershaft of this gearbox can be compared to the layshaft of a simple in-line manual transmission and the main/secondary shaft can be compared to the primary/mainshaft. Instead of the required gear being selected and engaged manually via a synchromesh dog clutch from the gear lever, the gears are changed by using a small clutch inside the gearbox for each gear, activated hydraulically and controlled electronically with an ECU.

Torque input to the gearbox from the engine is through a traditional torque converter with a lock-up clutch for maximum efficiency. The gear selector clutches are engaged via hydraulic oil pressure and controlled with solenoid operated shift valves. These shift valves in turn are activated by the automatic transmission ECU, which changes to the appropriate gear for driving conditions. It is also possible for the driver to select the required gear manually (a semi-automatic). Table 5.3 shows the operating conditions of the clutches for each of the available gears.

The latest development of this gearbox has reduced its overall length by 22 mm. This does not sound a lot, but in a modern engine bay, where space is already at a premium, this could be very advantageous. In addition, the internal component count is reduced by dispensing with the first gear one-way clutch. This means that the gearbox needs only four clutches and a servomechanism to provide all the required gears. In the development of this latest version specific problems had to be overcome.

In previous versions of the gearbox a one-way clutch was fitted to the first gear clutch to improve shift quality by transferring some torque during upshift. Without this element a drop in torque during the shift could be perceived by the driver, which adversely affects drivability. This happens because hydraulic clutches have a small, finite, delayed response caused by the necessary refilling of the piston cavity with hydraulic oil before clutch pressure is generated. The piston cavity is emptied of oil through a check valve after each operation to prevent displacement of the

piston due to centrifugal effects. To overcome this, a centrifugal cancellation mechanism is fitted to the first and second gear clutch hydraulics (Figure 5.45), which allows precise operation and timing of the first and second gear clutch operation for smooth upshifting. This precision timing is achieved with high-performance linear solenoids, which can give the required degree of control. In addition, the mainshaft speed and acceleration are monitored by the automatic transmission ECU, so that shifting can be monitored and optimised in real time operation by the ECU.

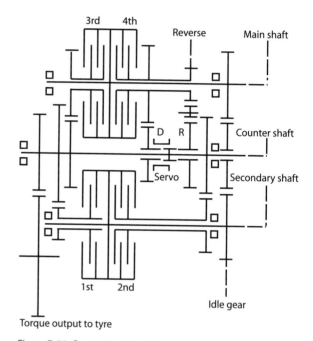

Figure 5.44 Gear train schematic

Table 5.3 Operating conditions

Elements Engaged	Clutch				Servo
Actual car	1st	2nd	3rd	4th	D/R
1st	•				D
2nd		•			D
3rd			•		D
4th				•	D
Reverse				•	R

Figure 5.43 Four-speed all clutch-to-clutch system

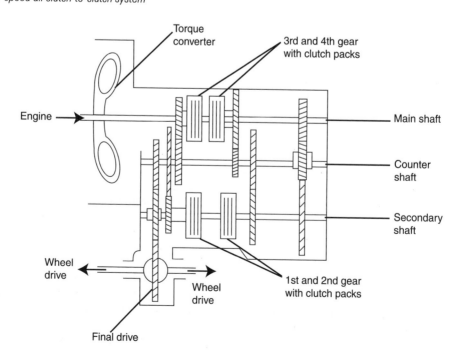

Catastrophic failure of the gearbox at speed and a consequential downshift to first gear due to control system failure would cause over-revving of the engine and possible road-wheel lock. This was previously prevented by using a one-way clutch to stop drive through the first gear being engaged under these conditions. Since the current design dispenses with the one-way clutch, a safety mechanism must be used to prevent engagement of first gear. This is done with direct hydraulic control using linear solenoids and new shift logic with three solenoids, plus a fail-safe valve. Thus gears are shifted through a combination of eight solenoid signals (Figure 5.46) and this provides the fail-safe mechanism.

The overall dimensions and form of this gearbox are ideal for front-wheel drive vehicles, providing safety and improved drivability for the user.

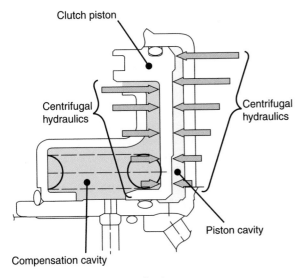

Figure 5.45 *Clutch piston mechanism*

Key Points

Tiptronic is the name used by Porsche (and others now) to describe a sequential shift automatic gearbox with intelligent shift strategy adaptation

Features such as 'gear hold in manoeuvres' can be provided. With this feature, lateral acceleration is detected and the current gear is maintained for maximum stability

For transverse front-engine–front-wheel drive, a solution in use by Honda is closer to a manual gearbox in form

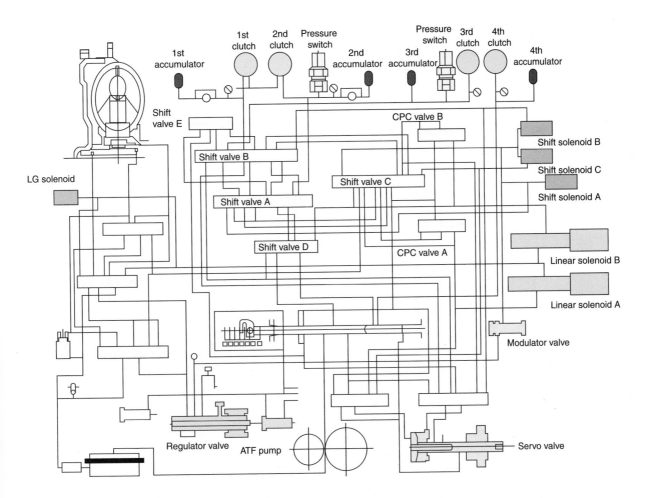

Figure 5.46 *Hydraulic control system*

5.10 CONTINUOUSLY VARIABLE TRANSMISSION (CVT)

5.10.1 Introduction

A problem with any combustion engine is that maximum power, torque and fuel economy all occur at different engine speeds within the range of normal operation. In a conventional, selectable, fixed ratio gearbox, in any particular gear, the engine speed and vehicle speed have a fixed relationship, so maximum torque, power or economy can be achieved only at one road speed per target in each gear. Driving a car along a road is transient in nature, so achievement of any of these targets for any reasonable period of time, will be nearly impossible.

Figure 5.47 shows that only a limited fit to the ideal curve can be achieved with a standard transmission. A continuously variable transmission (or CVT), as its name implies, can provide an infinite number of ratios between some absolute limits. Thus this transmission system can give a powertrain performance curve that is capable of matching the ideal tractive effort curve for a particular vehicle.

CVT transmissions can be operated mechanically, hydraulically or electrically and various designs have been developed, proposed and utilised, although they have never made the market breakthrough that was anticipated. One popular design, adopted by DAF and Volvo for small cars, was the Variomatic system shown simplified in Figure 5.48.

The Volvo system satisfied the basic requirements for a CVT for light vehicle applications. However, the technology was considered 'quirky' within the market place and the system layout was not easily adaptable for general application in the front-engine–rear-drive cars that were popular at the time that the system was developed. The system needed a specific powertrain layout (a front engine, with rear drive via a transaxle (Figure 5.49)). Composite rubber drive belts were used, which needed adjustment and replacement. These belts limited the maximum torque transfer possible, so the system was suitable only for small cars.

The next generation of CVT developed for compact cars used a steel belt instead of a rubber one. The packaging is clearly different as the application is for front-wheel drive vehicles (Figure 5.50) but the principle of operation is exactly the same as that of the Variomatic system. One important difference is that this steel belt is actually used in compression to push, rather than pull, the drive force. A major advantage of this system is that parasitic losses inside the gearbox are significantly reduced compared with the losses in a traditional automatic gearbox.

The system incorporates the differential assembly and forms a compact single unit. The steel belt limits the torque that can be transferred, so the system can be used only with smaller engines of up to 1.6 litres displacement.

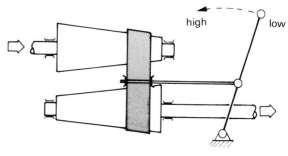

Figure 5.48 CVT system

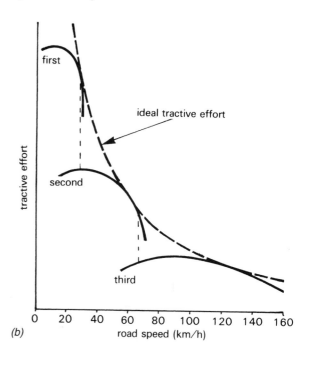

Figure 5.47 Tractive effort curves
a Ideal tractive effort curve
b Curve for conventional stepped transmission

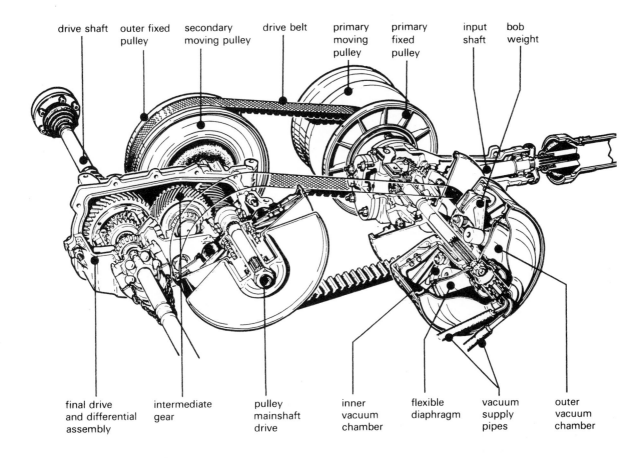

Figure 5.49 Variomatic transmission

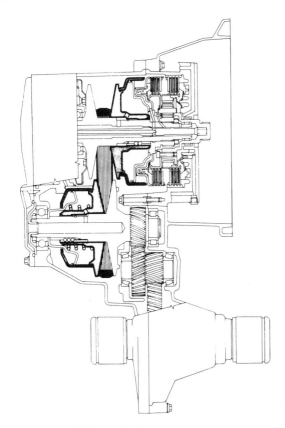

Figure 5.50 Ford CTX transmission

Basic outline of CVT transmission operation

The CVT systems described above both work on the same basic principle. They have similarly constructed driving and driven members that consist of opposed cones both mounted on the same shaft. These effectively form pulleys with v-shaped grooves, with a belt running between them to transmit torque. The cones that form the pulley on the primary (driving) side can be moved closer together or further apart: it is through this mechanism that the overall gear ratio can be varied infinitely. In operation, with a fixed width belt, if the pulley sides (cones) are moved apart, the effective working diameter of the belt is reduced. If they are moved together, the diameter is increased (Figure 5.51).

Gear ratios are shifted via an actuator: by moving the relative positions of the cones on the primary pulley, the actuator changes the effective working diameter of this pulley and consequently the gear ratio. The secondary (driven) pulley has the cones spring-loaded against each other, which maintains the correct belt tension as the ratio varies with the fixed length belt.

The CVT has great potential to reduce fuel consumption and emissions because the engine can be operated continuously at its optimum operating point. The greatest problem is the power loss caused by the internal energy requirements of the transmission. With electronic systems, oil flow and pressure can be

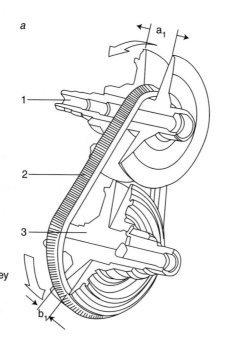
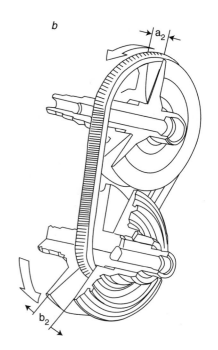

a 'Low' ratio
b 'Overdrive' ratio
1 Input (primary) pulley
2 Push-belt or chain
3 Output (secondary) pulley

a_1, b_1 'Low' ratio
a_2, b_2 'Overdrive' ratio

Figure 5.51 Simple CVT

controlled accurately to suit the working conditions of the gearbox, so overall efficiency can be significantly improved. A most important factor is the availability of reliable sensors and actuators to support reliable implementation of the control strategy.

Basic functions of the transmission

As well as the variable-ratio pulley assembly, additional components are needed in the transmission system for it to be suitable for road vehicles. These are:

- mechanisms to provide a neutral gear (disengagement of the drive to the road wheels) and a reverse gear
- an arrangement to allow the progressive take-up of drive from standstill, such as an electric or multi-plate clutch or torque converter, which should also allow the vehicle to 'creep' at low speeds for manoeuvring
- an appropriate fixed gear assembly to drive the final drive/differential at the appropriate speed and divide torque equally between the driving wheels
- a suitable control system to select the correct ratio according to driver's requirements and driving conditions. This could be a hydraulic system, but the preferred solution for a modern vehicle would be electronic or electro-hydraulic.

Electronic control functions

The control system for a CVT could also incorporate the following specific requirements.

- Contact pressure control – this provides adjustment of the belt clamping force in relation to load forces.

It prevents excessive forces being used, which waste power and reduce efficiency, but maintains sufficient pressure to prevent belt slip.

- A driving program – this enables preselected driving modes to be implemented as well as adaptive functions, and the selection of fully automatic or semi-automatic (sequential) modes.
- Torque converter lock-up – this improves transmission efficiency by bypassing torque converter slip.
- Pump control – control of the pump flow rate improves transmission efficiency and prevents excessive flow at high speed.
- Limp home mode – in the event of failure, limp home and fail-safe features must be built into the control system structure, in addition to diagnostic monitoring capability.

Key Points

A CVT system has only two gears – forward and reverse

CVT transmission can be operated mechanically, hydraulically or electrically

Gear ratio shifting is implemented through an actuator which alters the relative positions of the cones

In most CVT boxes the drive belt is pushed – not pulled

CTX (the Ford transmission) stands for constantly variable transaxle

5.10.2 Case study: Audi Multitronic transmission

Introduction

Audi has taken the principle of the basic CVT system and extended its capability to make it suitable for applications in larger vehicles where the torque transfer requirements are much higher. By adapting and improving some of the basic mechanical parts, particularly those that limit the capabilities of the traditional CVT, and with the addition of sophisticated electronic control, Multitronic transmission (Figure 5.52) gives improved fuel consumption compared with a traditional automatic transmission. The acceleration performance of the vehicle is also marginally improved when compared with a normal five speed manual transmission.

Overall the system provides very wide ranging gear ratios of up to 6.05 to 1, both higher and lower ratios than any other automatic transmission. With this system Audi has produced a highly efficient CVT with broader application possibilities and some important technical developments and improvements.

System highlights

- **Link plate chain drive** – The component that limits torque transfer in a CVT is the connecting element between the driving and driven parts of the variator. Early designs used rubber belts (DAF 66, Volvo 340). Later designs, as mentioned above, use a steel thrust belt designed by Van Doorne. Both are limited in terms of the maximum torque that they can transfer. For the use in the Audi application the belt must transfer nearly 300 Nm of torque! The solution was the development of a link plate chain drive, designed jointly with LuK (Figure 5.53). This chain is constructed of 1025 links with 75 pins, all made

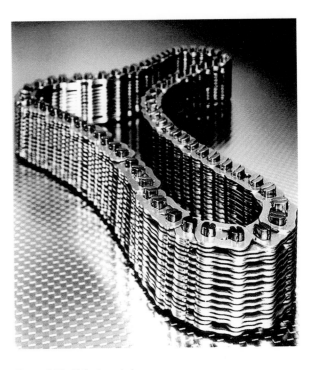

Figure 5.53 Link plate chain

of high-strength steel. Torque is transferred through the contact between the pulley flanks and the ends of the pins.

- **Multi-plate clutch** – A wide range of gear ratios is available, so the torque converter is replaced by a much more efficient, hydraulically operated, wet multiplate clutch. This avoids the traditional losses associated with a torque converter but also, with electronic control, allows implementation of a number of starting strategies according to driver preference. These strategies are established via monitoring of throttle demand and rate of change. An additional feature is a 'creep' function that is automatically initiated by the electronic control system for low speed manoeuvres.

- **Dual piston variator with torque sensor** – This technology ensures that the variator grips the chain with sufficient pressure, depending on torque transmitted, to prevent slip but with no more pressure than is necessary. This is measured by the transmission ECU monitoring the clamping forces (via the torque sensor) and variator speeds (via speed sensors); the hydraulic pressures are then adjusted accordingly. The advantage is that this keeps the internal gearbox power requirements to the absolute minimum, thus increasing efficiency, as well as reducing heat build-up. The dual piston arrangement for the variator (one piston for clamping the chain and a smaller piston for ratio change) ensures that the required dynamic response can be obtained with a small, more efficient hydraulic pump (Figure 5.54).

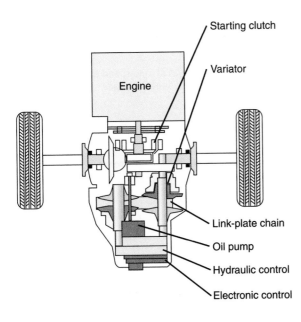

Figure 5.52 Multitronic system overview

Figure 5.54 Variator with torque sensor

- **DRP (dynamisches regelprogramm – dynamic control program)** – The transmission control module (mounted on the gearbox itself) has a highly dynamic program for calculating the target transmission input speed. Based on driver input and operating conditions, the system can determine the appropriate driving style and shift pattern selection, for example performance or economy. The driving feel is designed to be similar to the feel of a manual shift mode. The system also eliminates the so-called 'rubber band' effect typical of traditional CVTs: it ensures that the engine speed increases proportionally with road speed in a similar way to a manual transmission when accelerating. Probably the most intriguing feature is the manual, sequential shift mode. This allows six predefined ratios (even though there are an infinite number available) to be

selected by the driver manually with the shift lever or steering wheel mounted buttons. This gives the driver more control over shifting and a more sporty driving experience (Figure 5.55).

5.10.3 Case study: Nissan electronic control

Introduction

Nissan has recently been at the forefront of the development, improvement and integration of CVT technology in its vehicle range. As noted earlier, this technology is only suitable for smaller, lower-power vehicles. Nissan has added significant technical features to the basic belt drive CVT to extend its application to more powerful vehicles up to the 2.0 litre engine class. In addition, the inclusion of an electronic control system has increased the efficiency, improved performance and extended the driving appeal of a CVT equipped vehicle.

Technical highlights

The main focus of the development was to:

- improve power and economy
- improve acceleration in terms of performance and drivability
- provide a manual, sequential shift mode.

To achieve these targets the technical developments were as follows.

1 **Torque converter with lock-up clutch** – This component was added to the transmission system to provide improved acceleration from rest; an additional benefit was smoother transmission through the damping properties of the torque

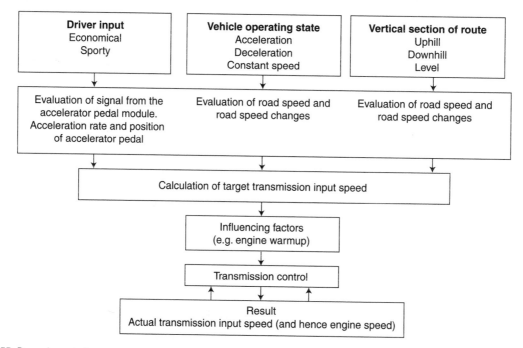

Figure 5.55 Dynamic control program

converter. An electronically controlled lock-up clutch ensures that the efficiency of the transmission remains high. This clutch also features a highly durable facing material that allows lock-up at lower speeds than is normal (down to 20 km/h), which gives a further improvement in economy.

2 **Expanded belt width** – The belt width is increased by 25%, and, by optimisation of the pulley ranges, the wider belt can easily accommodate the torque generated by a 2.0 litre engine.

3 **Electronic control system** – The system consists of sophisticated electro-hydraulic elements with a fully electronic control system (ECU). This system monitors and controls all aspects of transmission operation to optimise performance and economy. The system overview is shown in Figure 5.56.

4 **Manual mode** – To enable greater driver interaction, a multi-speed manual mode is included. This has sequential shifting to allow the driver to select and hold gears during sports driving.

Summary

The system shows measurable benefits in terms of economy and performance. The fuel economy is improved by 20% compared with the standard four speed automatic. This is possible because of the extended range through which the lock-up clutch can operate (reducing slip losses) and because the system hydraulic pressure adapts to engine load (via the electronic control system) to reduce internal energy losses.

The torque multiplication capability of the torque converter improves acceleration performance by 30%, and drivability is increased through the smooth, stepless torque delivery of the CVT system. The manual shift mode is an enhancement which will be appreciated by drivers who want a greater level of interaction for a more rewarding driving experience.

Key Points

The Audi Multitronic system provides a very wide range of gear ratios (from 6.05:1 to 1:1). The system does not use a torque converter

The Nissan system monitors and controls all aspects of transmission operation to improve performance and economy

Using a wider belt can increase the torque capacity and allow CVT systems to be used with larger engines

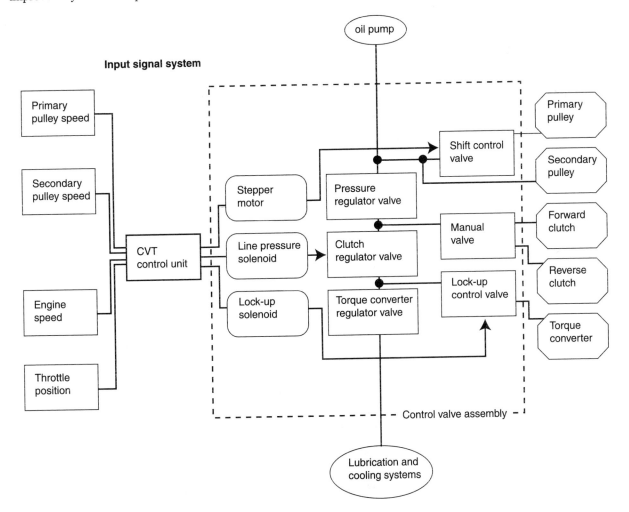

Figure 5.56 System overview

5.11 LIGHT HYBRID POWERTRAIN TECHNOLOGY (STARTER–GENERATOR)

5.11.1 Introduction

A hybrid powertrain is one with more than a single prime mover and can incorporate a number of technologies for power conversion and energy accumulation. The prime objective of a hybrid drive is to harness the advantages of each particular drive technology under its optimum operating conditions. The consequential increase in efficiency of the powertrain as a whole offsets the increased initial cost and reduces the harmful exhaust emissions from the vehicle.

The internal combustion engine and electric motor can both be considered as torque sources or prime movers; their respective attributes are show in Table 5.4.

Table 5.4 Internal combustion engine and electric motor comparison

	Internal combustion engine	Electric motor
Torque Response	Uni-directional Slow: > 300 ms at low speed	Bi-directional Fast: < 5 ms
Characteristic	Maximum torque not available at lower speeds	Maximum torque available at lower speeds and from zero

The hybrid drive solution offers great potential for improving fuel consumption and reducing emissions during low- to medium-speed operation of the vehicle. This is because the internal combustion engine has greatly reduced efficiency under part-load conditions. It is likely that hybrid powertrain designs will become commonplace in future as the technology develops and improves. Figure 5.57 shows the classification of hybrid drives.

A full hybrid drive powertrain with integrated control needs to be a fundamental part of a vehicle's initial design. It is is impossible to introduce a hybrid drive retrospectively into an existing vehicle without considerable reworking of the powertrain (to accommodate both the internal combustion engine and the electric drive) as well as the vehicle chassis (to accommodate the energy storage medium – the battery).

5.11.2 Light hybrids

A compromise can be found in the form of the integrated starter–generator (ISG), which is a natural progression in the development of automotive electrical systems because of the continuously growing demand for electrical power in the modern vehicle. It is expected that electrical power of up to 10 kW could be needed in future and the standard 14 V electrical system will need

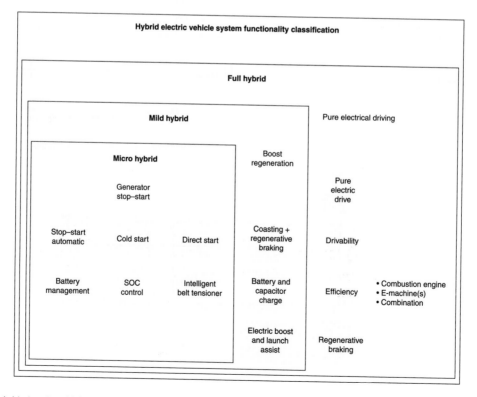

Figure 5.57 Hybrid electric vehicle classification

to be supplemented or replaced by a 42 V system (Figure 5.58). The separate starter and generator units used in modern vehicles can be easily integrated into a single unit to start the IC engine, provide on-board electrical power and recharge the battery. This unit, depending on the installation, could also provide a number of additional features such as:

- a short-term power boost function to supplement the internal combustion engine during acceleration, particularly in the lower speed ranges
- a retarder to supplement the brakes, which could also regenerate energy during deceleration: the electric motor/generator is highly efficient at doing this and can achieve efficiencies of up to 80% under these conditions
- an engine stop/start function for use in stationary traffic to reduce harmful emissions; engine starting times of less than 0.5 seconds can be achieved.

A considerable advantage of this technology is that it can be integrated into an existing design with minimal effort. Basically the system consists of:

- a three-phase AC motor integrated with the internal combustion engine design
- an AC/DC converter which rectifies the AC electricity generated by the three-phase motor
- a DC/DC converter that provides the required voltage levels
- a control electronics system for the ISG powertrain system
- an energy management system controlling the ISG and the vehicle power requirements.

There are two principal designs for an ISG currently proposed or under development by manufacturers (see Figure 5.59), which are discussed in more detail below.

Micro hybrid
Belt driven SG
Generator/starter
stop–start

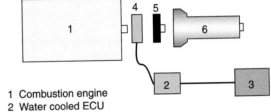

1 Combustion engine
2 Electric machine (SSG)
3 Air cooled ECU
4 Smart switching unit
5 14 V battery
6 DLC (supercapacitors)

Mild hybrid
Intergrated SG
Micro hybrid functionalities
+ Boost
+ Regeneration

1 Combustion engine
2 Water cooled ECU
3 DLC (supercapacitors)
4 Electric machine
5 Clutch
6 Gearbox

Figure 5.59 Micro and mild hybrid systems

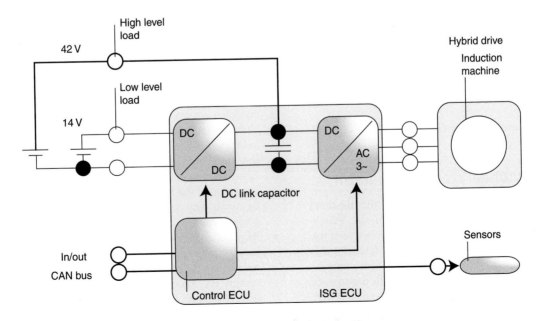

Figure 5.58 Integrated starter–generator control system

5.11.3 Belt driven starter–generator

The belt driven starter–generator is also known as a micro-hybrid system (Figure 5.60). It consists of a belt driven electric machine mounted at the front of the engine, with a control unit and belt tensioner. It provides start/stop functionality as well as starting and charging functions. The system works at 14 V and as such does not require major modifications to the vehicle electrical system: the standard starter battery technology is used. This means that the system can be retrofitted to existing engine designs, since it can be fitted in place of a conventional alternator using the same fixings, freeing up the space where the starter would normally appear on the engine, which also gives a small weight saving.

In starter mode, the machine can start the engine silently (with its belt drive) and up to three times quicker than a traditional starter with a ring gear. In generator mode, the machine is over 80% efficient, up to 15% more so than a standard alternator because of the advanced power management system.

In operation, when the vehicle is at a standstill in traffic, the engine cuts out, so all sources of noise and pollution are eliminated and fuel consumption is zero. When required, the engine restarts automatically and immediately in less than half a second; this is possible because of the high torque/inertia ratio of the electric machine. In modern traffic conditions, in suburban areas, vehicles are standing for up to 35% of journey time: overall fuel consumption in these conditions can be improved by up to 10%.

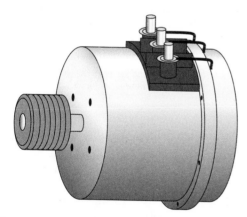

Figure 5.60 Belt driven starter–generator

5.11.4 Flywheel starter–generator

Also known as a mild hybrid system, the flywheel starter–generator is mounted in place of the vehicle flywheel and acts directly at the crankshaft between the engine and transmission (Figure 5.61). Typically this unit is a highly efficient synchronous or asynchronous AC machine running at up to 60 V. Normally a system of this type is integrated within a vehicle electrical power system incorporating a higher voltage line, at 42 V, for more efficient transmission and conversion. It is clear

Figure 5.61 Flywheel starter–generator

that, with these constraints, this technology must be incorporated into the powertrain design. It would be more difficult to incorporate this system than some others and retrofit would not be feasible.

The system has a high performance, providing up to 200 Nm of torque for short durations. The unit is capable of generating up to 8 kW of electrical power continuously for the electrical system. A flywheel starter–generator is usually fully integrated with a vehicle's power management system. Managed by the powertrain control system as an available torque source, the system is integrated via a standard interface, such as a controller area network (CAN). A torque management system will then distribute the torque from the starter–generator and the internal combustion engine according to driver requirements and driving conditions.

In addition to providing engine starting and stop/start functions (as does the belt drive starter–generator), the flywheel starter–generator can be configured to improve efficiency, because it is far more integrated with the powertrain control system. Additional features that can be added to do this include the following.

- A torque booster can provide additional torque to complement an internal combustion engine under certain conditions. The torque booster also gives the vehicle designer the option of using a smaller internal combustion engine. An important factor here though is the battery state: the charge condition of the battery must be monitored carefully to avoid any significant deterioration in vehicle performance.
- Regenerative retarder – The ISG can be used to recover energy during braking, and can be incorporated into an active brake management system for maximum benefit. Again though, the battery's state of charge is a critical factor: there must be enough capacity to store all the energy recovered.

The ISG system can be part of an intelligent powertrain management system, controlling and managing all available torque sources, and deploying the most efficient one depending on operating conditions. As well as managing traction demands, the system also manages the vehicle's power usage. It controls the entire drive train by enabling communication between all electronic units in the vehicle. It constantly monitors and exchanges data between the internal combustion engine, the powertrain, and the electrical control systems, such that the auxiliary drive system always has sufficient electrical power for the engine to be able to self-start when required.

Key Points

A hybrid powertrain is one with more than one prime mover (an engine and a motor)

ISG stands for integrated starter–generator

A mild hybrid can provide a short-term power boost, a retarder function to supplement brakes and an engine stop/start function to reduce harmful emissions in static traffic

A micro-hybrid system has a belt driven electric machine mounted at the front of the engine (a combined starter and alternator)

5.12 ELECTRONIC DIFFERENTIAL AND FOUR-WHEEL DRIVE CONTROL

5.12.1 Introduction

The rapid development of electronic systems controlling the modern motor vehicle powertrain has progressively extended from the engine, to the transmission and more recently to the final drive system. Electronic control is integrated into modern vehicles to ensure that torque delivered by the powerpack (engine and transmission) is efficiently and effectively transferred as tractive force. Vehicle electronic control systems interact to maximise the potential of the vehicle propulsion system to improve safety and performance.

Vehicle wheels are often in contact with surfaces where the adhesion varies significantly, so optimisation of the tractive force is essential. Nearly all vehicles have a standard mechanical differential, which, under normal driving conditions, provides uniform torque distribution between the driving wheels, giving predictable vehicle behaviour. However, the force is always distributed evenly, irrespective of speed; so, if one wheel lacks grip and slips, no force is transmitted, so the other wheel also transmits no force and the vehicle is immobilised. Stability is another important issue with modern vehicles. Powerful engines can produce more force to accelerate the vehicle than the system can transmit. Depending on the road surface and driver behaviour, the wheels can spin, leading to loss of traction and erratic performance.

Several electronic control solutions are available to deal with these problems, and to enhance vehicle performance as a whole.

Automatic brake differential (ABD)/traction control (ASR)

An automatic brake differential is not a differential lock in the traditional sense: it is not like a mechanical lock, which positively locks and prevents differential action completely. ABD uses the anti-lock brake system infrastructure (wheel speed sensors, hydraulics, etc.) and detects any difference between the rotational speeds of the driving wheels. When it detects a speed difference, the system can activate the brake on the offending wheel to counteract the slip. This is done in a progressive manner, allowing controlled transfer of torque via the open differential to the driving wheel with the greatest adhesion. There are some limitations with this system: it cannot operate effectively at zero speed and therefore is of no use for true off-road applications; and because of the temperature limits of braking systems, it is not available at higher vehicle speeds (greater than 25 mile/h).

The system normally operates in conjunction with the engine control electronics to provide active traction control: as well as decelerating the slipping wheel with the brake, the ECU can actively reduce engine power to further control the torque distribution. The engine torque is usually controlled via the electronic throttle (e-gas) actuator and the ignition timing (spark retard). The control units communicate using the high speed CAN bus line.

Electronic control of differential

The above system is not specifically suitable for off-road vehicles or sports utility vehicles (SUVs). So, for such use, it needs to be supplemented by another system, capable of sustained prevention of the differential action on the driving axles for maximum traction at low speed. Mechanical solutions here include differential locks and limited slip differentials (LSDs). However, these solutions require manual intervention by the driver (the former) or can only respond in a simplistic way (the latter). An electronic control system provides the following benefits:

- a smart system that can respond proactively, not only to speed differences, but also to other parameters monitored by the vehicle electronic control systems (wheel speeds, throttle demands, engine load, etc.)
- a differential action that can easily be integrated with other vehicle systems, such as ABS, traction control and stability control.

The system can be configured in a number of ways but Figure 5.62 shows a solution for a live rear axle. It consists of a standard differential, but with the addition of multi-plate clutches between the planet wheels and differential cage. These clutches are engaged electromagnetically by a current in the coil. This current determines and is proportional to the torque transfer. When activated, the current coil creates a magnetic field which pulls the cone into frictional engagement with the differential cage. The frictional torque created by the cone causes the balls to ride up a ramp machined into the side gear. The lateral movement of the side gear applies a force onto the centre block and that load is transmitted from the centre block to the opposite side gear, compressing the clutch pack and locking the differential.

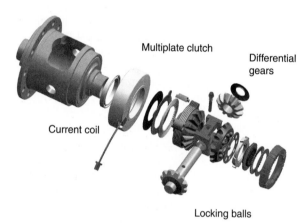

Figure 5.62 *Electronically controlled differential*

This design is particularly intelligent as it does not require any additional hydraulic or pneumatic power and hence is highly efficient. It can easily be integrated into an existing installation simply by adding the hardware and driver stage to an existing powertrain ECU. It does not need to have its own specific control unit.

Figure 5.63 shows excitation current plotted against locking torque.

Integration of safety systems

A clear benefit of these solutions is that it is possible to connect the differential control system to other vehicle dynamics controllers to provide a harmonised efficient system with maximum tractive force control, providing greater safety. The systems that could be linked include:

- anti-lock braking (ABS)
- traction control (ASR)
- brake force distribution (EBD)
- cornering stability control (CSC)
- dynamic drift control (DDC).

These systems could either be directly integrated in a powertrain control unit (PCU), or they could communicate with each other on a high-speed bus system (e.g. CAN).

5.12.2 Case study: Porsche traction management (PTM)

Introduction

The Porsche Cayenne is equipped with one of the most sophisticated four-wheel drive systems. The system mechanics are similar to any off-road or SUV with full-time 4WD, and the system intelligence lies in the electronic controls. The fundamental principle is extremely simple: to actively distribute torque to those wheels that can utilise it most efficiently.

Dynamometer test showing the relationship between bias torque and coil current. The tight wheel was held to zero RPM, the differential was driven at 50 RPM, and the loose wheel was allowed to freely rotate at 100 RPM. The coil current was slowly increased until the tight wheel torque reached 18,000lb in.

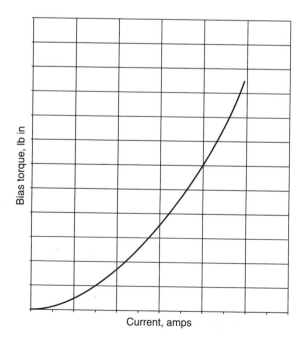

Figure 5.63 *Control current: excitation current v locking torque*

The system consists of:

- a transfer case incorporating epicyclic differential and range selection, with an electrically operated progressive differential lock via a multiplate clutch (Figure 5.64)
- a front axle with electrical (ABD) lock capability
- a rear axle with electrical, progressive differential lock via a clutch
- harmonised electronic control and monitoring of brakes, traction and stability.

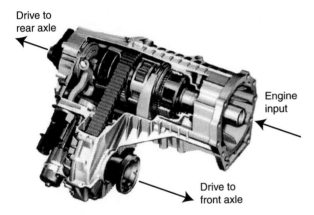

Figure 5.64 Four-wheel drive traction management unit

Operation

The system provides permanent torque distribution between the front and rear axles which, under normal conditions, is a 38/62% front/rear split. This rear wheel bias provides stable grip on almost any surface and gives the driver the level of road feel and chassis feedback that would be expected from a high-performance vehicle.

The transfer boxes provide high- and low-gear ratios for on/off road use. The set of ratios is selected with a toggle switch near the gear lever. The functions are progressive and sequentially selected and shift between, for example, on- and off-road conditions.

- The first actuation of the switch selects 'low' range through the transfer box. This is engaged via a selector fork and electric motor actuator. In addition, with the vehicle sensors, the active electronic system continuously measures traction at the wheels, as well as vehicle speed, lateral acceleration, steering angle and operation of the accelerator pedal. From this, the system automatically calculates the optimal degree of locking for the differentials at the drive axles. In this way, more power is applied at the front or rear wheels, depending on the driving situation.
- The second actuation of the switch fully locks the centre differential using a clutch and an electric motorised actuator.
- The third actuation of the switch fully locks the rear differential, again using a clutch and actuator for maximum off-road traction.

The front final drive does not have a mechanical differential lock. Potential slip of one front wheel is prevented by the automatic brake differential (ABD, see above). The negative effects of a mechanical differential lock, such as increased weight and limitations on steering and handling can thus be avoided. If both wheels on one axle are in danger of slipping, the control system intervenes through the electronic engine management and reduces power in order to maintain grip. By combining these functions, the PTM ensures optimum traction on almost every surface.

All the PTM functions are fully automatic, resulting in inherently more dynamic handling characteristics, as well as greater active safety.

5.12.3 Case study: Haldex coupling

Introduction

Four-wheel drive transmissions (4WD) have been in production models of performance cars for some 25 years. During this time the mechanics of these transmissions have evolved to improve further the traction efficiency of the system as a whole. The heart of a 4WD system is the centre differential which divides the torque between the front and rear axles. Over the years this technology has evolved from simple locking differentials, to limited slip differentials, to viscous differentials, and, the latest iteration, the Torsen differential. This development process has improved the performance of 4WD vehicles, but all of these systems suffer from the same shortfall: wheel slip can be recognised only by a difference in shaft speeds between the front and rear axles. The problem is that although these systems can sense slip, they are not able to detect the cause of it.

Developments in electronics have moved this technology forward significantly with the introduction of the Haldex coupling, which is now used by a number of large motor manufacturers. Owing to the mechatronic nature of this system, the coupling is fully controllable and can take into account not only slip but also vehicle dynamic state.

Overview and operation

The Haldex coupling is mounted in the rear differential assembly and is driven by a propshaft connected to the front transaxle (Figure 5.65). Engine torque is transmitted via this propshaft from the front transaxle, directly from the front differential drive. There is effectively no centre differential. Inside the unit the input shaft is connected to the output shaft and rear axle via the Haldex multi-plate coupling; torque to the rear axle is provided and controlled through this coupling.

The basic operation of the mechanics and hydraulics of the system are as follows (Figure 5.66). When a speed difference occurs between the input and output shafts of the coupling, the swash plate drives the small oil pump plungers and this generates oil pressure. This pressure is used in the clutch pistons to compress the

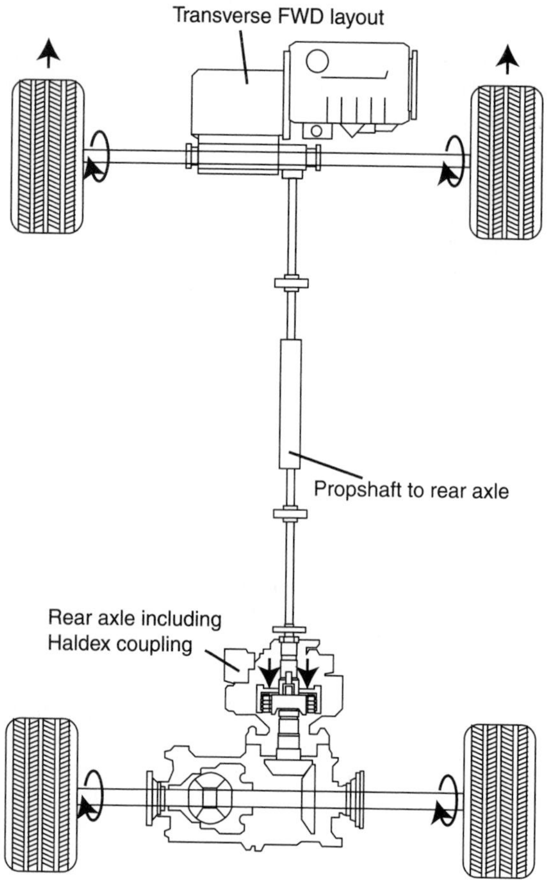

Transverse FWD layout

Propshaft to rear axle

Rear axle including
Haldex coupling

Figure 5.65 Four-wheel drive control layout

clutch plate pack and hence engage the clutch. Once the clutch is locked then 100% of the torque is transmitted through the coupling. The clutch pressure is maintained by a regulating valve. The system includes an electric oil pump which runs at engine speeds above 400 rev/min. This provides a background system pressure of 4 bar which pre-loads the clutch pack to remove any play and ensures a minimum system response time.

Electronic control system

The ECU for the 4WD system/Haldex coupling is mounted directly at the rear axle casing. This is in line with current trends for powertrain control systems: there is a fully integrated mechatronic control module including electronics and hydraulics, with minimal external connections and interfaces, to improve reliability. Figure 5.67 shows the system overview.

The sensors and interfaces used in the system are:

- a CAN interface to the engine ECU, providing information about engine speed and load through crankshaft position and throttle position sensors

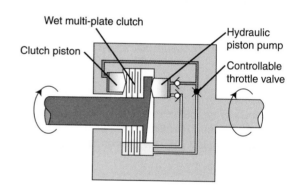

Wet multi-plate clutch

Clutch piston

Hydraulic piston pump

Controllable throttle valve

Figure 5.66 Hydraulically controlled clutch assembly

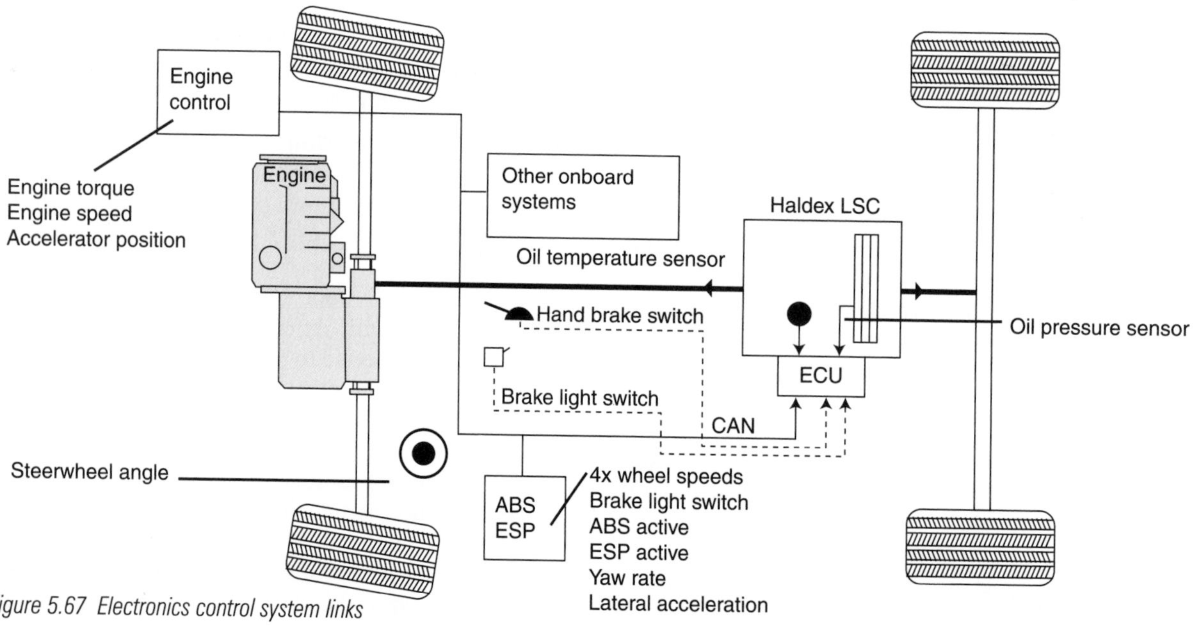

Engine control

Engine

Engine torque
Engine speed
Accelerator position

Other onboard systems

Oil temperature sensor

Haldex LSC

Hand brake switch

Oil pressure sensor

Brake light switch

ECU

CAN

Steerwheel angle

ABS
ESP

4x wheel speeds
Brake light switch
ABS active
ESP active
Yaw rate
Lateral acceleration

Figure 5.67 Electronics control system links

- a CAN interface to the ABS ECU, providing information about the vehicle dynamic state, including wheel speed, vehicle acceleration, brake status (on or off) and handbrake status (on or off)
- a temperature sensor for the Haldex coupling, enabling the coupling to react to changes in oil temperature, and to detect high temperature or overload conditions so the system can protect itself in extreme conditions.

The actuators are:

- a positioning motor for the regulator valve (controlled directly by the ECU) which controls the clutch pressure and hence the operation and control of the system
- an oil pump, which provides background system pressure and lubrication while the unit is in standby mode.

The system's main features and advantages are:

- active torque distribution via an electronically controlled multi-plate clutch, with instant activation and high torque transfer for maximum traction when required; an alternative separate off-road mode (switch) can lock the coupling

- an extremely fast responding, highly dynamic system but with the feel of a normal two-wheel drive car for predictable handling
- no strain on system components or the vehicle during low-speed manoeuvring
- compatibility with different tyre sizes, for example, when a space saving spare wheel has to be fitted; an algorithm in the ECU detects differences in the diameters of the tyres and adjusts the characteristics accordingly
- no restriction on towing or testing (a chassis dynamometer or brake test) of the vehicle, because the system is inactive when the engine is not running
- full compatibility with other vehicle dynamic control systems such as ABS, EDL, TCS EBD and ESP; the coupling communicates on-line with safety systems in the vehicle.

Key Points

The fundamental purpose of four-wheel drive traction management is to distribute actively torque to the wheels that can utilise it most efficiently

Four-wheel drive control systems are fully integrated with other dynamic control systems for maximum driver safety and benefit

TRANSMISSION DIAGNOSTICS

5.13.1 Introduction

Although they are sophisticated pieces of modern electromechanical technology, like anything else, electronically controlled transmissions can and do go wrong. Generally, considering the environment in which they operate, these units are extremely reliable. In most cases, failure of a sensor or actuator initiates the limp home failure mode which means that the vehicle can still be driven (although with reduced performance) for repair or to get the occupants home.

An important point though is that the working components are expensive and can be difficult to replace if they are deeply embedded inside the transmission unit. So correct diagnosis of the cause of faults is important to prevent wasted time and the unnecessary replacement of parts.

5.13.2 Typical diagnostic procedure

A logical approach is essential! For diagnosis, analysis of a system should be broken down into its elemental, functional parts. A typical test procedure would involve some or all of the following.

- **Simple, basic manual and visual checks** – The most basic checks should be done first, for example, the lubricating fluid level and condition. The transmission should be at the correct temperature when the fluid level is checked (see manufacturers' data). Then a visual check should be made for obvious problems, such as fluid leaks or damaged electrical connections.
- **A road test and report** – A complete understanding of the problem is essential in order to be able to diagnose a fault efficiently. This can be achieved through a test drive. Findings should be recorded efficiently as a report during or after the test drive. Malfunctions and correctly functioning components should be noted. Particular attention should be given to shift quality, both downshifts and upshifts. A stall test should be performed. It is necessary to test the correct operation of different shift programs and converter lock-up clutch operation (by driving feel).
- **System mechanical checks** – Basic checks should be performed on the mechanical and hydraulic components. The whole system can operate correctly only if the system pressure is correct. If

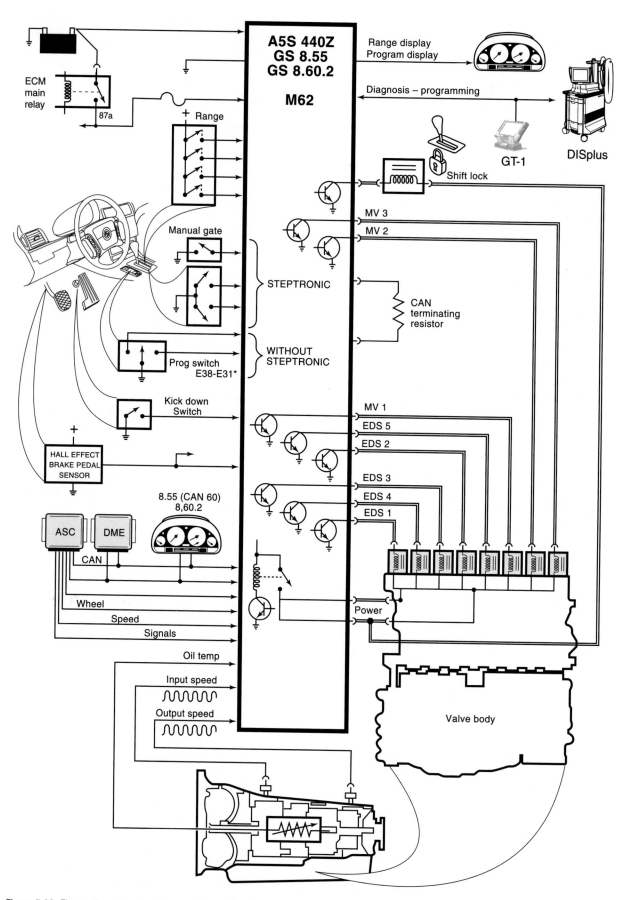

Figure 5.68 Electronic system overview

possible a pressure gauge should be used to take readings under operating conditions, so that these can be compared with manufacturer specifications. If there is a throttle cable, adjustment of this should be checked. Incorrect adjustment can cause problems with shifting (shift points).

Check resistances of sensors and actuators

Depending upon the nature of the problem, it may be necessary to check various components for correct resistance readings with a multimeter. Manufacturer information is essential for this to compare the measured value with the correct value. Changes in ambient temperature can affect resistance readings in electromagnetic coils, so a realistic tolerance must be allowed for this. To prevent damage to sensitive electronic components and false readings, general multimeter etiquette must be followed, with components completely disconnected from the circuit when they are checked.

Check signals (waveforms) and voltages at sensors and actuators

However, just because a sensor or actuator has the correct resistance doesn't mean that it is working properly when installed. Intermittent faults are particularly difficult to find as they usually occur only when the vehicle is being operated. Therefore, if possible, measure the signal at the sensor or actuator under running conditions. In most cases, an oscilloscope will give much more information than a multimeter. The voltage signals at some sensors and most actuators are quite dynamic in nature and a multimeter is not able to process the signal appropriately. There are many portable, cheap oscilloscopes on the market ideal for this purpose and robust enough for workshop use.

Check system electronics via diagnostic interface

Nearly all vehicle electronic systems have a diagnostic interface. In newer vehicles (2001 on), this interface is a standardised on-board diagnostic (OBD) connector and there are a number of generic scan tools available that can access fault codes from the transmission ECU (as well as from the engine ECU). The fault codes have

a standardised protocol, which aids diagnostics quite considerably. Older vehicles tend to have diagnostic interfaces specific to their manufacturer. Generally, specific equipment protocols exist, which must be used to access the information. On some vehicles (particularly Japanese ones) there is a blink code indication, which, although limited in the information it provides, can be a useful aid.

Diagnostics summary

Irrespective of its type (CVT, DSG, etc.) an electronic transmission is a complex unit and a systematic approach is needed when dealing with any technical problems. An electronic transmission is, though, simply a system (Figure 5.68). It has inputs which are processed, giving outputs with the desired reactions or responses. From first principles, therefore, the inputs to the system must be confirmed as correct. If this is so, then the outputs can be checked for correct action. If actions are incorrect, then the actuators should be checked or tested. If they are OK, then the connection between the actuators and ECU should be checked, etc., etc. This approach will solve most problems that might occur.

Another point to consider when diagnosing faults is that a good understanding of the system and its inputs and outputs is especially important, with so many variables changing at the same time in such a complex way. Make your life easy! Get as much information as possible about the system. Try to get a good understanding of the system in overview and how all the components fit together and work together in normal operation. This information can be obtained from the manufacturer through training documentation or from workshop manuals – as well as from good textbooks of course!

Key Points

A logical approach is essential for diagnostics

Consider systems as black boxes and check all inputs and outputs

Understand the system operation as well as the diagnostic procedures

Check sensor signals and supply signals using an oscilloscope as well as a multimeter

---

5.14 TRANSMISSION SUMMARY

5.14.1 Outline of electronic control

It is clear that the development of electronic control for transmission systems will continue to move at a swift pace. Technical developments in mechatronics and microelectronics now allow great freedom and flexibility in terms of packaging of control units and interfacing between vehicle control systems. These

developments are making electronic control of the transmission, even automatic shifting, more attractive in markets where an automatic gearbox would once have been shunned, for example, in high performance cars.

Highly integrated vehicle systems can provide sophisticated control algorithms to improve driver comfort and safety. Together with adaptive strategies that take into account additional operating parameters and boundary conditions, systems can optimise vehicle performance.

In summary, the main types of transmission currently available are:

- manual constant mesh transmissions
- automatic transmissions, with a planetary gearbox and torque converter
- continuously variable transmissions, with a belt driven variator.

Electronically controlled transmissions, in conjunction with advanced powertrain control systems, can provide improved vehicle performance and efficiency. The following powertrain systems have all seen the benefits of the implementation of electronic controls:

- manual transmission – electronic clutch and shifting for improved economy and/or vehicle performance
- automatic transmission – sophisticated shift strategies and control systems to improve efficiency and driver interaction
- continuously variable transmission – control of shifting to improve driver feel, and more control over hydraulics for greater efficiency
- four-wheel drive – improved traction and extended functionalities through integration with other control systems
- axle/traction control – better tractive force management on surfaces with limited or no grip.

Current developments show that integrated powertrain control will be the basis of future developments. To improve performance, as well as to meet legislative requirements on harmful vehicle emissions, it is no longer appropriate to treat the powertrain system as separate, mechanically connected units (the combustion engine, gearbox, axle, etc.). The powertrain system, consisting of these elements, must be considered as a single unit and calibrated and optimised during development for significant improvements to be made.

5.14.2 Future developments

Vehicle manufacturers are under increasing pressure to reduce vehicle emissions. Advanced powertrains will play a major part in achieving future goals of emission reduction and improved efficiency to conserve natural resources. A critical factor to be overcome is the reduced efficiency of the combustion engine at low speeds, and its polluting effect at idle where no power is required at all by the vehicle for motion.

This is an area of great interest, with large potential for improvement, and the current trend is towards hybrid powertrains. The hybrid vehicle combines the positive attributes of an electric drive (high efficiency, quiet, full torque at low/zero speed) with those of a combustion engine (high specific power to size ratio, long driving range between refuelling). This technology needs a sophisticated control system for the prime movers to work together in a harmonious and efficient way. This can easily be achieved with an electronic control system but there are a number of factors that impede the acceptance of this technology in the market place:

- battery technology – current units are expensive and heavy, and this technical hurdle must be overcome to move the technology forward significantly
- the existing electrical system voltage – the standard voltage for vehicle systems is 12 volts, which is far too low to transmit power efficiently at the level required for tractive force; higher voltage systems will be developed to cope with increasing power demands, which will be essential for the adoption of full hybrid systems
- motor size – although highly efficient, modern electric motors are still quite large relative to their power output; as technology develops, motors of the appropriate power rating will become smaller and will be easier to integrate into a combined vehicle propulsion system.

Manufacturers are currently working hard to overcome these issues, as well as introducing light hybrid systems that can be integrated within current vehicle ranges as an intermediate step. This allows them to introduce the technology into the market place and gauge customer reaction to it.

> **Key Points**
>
> Transmission management is used primarily to improve economy and vehicle performance, as well as driver interaction
>
> Hybrid solutions are likely to be the future …

Web links

Transmission systems information
www.zf.com
www.porsche.com
www.luk.de
www.bosch.co.uk
www.haldex-traction.com
www.siemensvdo.com
www.audi.com
www.vw.com
www.sae.org

Teaching/learning resources

Online learning material relating to transmission systems:

www.auto-training.co.uk

INDEX